A Text Book of

MOBILE COMPUTING

FOR
M.C.A. : MANAGEMENT : SEMESTER - IV
SUBJECT CODE : IT42

AS PER NEW REVISED SYLLABUS OF PUNE UNIVERSITY

MAHEK SHAIKH
M.Sc. (Computer Science)
Lecturer, M.E.S.'s Abasaheb Garware College
Pune

NIRALI PRAKASHAN

MOBILE COMPUTING (M.C.A. IV)　　　　　　　　　　　　　ISBN 978-93-83750-11-5

First Edition : January 2014

© : Author

The text of this publication, or any part thereof, should not be reproduced or transmitted in any form or stored in any computer storage system or device for distribution including photocopy, recording, taping or information retrieval system or reproduced on any disc, tape, perforated media or other information storage device etc., without the written permission of Authors with whom the rights are reserved. Breach of this condition is liable for legal action.

Every effort has been made to avoid errors or omissions in this publication. In spite of this, errors may have crept in. Any mistake, error or discrepancy so noted and shall be brought to our notice shall be taken care of in the next edition. It is notified that neither the publisher nor the authors or seller shall be responsible for any damage or loss of action to any one, of any kind, in any manner, therefrom.

Published By :　　　　　　　　　　　　　　　　　　　　　　　　　　**Printed By :**
NIRALI PRAKASHAN　　　　　　　　　　　　　　　　　　　　Repro Knowledgecast Limited,
Abhyudaya Pragati, 1312, Shivaji Nagar,　　　　　　　　　　　　　　　　　　　　Thane
Off J.M. Road, PUNE – 411005
Tel - (020) 25512336/37/39, Fax - (020) 25511379
Email : niralipune@pragationline.com

DISTRIBUTION CENTRES
PUNE

Nirali Prakashan　　　　　　　　　　　　　　*Nirali Prakashan*
119, Budhwar Peth, Jogeshwari Mandir Lane　　　S. No. 28/27, Dhyari,
Pune 411002, Maharashtra　　　　　　　　　　　Near Pari Company, Pune 411041
Tel : (020) 2445 2044, 66022708, Fax : (020) 2445 1538　　Tel : (020) 24690204 Fax : (020) 24690316
Email : bookorder@pragationline.com　　　　　Email : dhyari@pragationline.com
　　　　　　　　　　　　　　　　　　　　　　　bookorder@pragationline.com

MUMBAI
Nirali Prakashan
385, S.V.P. Road, Rasdhara Co-op. Hsg. Society Ltd.,
Girgaum, Mumbai 400004, Maharashtra
Tel : (022) 2385 6339 / 2386 9976, Fax : (022) 2386 9976
Email : niralimumbai@pragationline.com

DISTRIBUTION BRANCHES

NAGPUR　　　　　　　　　　　　　　　　　　**JALGAON**
Pratibha Book Distributors　　　　　　　　　　*Nirali Prakashan*
Above Maratha Mandir, Shop No. 3, First Floor,　34, V. V. Golani Market, Navi Peth, Jalgaon 425001,
Rani Jhanshi Square, Sitabuldi, Nagpur 440012,　Maharashtra, Tel : (0257) 222 0395
Maharashtra, Tel : (0712) 254 7129　　　　　　Mob : 94234 91860

BENGALURU　　　　　　　　　　　　　　　**KOLHAPUR**
Pragati Book House　　　　　　　　　　　　　*Nirali Prakashan*
House No. 1, Sanjeevappa Lane, Avenue Road Cross,　New Mahadvar Road,
Opp. Rice Church, Bengaluru – 560002.　　　　Kedar Plaza, 1st Floor Opp. IDBI Bank
Tel : (080) 64513344, 64513355,　　　　　　　Kolhapur 416 012, Maharashtra. Mob : 9850046155
Mob : 9880582331, 9845021552
Email:bharatsavla@yahoo.com

CHENNAI
Pragati Books
9/1, Montieth Road, Behind Taas Mahal, Egmore,
Chennai 600008 Tamil Nadu, Tel : (044) 6518 3535,
Mob : 94440 01782 / 98450 21552 / 98805 82331, Email : bharatsavla@yahoo.com

RETAIL OUTLETS
PUNE

Pragati Book Centre　　　　　　　　　　　　　*Pragati Book Centre*
157, Budhwar Peth, Opp. Ratan Talkies,　　　　676/B, Budhwar Peth, Opp. Jogeshwari Mandir,
Pune 411002, Maharashtra　　　　　　　　　　Pune 411002, Maharashtra
Tel : (020) 2445 8887 / 6602 2707, Fax : (020) 2445 8887　Tel : (020) 6601 7784 / 6602 0855

Pragati Book Centre　　　　　　　　　　　　　*PBC Book Sellers & Stationers*
Amber Chamber, 28/A, Budhwar Peth,　　　　　152, Budhwar Peth, Pune 411002, Maharashtra
Appa Balwant Chowk, Pune : 411002, Maharashtra,　Tel : (020) 2445 2254 / 6609 2463
Tel : (020) 20240335 / 66281669
Email : pbcpune@pragationline.com

MUMBAI
Pragati Book Corner
Indira Niwas, 111 - A, Bhavani Shankar Road, Dadar (W), Mumbai 400028, Maharashtra
Tel : (022) 2422 3526 / 6662 5254, Email : pbcmumbai@pragationline.com

Dedicated To …
    My Mother & Father
    Mrs. Supriya Datta Joglekar,
    Mr. Datta Shankar Joglekar

Special Thanks to My Husband
    Mr. Javed Shaikh
    and My Daughter Kashish

… **Mahek Shaikh**

PREFACE

It gives me an immense pleasure in presenting this book, 'Mobile Computing'. This book has been designed to serve as a text book for students of Master of Computer Application (MCA), Semester – IV.

The goal of presenting this book is to introduce and explain the basic concepts of Mobile Computing as well as android application development. This book is an introduction to the field of mobile communications and it also explains about all the aspects of mobile communication, a brief knowledge of Internet and networking. The last chapters of this book contain the introduction to new operating system, android environment. This will surely help students to understand the practical aspect of this system along with theory. This book will assist students to write complete software application using android development environment. For the students familiar with Java Programming language, this book will be an accelerated guide and a comprehensive reference for developing application using android.

This book has been written which reflects the newly revised syllabus of University of Pune. I have tried to keep the language as simple and lucid as possible. It highlights important concepts by giving suitable examples wherever necessary. It comprises a wide collection of methods and constructors along with syntax and their appropriate explanation.

A special attention has been paid to develop the interest of students in today's most popular android application development. Throughout the book, I have taken all the efforts to keep students interested in the objective of learning this new operating system.

There are many people who have helped me a lot while constructing this book.

I sincerely thank **Shri. Dineshbhai Furia** and **Shri. Jignesh Furia**, the publishers for showing the confidence and giving me an opportunity to reach out to the students of management studies.

My special appreciation goes to Mr. Mahesh Swami and Ms. Pradnya Jagtap who were involved in designing and developing the contents of this book.

I thank Prof. Gautam Bapat, Mr. Ilyas Shaikh, Ms. Chaitali Takale, Mr. Vijay Shete and all the staff members of Nirali Prakashan, Pune for their important inputs and valuable suggestions to make this book presentable.

Suggestions and positive criticism to improve this book are most welcome!!!

Author

SYLLABUS

1. **Introduction to Mobile Communications and Computing**
   1.1 **Mobile Computing (MC):** Introduction to MC, applications, limitations, and architecture.
   1.2 **Cellular Overview**
   Cellular networks, Cellular concept, Location management, Handoffs.

2. **Wireless LANs and Application Overview**
   2.1 WLAN
   2.2 Wireless applications
   2.3 Mac issues (Hidden and exposed terminals, Near and far terminals),
   2.4 Mobile IP
   2.5 Mobile ad-hoc Networks (MANET)
   2.6 TCP Issues
   2.7 Disconnected operations
   2.8 Data broadcasting
   2.9 Mobile agents

3. **GSM**
   3.1 GSM
   - Air-interface, channel structure, timing
   - Mobile Services (Bearer, Tele-and supplementary services)
   - System Architecture
     - Radio subsystem
     - Network and switching subsystem
     - Operation subsystem
   3.2 Protocols
   Localization and calling
   Handover
   Value Added Services
   - SMS
   - Cell Broadcast Service
   - MMS
   - Location Services
   3.3 WAP
   - Architecture
   - Protocol stack
   - Application environment - Application demo

4. **Access Technologies**
   4.1 Blue Tooth, GPRS, 802.11, CDMA 3
   4.2 Mobile Phone Technologies (1G, 2G, 2.5G, 3G)

5. **Database Issues**
   5.1 Hoarding techniques
   5.2 Caching invalidation mechanisms
   5.3 Client server computing with adaptation,
   5.4 Power-aware and context-aware computing,
   5.5 Transactional models, query processing, recovery, and quality of service issues.

6. **Platforms/Operating Systems for Application Development**
   6.1 Palm OS
   6.2 Windows CE

    6.3   Embedded Linux
    6.4   J2ME (Introduction)
    6.5   Symbian (Introduction)

7. **Android Application Development**
    7.1   Overview of Android
    7.2   Devices running android
    7.3   Why Develop for Android
    7.4   Features of android
    7.5   Architecture of Android, Libraries
    7.6   Software development kit

8. **Designing the User Interface**
    8.1   Introducing views and view groups,
    8.2   Introducing layouts, Creating new views,
    8.3   Creating and using Menus

9. **Starting with Application Coding**
    9.1   Introducing Intents
    9.2   Introducing Adapters
    9.3   Using Internet Resources
    9.4   Introducing Dialogs
    9.5   Capturing Date and Time
    9.6   Validating and Handling Input data

10. **Accessing Location Based Services Application**
    10.1   Selecting Location Provider
    10.2   Finding your location.
    10.3   Creating map based activities

11. **Data Storage, Retrieval and Sharing**
    11.1   File system in android
    11.2   Internal and external storage
    11.3   Saving and loading files
    11.4   File Management tools

12. **Introduction to SQLite**
    12.1   Creating SQLite database,
    12.2   Editing Tasks with SQLite
    12.3   Cursors and content values
    12.4   Working with Android database

13. **Peer-to-Peer to Communication**
    13.1   Accessing Telephony Hardware
    13.2   Introducing Android Instant Messaging
    13.3   GTalk Service : Using, binding & Making connection
    13.4   Managing chat Sessions
    13.5   Sending and receiving Data messages
    13.6   Introducing SMS
    13.7   Using, sending & Listening SMS Messages

14. **Accessing Android Hardware**
    14.1   Audio, Video and using the camera.
    14.2   Introducing Sensor Manager
    14.3   Android Telephony
    14.4   Using Bluetooth
    14.5   Manage network and Wi-Fi connections

15. **Publishing Android Application to Market**

CONTENTS

1. Introduction to Mobile Communications and Computing — 1.1 – 1.26
2. Wireless LANs and Application Overview — 2.1 – 2.42
3. GSM — 3.1 – 3.32
4. Access Technologies — 4.1 – 4.30
5. Database Issues — 5.1 – 5.22
6. Platforms/Operating Systems for Application Development — 6.1 – 6.26
7. Android Application Development — 7.1 – 7.48
8. Designing the User Interface — 8.1 – 8.34
9. Starting with Application Coding — 9.1 – 9.52
10. Accessing Location Based Services Application — 10.1 – 10.26
11. Data Storage, Retrieval and Sharing — 11.1 – 11.30
12. Introduction to SQLite — 12.1 – 12.18
13. Peer-to-Peer Communication — 13.1 – 13.18
14. Accessing Android Hardware — 14.1 – 14.24
15. Publishing Android Application to Market — 15.1 – 15.10

Chapter 1...

INTRODUCTION TO MOBILE COMMUNICATIONS AND COMPUTING

1.1 Introduction to Mobile Computing
    1.1.1 Mobile Computing
    1.1.2 Mobile Computing Devices
    1.1.3 Mobile Communication Applications
    1.1.4 Limitations of Mobile Computing
    1.1.5 Mobile Computing Architecture
1.2 Cellular Concept
    1.2.1 Basic Principle of Cellular System
    1.2.2 Mobility Management
    1.2.3 Location Management
    1.2.4 Handoff
    • Practice Question

1.1 Introduction to Mobile Computing

Mobile computing is human-computer interaction which involves mobile communication, mobile hardware and mobile software. Computing is based on ad hoc and infrastructure networks as well as communication properties, protocols and data formats. Hardware includes mobile devices or device components. Mobile software that deals with the characteristics and requirements of mobile application.

- Man is a social human being. It is his primary need to communicate with each other for day to day transactions. For short distances we can talk directly but for long distances we cannot talk directly due to weak sound. In a broad sense the purpose of communication is to establish a link between two points. These points may be situated on the earth or on the other in space.
- A new era was established a link for communication by sending first telegraphic message by Samuel F.B. Marse in 1836. This is called Electrical Communication.
- Communication is a transmission and reception of data streams that may be voice data or multimedia streams. This streams are past through fiber, wire or wireless medium.

- During transmission the transmitter sends the signals according the define regulations, recommended standards and protocols.
- When communication is held on long distance it is called as telecommunication.
- Depending upon the type of information to be sent and received different electronic communication systems namely radio telephony, telegraphy, broad casting, radar, computer communication, point to point and mobile communication systems has been developed over the years.

Mobile computing provides mobility to device which can carry all necessary files and software to operate the application. It also provides the ability to use computing capability without a pre defined location.

- Depending upon the type of communication used for transmission of electromagnetic signals the communication system can be classified into two groups as follows
  1. Wire Communication
  2. Wireless Communication
- These conventional telephone systems have some limitations
  1. Limited service Capability
  2. Poor service performance
  3. Inefficient frequency spectrum utilization

1.1.1 Mobile Computing

The first public radio mobile system in the USA was introduced in the year 1946 and it is considered to be the beginning of era of public mobile communication services.

The cellular concept was developed by AT&T bell laboratories of USA in the year 1947 and in the year 1962. This was the first test conducted to explore commercial applications.

With the development of highly reliable miniature, solid state radio frequency (RF) hardware in the 1970's, the wireless (Radio) communication era was born.

Definition: A technology that allows transmission of data, via a computer, without having to be connected to a fixed physical link.

With rapidly increasing penetration of laptop, computers which are primarily used by mobile users to access internet services (Email and www), henceforth the need for access the internet services in a mobile environment was an emerging requirement.

- Mobile computing is used for computing physical mobility environment of a user. While moving a user must be able to access information, data or other logical objects from any device in any network.
- For optimal use of resources and to increase productivity mobile computing should be spread over wired as well as wireless media.

- Mobile station can move anywhere, local (offline) and remote (real time) services must be available to it.
- It provides global service portability which makes services portable and available in every environment.
- For accessing the location of a user (virtual home environment (VHE)) should be established in which user recite in foreign network still it may get computing environment of its home network.

Mobile Computing Functions

A computing environment is said to be mobile if it supports few of the characteristics mentioned below :

- User mobility – the user should be able to move with same set of services from one physical location to another i.e. may be in home network or remote network.
- Network mobility – Network mobility can be defined in two ways:
    1. User mobile is moving from one network to another network and avails the same set of services. For e.g. - a user can move from 3G network to Wi-Fi network while using the same services.
    2. The network itself is moving for e.g. – mobile adhoc network (MANET). In this each node is identified with host and a router. When a mobile moves router changes the routing table structure for e.g. – These are mostly used in sensor networks where nodes are moving constantly.
- When user moves from one bearer to another, he should be able to use the same application. For e.g. – a user uses WAP bearer service in Delhi now he moves to Mumbai where WAP is not supported then the same application can be accessed by using voice or sums bearer.
- Device portability should be provided to user, to access the same application.
- A user must be able to access the same session even if he moves from one user agent environment to another. For e.g. – a user using his application through CDMA (Code division multiplexing access) in network. The user entered in basement to park his bike and got disconnected from CDMA network. He goes to home office and start using desktop so that unfinished session moves from mobile device to desktop.
- The device can be either client or server. When it is server, IP mobility needs to be taken care of.

1.1.2 Mobile Computing Devices

- There are two categories of mobile computing devices. It may be a computing or a communication device.
    - Computing devices may be are laptop, palmtop or desktop.
    - Communication devices are fixed to telephone line, mobile or digital TV.

- Mobile computing uses different kinds of networks. These can be fixed telephone networks, GSM, GPRS, ATM (Asynchronous Transfer Mode) Frame relay, ISDN (Integrated service digital network), CDMA, CDPD (Cellular Digital Packet Data), DSL (Digital Subscriber Loop), Dial up WIFI (Wireless Fidelity), 802.11, Bluetooth and Broadband etc.

1.1.3 Mobile Communication Applications

- In today's era, all people need data and information through mobile computing services.
- The list of mobile computing applications is unending. It depends on the basis of the lifestyle and the business need of an individual person and accordingly they can be grouped in different categories.
- It includes applications on personal, youth, news, weather, related to shopping, entertainment, corporate level, virtual office, sports, telebanking, Digital Library, application, for speech/hearing challenges people and so on.
- It also has telemedicine, healthcare, virtual laboratories, job facilitator, alerts and notification.
- These applications help in making our day to day transactions to be solved in sorted manner.

1.1.4 Limitations of Mobile Computing

1. **Range and Bandwidth**
   - Mobile internet access is generally slower than direct access from cable connection.
   - Mobile devices uses technologies such as GPRs, EDGE more recently HSDPA and HSUPA, 3G and 4G networks.
   - These networks are available only in the range of commercial cell phone towers.
   - Higher speed wireless LAN is inexpensive but has very limited range.

2. **Security Standards**
   - Security is a major concern while considering the mobile computing standards on the fleet. One can easily attack the VPN through a huge number of networks interconnected through the line.

3. **Power Consumption**
   - Mobile notes must rely entirely on battery power combined with compact size of mobile device.
   - When a power outlet or portable generator is not available mobile device depends on battery, so it must provide good battery life.
   - Combined with the compact size of many mobile devices, this often means unusually expensive batteries must be used to obtain the necessary battery life.

4. **Transmission Interference**
   - While moving a mobile device, may have range problem with nearest signal point. Reception of signal in tunnels, some buildings and rural area is often poor.

5. Potential Health Hazards
- Now a days many questions concerning mobile phone radiations and health have been raised.
- People who use mobile devices while driving are often distracted from driving and are thus assumed more likely to be involved in traffic accidents. Cell phones may interfere with sensitive medical devices.

6. Human Interface with Device
- User interacts with mobile phones through screens and keyboard.
- Screens and keyboards tend to be small, which may make hard to use and alternate input method such as speech and handwriting recognition needs training.

Advantages of Mobile Computing

The advantages of Mobile Computing have been highlighted in many fields of which a few are described below:

- **For Estate Agents:** Estate agents can work either at home or out in the field. With mobile computers they can be more productive. They can obtain current real estate information by accessing multiple listing services, which they can do from home, office or car when out with clients. They can provide clients with immediate feedback regarding specific homes or neighborhoods, and with faster loan approvals, since applications can be submitted on the spot. Therefore, mobile computers allow them to devote more time to clients.
- **Emergency Services:** Ability to receive information on the move is vital where the emergency services are involved. Information regarding the address, type and other details of an incident can be dispatched quickly, via a CDPD system using mobile computers, to one or several appropriate mobile units which are in the vicinity of the incident.
- **In courts:** Defense counsels can take mobile computers in court. When the opposing counsel references a case which they are not familiar, they can use the computer to get direct, real-time access to on-line legal database services, where they can gather information on the case and related precedents. Therefore mobile computers allow immediate access to a wealth of information, making people better informed and prepared.
- **In companies:** Managers can use mobile computers in, say, critical presentations to major customers. They can access the latest market share information. At a small recess, they can revise the presentation to take advantage of this information. They can communicate with the office about possible new offers and call meetings for discussing responds to the new proposals. Therefore, mobile computers can leverage competitive advantages.

- **Stock Information Collation/Control:** In environments where access to stock is very limited i.e.: factory warehouses. The use of small portable electronic databases accessed via a mobile computer would be ideal.

  Data collated could be directly written to a central database, via a CDPD network, which holds all stock information hence the need for transfer of data to the central computer at a later date is not necessary. This ensures that from the time that a stock count is completed, there is no inconsistency between the data input on the portable computers and the central database.

- **Credit Card Verification:** At Point of Sale (POS) terminals in shops and supermarkets, when customers use credit cards for transactions, the intercommunication required between the bank central computer and the POS terminal, in order to effect verification of the card usage, can take place quickly and securely over cellular channels using a mobile computer unit. This can speed up the transaction process and relieve congestion at the POS terminals.

- **Taxi/Truck Dispatch:** Using the idea of a centrally controlled dispatcher with several mobile units (taxis), mobile computing allows the taxis to be given full details of the dispatched job as well as allowing the taxis to communicate information about their whereabouts back to the central dispatch office. This system is also extremely useful in secure deliveries i.e.: Securicor. This allows a central computer to be able to track and receive status information from all of its mobile secure delivery vans. Again, the security and reliability properties of the CDPD system shine through.

- **Electronic Mail/Paging:** Usage of a mobile unit to send and read emails is a very useful asset for any business individual, as it allows him/her to keep in touch with any colleagues as well as any urgent developments that may affect their work. Access to the Internet, using mobile computing technology, allows the individual to have vast arrays of knowledge at his/her fingertips.

  Paging is also achievable here, giving even more intercommunication capability between individuals, using a single mobile computer device.

1.1.5 Mobile Computing Architecture

Mobile computing architecture allows in maintaining the connection of internal network with the user wherever it moves.

Important Components of Mobile Architecture

1. **Scalability:** It must provide all recovery requirements on both small and large scale.
2. **Secure:** Encryption plays important role in terms of security. Transmissions protocols must support encryption (SSL) via secure transits HTTPs.
3. **Reliable:** Mobile architecture should provide reliability.

4. **Best Practices:**
   - Data should be populated for data base views.
   - Use version number to track updates during synchronization.
   - Middle ware should maintain only necessary information of the user.
   - UI on multiple screens should have common elements.

The network centric mobile computing architecture is based on three tiers.
- In the three tier architecture the first layer is the user interface or presentation tier. This tier handles user services such as session, dialogue and display management, text inputs etc. It recites on user system interface.
- The second tier is the process management or application tier. In this layer business logic and rules are executed for application programs or process management. It also ensures reliable completion of all transactions.
- The third tier is database management or data tier. It provides increased performance, flexibility, maintainability, reusability, scalability. It hides the complexity of distributed processing from user.
- Considering the mobile computing we have to consider that the network can be access through any network, bearer agent and device. To access the network server it should be always connected to the internet. For that device needs any web browser it can be Internet explorer, Mozilla or Chrome.
- Mobile three tier architecture consists of presentation, application and data tier. This layer can be further sub layered according to instances.

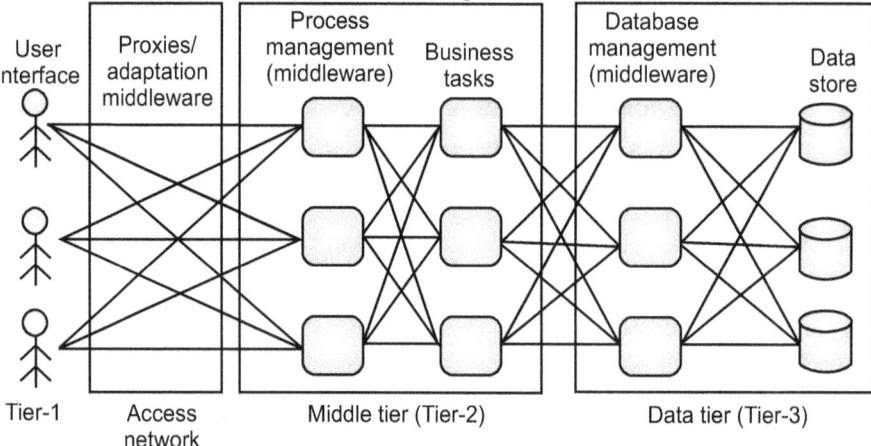

Fig 1.1: Three-tier architecture for mobile computing

Presentation Tier

This tier directly interacts with the user. It provides agent applications and systems.
- These applications run on client side and user may interact through visual or audio means to receive information .they also use keyboard (laptop, computer or cell phone),pen(tablet PC, palmtops),touch screen(kiosks0 or voice 9telephone0 to give input to the system.

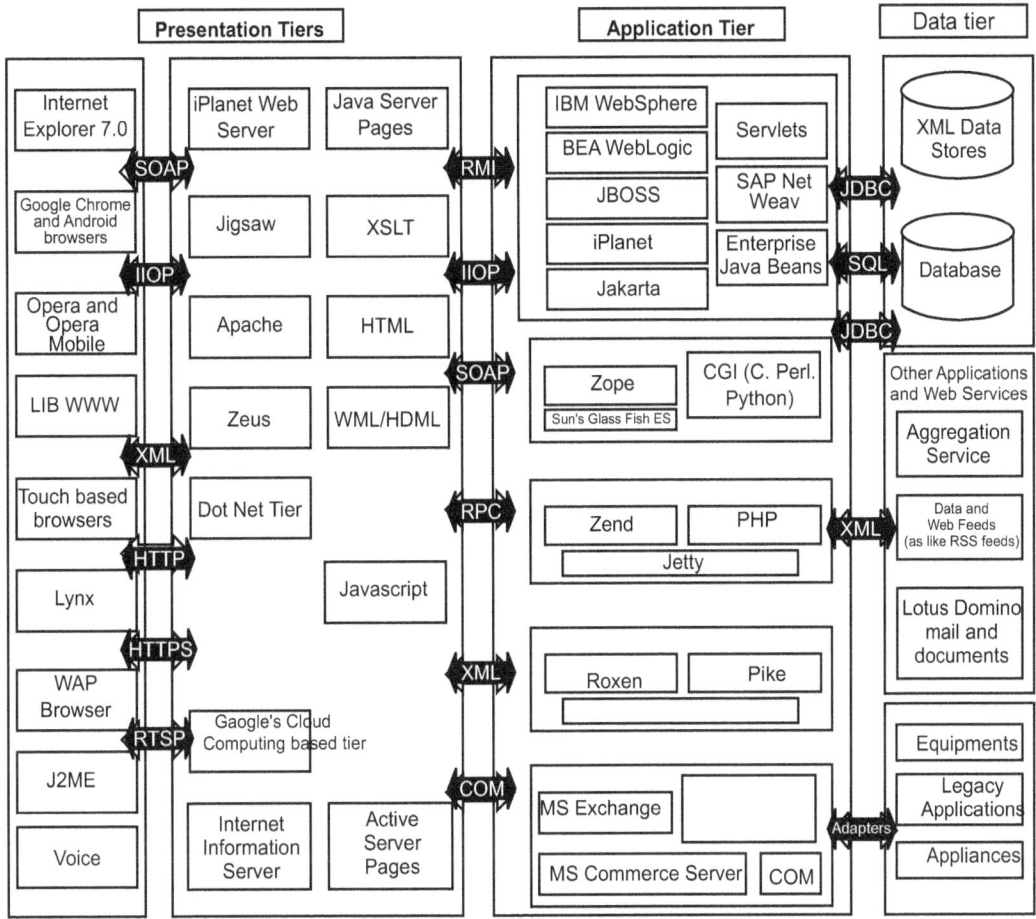

Fig. 1.2: The mobile computing architecture

- This layer includes web browser (like Mozilla, lynx, Internet Explorer and Netscape navigator), WAP browser and customized client programs. These all act as software agent in the client device.
- Some of the agents work as a web scraper. Functionality of HTTP browser and an automate web browsers are embedded within a web scraper.
- Role of web scraper is to filter off the data which is taken from web page, according to predefined templates.
- These applications can be work in B2B (business to business), B2C (business to consumer), B2E (business to employee), M2M (machine to machine) space. Applications range from simple task of accessing other application, ecommerce, supply chain management up to legacy system.

Application tier:

This is the middle tier which acts as business logic processes inputs, make decision to retrieve output.

- This layer include technologies like CGIs, Java, JSP, .Net services, PHP or cold fusion, deployed in products like apache, webspere, weblogic, iPlanet, JBoss or ZEND.

- Mobile computing environment demands more management functions besides applying business logic. Such as decisions on rending, network management, security, data store access. These are implemented by using middle ware software, that works between operating system and user facing application.
- In a net-centric architecture middleware framework works in between an agent and business logic.
- Middleware framework has wide variety of groups :
  1. Message –oriented middleware
  2. Transaction processing middleware
  3. Database middleware
  4. Communication middleware
  5. Distributed objects and components middleware
  6. Transcoding middleware.

1. **Message oriented middleware (MOM):**
   MOM is mostly used in event driven application. It connects through asynchronous exchange of data.
   - The message can contain formatted data, requests for action or unsoldered application.
   - The publisher application has responsibility to notify all subscribers that event has happened e.g. message queue (MQ series) from IBM, Java message Service in Java.

1. **Transaction processing middleware:**
   It provides tools and an environment for developing transaction based distributed application.
   - This middleware is able to put input at the point of information source in the system and output the data at the point of sink in the system.
   - It maps various client requests through application service routines to various application tasks.
   - It can optimize the use of resources which are required by client functions by multiplexing them into smaller set of application service routine.

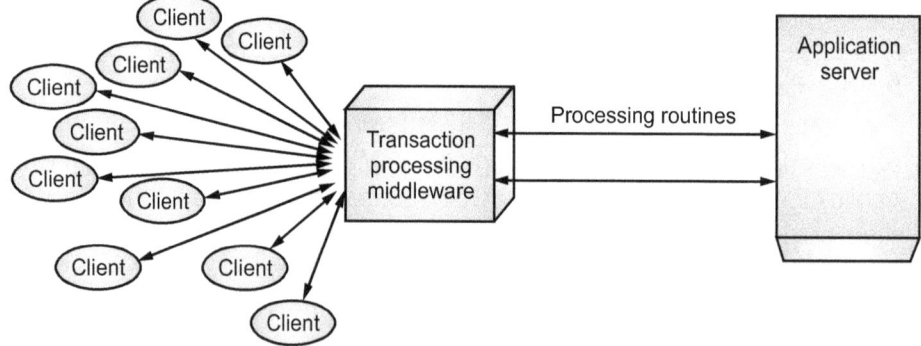

Fig 1.3: Transaction processing middleware

E.g. CICS (Customer Information Control System) in IBM mainframe computers.

3. Communication middleware

In this middleware, like connecting one application to another through telnet.

- Meditation server automates the telnet protocol to interact with these nodes in network.

1. Distributed object and components middleware

An example of this is CORBA(Common Object Request Broker Architecture).

- It is very useful; with this any situation can be handled easily as it integrates so many vendors, with sizes ranging from mainframes through minis and desktops.

1. Transcoding middleware

It is used to translate the code so that communication may be held easily between different clients.

- E.g. we want to access page from mobile phone which is supported by WAP (Wireless Application Protocol). Then, the HTML page should be converted from HTML to WML (Wireless Markup Language).
- Technically Transcoding is used for content adaption to fit the need of the device. This content adaption needs to cope up with network bandwidth. E.g. some frames in video clip need to be dropped for low bandwidth. For content adaption IETF (Internet Engineering Task Force) allows the Intent Content Adaption Protocol (ICAP). ICAP is standardized and described in RFC 3507. It is described as follows.

Intent content adaptation protocol (ICAP)

It is used to transpose on HTTP messages as "remote procedure call "is executed on HTTP request.

- Client sends HTTP message in ICAP server, server executes its transformation service on message it may be HTTP request or HTTP response.
- Before document is displayed to all agent it is checked to all agent it is checked for virus.
- It works at the edge part of network.
- Data flow in ICAP environment :

1. A user agent makes a request to an ICAP capable surrogate for an object on an origin server.
2. The surrogate sends the request to the ICAP server.
3. The ICAP server executes the ICAP resource's service on the request and sends the possibly modified request or a response back to the ICAP client.

4. The surrogate sends the request, possibly different from the original client's request, to the origin server.
5. The origin server responds to the request.
6. The surrogate sends the reply (from either the ICAP or the origin server) to the client.

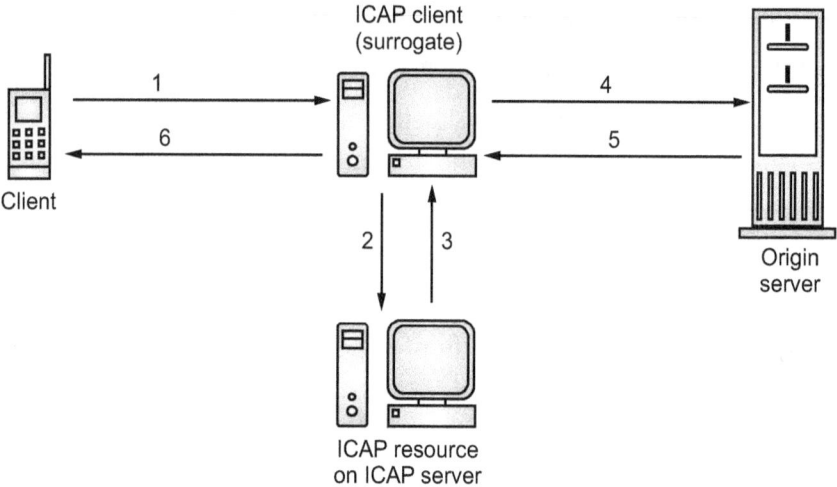

Fig. 1.4: Typical data flow in ICAP environment

Web services:

Web services provide exchange of information independent of variety of platforms and framework.

- It is software system identified by a URL, whose public interfaces & binding defined using XML.
- Web services are capable of :
  1. Exchanging messages
  2. Describing web services
  3. Publishing and discovering web service description.
- This involves the operations like publish, find and bind.

Data (tier 3)

This tier is used to store data needed by the application and acts as repository for both temporary and permanent data.

- It stores, simple text files, sophisticated relational database, legacy hierarchical database. In XML format it increases the interoperability of system with other system.
- In database middleware, the business logic should be independent of device capability. i.e. business logic should be independent database.

- It runs between application program and database. These acts as database connector. Database middleware allows business logic to be independent and transparent of the database technology and database vendor.

  e.g. ODBC, JDBC are such middleware, using this application can access data from any data store.

Cellular System:

The main aim of the early mobile radio system was to provide the coverage to a large area with the help of a signal high power transmitter having an antenna mounted on a fall tower. But this radio system suffers from the number of problems. It has limited radio coverage area and limited radio spectrum.

- Therefore this type of radio system is not used in practice.
- Hence it becomes necessary to restructure the mobile radio telephone system to enhance the user capacity, also the proper spectrum allocation in proportional with increasing demand and also larger coverage area.
- A cellular system spreads over a large geographical area, within a limited frequency spectrum.
- Base station transmitter is restricted to small geographical area called a cell for high capacity transmission. Same radio channel may be used by another base station located at same distance away.
- A switching technique called handoff performs uninterrupted calls when user moves from one cell to another cell.

1.2 Cellular Concept

The cellular concept was a major breakthrough in solving the problem of spectral congestion and user capacity. It offers very high capacity in limited spectrum allocation without any major technological changes.

- The cellular concept was developed by AT and T Bell Laboratories of United States in 1947, but the first tests were conducted in 1962 to explore commercial applications.
- A small geographic coverage area of a base station with the diameter of 2 to 50 km each of which allocated a number of radio frequency (RF) channels is called a cell. Thus cell represents the coverage area of base station, where it acts as a transmitter.
- The hexagonal shape of a cell shown in Fig. 1.5 (a) is a conceptual and a simplest model for a cell of the radio coverage for each station.
- It has been universally adopted, since hexagon permits easy and manageable analysis of a cellular measurements or propagation predication models.

- A group of cells is known as a cluster. Cluster size (n) is not fixed. It depends on the requirement.

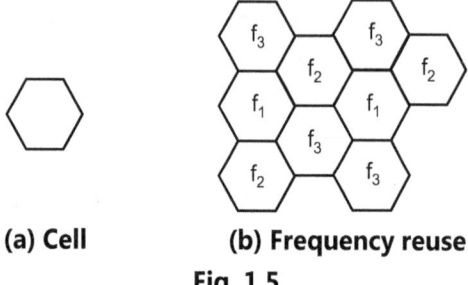

(a) Cell   (b) Frequency reuse

Fig. 1.5

The shape and size of a cell – The size of a cell is irregular usually and the coverage area in terms of cells is a typical topology for a cellular radio system. The hexagonal cell shape is simplified Model of the radio coverage for each base station. Hexagonal permit easy analysis of a cellular system

1.2.1 Basic Principle of Cellular System (April 2015)

The basic working of cellular system is based on frequency reusable system.

In the basic cellular concept BS (Base Station) antennas are designed to achieve the desired coverage within the particular cell. By limiting the coverage area, same groups of channels may be used to cover different cells that are separated from one another by distance to keep interference level (co-channel interference) within tolerable limits. The process of selecting and allocating channel groups for all cellular base stations within a system called Frequency Reuse. [Refer Fig. 1.5 (b)].

- The basic principle of a cellular (radio) system is to divide a large geographic service area into cells with diameters from 2 to 50 km each of which is allocated a number of radio frequency (RF) channels.
- The transmitter in each adjacent cell operates on different frequencies to avoid the interference.
- Since, however, transmit power and antenna height in each cell is relatively low, the cells that are sufficiently far apart can reuse the same set of frequencies without causing co-channels interference.
- As the demand for cellular mobile service grows, the additional cells can be added, and as traffic demands grows in a given area, the cells can be splitted to accommodate the additional traffic.
- A cellular (radio) system provides the capability to hand-off calls in progress, as the mobile terminal (user) moves between cells.
- Generally, fixed amount of frequency spectrum is allocated to a cellular system by the Federal Communications Commission's (FCC) in the United States.

- The multiple access techniques are then deployed so that many users can share the available spectrum in an efficient manner.
- The multiple access systems specify how signals from different sources can be combined efficiently over a given RF band and then separated at the destination without manual interference.
- The three basic multiple access technologies used in cellular systems are as under:
  1. Frequency Division Multiple Access (FDMA)
  2. Time Division multiple Access (TDMA)
  3. Code Division multiple Access (CDMA)
- The FDMA technique is used in analog cellular systems, where as the TDMA and CDMA techniques are used in digital cellular system.
- These technologies are used to avoid interference between transmitters by combining them with each other.
- When cellular system using FDM combined with TDM is used the following allocation of frequencies can be held:
  1. Fixed channel Allocation, in which fixed frequencies are assigned to the clusters. FCA is used in GSM system as it is much easier to implement.
  2. Borrowing channel allocation scheme is used when there is a case of having heavy traffic load in one cell and light traffic load in another cell. More frequencies are allocated dynamically to the loaded cell.
  3. Dynamic channel allocation, it is implemented in DECT (Digital Enhanced Cordless Telecommunication), here frequencies can only be borrowed, with this the danger of interference increases.
- When cellular system uses CDM users are separated by the code. In this scheme CDM cell shrinks if the load increases. If more users are added it increases the noise, it leads to path loss and transmission errors. Finally mobile stations move away from base station and drop out of the cell.

Cell Splitting

Cell splitting is the process of subdividing a congested cell into smaller cells. Each with its own Base Station and corresponding reduction in antenna height and transmitter power.

- Cell splitting increases the capacity of a cellular system since, it increases the number of Times the channels are reused.
- By defining a new cell which has a smaller radius than the original cell and by installing this smaller cell called micro cells between the existing cells.

- Capacity of network increases due to the additional number of channels per unit area.
- Cell splitting allows a system to grow by replacing large cell with smaller cells while not Upsetting the channel allocation scheme required to maintain the minimum co-channel Reuse ratio Q between co-channel cells
- After cells are spitted into the smaller cells the Base Stations are placed at corners of the cells and the area Served by Base Station A is assumed to be saturated with traffic i.e. the blocking of base Station A exceeds acceptable rates.
- New base stations are therefore needed in the region to increase the number of channels in the area and to reduce the area served by the single base station.
- In this Fig. 1.6 the original base station A has been surrounded by six new microcell bases Station.

Fig. 1.6: Cell Splitting

- In this smaller cells were added in such a way to preserve the frequency reuse plan of the System.

1.2.2 Mobility Management

It allows locating roaming MTS at any time to deliver its services and to maintain connections as the mobile station moves from one location to another location.

- In PCS (Personal Communication Service) network the most important issue is Mobility Management. The PCS network gets affected by the way the network manages the movement of mobile users.
- The mobile service area is covered by a set of Base Stations (BSs) which are responsible for relying the call to and from mobile station (MSs) located in the same coverage area. All base stations are connected to Mobile Switching Center (MSCs) by land links.

- MSC is nothing but the telephone exchange, configured for all mobile applications. As mobile user moves from one location to another location, to locate the current destination of mobile user two databases are used that are home location register (HLR) and visitor location register (VLR).

Mobility management consist of two components:
- 1. **Location management:** To locate the mobile station to deliver incoming calls to them at reasonable cost.
  2. **Handoff or Handover management:** To transfer ongoing calls to adjacent cells as mobile station moves from one access point in the network to another.

1.2.3 Location Management
- To update the location the following schemes are used :
  1. Static or global schemes: LU (Location Updater) is triggered based on the topology of network.
  2. Dynamic or local schemes: A mobile station sends a message to Location updater according to the time elapsed (time based method), the number of cells visited (movement based method) or the distance in terms of cell traversed. (Distance based method).
  3. Time based method is applied to signal strength, Time of Arrival (TOA), or Difference of Arrival (TDOA) as measurement for location estimation.
  4. In Movement based method, each mobile station keeps a counter of the number of cells visited.
- A location update is performed when this counter exceeds a predefines threshold value (d).
- Centre cell is the cell where the last location update occurred.
- Residing area of the mobile station is the area in which the mobile can be located and this area is within a maximum distance of d-1 from the centre cell.
- Polling cycle the process which is done by the network when a call arrives to a mobile station, the network send polling signal to target cell in the residing area and wait for response.

Distance based method:
- The distance between two points is taken as common metric so as to see the similarity among the components of population. The commonly used distance measure is the Euclidean which defines the distance between two points p = (p1, p2...) and q = (q1, q2...) is given by Formula, $d(p, q) = d(q, p) = \sqrt{(q_1 - p_1)^2}$.
- It assigns a distance measured between data.
- It finds a partition such that distance between objects within a partition (i.e. same cluster) is minimized; distance between objects from different clusters is maximized.

1.2.4 Handoff

Necessity of Handoff

The mobile telephone switching office (MTSO) monitors the level of every signal in the cellular system. If the strength of the signal diminishes by any means, then the MTSO seeks new cell that can accommodate the better quality of communications.

This intelligent decision has to be made by the MTSO quite early.

In such situations, there is necessity of hand-off in cellular mobile radio systems to handle the signal off from current channel to a new channel by MTSO, when the level of received signal in mobile phone becomes weak.

- The hand-off is always implemented on the voice channel.
- The hand-off is needed in two situations where the cell sites receives weak signal from the mobile phone;
    (1) at the cell boundary, say – 100 dBm, which is the level for requesting a hand-off in a noise limited environment and
    (2) when the mobile phone is reaching the signal strength holes (gaps) within the cell site.
- The scenario for handover is when a mobile user is engaged in conversation the MS (Mobile Station) is connected to a Base Station (BS) via a radio link. If the mobile user moves to the coverage area of another BS, the radio link to the old BS is disconnected and a radio link to the new BS should be established to continue the conversation. This process is referred to as automatic link transfer.
- Three strategies have been proposed to detect the need for handoff:
    (i) Mobile Control Handoff (MCHO) In Mobile Controlled Handoff (MCHO) the MS (Mobile Station) continuously monitors the signals of the surrounding BSs and it initiates the handoff process when some handoff criteria are met. MCHO is used in cordless (DECT) and low tier (PACS).
    (ii) Network Controlled Handoff (NCHO) In Network-Controlled Handoff (NCHO), the surrounding Base Stations (BSs) measure the signal from the Mobile Station (MS) and the network initiates the handoff process when some handoff criteria are met. NCHO is used in CT-2 plus and AMPS.
    (iii) Mobile Assisted Handoff (MAHO) - In Mobile-Assisted Handoff (MAHO), the network asks the MS to measure the signal from the surrounding BSs. The network makes the handoff decision based on reports from the MS. MAHO is used in GSM and IS-95 CDM.

1.2.4.1 Concept of Hand-off

When the cellular mobile phone unit moves out of the coverage area of a particular cell site, while the conversation is in progress the reception becomes weak. The present cell site requests the Mobile Switching Centre (MSC) to transfer the call to a new frequency channel in a new cell site without either interrupting the call or altering the user. So the MSC automatically transfers the call to a new frequency channel belonging to the new base station. The call continues as long as the user is talking. This operation is called Hand-off.

- The hand-off operation not only involves identifying a new base station, but also requires that the voice and control signals be allocated to channels associated with the new base station.
- The hand-off was first used by the AMPS (Advanced Mobile Phone Service) and then it is renamed as handover by the European systems. The user does not notice the hand-off occurrences.
- In deciding when to hand-off, it is important to ensure that the drop in the measured signal level is not due to momentary fading and that the mobile is actually moving away from the serving base station.
- In order to ensure this, the base station monitors the signal level for a certain period of time before a hand-off is initiated.
- This running average measurement of signal strength should be optimized so that unnecessary hand-offs are avoided, while ensuring that necessary hand-offs are completed before a call is terminated due to proper signal level.
- The length of time needed to decide if a hand-off is necessary depends on the speed at which the vehicle is moving.
- If the slope of the short term average received signal level in a given time interval is sleep, then the hand-off should be made quickly.
- The information about the vehicle speed is very useful in hand-off decision.
- The hand-off is the most important feature of cellular system that allows the cellular system to operate effectively in practice.
- The main criteria for call hand-off to avoid the dropped calls is the quality of transmission for hand-off to optimize global interference in the up-link and down-link transmission quality corresponding to each neighboring cell to which the mobile station could potentially be handled over.

1.2.4.2 Definition of Hand-off

- Hand-off is a process of automatically transferring the call to a new frequency channel belonging to a new base station (i.e. cell site), when the cellular mobile phone moves into a different frequency zones so that the conversation can be continued in a new frequency zone without dialing.

- The hand-off is nothing but handling the signal off from current channel to a new channel by MTSO.
- The process in which the mobile station changes from one cell to another i.e., one base station to another and the mobile station remains connected to the called person is known as hand-off operation of the base station.

1.2.4.3 Hand-off Strategies
- The processing of hand-off is an important task in cellular telephone system.
- In the hand-off strategies, higher priority is given to the hand-off request than the call initiation request in the cellular system.
- The procedure of hand-off should be performed successfully and it should not be repeated frequently.
- The system designers must specify the optimum signal level at which the hand-off is to be initiated.
- The minimum signal level Pr, minimum is first decided for maintaining the call. Then the slightly stronger signal level is used as the hand-off Pr, threshold for maintain the call.
- The difference between these two levels of the signal is denoted by a symbol delta, (Δ) and it is given by,

    Δ = Pr handoff minimum usable.
- As the value of delta (Δ) is very critical, it should not be too small or too large.
- If the value of delta (Δ) is too small, then the call may lost due to weak signal and if the value of delta (Δ) is too large, then unnecessary hand-off may take place at any time.

1.2.4.4 Advantages of Hand-off
- It avoids the drop calls when a subscriber crosses the boundary of one cell and moves into neighboring cell.
- It improves the global co channel interference level.
- It improves the load balancing between adjacent cells.

1.2.4.5 Types of Hand-off

1. Soft Hand-off

The Soft Hand-off is applied to only one kind of digital cellular system called CDMA.
- The Hand-off from CDMA cell to CDMA cell at the same CDMA frequency is called Soft Hand-off. It means that an identical frequency assignment between the old base station and new base station.

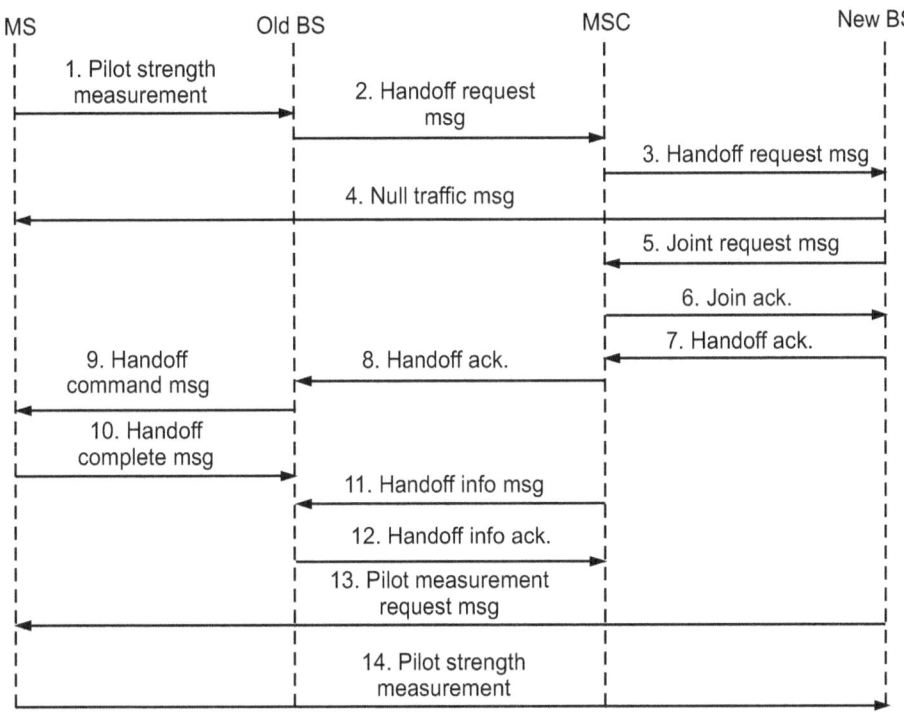

Fig. 1.7: Adding a New BS

2. Hard Hand-off

The Hard Hand-off is applied to only one kind of digital cellular system named CDMA.

- If a mobile station transmits between two base stations with different frequency assignment then it is called Hard Hand-off.
- It occurs when
    1. The mobile station is transferred between disjoint active sets.
    2. The CDMA frequency assignment changes.
    3. The frame of set changes.
    4. The mobile station is directed from a CDMA traffic channel to an analog voice channel.

3. Delayed Hand-off

The hand-off is necessary, when the level of the received signal becomes weak.

- It is implemented with two level hand-off algorithms and the hand-off is requested after certain delay of time. This is called delayed hand-off.
- If the mobile unit is moving randomly and counter is not even, then the strength of the signal received by the mobile phone unit fluctuates up and down.
- If the mobile phone unit is in the weak spot (i.e., hole) in the cell for the less than 5 seconds, then the delayed hand-off occurs.

4. Queued Hand-off

The MTSO will queue the requests of hand-off cells instead of rejecting them, if the new cell sites are busy or the call traffic is heavy. This operation is called as queuing of hand-off.

- A queuing scheme becomes effective only when the requests for hand-off arrive at the MTSO in batches or bundles.
- The queuing of hand-off is more effective than two-threshold level or delayed hand-off.
- The delay time and size of the queue are determined from the traffic pattern of the particular service area.
- It should be noted that the queuing does not guarantee the zero probability of forced termination.

5. Mobile Assisted Hand-off (MAHO)

In the second generation (2G) cellular systems, the hand-off decisions are mobile assisted. In short, the mobile assisted hand-off is known as MAHO.

- In the digital cellular system, the mobile receiver is capable of monitoring the signal strength of the set up channels of the neighboring cells while serving a cell.
- In MAHO, every mobile station measures the received power from surrounding base stations and continuously reports the results of these measurements to the serving base station.
- A hand-off is initiated, when the power received from the base station of a neighbouring cell begins to exceed the power reached from the current base station by a certain level or for a certain period of time.
- The MAHO method enables the calls to be handed over between the base stations of a much faster rate than in first generation analog systems, since the hand-off measurements are made by each mobile phone unit and mobile station it centre, it no longer constantly monitors signal strength.
- MAHO is particularly suitable for microcellular environments where the hand-offs are to be followed more frequently.

1.2.4.6 Inter-BS Handoff

In inter BS handoff the handover is in between the old and new BS, both (i.e. changing) BS are connected to the same Mobile Switching Center (MSC).

We assume that the need for handoff is detected by the MS, the following action are taken-

1. The MS suspends conversation and initiates the handoff procedure by signaling on the idle or currently free channel in the new BS then it resumes the conversation of the old BS in 1st step.

2. Upon the receipt signal the MSC transfers the encryption information to the selected idle channel of the new BS and sets up the new conversation path to the MS through the channel.

   The switch bridges the new path with the old path and informs the MS to transfer from the old channel to the new channel in step 2.

3. After the MS has been transferred to the new BS, it signals the network and resumes conversation using the new channel in step 3.

4. In last step handoff completion signal, the network removes the Bridge from the path and release resources associated with the old channel.

   - The whole process must be completed as quickly as possible, to ensure that the new link is established before the old link fails.
   - The handoff procedure is used with mobile controlled handoff strategy. For this all the handoff signaling messages are exchanged between MS and old BS through the failing link.
   - If the new BS does not have idle channel the handoff call may be dropped or force to terminate
   - If the no channel is available then the handoff is blocked and call is held on the current channel in the old cell until the call is completed. It is called non prioritized scheme.
   - To reduce forced termination and to promote call completion. Three channel schemes have been proposed.

1. Reserved channel scheme: It is similar to the no prioritize scheme, except that some channels in each BS are reserved for handoff calls.

2. Quelling priority scheme: When the adjacent coverage areas of BSs overlap. Then there is an area where a call can be handled by either BS. This is called handoff area.

- If no channel is available in the new BS during handoff, the new BS buffers the handoff request in waiting queue.
- The MS continues to use the channel with the old BS until the new BS become available or the MS moves out of the handoff area and the call is forced to terminate.

3. Subrating scheme: It creates a new channel a handoff call by sharing resources with an existing call if no channel is available in new BS.

- Subrating means an occupied full rate channel is temporarily divided into two channels at half the original rate. One to serve the existing call and other to serve handoff request.

- In the inter system handoff the new and old BSs are connected to different MSCs that is MSC are changing.
- Trunk connection after and before the intersystem handoff.
- Mobile users move from the BS which is controlled by MSC A and enters into the area covered by MSC B.

The intersystem needs the following steps to complete the intersystem handoff

1. MSC A request MSC B to perform handoff. MSC B then selects a candidate BS1, BS2 and interrogates it for signal quality parameter values, along with other relevant information to MSC A.

2. MSC A checks if the MS has made too many handoffs (i.e. handoffs between BS1 and BS2 and where MS is overlapped area) or intersystem trunks are not available. If so MSC A exists the procedure otherwise MSC A ask MSC B to setup a voice channel. That voice channel is available in BS2, MSC B instructs MSC A to start the radio link transfer.

3. MSC A sends the MS handoff order. MS synchronizes to BS2. After connected, the MSC B Informs MSC A that handoff is successful, MSC A then connects the call path (trunk) to MSC B and completes the handoff procedure.

There are 4 steps or cases for this –

1. **Handoff Forward:** when MS moves from one MSC to another MSC the reestablishment of a new path between MS and new MSC needs extra setup operations in PSTN (Public Switched Telephone Network) which is not available or not cost effective.

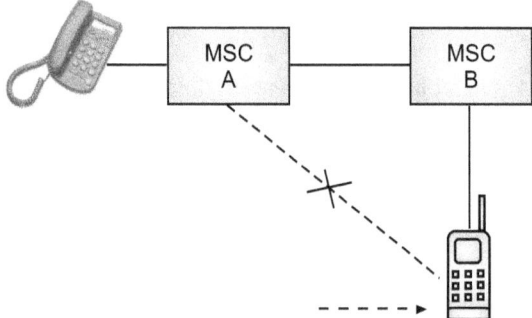

Fig. 1.8: Handoff Forward

2. **Handoff Backward:** If the MS moves back again in MSC A that is the old MSC, then connection between MSC A and MSC b is removed.

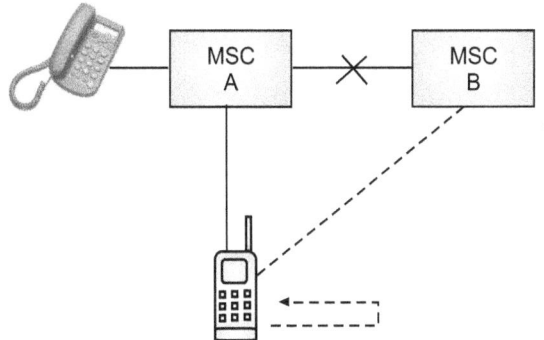

Fig. 1.9: Handoff Backward

3. **Handoff to the Third:** if MS moves from the MSC B to MSC C i.e. to the third MSC, then MSC B will be in the call path.

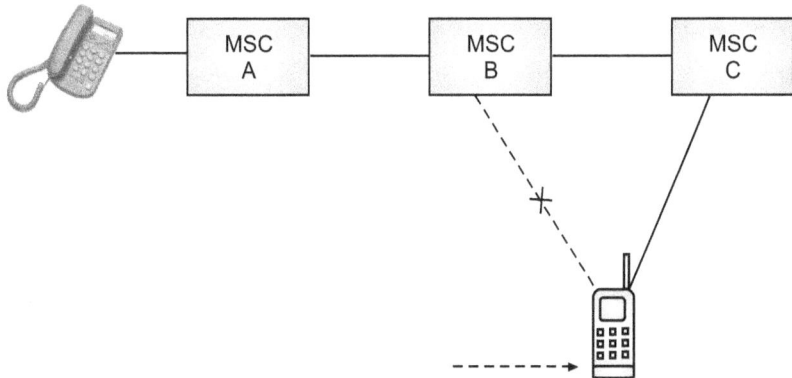

Fig. 1.10: Handoff to the Third

4. **Path Minimization:** When MS moves to the third MSC, the second MSC may be removed from the call path. That is link between MSc B and MSC A is disconnected and MSC C connects to MSC A directly. This process is called path minimization.

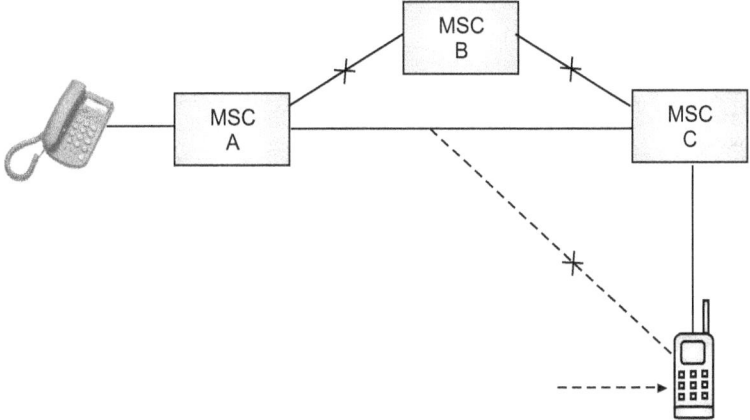

Fig. 1.11: Path Minimization

Call Roaming:

When a mobile user moves from one PCS system (e.g. system in Goa) to another (system in Mumbai), then the system should be updating the current location of the user. This is called that the system is in Roaming. This would make possible to deliver the services to mobile user.

There are two operations in Roaming:

1. **Registration or location update:** It is the process where a MS informs the system of its current location.
2. **Location tracking:** The process during which the system locates the MS. It is required when the network attempts to deliver a call to the mobile user. How the roaming management system tracks the location of the user.

The roaming management has two level strategies in that a two-tier system of home and visited location registers.

(i) **HLR:** When a user subscribe the services of PCS network, a record is created in the system's database called Home Location Register. This register keeps all the data related to all subscriptions. HLR manages and stores the data related to directory number, current location and validation period.

(ii) **VLR:** When the mobile user visits a PCS networks other than home system a temporary record for the mobile user is created in visitor location register of the visited system. VLR temporarily stores subscription information for the visiting subscribers so that corresponding MSC can provide service.

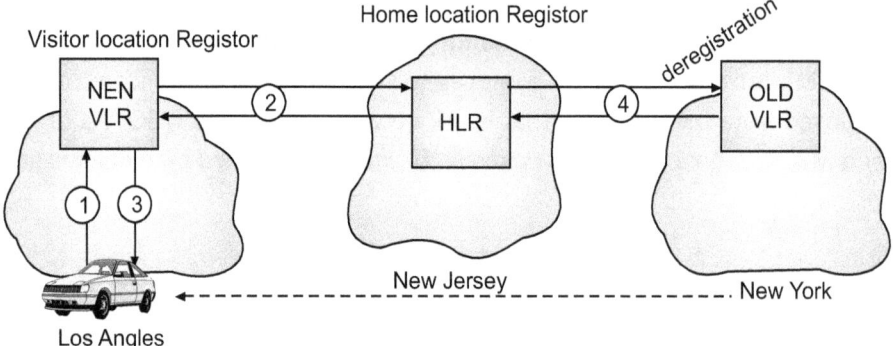

Fig. 1.12: MS Registration Process

1.2.4.7 Registration Process During Roaming

Steps for the registration process during Roaming are as follows:

Step 1: Suppose that the home system of a mobile user is in Mumbai, when the mobile user moves from one visited system i.e. Mumbai to another e.g. Goa. It must register in the VLR of the visited system.

Step 2: The new VLR informs HLR of the subscriber (user) the address of new VLR. The HLR sends an acknowledgement, which includes the MS's profile to the new VLR.

Step 3: The new VLR informs the MS of the successful registration.

Step 4: After Step 2, the HLR also sends a deregistration message to cancel the obsolete location record of the MS in the old VLR. The old VLR acknowledges the deregistration.
- To originate a call the MS first contacts the MSC in the visited PCS network.
- The call request is forwarded to the VLR for approval. If the call is accepted, the MSC set up the call to the called party by standard PSTN call setup procedure.

1.2.4.8 Call Delivery

Call delivery procedure are as follows:

Step 1: If a wire line phone attempts to call a mobile subscriber, the call is forwarded to a switch, called the originating switch in the PSTN.
- Which queries the HLR to find the current VLR of the MS for getting a routable address?
- If the originating switch is not capable of querying the HLR then the call is routed through the PSTN to the subscriber's gateway MSC, this queries the HLR to determine the current VLR serving the MS.

Step 2: The VLR returns the routable address to the originating switch through the HLR.

Step 3: Based on the routable address, a truck (voice circuit) is setup from the originating switch to the MS through the visited MSC.

Practice Question

1. What is frequency reuse channels ?
2. Explain basic architecture of cellular system.
3. What is cell splitting ? Why it is needed ?
4. Explain step by step inter system handoff.
5. Explain various generation of mobile communication system.
6. Explain the concept of hard handoff and soft handoff.

Chapter 2...

WIRELESS LANs AND APPLICATION OVERVIEW

- 2.1 WLAN
    - 2.1.1 Design Issues of Wireless LAN
    - 2.1.2 Wireless LAN Advantages
    - 2.1.3 Disadvantages of WLAN
- 2.2 Wireless Application
    - 2.2.1 Wireless LAN Architecture
    - 2.2.2 Types of Wireless LAN
    - 2.2.3 Ad hoc Versus Infrastructure Mode
    - 2.2.4 Protocol Architecture
    - 2.2.5 Description of IEEE 802.11 Layers
- 2.3 MAC Issues
    - 2.3.1 The MAC Layer Architecture
    - 2.3.2 Hidden and Exposed Terminal
    - 2.3.3 Near and Far Terminal
- 2.4 Mobile IP
    - 2.4.1 Goals, Assumptions and Requirements
- 2.5 Mobile Ad-hoc Networks
- 2.6 TCP Issues
    - 2.6.1 Implication on Mobility
    - 2.6.2 TCP over 2.5/3G Wireless Network
- 2.7 Disconnected Operations
    - 2.7.1 Overview of Coda files System
- 2.8 Data Broadcasting
    - 2.8.1 Organization of Broadcast Data
- 2.9 Mobile Agents
    - 2.9.1 Architecture
    - 2.9.2 How Does Mobile Agent Works?
    - 2.9.3 Security Concern Regarding Mobile Agents
    - 2.9.4 Events in Mobile Agent's Lifetime
    - • Practice Questions

2.1 WLAN

A Wireless Local Area Network (WLAN) is used to link two or more devices using wireless distribution method and these devices are connected to the wider internet network through an access point. This access point provides the mobility to the user who is able to move in LAN and can access the internet by using an access point it was firstly named as LAWNs (Local Area Wireless Networks), modern WANs are based on IEEE 802.11 standards, and these are marketed under WI-FI band.

- Two or more devices are connected on the base of some wireless distribution method, to create a wireless local area network. This is accessed by access point.

- The world's first wireless network is developed by the professor Norman Abramson from the University of Hawaii. This is deployed using seven computers distributed over four islands. They communicate through a central computer without using phone lines.

- For implementing wireless local area network (WLAN), a set of medium access layer (Mac) and physical layer of IEEE 802.11 is used. These are created and followed according to IEEE LAN/MAN standards.

- Network is restricted in their diameter to build a campus, single room etc and is operated by individuals not by large scale network providers.

- The goal of WLAN is to access to the internet while moving from one location to another and to introduce a higher flexibility for ad-hoc communication e.g. group meetings.

- It is also commercially known as Wi-Fi (Wirelss Fidelity)

Generations of WLAN:

First generation: It was published in June 1997 and IEEE assumed to be responsible to establish all the standards for wireless Ethernet.

Second generation: It introduced 11-Mbps 802.11b standard in September 1999.and standards like 802.11 a, 802.11g offered much higher bandwidth to access the data.

Third generation: It eliminates the boundaries between public wireless systems for seamless roaming and LAN (wired and wireless), it integrates with #G telecom networks and vertical roaming also possible in this generation. These provide application for mobile IP standards and security is being extended, this is possible in standards like 802.11f and 802.11i.

- There are four types of wireless network

Table 2.1

Type	coverage	Performance	standards
Wireless pan	Within reach of a person	moderate	Bluetooth,IEEE802.15, IrDA cable replacement for peripherals
Wireless LAN	Within building	high	IEEE 802.11,Wi-Fi, Hiper LAN
Wireless MAN	Within a city	high	Proprierity,IEEE802.16 And WIMAX
Wireless WAN	Worldwide	Low	CDPD(Cellular Digital Packet Data) and cellular 2G, 2.5G and 3G

2.1.1 Design Issues of Wireless LAN

Wireless development started in an unstructured form. Wireless communication started between the corporate LANs and mobile devices (like laptop etc.)

By using this concept IEEE is responsible for maintaining Ethernet LAN standards by assuming and maintaining the Ethernet LAN responsibilities.

- **Global operation:** WLAN is implemented in many countries, considering national and international frequency regulations. LAN equipment may be moved from one country to other country, this operation should be legal.
- **Low power:** Wireless communication should take into consideration that wireless devices runs on battery power so, it should be implemented with power saving modes and power management.
- **License free operation:** The equipment must operate in license free band, such as 2.4 GHz Ism band.
- **Robust transmission technology:** WLAN can work under difficult conditions. WLAN cannot be perfect in standard office or production environment, as antennas used are omnidirectional, not directed, so sender and receiver may move.
- **Simplified spontaneous cooperation**: WLAN should operate spontaneously after power up.
- **Protection of investment:** WLAN should be interoperable in an existing network, as lot of money is invested in constructing the previous network.
- **Safety and security:** Wireless LAN should be safe to operate, it should also consider the user privacy.

2.1.2 Wireless LAN Advantages

- **Mobility:** User can have an access to the network from anywhere and anytime. The work productivity can be increased with the help of decision making capability which is based on real time information.
- **Low implementation cost:** WLANs are easy to implement. Its set up and relocation is easy for the networks that frequently changes and also where the cabling is impossible to implement.
- **Network expansion:** It reaches where wires cannot be reached.
- **Installation speed and simplicity:** It is easy to install through walls and ceilings.
- **Design:** Wireless network allow for the small, independent design of devices, which can be even put into the packet cables for which they are not restrict the users.
- **Reduced cost of ownership:** It provides long term cost benefits as installation and maintenance cost is low as compared to wired network. It is suitable for dynamic environments.
- **Reliability:** WLANs gives more reliability than wired network which causes failure due to fault in cable.
- **Scalability:** According to need of specific application and installation WLAN can be configured to different types of topologies. The range of network starts from a small number of groups of users. To full infrastructure networks of thousands of users that allows roaming over a broad area.

2.1.3 Disadvantages of WLAN

The disadvantages of the WLAN are as follows:

1. **Quality of service:** WLAN offer lower quality than the wired network.
2. **Safety and security:** In WLAN data transmission might be interface with other high-tech equipment for example, instruments that are used in hospitals.
3. **Restrictions:** All wireless products have to be completely with national regulations.
4. **Security:** Wireless LAN transreceivers are designed to serve computers throughout a structure with uninterrupted service using radio frequencies. Because of space and cost, the antennas typically present on wireless networking cards in the end computers are generally relatively poor. In order to properly receive signals using such limited antennas throughout even in a modest area, the wireless LAN transreceiver utilizes a fairly considerable amount of power.
5. **Range:** The typical range of a common 802.11g network with standard equipment is on the order of tens meters. While sufficient for a typical home, but it will be insufficient in a larger structure.

6. **Reliability:** Like any radio frequency transmission, wireless networking signals are subject to a wide variety of interference, as well as complex propagation effects (such as multipath) that are beyond the control of the network administrator. In the case of typical networks, modulation is achieved by complicated forms of phase-shift keying (PSK) or quadrature amplitude modulation (QAM), this makes interference and propagation effects all the more disturbing. As a result, important network resources such as servers are rarely connected wirelessly.
7. **Speed:** The speed on most wireless networks (typically 1-108 Mbit/s) is reasonably slow compared to the slowest common wired networks (100 Mbit/s up to several Gbit/s). There are also performance issues caused by TCP and its built-in avoidance. For most users, however, this observation is irrelevant since the speed bottleneck is not in the wireless routing but rather in the outside network connectivity itself.

2.2 Wireless Application

There are many application areas of wireless LAN. WLAN configuration is very useful in big campuses like office environments and buildings, where user frequently moves from one location to other. e.g. offices, university campus, hotels, hospitals etc.

- **Factory shop floor:** In the environments like factory shop floor, warehouse, exhibition sites, retail shops, labs etc, where floor layouts are frequently changed and objects are also constantly moving. To implement the wired network and setting up a wired LAN in such an environment is impossible. Wireless LAN can be useful in such an environments.
- **Homes:** These will include networking of different home devices like phones, computers and applications.
- **Workgroup Environment:** WLAN can be applied in between groups as small workgroups or teams that needs to work together. This may include the two teams working from neighbouring buildings or survey team on top of a hill or rescue members after a natural disaster or an accident site. It is also useful in construction sites.
- **Public Place:** This includes airports, railways station or place where many people assemble and need to access the information.
- **War/Defence sites:** If there is a war in any area then it provides the network access for some research.

2.2.1 Wireless LAN Architecture

Wireless LAN can be formed by a single cell or it may be a group of multiple cell structures. It may have single or multiple access points. These access points are connected through the type of backbone, this backbone is called as Distribution system.

- Distribution system is typically Ethernet and in some cases it is wireless itself.
- The whole interconnected WLAN includes different cells and their respective access point and Distribution system. (Refer Fig. 2.1)

Portal is used to interconnect between 802.11 to another 802.11 network.

802.11 standards define the concept of portal.

Architecture

Wireless LAN can exhibit two different basic system architecture as.

1) Infrastructure based
2) Ad-hoc based

Station:

Stations are refereed as the components that are connected to a wireless medium, all stations are equipped with wireless network interface controllers, wireless stations are maybe an access point or client machines. Access points are normally routers, which are base station for the network. Wireless clients can be mobile devices such as laptops, personal digital assistance, IP phones and other smart phones or fixed devices such as desktops and workstations.

The components of an infrastructure and a wireless part as specified IEEE 802.11. Several nodes, called stations STA(i) are connected to access points(AP).

Following are the technologies defined in the architecture:

1. Basic Service Set:

The Basic Service Set is a set of all stations that can communicate with each other .Every BSS has an identification called BSSid, it is the MAC address of the access point of that BSS. There are two types of BSS i.e. independent BSS which is an ad hoc network that contains no access points, they can not be get connected to another BSS and another type is infrastructure BSS.

2. Extended Service Set:

Set of inter connected BSSs is called as an Extended Service set(ESS).all access points of the BSSs are connected to each other by a distribution system, each ESS has an ID SSID(Service Set Identifier) which is a 32 byte (maximum)character string.

3. Distribution System:

- A distribution system connects all access points of the BSSs in ESS distribution system can be used to increase network coverage through roaming between cells. Distribution system can be wired or wireless. Current wireless distribution systems are based on WDS (Wireless Distribution System) or MESH protocols.
- A WDS enables the wireless interconnection of access points in an IEEE 802.11 network. It helps a wireless network to be expanded using multiple access point without using wired network. The notable advantage of WDS over other solutions is that it preserves the MAC addresses of client packets across links between access points.

- An access point can be either a main, relay or remote base station. A main base station is connected to the wired Ethernet. A relay base station relays data between remote base station, wireless clients or other relay stations to either a main or another relay base station a remote base station accepts connections from wireless clients and passes them to relay or main stations.

- All base stations in a wireless distribution system are configured to use the same radio channel, and share WAP keys if they are used.

- WDS may also be referred to as repeater mode because it appears to bridge and accept wireless clients at the same time (unlike traditional bridging).

- When it is difficult to connect all of the access points in a network by wires, it is also possible to put up access points as repeaters.

2.2.2 Types of Wireless LAN

Following are the different types of wireless local area networks:

- **802.11:** It was the first standard specified by IEEE in June 1997.This standard served local area network of bandwidth of maximum up to 54Mbps .It offers 2.4 GHz frequency band with data rate of 1 Mbps and 2 Mbps, it has many variations as 802.11a, 802.11b, 802.11g etc.

- **HyperLAN:** ETSI Broadband Radio Access Network Group specified HyperLan standard in Europe in 1996.the current version HyperLAN /1works at 5GHz band and offers 24 Mbps bandwidth. Next version HyperLAN/2 will be able to carry Ethernet frames, ATM cells, IP packets and support data, video, voice and image.

- **Home RF:** It is the industry standard which uses shared wireless Access Protocol (SWAP) specified by Home RF working group. This standard offers the interoperability between electronic devices and PC within home. SWAP uses frequency hopping spread spectrum modulation and offers 1 and 2 MBPS at 2.4 GHz frequency band.

- **Bluetooth:** Big industry experts like IBM, Erricsson, Intel, Lucent, Microsoft, Nokia, Motorola, Toshiba introduced this wireless personal area network i.e. PAN, as they believe in the theory of "world with cooperation and interoperability", which is preached by Danish King Harold, it offers 2.4 GHz band and 1Mbps data rate.

- **MANET:** MANET itself is a working group in IETF which develops the standard for mobile and ad-hoc networks. IEEE 802.11 standards:

2.2.3 Ad-hoc versus Infrastructure Mode

There are two types of wireless network: (1) Infrastructure mode and (2) Ad-hoc mode.

(1) Infrastructure Mode:

Infrastructure works as a star topology where all the mobile stations (ms) are connected to a base station, through access point. An mobile stations can communicate to each other. It provides the ease to access other network and includes forwarding functions, medium access control etc.

- In infrastructure mode 802.11 LAN follows cellular architecture in which system is divided into small clusters or cells. Each cell is called Basic service set (BSS). one BSS is connected to other BSS according to topology. Two BSS communicate with each other through access point.
- Multiple BSS using different carrier frequency may forms one ESS (Extended service set) which act a backbone for LAN or distribution system.

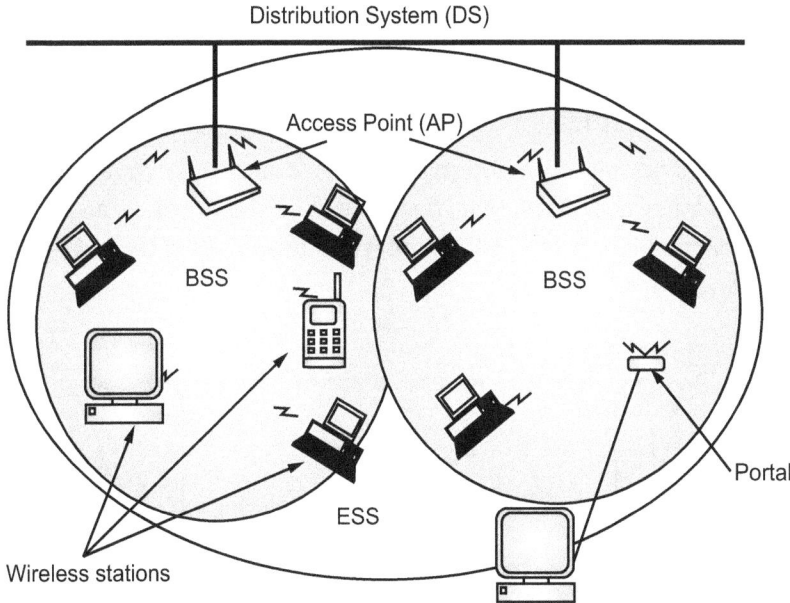

Fig. 2.1: Wireless LAN in Infrastructure Mode

(2) Ad-hoc Mode:

An Ad-hoc network (not the same as a Wi-Fi Direct network which is a network where stations communicate only (peer to peer) P2P. There is no base and no one gives permission to communicate. This is accomplished using the Independent Basic Service Set (IBSS).

- In an ad-hoc network, mobile stations forms a cluster to communicate with each other and there is no access point.
- In ad-hoc network BSS is completely independent.

- It does not specify any special nodes that support routing ,forwarding of data or exchange of topology information.

E.g. HyperLAn/1, bluetooth.

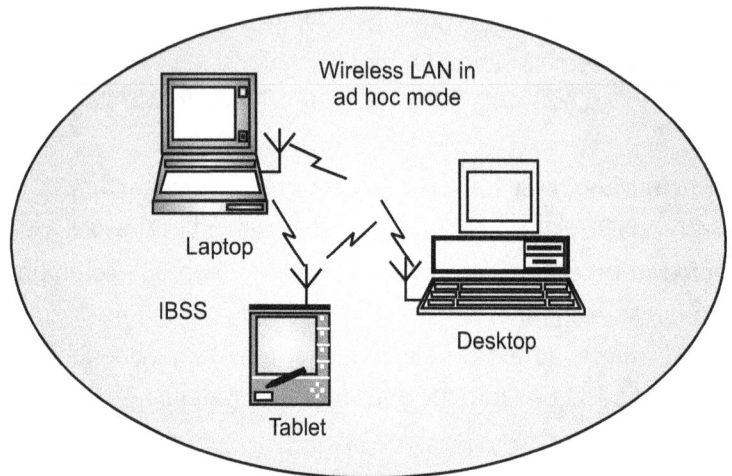

Fig. 2.2: Wireless LAN in Ad-hoc Mode

2.2.4 Protocol Architecture:

In 802.11, one cell or one BSS is controlled by one access point (hot spot). Installation of mobile stations to a network and connection of mobile station to an access point is done with the help of distribution system. This architecture forms one extended service set, which is seen in upper layers of OSI model.

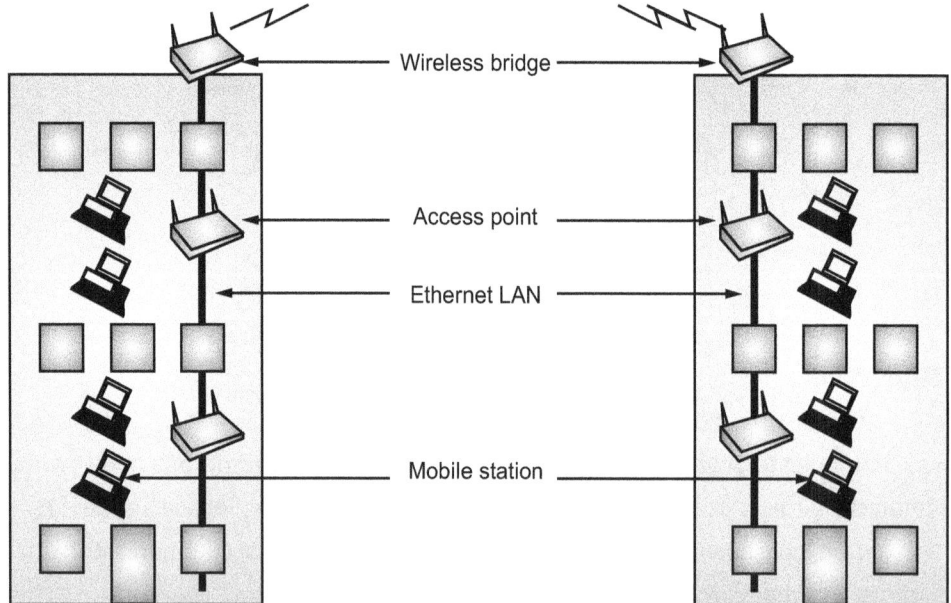

Fig. 2.3: Two access as part of the distribution system

- Neighbouring cells works on different frequencies so that there is no interruption when LAN cards transmit the signal.
- In order to avoid interference the DSSS (Direct Sequence Spread Spectrum) standard define 13 channel frequencies, these are non overlapping frequencies i.e. it works on different radio spectrum and band.

Table 2.2: Channels within the 2.4 GHz band

Channel No.	Frequency (GHz)
1	2.412
2	2.417
3	2.422
4	2.427
5	2.432
6	2.437
7	2.442
8	2.447
9	2.452
10	2.457
11	2.462
12	2.467
13	2.472

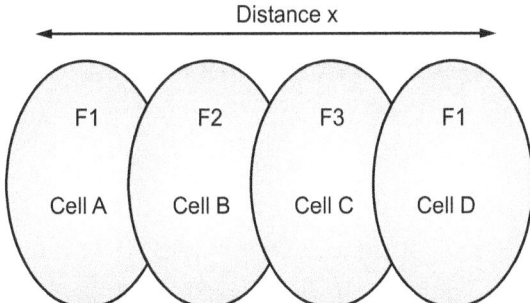

Fig. 2.4: Cell design in a WLAN

2.2.5 Description of IEEE 802.11 Layers

IEEE 802.11 has three physical layers which interacts with single MAC layer, the three physical layers are:

(1) Frequency hopping spread spectrum

(2) Direct sequence spread spectrum

(3) Infrared it also performs the other functions like fragmentation, packet retransmission and acknowledgements.

802.2	Data link layer			
802.11 MAC			MAC layer	
Frequency hopping	Direct sequence	Infrared	Physical layer	PLCP sublayer
				PMD sublayer

Fig. 2.5: The 802.11 stack

(1) Physical Layer (Layer 1) Architecture

- This layer constitutes from two sublayers:
  (1) PLCP (Physical Layer Convergence Procedure)
  (2) PMD (Physical Medium Dependent).
- **PLCP:** It uses carrier sense multiple access/collision avoidance protocol, PLCP performs the carrier sense part of it. It prepares MAC protocol Data Unit (MPDU) for transmission, it sends the incoming frames to mac layer. It creates the PLCP protocol data unit frame and its header contains the logical information that allows the receiving station's physical layer to synchronize with each incoming packet.
- **PMD:** This sublayer performs modulation /demodulation of the transmission. It performs the actual transmission and reception of physical layer entities through wireless media.
  - Physical layer uses the spread spectrum technique which involves spreading the bandwidth needed to transmit data. In a transmission system, the information is modulated with a carrier signal and then transmitted through a medium.
  - In spread spectrum the transmission signals bandwidth is much higher than the information bandwidth.
  - When all the power of signal is transmitted around a particular frequency. The frequency represent a specific channel of narrow band.
  - There are numerous ways to cause a carrier to spread.
  - Spread spectrum system can be viewed as two steps of modulation:
1. The data to be transmitted is modulated.
2. The carrier is modulated by the spreading code, causing it to spread over a large bandwidth.

(2) Frequency Hopping Spread Spectrum

Frequency hopping spread spectrum defines the co-existence of multiple networks in the same area by separating different networks using different hopping sequences.

- It is used to synchronize the sender's clock with the receiver's clock, the frame which is created by using FHSS consists of two parts one is PLCP (preamble and header) and other is payload part.
- The fields of FHSS PLCP are as follows:
  1. **SYNC:** This pattern starts with 80 bit synchronization which is made up of alternate zeros and ones i.e.10101010.....this pattern is used to synchronize the sender with the receiver.
  2. **Start frame delimiter:** This is transmitted by using 16 bit. This shows the beginning of the frame and it always contains the same pattern as 00001100111101.
  3. **PSDU length word (PLW):** This field indicates the length of payload in octets.
  4. **PLCP signaling (PSF):** This is 4 bit field which indicates the data rate of payload. PLCP premable always sent at the rate of 1 Mbps irrespective of the data rate of a wireless LAN and this field contains information about the link.
     0000-1mbp s(lowest data rate)
     0010-2mbps
     0111-4.5 mbps
     1111-8.5mbps
  5. **Header Error check:** This field has CRC (Cyclic Redundancy Check) according to CCITT CRC-16 algorithm.

80 bits	16 bits	12 bits	4 bits	16 bits	Variable PLCP service data unit
SYNC	Start frame delimiter	PLW	PSF	Head error check	

Fig. 2.6: Frequency hopping spread spectrum PLCP

- In frequency hopping spread spectrum system the total available bandwidth is split into many channels of smaller bandwidth plus guard spaces between the channels.
- The transmitter and receiver stay on one of these channels for a certain time and then hop to another channel. This pattern of channel is called hopping sequence.
- FHSS is further divided into two types:
  (a) Slow hopping, (b) Fast hopping.
- **(a) Slow hopping:** In slow hopping the transmitter uses one frequency for several bit periods.
- **(b) Fast hopping:** In fast hopping the transmitter changes the frequency several times during the transmission of signal bit.

FHSS Transmitter

Step 1: FHSS transmitter is the modulation of user data according to one of the digital to analog modulation scheme. The result is a narrowband signal.

Step 2: Frequency hopping is performed on based of hopping sequence. Hopping sequence is fed into the frequency synthesizer generating the carrier frequency. The second modulation uses the modulated narrowband signal and the carrier frequency to generate a new spread signal frequency.

FHSS Receiver

The receiver of FHSS system has to know about the hopping sequence and synchronized, it then perform inverse operation of the modulation to reconstruct the user data.

(3) Direct Sequence Spread Spectrum:

Direct sequence spread spectrum is typically used to transmit digital information. A common practice in direct sequence system is to mix the digital information stream with a pseudo random code.

DSSS system take a user bit stream and perform an XOR with this it is called as a chipping sequence. The example shows that the result is either the sequence 0110101 (if user bit is equal to 0) or is complement 1001010 (if user bit is equal to 1).

The chipping sequence consists of smaller pulse called chip with a duration of 'tc'. If chipping sequence is generated properly then it appears as random noise then this sequence is sometime called pseudo-noise sequence.

- This is responsible for synchronizing sender and receiver by checking its data bits, which is separated by code not by frequency.
- The frame format consists of two parts one is PLCP (preamble and header) and other is payload part.
- The fields of DSSS PPDU is as follows:
    1. **SYNC:** The first 128 bits are used to synchronize the sender's and receiver's clock. And it is also used to check setting, energy detection, frequency offset compensation.
    2. **Start Frame Delimiter (SFD):** This is 16 bit field used for synchronization at the beginning of a frame and consists of the pattern 1111001110100000.
    3. **Signal:** This field states the type of modulation the receiver must used to demodulate the signal.
    4. **Service:** This field is not used and reserved for future. Usually it is 0, it indicates IEEE 802.11 complaint frame.
    5. **Length:** It defines the length of payload in microseconds. This is used by receiver to synchronize with the clock to determine the end of the frame.
    6. **Frame check sequence:** This is 16 bit checksum based on CCITT CRC-16 algorithm.

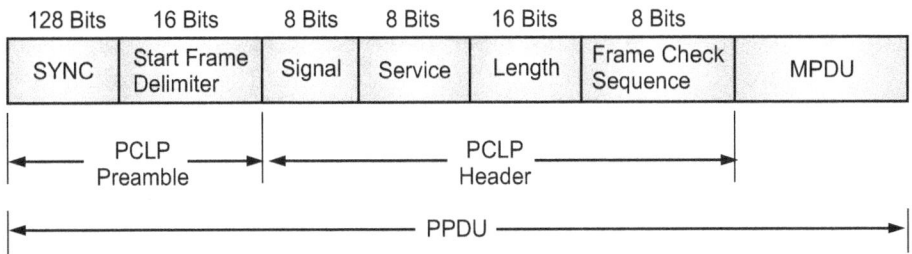

Fig. 2.7: Direct sequence spread spectrum PLCP protocol data unit

DSSS Transmitter

For spreading using DSSS. It needs additional components.

Step 1: DSSS transmitter spreads the user data with the chipping sequence.

The spreading signal is then modulated with the radio carrier. The radio carrier then shifts the signal to the carrier frequency. The signal is then transmitted.

DSSS Receiver

Step 2: With additional component of DSSS Receiver.

In this receivers demodulates the received signal. This is achieved from same carrier by receiving the modulation.

Receiver knows the original chipping sequence and generates the same pseudo random sequence as the transmitter.

Receiver calculate the product of a chip and XOR it. Integrator adds all the product of chips and signal and this is called correlator.

Each bit period of decision unit represent the sum generated by integrator in binary 0 or 1.

2.3 MAC Issues

2.3.1 The MAC Layer Architecture

The two access methods are defines by a MAC layer as Distributed Coordination Function and Point Coordination Function.

- The basic access method is CSMA/CA which is defined as Distributed Coordination Function by IEEE standard 802.11. As compared to wired LAN e. g Ethernet which uses CSMA/CD as a access method where collision can be detected and every mobile station connected in LAN can sense the collision message.

- When wireless LAN is considered CSMA/CA is used as it is not possible to detect the collision in the mid of the air.

2.3.2 Hidden and Exposed Terminal

- Consider the scenario with three mobile nodes A, B, C.
    1. The transmission range of A reaches B but not C. The transmission range of C reaches B but not A, however the radio signal of B reaches both A and C. A is not reachable to C and vice versa.
    2. A starts sending to B, C does not receive this transmission. At the same time, C also wants to sent to B. It senses the medium as idle and sends to B, thus C starts causing collision at B. A also does not get transmission of C and keeps on sending data to B.
    3. Therefore A is called "hidden" to C and vice versa.

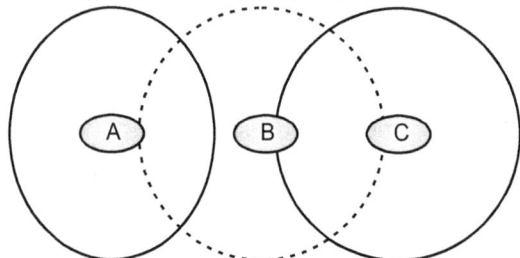

Fig. 2.8: Hidden terminal

- Consider another scenario
    1. The radio transmission signal of A reaches C and B.A and D are in the transmission range of C, A wants to communicate to B and A starts sending to B.C wants to communicate with D it senses the medium and finds A is communicating to B, C waits till the time A is sending signal to B. Although D is out of range of A therefore waiting is not necessary.
    2. Although A, B, C and D can communicate simultaneously, without any collision, but protocol doesn't allow this A and C are "exposed".

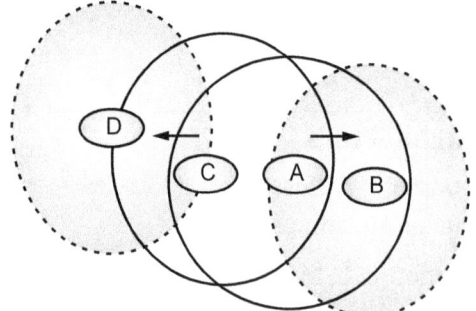

Fig. 2.9: Exposed terminal

2.3.3 Near and Far Terminal

In near and far terminal problem receiver is not able to detect the weak signals as it captures a strong signal. It is difficult to handle this problem in CDMA as transmitters shares different transmission frequencies and time.

- Consider a receiver and two transmitters one is near and another is far away, both are transmitting simultaneously at the same rate of power. Receiver will receive more power from nearer transmitter according to inverse square law. Since one's transmission signal treated as noise to other, the signal to noise ratio (SNR) is much lower for farther transmitter.
- If nearer transmitter transmits in order of magnitude higher than the farther transmitter then for farther transmitter SNR ratio will be below detectability and it keeps on transmitting, this creates congestion in channel.
- Taking this analogy to wireless communication, farther transmitter has to increase its transmission power which is not possible.
- The optimal solution on this problem is that the closest transmitter should use less power so that SNR for all transmitters will be same at receiver, this will depend on distance from a base station while maintaining the good SNR ratio, network sometimes drops out and situation leads to" power run away"
- Other Possible solutions to this problem are:
  1. Increase the receiver's dynamic range
  2. Dynamic output power control
  3. Implementation of TDMA and FDMA

2.4 Mobile IP (April 2015)

In wireless network the communication between the nodes is unstable, since the network where nodes reside is fluctuating rapidly. As we consider the wireless nodes are very small in size as compared to traditional nodes and it is generally not suitable to design the algorithms with a large processing power or memory footprint.

For this reason wireless network protocols has to be able to assess their performance, this can be achieved by following two strategies:

Using tested implementation (i.e. develop the protocol exactly according to theory stated earlier) and another is implement it using simulation i.e. real world is modeled in mobile network simulation software.

Mobile IP which adds mobility support by allowing the mechanism to the internet network layer (protocol IP).

Another kind of mobility is supported by DHCPC (Dynamic Host Configuration Protocol). It has mobility portability of equipment.

The protocol for Mobile IP is presented by a standard (RFC 2002,perkins,1996a) is perkins (1997) and Solomon(1998)and it describe the development of mobile IP, all packet formats and mechanisms.

2.4.1 Goals, Assumptions and Requirements

The internet is a network of data communication of large amount of moving nodes, to get the proper location of the mobile node, it should be always connected to its home network where the mobile node is registered previously. The node is not able to receive a single data packet as it moves from its home network.

The IP address of mobile node can be traced with the help of routing algorithms, in routing table only prefixes are stored and further optimization are applied.

Following are may be **quick solutions** to locate the node while it is moving:

1. To assign new topologically correct address, this can be done with the help of DHCP, but it is impossible to find the new IP address of the node.
2. An update of the mapping logical name (home network) - IP address is maintained with the help of Dynamic DNS. Time is needed to update new IP address in the internal routing table, but this would not be efficient in case where mobile node is moving rapidly.
3. TCP connection is identified by a socket pair(source IP address, source port address, destination IP address, destination port address), as mobile node moves its IP address changes which will affect to its port address too, as TCP connection breaks down.

Quick solutions cannot be work properly in all situations. a more rigid architecture is needed, and mobile IP standards have to be established to fulfill the following requirements:

1. **Compatibility:** Mobile IP must be compatible to all existing operating systems and applications which run on it. It has to be compatible to all lower layers standards, non-mobile too. Users must be able to access other applications and communication with fixed systems in the internet.
   - A new standard can not introduce changes for application or network protocols already in use.
   - Mobile IP must not require special media or protocol. So it uses the same interface and mechanism to access the lower layers as IP does.
   - Mobile IP has ensure that users can still access all the other servers and systems in the internet using the same address format and routing mechanisms.
2. **Transparency:** Higher layer protocols and application must be sustained when the mobile node is moving and changing its IP address. So only effect of mobility is higher delay and lower bandwidth.
   - Solution is to keep the transparency by using Mobile IP address.

- Mobile should remain invisible for higher layer protocol and applications.
  (i) Even if the lower band width and some interruption in services of higher layer.
  (ii) Introduced work even if the mobile computer has changed its point of attachment to the network.
  (iii) For TCP this means computer must keep IP address.
3. **Scalability and efficiency:** While enhancing the mobile IP standards it should not generate too many messages to maintain the mobility of the node. Myriad devices like cars, trucks, mobile phones are also participating in the internet traffic where IP implementation must be embedded into their systems; it should be scalable over a large number of participants in the whole internet.

   In much mobile system have a wireless link to an attachment point so only some additional packets should be between a mobile system and node in the network.
4. **Security:** The IP layer must provide the security that it forwards a packet to an authenticated mobile node in the internet.
   - The IP layer must be sure that if it forwards a packet to a mobile host that this host receives the packet. The packet only guarantees that IP address of the receiver is correct.
   - Higher layers have the responsibility to identify the fake IP address.
   - That means "mobility should be preserved while maintaining the scalability, efficiency and compatibility with respect to existing applications and protocols".

Entities and Terminologies:
- RFC 3344 standard defines the following terms needed to understand the mobile IP.
  1. **Mobile node:** A mobile node is an end system or router which is having different IP address as it moves in to the different network. Its keeps its IP address updated in the internet as long as link layer connectivity is given.
  2. **Correspondent node:** The CN can be mobile or fixed .it is a node with which MN (Mobile Node) is communicating.
  3. **Home Network:** MN initially belongs to the home network with respect to its IP address. Mobile IP support is not needed in the home network.
  4. **Foreign network:** This is the subnet where MN currently resides, which is not similar to home network.
  5. **Foreign agent:** It works as a guide of MN in foreign network; it acts as tunnel end point and forwards packets to MN. It acts as a security point of MN in foreign network.

6. **Care of address:** FA (Foreign Agent) is responsible to provide COA (Core of Address), which defines as a current location of the mobile node. All IP packets are delivered to COA rather than the IP address of MN. There are two situations where COA can be located:
   (a) **Foreign agent COA:** IP address of FA acts as a COA, FA is tunnels endpoint and forwards packets to the MN.
   (b) **Co-located COA:** If MN temporarily acquires an additional IP address it acts as co-located COA.
7. **Home agent:** HA (Home Agent) maintains the location registry in home network of the MN. It can be implemented on a router that is responsible for home network, on arbitrary node in the subnet or on router acting as a manager.

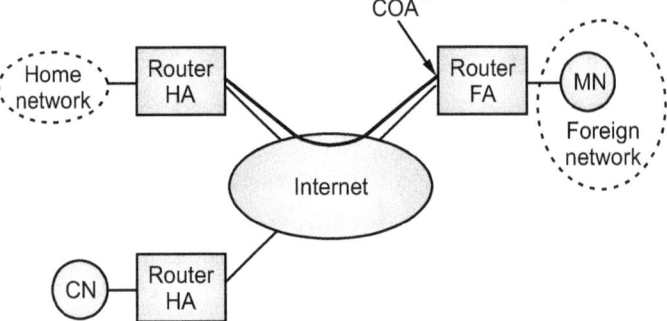

Fig. 2.10: Mobile IP example network

IP Packet Delivery

Step 1: Correspondent node CN wants to communicate with the MN, it sends the IP packet with CN IP address as a source and MN IP address as a destination inspite of knowing the current location of the MN.

Step 2: Home Agent HA intercepts the packets and searches for MN in its home network first, as it is moved to foreign network, it encapsulates the packet with the new header showing HA as a source address and new COA as a destination address.

Step 3: The Foreign Agent (FA) agent encapsulates the packet and gets original header as (Correspondent Node CN as a source, Mobile Node MN as destination).

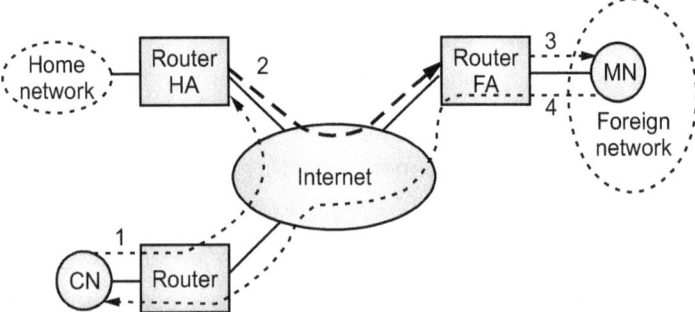

Fig. 2.11: Packet delivery to and from the mobile node

Step 4: Once the current location of MN detected, CN will continue to send packets directly to the IP address of MN, if MN moves again, for this the above steps are followed.

Step 5: To locate the home agent and foreign agent, agents itself broadcast the advertisement messages.

Step 6: Tunneling and encapsulation can be done in three ways: (1) IP in IP encapsulation (2) Minimal encapsulation (3) Generic routing encapsulation.

Agent Discovery

To find a foreign agent from MN's point of view is a complex task for this the home agents and foreign agents are needed to be located. The two discovery methods are:

1. Agent advertisement
2. Agent solicitation

(1) Agent advertisement

Generally the foreign agents and the home agents advertise about their presence through Periodical agent advertisement message. They are seen as beacon broad cast into subnets.

- Internet Control Message Protocol (ICMP) message as per RFC 1256 is used for producing the advertisement. Some extensions are used for mobility status.

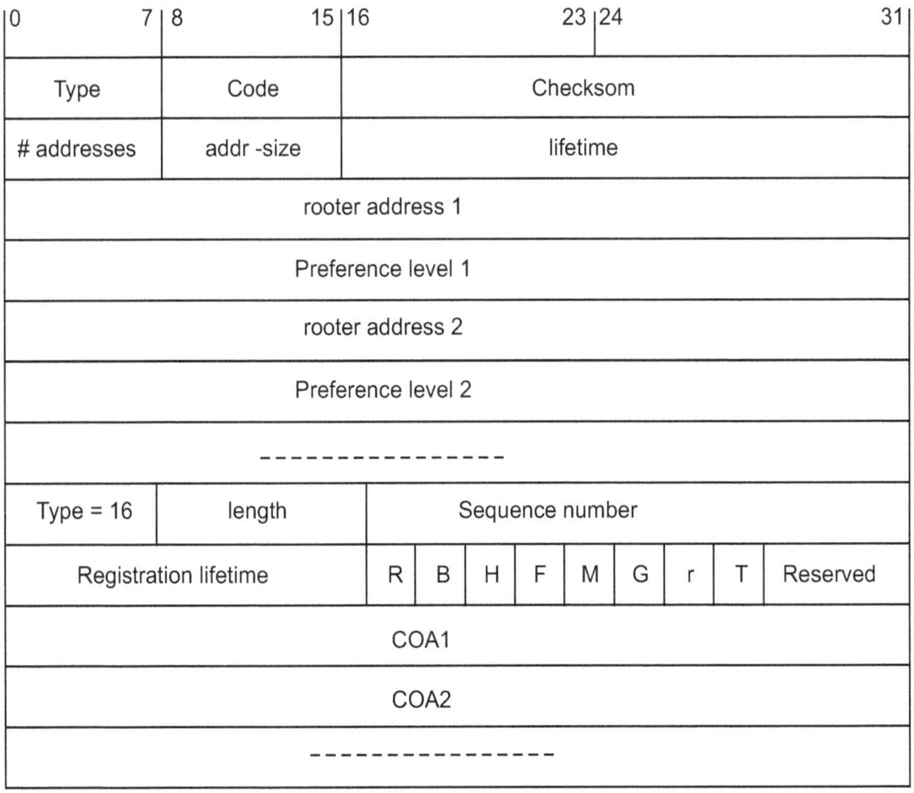

0	7	8	15	16	23	24	31
Type		Code		Checksom			
# addresses		addr -size		lifetime			
rooter address 1							
Preference level 1							
rooter address 2							
Preference level 2							

Type = 16		length		Sequence number			
Registration lifetime				R	B	H	F	M	G	r	T	Reserved
COA1							
COA2							

Fig. 2.12: Agent advertisement packet

- The upper part of packet represent ICMP packet where as the lower part has all the entries that are needed for the mobility extension. Some of the fields that are necessary on lower for agent advertisement are not shown here. The Fields are namely type, code, lifetime, address preference levels, length etc.
- The Time to Live (TTL) field of the packet will be set to 1, for all the advertisements. So as to avoid the forwarding process. The mobile node has to be coached with connected link layer's address
- The respective fields in the ICMP are usually defined as the type is set to a value 9, next the code is set to 0, when the agent routes the traffic from the non-mobile nodes or 16, if it does not route anything other than mobile traffic.
- The foreign agents are required to send their packets from the mobile nodes and the number of address advertised with this packet is given in address.
- The length of time for which these advertisements are valid is called as lifetime.
- Reference levels are available for each address which helps the node to select the router that is interested to receive a New Node (NN).

Agent Solicitation

- In case if there is no agent advertisement presented and if mobile node (MN) did not receive any COA then the MN should send an agent solicitation message. These solicitations are again based on RFC 1256 for router solicitations.
- But it is important to monitor that these agent solicitation message do not flood the network. A mobile node can send three solicitation messages (one per second) as soon as it enters a new network. Basically the solicitation messages are sent by MN to search a foreign agent.
- For highly dynamic wireless network with moving MN and with applications it requires continuous packet streaming even a time interval of one second between solicitation message is too long. Discovering a new agent can be done any time if MN is not connected to one.
- By their advertisements as solicitations a MN may get a COA. If MN is in foreign network then the next step will be registration with Home Agent (HA).

Registration

- Registration process is used to intimate the home agent about the current location of the mobile node.
- Mobile Node Make use of registration (authenticated) procedure to intimate the care of address to a home agent.
- The registration can be done in two different ways depending on the location of the COA.

There are two ways to register the address:
- The first way is when the COA is at the FA, then the registration is done by following way:

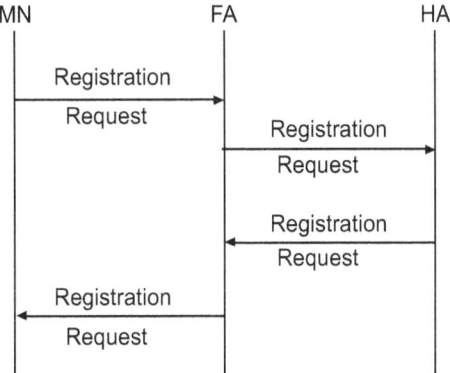

Fig. 2.13: Registration of a mobile node via FA

- In this the MN sends its registration request containing the COA to the FA which is forwarding the request to the HA.
- The HA setup the mobility binding containing the MN home IP address and current COA.
- Mobility Binding contains the lifetime of the Registration process. And it expires automatically after the lifetime is deleted so MN should register before it expires. This mechanism is used to avoid mobility binding which is no longer used.
- After setting up the Mobility binding the HA sends a reply message back to FA which forwards it to MN.
- In the second way COA is co-located then the registration process can be simpler as first way.

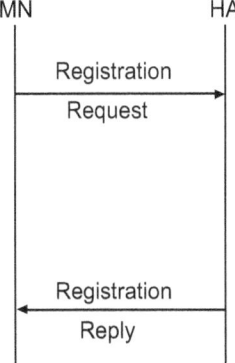

Fig. 2.14: Directly registration with HA

- The MN may send the request directly to HA and vice versa.

- By this Registration process for MN which is returning to their home network. Here registration is done directly with HA.
- If R bits is set in the advertisement then that advertise id published by FA. And mobile node should register the advertisement via FA.

Registration Process

- Registration procedure requires two processes:

    (1) Registration Request, (2) Registration Reply.

1. **Registration Request**

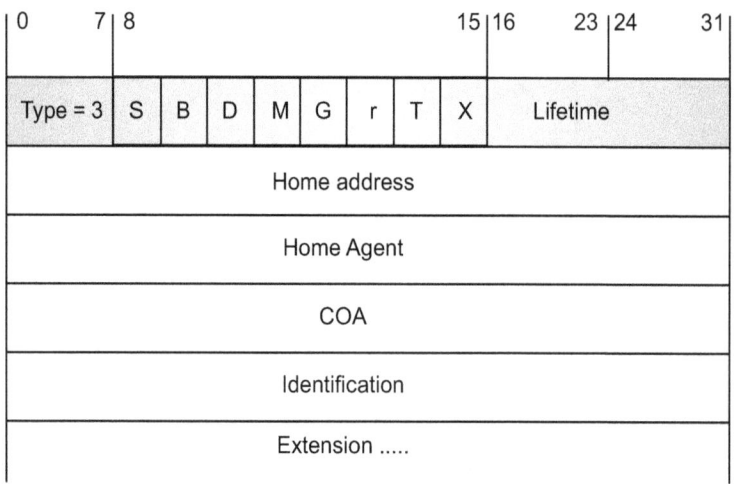

Fig. 2.15: Registration request

- UDP packet is used for registration for better performance.
- The first field types are set 1 for a registration request. This allow binding with the S bit an MN can specify if it wants the HA to retain the mobility bindings. The following bits denote the requested behavior for packet forwarding. The B bit indicates that MN wants to receive the broadcast packets which are received by HA in home network. The D bit indicates care of decapsulation at tunnel endpoint.
- The M and G bits denote the use of minimal encapsulation and T indicates the reverse tunneling.
- Lifetime denotes the validity of registration in seconds
- Home address is fixed IP address of MN, home agent is the IP address of the HA and COA represent tunnel end point.
- 64 bit Identification is generated by MN to identify request and reply.
- Extension must at least contain parameters for authentication.

2. Registration Reply

0	7	8	15	16	31
Type = 3		Code		Lifetime	
Home address					
Home agent					
Identification					
Extension					

Fig. 2.16: Registration reply

- Registration reply contain a type field set to 3 and code indicating the result of the registration request.
- The lifetime field, indicates how many seconds the registration is valid if it successful.
- Home address and home agent are the address of the MN and the HA.
- The 64-bit identification is used to match registration request with replies.
- The value is based on the identification field from the registration and the authentication method.

Tunneling and Encapsulation

- It is used for forwarding packets between HA and the COA.
- A virtual pipe as a tunnel is established for sending the data packets. These data packets travel from tunnel entry point to tunnel exit point that is kept unchanged.
- Tunneling is the process of sending a packet through the tunnel and it is achieved by an encapsulation.

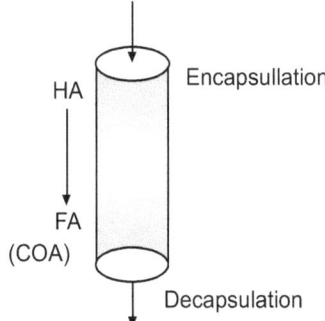

Fig. 2.17: Encapsulation and Decapsulation

Encapsulation

- Every packet has two parts as Header and Data part. Encapsulation is the mechanism putting one packet into the data part of another packet.

Decapsulation
- The reverse operation taking the packet out of the data part of another packet is called decapsulation.
- Whenever a packet is send form higher to lower or lower to higher protocol layer these two operations are performed. These encapsulation and decapsulation are performed within the same layer.

Tunneling
- Even while mobile nodes are moving from one location to another location (roaming) on foreign networks, it maintains the appearance of it to be in home network only. Mobile nodes send packets using its home IP address. Its movements are transparent to correspondent node.
- Data packets addressed to the Mobile Node are routed to its home network, where the HA now intercepts and tunnels them to the care-of address towards the mobile node.
- Tunneling has two primary function:
    1. Encapsulation of the data packet to each the tunnel end point and
    2. Decapsulation when the packet is delivered at that end point default tunnel node is IP encapsulation.
- Typically the Mobile Node sends packet to the Foreign agent, which routes them to their final destination the correspondent node as shown in Fig.

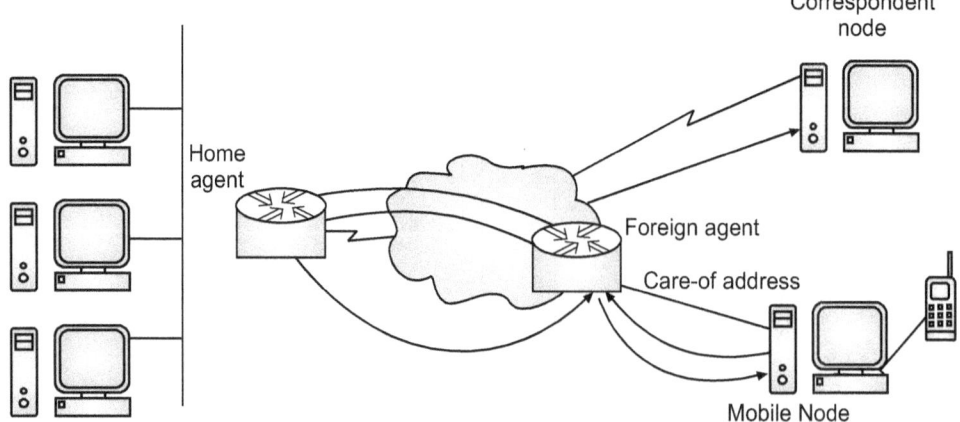

Fig. 2.18: Packet Forwarding

- However, this data path is topologically incorrect because it does not reflect the true IP network source for the data rather it reflects the home network of Mobile Node. Format of IP Encapsulation

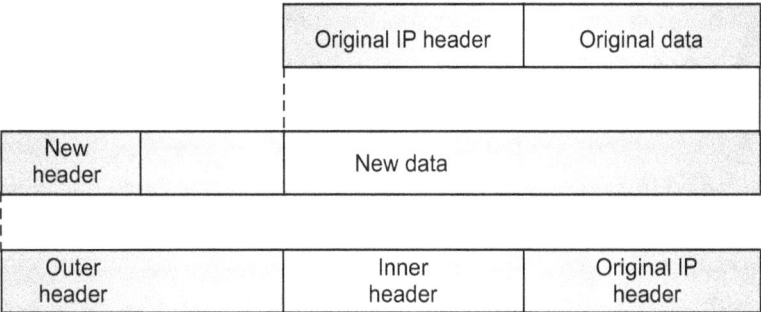

Fig. 2.19: IP encapsulation

- In this format the new header is called outer header and inner header is identical to original header.
- HA (Home Agent) at the tunnel entry takes the original packet with the MN as destination IP address puts it into the data part of a new packet and sets the new IP header in such a way that the packet is routed to the COA. The new header is called outer header and the inner which is identical to the original header.

Ways of IP Encapsulation

- There are three ways of performing IP encapsulation
    1. IP-in-IP Encapsulation
    2. Minimal Encapsulation
    3. Generic rooting Encapsulation

(1) IP-in-IP Encapsulation

Version	IHL	DS (TOS)	Length		
IP identification			Flages		Frogment offset
TTL		IP-In-IP	IP checksom		
Source IP address of HA					
Destination care-of-address of COA					
Version	IHL	DS(TOS)	Length		
IP identification			Flage		Fragment offset
TTL		Layer and protocol	IP checksom		
IP address of CN					
IP address of MN					
TCP/UDP/ ....../pay load					

Fig. 2.20: IP in IP Encapsulation

- In this encapsulation packet is inside the tunnel. IP-in-IP is a type of protocol it is used as IP payload and set to 4.
- The outer header fields, the version is set to 4 for IP version 4, the Internet Header Length (IHL) denotes the outer header length in 32 bits. DS (TOS) is type of service that is copied from the inner header to cover the encapsulated packet.
- IP address of home agent (HA) is entry source address and care of address (COA) is destination.
- When showing original sender CN and the receiver MN of packet only change TTL (Time to Live) is decremented by 1. i.e. whole tunnel act as a single hop from the point of view of original packet.

(2) Minimal Encapsulation

Minimal encapsulation method used for mobile IP. Here both tunnel entry and end point are clearly specified. The header fields consist of the value 55 for minimal encapsulation protocol.

- The inner header is different here. The address of MN is needed.
- A bit S is maintained as a field content. The original sender address of CN is included. S - If bit S is set, it means that original sender is included.

Version	IHL	DS(TOS)	Length	
IP identification			Flags	Fragement affset
Time to live (TTL)	Minimal encapsulation		IP checksom	
Source address (IP address of HA)				
Destination address (Care-of address of COA)				
Layer 4 protocol	S	Reserved	IP checksom	
IP address of MN				
Original sender IP address when S in set				
TCP/UDP/ .... Payload				

Fig. 2.21: Minimal Encapsulation

- TTL - should be high so that packet will reach endpoint.

(3) Generic Routing Encapsulation (GRE)

The GRE allows the encapsulation packet of one protocol suite into the payload portion of a packet of another protocol suite.

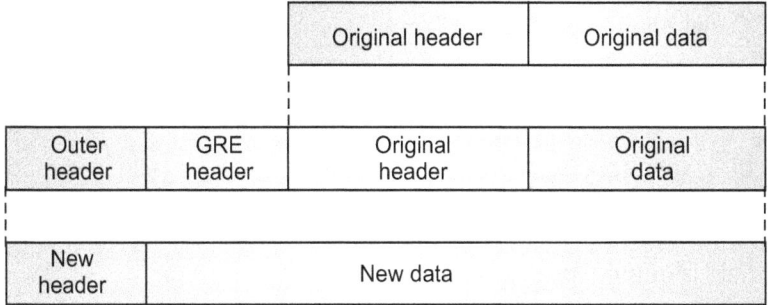

Fig. 2.22: Generic routing encapsulation

Here original data header and GRE form the new data, the header of second protocol suit will put in the front end of the frame.

Version	IHL	DS(TOS)	Length		
IP identification			Flags	Frogment offset	
TTL		GRE		IP checksom	
IP address of HA					
Care-of address of COA					
C R K S s rec rsv ver				Protocol	
Checksom (Optional)			Offset (Optional)		
Key (Optional)					
Sequence number (optional)					
Routing (Optional)					
ver	IHL	DS (TOS)	Length		
IP identification			Flags	Fragment offset	
TTL		Layer for protocal		IP checksom	
IP address of CN					
IP address of MN					
TCP/UDP/..... payload					

Fig. 2.23: Protocol fields for GRE according to RFC 1701

- The minimal value of header is only 4 bytes.
- The C bit field is set if the checksum of field consist of a valid IP checksum of header and the payload data.
- The R bit is set if routing and offset field are present with valid information.
- The routing field has variable length and it consist of field for the source routing.
- A key field is offered for GRE authentication.
- There is a field in GRE called recursion control field that differentiates GRE from other encapsulation methods.

Optimization

- In the mobile IP protocol the entire data packet to the mobile node should go through home agent. Because of this latency got increases as there are unwanted overheads between HA and CN in network. Thus it is important to optimize the routes in the network. For this the CN has to be informed about current location of the MN. An optimized mobile protocol requires four additional messages. They are as follows :

1. **Binding request:** If a node wants to know about mobile node. It sends a request to HA.
2. **Binding Acts:** On that request the node will return this message after getting binding update message.
3. **Binding update:** This is a message sent by HA to CN mentioning the correct location of MN.
4. **Binding warning:** The message is send by a node if it decapsulates a data packet for MN but it is not present in FA. For this MN sends a binding warning. The message contains target node address and MNs home address. In turn a binding update message will be sent to the node by HA.

Reverse Tunneling

- The return path from MN to CN is already traced in IP packet delivery. It can directly sends its packet to CN in any other standard IP situation. But there is several problems associated with this solution. To correct or handle this problems reverse tunneling is introduced. Problems are:

1. **Firewalls:** Firewalls only allow packet that have correct address to pass. But MN still sends packet with its fixed IP address as source which is not correct in a foreign network.

2. **Multi-cast:** The nodes in the home network participate in multicast group. An MN is a foreign network can not transmit multicast packets from its home network without a reverse tunnel.
- To solve the above problems reverse tunneling was added to mobile IP and creates a triangular routing problem in reverse direction.
- All packets from MN to CN go through HA.
- Reverse tunneling also provide some security issues that are not be solved up to now.
- Reverse tunneling solves the problem by having foreign Agent tunnel packet back to home agent when it receives them from the mobile node.

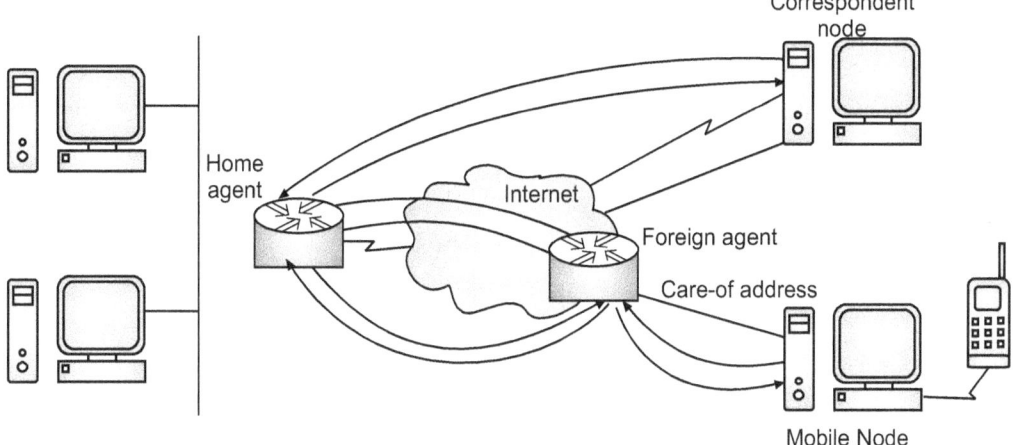

Fig. 2.24: Reverse Tunnel

2.5 Mobile Ad-hoc Networks

Cellular phone networks requires base stations infrastructure network etc. However there are several situations where user network cannot rely on an infrastructure because it is too expensive. Therefore there is a need of mobile ad hoc network.

In Mobile ad-hoc networks Mobile IP requires home agent, tunnels and default routers. In this situation mobile ad-hoc networks are only the choice. There network should be mobile and use wireless communication

- To locate the proper location of the mobile node, some infrastructure is needed i.e. mobility is provided when there is some infrastructure. Mobile IP requires home agent, tunnels, and default routers. DHCP requires servers and broadcasts capabilities of the medium to reach MN. Cellular phone requires base station and infrastructure networks.
- There are many situations where the infrastructure is not available or it is not affordable to MN to rely on it. In these situations, the mobile ad-hoc network is constructed.

- These networks should be mobile and agrees upon wireless communication, in particular situation multi hop ad hoc network is taken into consideration.
- **Instant infrastructure:** To service the unplanned meetings or spontaneous interpersonal communication is to be held, it will take time to create the network with administration. In these situations ad hoc infrastructure is created.
- **Disaster relief:** Network usually crashes in disaster areas, on emergency terms ad hoc infrastructure gives extremely fast and reliable network.
- **Remote areas:** Remote areas are nothing but most populated network of mobile nodes, depending upon the communication pattern and to reduce the cost of fixed infrastructure the ad-hoc network is constructed.
- **Effectiveness:** Existing infrastructure may offer the application at higher cost so here in case a small packet oriented network might be a better solution.
- Ad-hoc networking has attracted a lot of research this let to the creation of a working group that is focusing on mobile ad-hoc networking called MANET.
- MANET research is responsible for developing protocol and components to enable adhoc networking between the mobile devices.

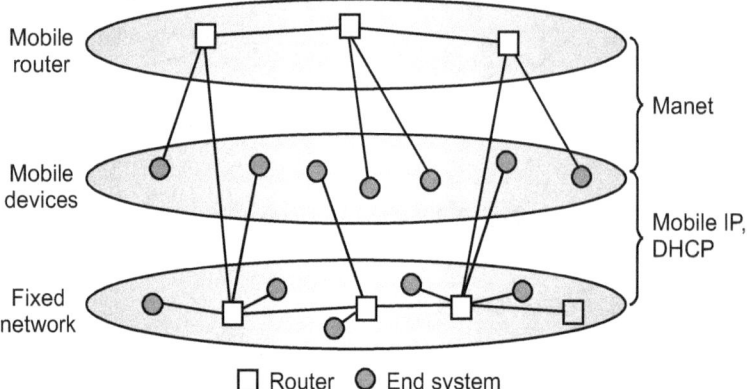

Fig. 2.25: MANETs and mobile IP

- The Fig 2.25 shows the relation between IP and DHCP.
- Mobile IP and DHCP handle the connection of mobile device to a fixed infrastructure and MANET comprises mobile routers using mobile IP for mobility and DHCP as a source of many parameters such as IP address.
- Mobile IP and DHCP interact with the fixed network and MANET interacts with mobile routers. It helps for developing protocols and components to enable the ad-hoc network. There is a logical separation in between the router and end systems.
- One of the first ad hoc network was developed is in Advanced Research Project Agency (ARPA) in 1973, which is of 138 nodes in packet radio network. This connects it to Arpanet (starting point of today's internet).

- In 1992(Perlman) distant vector variant is applied to ad hoc networks, in which each nodes advertises the routing information, depending upon the distance vector algorithm each node updates the local routing table.
- Difference between wired network and ad-hoc wireless networks related to routing is stated as follows :
1. **Asymmetric links:** Node A receives a signal from node B. But this does not tell us anything about the quality of connection in reverse. B might receive nothing it have a weak link as even better link than the reverse direction. Routing information collected for one direction is almost having no use for the other direction.
2. **Redundant link:** Wired networks have redundant links to survive link failure, there is some redundancy in wired network which automatically controlled by network administrator. In ad-hoc network nobody controls redundancy so there might be many redundant links up to extreme of a completely meshed topology.
3. **Interference:** In wired network links exist only where a wire exists and the connections are planned by network administrates. In ad-hoc network links are come and go depending on the transmission characteristics.

Routing for ad-hoc network

In case of infrastructure network, the base station is always reaches all mobile nodes but in ad hoc network a destination node is not always in the range of source or base node, so routing is needed to find a path between source and destination to send the data packets.

- In ad-hoc network each node must be able to forward data for other nodes this creates problems.
- In ad-hoc network each node is able to forward data to other node this creates problem.
    1. There are hardware limitations in ad hoc network, due to this all mobile nodes face the problem while sending the data, there is a bigger problem of wastage of battery power because it has the limitation over the routing algorithms.
    2. There is Interference between two or more transmission for the same node for forwarding. If we shielded wire correctly then there is no interference.
- To solve these problem routing can be made for ad-hoc networks with moving the nodes.

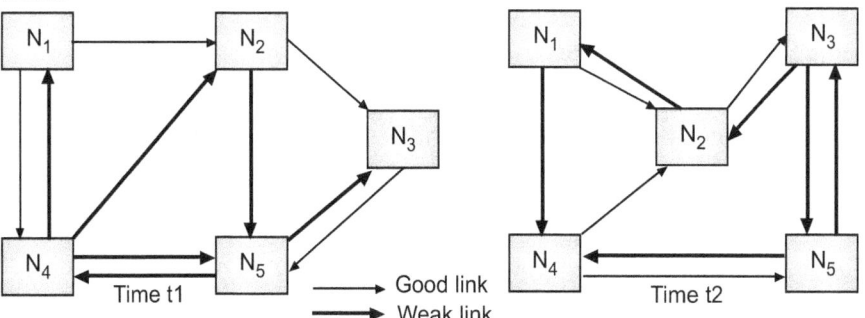

Fig. 2.26: Example of ad-hoc network

- Traditional routing algorithm known from wired network will not work efficiently (e.g. distance vector). For adhoc network.
- Centralized approaches will not work really because it takes too long to collect the current status and disseminate it again.
- Many nodes need routing capabilities while there might be at least one route that has to be within the range of each node.

Routing algorithms for ad hoc networks

(1) Destination Sequence Distance Vector
- Destination Sequence Distance Vectors (DSDV) routing is an enhancement to distance vector routing for ad-hoc networks.
- Distance vector routing is used as routing information protocol in wired networks. It performs extremely poor with certain network changes due to the count-to-infinity problem. Each node exchanges its neighbour's table periodically with its neighbor's.
- Changes at one node in the network propagate slowly through the network step by step with every exchange.
- The strategies to avoid this problem which are used in fixed networks do not help in case of wireless ad-hoc network due to rapidly changing topology. This might create loops as unreachable regions within the network. DSDV now adds two things to the distance vector algorithm.

    1. Sequence number: Each routing advertisement comes with a sequence number. Within ad-hoc network, advertisements may propagate along the many paths. Sequence number helps to apply the advertisements in correct order. This avoids the loops that are with the unchanged distance vector algorithm.

    2. Damping: Transient changes in topology that has short duration and should not destabilize the routing mechanism. Advertisements containing changes in the topology currently stored are therefore not disseminated further. A node waits with dissemination if these changes are probably unstable. Waiting time depends on the time between the first and the best announcement of a path to a certain destination.

- DSDV has low memory requirements and quick convergence via triggered updates.

(2) Dynamic Source Routing (DSR)

In an ad-hoc network where nodes, exchange packets from time to time i.e. network is only lightly loaded and DSDV or one of the traditional distance vector or link state algorithm is used for updating routing tables.

Although only some user data has to be transmitted the nodes exchange routing information to keep track of the topology. These algorithms maintain routes between all nodes, although there may be currently no data exchange at all. This causes unnecessary traffic and prevents nodes from saving battery power.

Dynamic Source Routing (DSR) therefore divides the task of routing into two separate problems.

1. **Route discovery:** A node only tries to discover a route to a destination if it has to send something to this destination and there is currently no known route.
2. **Route maintenance:** If a node is continuously sending packets via a route it has make sure that the route is held upright. As soon as a node detects problems with the current route, it has to find an alternative.

- The basic principle of source routing is also used in fixed networks e.g. token rings.
- Dynamic source routing eliminates all periodic routing updates and works as follows.
- If a node needs to discover a route, it broadcasts a route request with a unique identifier and the destination address as parameter. Any node that receives a route request does the following:
- If the node has already received the request, it drops the request packet.
- If the node recognizes its own address as the destination, the request has reached its target.
- Otherwise, the node appends its own address to a list of transverse hops in the packet and broad cast their updated route request.

Using this approach, the route request and collects a list of address that representing a possible path towards the destination. As soon as the request reaches the destination, it can return the request packet containing the list to the receiver using this list in reverse order.

Algorithms such as DSDV and DSR only work for a smaller number of nodes. For larger network clustering of nodes are using different routing algorithm between and within the cluster.

2.6 TCP Issues

TCP has built in mechanism of" network friendliness", which helps it to detect the packet loss, intercogesion in a network and slows down the transmission rate when needed.

2.6.1 Implication on Mobility

- Mobility itself causes the packet loss. In many situations like when mobile node moves from one network to another network the old FA may not be able to forward the packets to new FA. or it is not able to buffer those packets. This leads to the rerouting traffic problem.
- The fundamental design issue of the TCP is the error control mechanism that is misused for congestion control mechanism i.e. it cannot differentiate acknowledgements that are missing due to transmission error and acknowledgements that are missing due to network overload. In both cases packets are lost.

- Standard TCP reacts with the slow start for the above issue which is not applicable over wireless links and doesn't help in handovers. However one cannot change the classical TCP just for the sake of mobility support.
- Every enhancement to TCP to support mobility should be compatible to classical TCP. Following are the research projects introduce to increase TCP performance in wireless and mobile environments.

Table 2.1: Overview of classical enhancement of TCP for mobility

Approach	Mechanism	Advantages	Disadvantages
Indirect IP	Splits TCP connection into two connections	Isolation of wireless link, simple	Loss of TCP semantics, higher latency at handover, security problems.
Snooping TCP	Snoops data and acknowledgements, local retransmission	Transparent for end-to-end connection, MAC integration possible	Insufficient isolation of wireless link, security problems
M-TCP	Splits TCP connection, chokes sender via window size	Maintains end-to-end semantics, handles long term and frequent disconnections	Bad isolation of wireless link, processing overhead due to bandwidth management, security problems.
Fast retransmit/ fast recovery	Avoids slow-start after roaming	Simple and efficient	Mixed layers, not transparent
Transmission/ time-out freezing	Freezes TCP state at disconnection, resumes after reconnection	Independent of content, works for longer interruptions	Changes in TCP required, MAC dependent
Selective retransmission	Retransmits only lost data	Very efficient	Slightly more complex receiver software, more buffer space needed
Transaction-required oriented TCP	Combines connection setup/release and data transmission	Efficient for certain applications	Changes in TCP not transparent, security problems

2.6.2 TCP over 2.5/3G Wireless Network

TCP should match the configuration optimization over the 2.5 /3G wireless WANS such as GSM/GPRS, UMTS or CDMA.

Following are the characteristics considered for deployment of application over 2.5/3 G wireless links:

1. **Data rates:** For typical 2.5 G network the data rates are 10-20kbit/s uplink, and 20-50kbit/s downlink. For future 3G network this may be replaced by 64kbit/s uplink and 115-384 Kbit/s downlink. Uploading is restricted with limited battery power. it is considered that in cellular system user will upload less as compared to downloading, so typically data rates are asymmetric. For broadcast systems (satellite system, digital radio) it is highly impossible to upload the data as the asymmetry ratio leads to 1000.resources are also shared according to the need so a scheduler must allocate and deallocate the resources for each user. This leads to periodic allocation and release of a channel.
2. **Latency:** Wireless systems elaborate the algorithms for error correcting and protecting, such as forward error correction, check summing and interleaving. The current GPRS system specifies the average delay of less than 2 seconds for the higher quality.
3. **Jitter:** Wireless system suffers due to delay variations. It mostly affects the audio and video files. This happens due to high priority traffic, increase in latency or handovers.
4. **Packet loss:** Packet loss is the major problem in wireless link. But in 2.5 /3G networks the corruption in packet loss is less as it implements link-level retransmission.

Based on these characteristics the following configuration parameters are suggested to adapt TCP wireless environments.

1. **Large window:** TCP should have a larger window size based on bandwidth delay product. This is implemented by using window scale option (more than one segment) and buffer size (more than 16kbyte).this will increase performance for short transmission.
2. **Limited transmit:** This specifies the extension to fast retransmission/fast recovery this is useful where small amount of data should be retransmitted (web service request)
3. **Large MTU:** To increase the larger congestion window faster TCP requires larger MTU(Maximum Transfer Unit)MTU path discovery should be used for transmission of larger segments.

4. **Selective acknowledgement (SACK):** It allows selective retransmission of the packets and it is beneficial as compared to standard cumulative scheme.
5. **Explicit congestion notification (ECN):** By setting ECN flag-on, receiver can inform the sender about the congestion. This mechanism will help in detecting the packet loss .this can be implemented only when ECN capable routers are deployed to the network.
6. **Timestamp:** Higher delay spikes can be handled by TCP with the help of timestamp without experiencing a spurious timeout.
7. **No header compression:** This mechanism should not be used as it does not perform when there is a packet loss and it is not compatible with TCP options like SACK or timeouts.

These standards are used in i-mode running over FOMA as deployed in Japan and are part of WAP 2.0 standard.

2.7 Disconnected Operations

Mobile computing should have ability to access critical data regardless of location. Data from shared files system must be available to programs that are running on mobile computers. Mobility may cause problem in providing these requirements.

Constraints of mobile computing: To access data from mobile devices is tedious because of three fundamental constraints:

1. As we compare given cost and level of technology, mobile elements are slower and have less memory space than static elements.
2. Mobile elements are more vulnerable to loss destruction than static elements, even if secretary is not considered here.
3. Elements of mobile must operate under a broader range of networking conditions. These constraints do not follow the concept of today's distributed system.

Ideally scalability and transparency are the real need of computing environment.

2.7.1 Overview of Coda files System

- Coda is a successor of AFS (Andrew File System) offers continued access to data in the face of server and network failures.
- Coda is a large collection of untrusted clients UNIX 1 clients and much smaller number of trusted UNIX file servers.
- It doesn't work for application like online transaction processing, whereas it is typically used for accessing and sharing patterns. Coda offers a mechanism to pre fetch of files while still it is connected called hoarding.

- Each of the coda clients has local disk and communicated with server over a high bandwidth network.

- Coda uses two mechanisms to achieve high availability, both rely on optimistic replica control strategy .system ensures detection and confinement of conflicting updates.

First mechanism is server replication, it allows volumes (i.e. subtree of file server) to read or write replicas at more than one server.

The set of replication sites for volume is called volume storage group (VSG), this mechanism is second high availability and key enabling technology for mobile computing.

- When client gets disconnected i.e. no server from its VSG is accessible. It happen when there is temporary interruption in mobile computing, such as short range, inability to operate underground, line of sight constraint. This is called involuntary disconnection. When client itself gets disconnection it is called voluntary disconnection.

- The changes made while disconnected can be recovered by operation log which is implemented on the top of transactional facility called RVM.

- To support disconnected operation it must be in one of the states .client remains with hoarding, emulation, and reintegration state.

- Client of coda system remains normally in hoarding state. It ensures that critical objects are in the cache at the moment of disconnection. (that is it represent while connected)

- When disconnection happens clients it represents 'Disconnection' enters emulation state. And it remains there over a period of disconnection.

- Upon reconnection, clients enters the reintegration state, resynchronizes its cache with its VSG, then to its returns hoarding state.

- It follows traditional caching algorithm i.e. recent reference history is cached. The following Fig. 2.27 shows three states of the client in a coda. The client only performs hoarding while a strong connection to the server exits. If the connection breaks completely, the client goes to emulating and user only cached replies. If client losses the strong connection but it has a weak connection then it does not undergo hoarding state rather it decides whether it should fetch the files from cache or not. The weak connection is not used for reintegration of files.

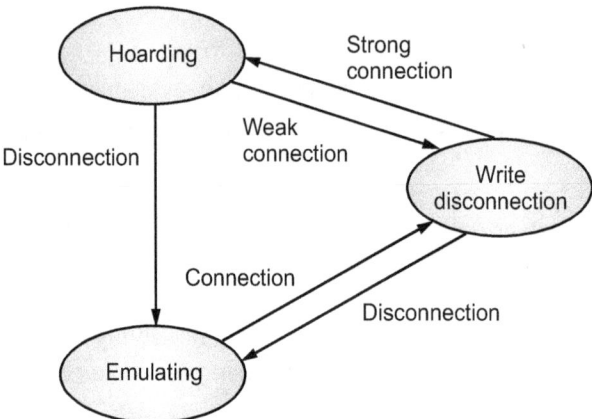

Fig. 2.27: States of a client in coda

2.8 Data Broadcasting

This method is used to broadcast the data items periodically according to predefined schedule.

- When data items are retrieved from storage device with non deterministic access time, the data item may not be ready .when it is required in broadcast cycle. This is called data –missing problem.
- There are two approaches to come over data missing problem. First approach reassess the require mobile client to retrieve data in next broadcast cycles.

And add-missing approach allows a mobile client to access missing data item in an attached missing data segment.

- Reaccess method is having poor performance than add missing in terms of access time and tuning time.
- Data broadcasting may be affected by communication asymmetry or network asymmetry i.e. downlink bandwidth exceeds uplink bandwidth.
- Data disseminated through broadcast can be accessed by number of clients.
- Data broadcasting can be achieved using
    1. **Selective broadcast:** It broadcasts selected subset of items and provide the rest on demand. It stores frequently requested data. Database is partitioned as 'publication group' and on demand group.
    2. **On demand broadcast:** The server chooses the next item to broadcast on every broadcast request from client. It may be broadcasted according to FCFS or page with maximum number of pending request.

2.8.1 Organization of Broadcast Data

- **Access time:** It is the time slice from when client requests for a data item till it is broadcasted to it.
- **Tuning time:** The amount of time spent listening to the broadcast channel.
- To organize the broadcast data it should have less access time and tuning time.
- Two parameters are needed for broadcasting
  - Number of disks.
  - for each disk
- Number of items and relative frequency to broadcast.
- The algorithm is needed to assign the items to disks and determines the interleaving of disks.

2.9 Mobile Agents

An agent is "an independent software program which runs on behalf of network user".

Mobile agent is nothing but a program, once it is launched by a user, can travel from node to node autonomously, and can continue to function even if the user is disconnected from the network.

It becomes viable, with recent technologies such as provided with java. It has potential to work in network application and yet not widely deployed.

Advantages of mobile agents:

1. They are efficient and have economical use of communication channels that may have low bandwidth, high latency, and may be error prone.
2. It provides peer-peer model, it supports in disconnected operation.
3. It doesn't require pre installation of application specific software at each site.
4. Mobile Agent enable the use of portable devices to perform complex task a even when the device is disconnected from network.
5. Synchronous operation and true decentralization is done with the help of mobile agents

2.9.1 Architecture

- Each host runs an agent server process these hosts are connected through links that can be low-bandwidth and unreliable.
- An agent is a serilizable object whose execution state can be frozen transportation and reconstituted upon arrival at a remote site.
- Mobile agents are nothing but objects so it contains state and its methods.

2.9.2 How Does Mobile Agent Works

- An agent is authenticated by host and roams the network to gather information.
- It accesses the needed information as it allows to work in disconnected paradigm, there is no sudden loss of data.
- When client reconnects, the agent return to the mobile device with the result.

2.9.3 Security Concern Regarding Mobile Agents

- **Authentication:** Agent must be authenticated for each host whereas agent server must authenticate itself to agent.
- **Encryption:** Agent encrypts its sensitive data.
- **Resource Access:** A host enforces strict access control to its resources.

2.9.4 Events in Mobile Agent's Lifetime

- **Creation:** A brand new agent is created and its state is initialized.
- **Dispatch:** An agent travels to new host.
- **Cloning:** A twin agent is born and the current state of the original is duplicated in the clone.
- **Deactivation:** An agent is put to sleep and its state is saved in persistent storage.
- **Activation:** A deactivated agent is brought back to life and its state is restored from persistent storage.
- **Retardation:** An agent is brought back from a remote host along with its state to the home machine.
- **Disposal:** An agent is terminated and its state in lost forever.
- **Communication:** Notifies the agent to handle messages incoming from other agents which is the primary means of inter agent correspondence.

Practice Questions

1. What are advantages and disadvantages of WLAN ?
2. What is maximum data rate specified for IEEE 802.11 WLANs ?
3. Write a short notes on :
   (a) Types of wireless LAN.

    (b) Near and far terminal

    (c) Data broadcasting.

4. How does mobile agent works ?
5. Explain mobile IP in details.
6. Explain important processes used in mobile IP.
7. What is requirement of mobile IP layer ?
8. Explain how mobile IP works.
9. Write detailed note on MANET.

Chapter 3...

GSM

3.1 GSM
    3.1.1 Mobile Services
    3.1.2 System Architecture
    3.1.3 Protocols
3.2 WAP
    3.2.1 Architecture of WAP
    3.2.2 Wireless Application Environment (WAE)
    • Practice Questions

3.1 GSM

Nowadays, Digital cellular network are the two segments of the market for mobile and wireless devices which is growing rapidly, this is an extension of PSTN or ISDN networks and allows seamless roaming with the same mobile.

- The worldwide market determines that, for cellular network the most popular digital system is GSM with approximately 30 percent of market.
- The GSM is a leading architecture to avoid the situation which is raised during early 1980s, that is analog mobile system working with different carrier frequencies, this evolution in second generation happens when group special mobile (GSM) was founded in 1982. Later, it is named as global system for mobile communications (GSM).
- GSM standard had replaced the first generation (1g) analog cellular networks, this standard was expanded by adding data communication firstly by circuit switched transport, then packet data transport via GPRS (General Packet Radio Services) and EDGE (Enhanced Data rates for GSM Evolution or EGPRS).
- The improvements lead towards the 3GPP which is developed by third generation (3G) UMTS standards followed by fourth generation (4G) LTE advanced standards.
- GSM is a second generation system, which primarily offers the user: e-mobile phone system to roam without the restriction of geographical area, but it doesn't offer the high data speed rate as compared to 3rd generation systems.

- The following are the versions of GSM system. Initial GSM deployed at 890-915 MHz for uplink and 935-960 MHz for downlink.

GSM 900 (DCS - Digital Cellular System)	1700-1785 uplink	1805-1880 downlink
PCS – (Personal Communication System)	18550-1910 MHz uplink	1930-1990 downlink

- In European countries GSM-Rail was introduced and it offers emergency calls with acknowledgements, Voice Groups Call Service (VGCS), voice broadcast service.

History of GSM:

- European Conference of Postal and Telecommunications Administrations (CEPT) created the 'Groupe Special Mobile' committee for digital cellular voice telephony in the year 1981. Later it supports the group technically. Firstly to deploy a common cellular telephony across the Europe, 15 representatives from 13 European countries signed memorandum and this decision helped to build a unified, open standard-based network which was larger than that in the United States.
- In February 1987, Europe produced the very first agreed GSM Technical Specification. In the same year many European countries declared their support to the Global Information Networks and the GSM MoU was tabled for signature in September.
- Parallel with this evolution, France and Germany signed a joint development agreement in 1984. UK and Italy joined them in 1986. In 1986 the European Commission proposed reserving the 900 MHz spectrum band for GSM.
- GSM specification with first phase were published in 1990.and the first call was made by former Finnish prime minister Harri Holkerito Kaarina Suonio who was mayor of the city on July 1, 1991. The network is build by Telenokia and Siemens and operated by Radiolinja, which is followed by Short Messaging Service, message in 1992 Vodafone UK and Telecom Finland signed the first international roaming agreement.
- In the year 1991, the GSM standard is expanded to the 1800MHz frequency band and the first 1800 MHz network became operational in the UK in 1993.telecom Australia became the first network operator to deploy a GSM outside Europe and the first practical hand-held GSM network outside Europe.
- In1995, fax, data and **SMS** messaging services were launched with 1900 MHz GSM network and it became operational in the United States and GSM subscribers exceeded worldwide.

- GSM network subscribers were spreading that time and it reached to 10 million in 1995 and fax, data and SMS messaging services were launched commercially. GSM with 1900MHz became operational in United States. 1996, GSM association was formed and pre paid GSM SIM cards were launched. By the 1998, GSM network subscribers reached up to 100 million.
- In the Y2K era the GSM network had been gone through milestones. The first commercial GPRS service was launched with GPRS compatible handsets. The year 2001 changed with the number of subscribers up to 500 million and first UMTS (W-CDMA) network was launched. Multimedia messaging (MMS) became popular in 2002. EDGE services became operational in a network in 2003 and the number of subscribers ended the year 2004 with the number 1 billion.
- In the year 2005, the first HSPDA capable network also became operational. Serving 1.5 billion subscribers. The first HSUPA network was launched in 2007, by the year 2008 almost two billion people started using GSM network.
- GSM network becomes most ubiquitous standard for cellular networks. GSM standard serves more than 80% of the global mobile market. GSM association accounted the users of GSM standard reached up to more than 5 billion people across the 212 countries.
- Macau planned to phase out its GSM network by June 4, 2015, making it the first region to decommission a GSM network.

Performance Characteristics of GSM

The following are the characteristics of GSM network according to performance:

1. **Communication:** Mobile, wireless communication which supports for voice and data services.
2. **Total mobility:** Different providers enables chip card by using access points it also provides international access.
3. **Worldwide connectivity:** The GSM network handles localization.
4. **High capacity:** It constructs the architecture of cells in smaller size and adds more subscribers per cell with better frequency.
5. **High transmission quality:** It provides higher audio quality and reliability for wireless, it handles uninterrupted phone calls at higher speed.
6. **Security functions:** It enable to authenticate subscribers via chip-card or PIN number.

3.1.1 Mobile Services

GSM offers the intercommunication of different voice and data services and to interact with existing network.

GSM offers three services :
   (1) Bearer
   (2) Tele
   (3) Supplementary Services.

GSM system works with the help of GSM –PLMN (Public Land Mobile Network) i.e. this is the infrastructure needed for it. A mobile station gets connected to this infrastructure through Um interface, and then this network may get connected to integrated services digital network (ISDN) or traditional public switched telephone network (PSTN).

(1) Bearer Services:

These services enable the transparent communication between the interfaces to the network. Bearer services acts as connection-oriented and circuit or packet switched.

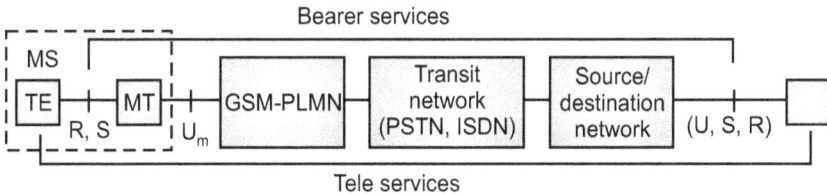

Fig. 3.1: Bearer and Tele Services Reference Model

- It offers all the transparent transfer of data from interface to the network. S in case of the mobile station and similar interface for other terminal. (SO and ISDN terminals).
- This service needs only three lower layers of ISO/OSI model.
- Mobile termination (MT) performs all network related tasks (TDMA, FDMA, Coding etc.) and offers an interface for data transmission to terminal TE
- Bearer services allow transparent and non-transparent, synchronous or asynchronous data transmission.
- **(a) Transparent Bearer Services:** These services use functions of physical layer for the transmission of data. It has constant delay and throughput if there is no error in transmission. Forward error correction helps in increasing the quality of transmission which converts redundancy to data stream and helps in recognizing original data. It does not recover data if there is loss due to error.

(b) Non-Transparent Bearer Services: Error correction and flow control is done by using protocols of second and third layer. This combines transparent bearer services with radio link protocol (RLP) with which High level data link control (HDLC) and selective-reject mechanism is possible.

- In both services data transmission can be full-duplex, synchronous with data rate 1.2, 2.4, 4.8 and 9.6 Kbit/s asynchronous from 300 to 9,600 bits/s.

(2) Tele Services:

Tele services involve encrypted voice transmission, message services, and basic data communication with terminals. The GSM primary goal is to transmit high quality digital voice at bandwidth of 3.1 KHz of analog phone systems.

- Another service offered is emergency number the same number should be used throughout the geographical area in spite of all service providers and service should be free of charge.
- GSM offers short message service (SMS) which permits a message up to 160 characters.
- The successor of SMS is extended message service (EMS), which permits 760 characters, animated pictures, small images and ringtones.
- MMS offers transmission of larger pictures (GIF, JPG, WBMP), short video clips etc.
- Group-3 wax is a non-voice service, fax data is transmitted as digital data over the analog telephone network according to ITU-T standards.

(3) Supplementary Services:

Supplementary services are served on top of teleservices or bearer services. The following are the supplementary services provided in GSM network.

- **Multiparty Service or conferencing:** Under this service a mobile subscriber can place a multiparty conversation i.e. simultaneous conversation between three or more subscribers to setup with the conference call. This is applicable to normal telephony.
- **Call Waiting:** This service let a mobile subscriber notify with an incoming call during a current conversation. The subscriber may answer, reject or ignore the incoming call. Call waiting is applicable to all GSM telecommunication services using a circuit switched connection.
- **Call Hold:** Service allows a subscriber to put an incoming call on hold and then resume this call. The call hold service is only applicable to normal telephony.

- **Call Forwarding:** This service used to divert the call from current number of recipient to another number, it is set up by the subscriber himself. It is normally used by subscriber when the original number of subscriber is unavailable so the calls coming to that number are diverted to another number. For example a sales person switch off his mobile and directed his incoming call to another number while in a meeting. So that he will be available to all the sales heads of the organization. And unavailable to rest of subscribers.
- **Number Identification:** There are following supplementary services related to number identification:
    - **Calling Line Identification Presentation:** This service provides the identification which shows calling party's phone number on the screen. This helps called person to recognize and to answer the caller.
    - **Calling Line Identification Restriction:** A person not wishing their number to be presented to others subscribes to this service. In the normal course of event, the restriction service overrides the presentation service.
    - **Connected Line Identification Presentation:** This service provides the number of the person to whom they are connected i.e. calling party, this happens in situations where calls are forwarded.
    - **Connected Line Identification Restriction:** There are times when the person called does not wish to have their number presented and so they would subscribe to this person. Normally, this overrides the presentation service.
    - **Malicious Call Identification:** This service helps in identification of annoying calls the victim who subscribes this service, they could recognize malicious calls in GSM network, using simple command this annoyed number is passed to the authority of action.
- **Advice of Charge (AoC):** This service was designed to give the subscriber an indication of the cost of the services as they are used. AoC for data calls is provided on the basis of time measurements. This service may be utilized by the service providers who wish to offer rental services to the subscribers without their Subscriber Identity Module (SIM).
- **Closed User Groups (CUGs):** This service is provided on GSM to enable groups of subscribers to only call each other. This type of services are being offered with special discount and is limited only to those members who wish to talk to each other
- **Unstructured Supplementary Services Data (USSD):** This allows operator-defined individual services

3.1.2 System Architecture

- A public land mobile network (PLMN) that is integrated to one GSM provider or administration, which includes all the elements, entities and interfaces.

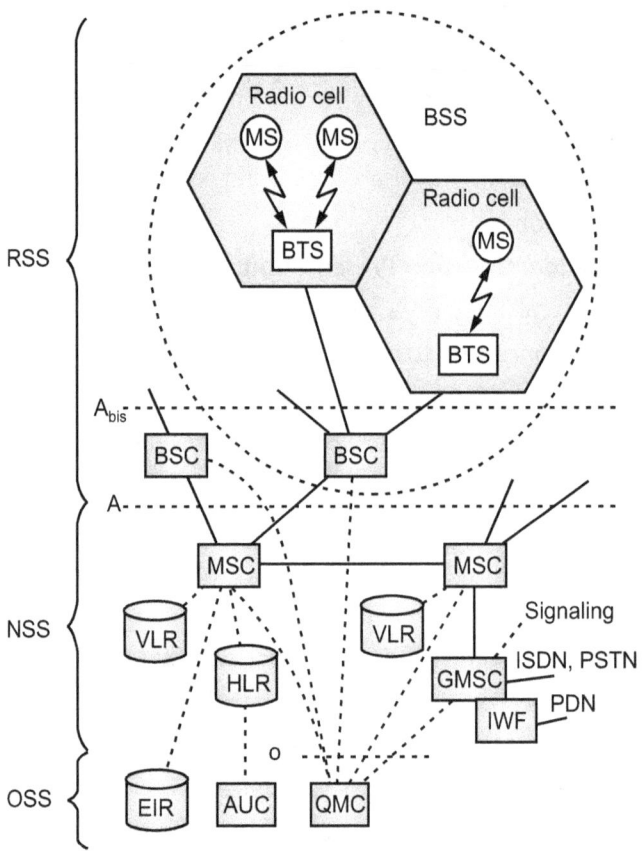

Fig. 3.2 : Functional Architecture of a GSM System

- A GSM system is hierarchical architecture of radio subsystem (RSS), network and switching subsystem (NSS) and operation subsystem (OSS).

3.1.2.1 Radio Subsystem

All radio specific entities such as mobile station (MS) and the Base Station Subsystem (BSS). 'A' interface enable radio subsystem to communicate with network and switching subsystem (solid lines) and connects it to operation subsystem with O interface (dashed lines). The 'A' interface is typically based on circuit switched PCM-30 systems (2.048 Mbit /s) carrying up to 30 - 64 Kbit/s connections, whereas O interface uses the signaling system No. 7 (SS7) based on X.25 network. A GSM network comprises many BSS, carrying management data to/from the radio subsystem.

- **Base Station Subsystem:** Base station controller (BSC) controls many BSSs in the GSM system. The BSS performs many functions necessary to:
  (a) Maintain radio connection to mobile station.
  (b) Coding/decoding of voice.
  (c) Rate adaptation to/from the wireless network part.
  Besides BSC, the BSS contains several BTSs.
- **Base Transceiver Station (BTS):** A BTS comprises of all radio equipment such as antennas, signal processing, amplifiers necessary for radio transmission. BTS can form a radio cell, which is having several ms.
- Mobile stations are connected to BTSs via Um interface (ISDN U interface for mobile user) and BSCs via Abis interface.
- Um interface contains all the mechanism needed for wireless transmission (TDMA, FSMA).
- A_{bis} interface consists of 16 or 64 Kbit/s connections.

Um

This is the air interface in between the mobile station (MS) and BTS. This interface has the functions like signaling, to conduct call control, measurement reporting, handover power control, authentication, authorization, location update and so on. Traffic and signaling are sent in bursts of 0.577 ms at intervals of 4.615 ms, to form data blocks each 20 ms. these all functions works on LAPDm protocol.

LAPDM is the link access procedure for D-channel in ISDN network (LAPD) Time Division Multiplexing.

Abis

This is the interface between the BTS and BSC it uses TDM subchannels for traffic (TCH), LAPD protocol for BTS supervision and telecom signaling and carries synchronization from the BSC to the BTS and MS.

A

This interface lies between BSC and MSC, it is used for carrying traffic channels and the BSSAP user part of the SS7 stack. These are usually transcoding units between BSC and MSC, the signaling communication takes place between these two ending points and the transcoder unit doesn't touch the SS7 information, only the voice or CS data are transcoded.

Ater

This is the interface between the BSC and transcoder. It is a proprietary interface whose name depends on the vendor (for example Ater by Nokia), it carries the A interface information from the BSC leaving it untouched.

Gb

It connects the BSS to the SGSN in the GPRS core network.

- The Base transreceiver station, are having the equipments for transmitting and receiving radio signals, antennas, and equipment for encryption and decryption communications with the base station controller. One picocell has several transreceivers which allow sending and receiving information on different frequencies and different sectors of the cell.
- BSC controls all BTSs via base station control function (BCF), it is implemented as a discrete unit and it provides an Operations and Maintenance (O and M) connection to the network management system and manages operational states of each transcreceivers as well as software handling and alarm collection.

The function of BTS varies depending on the cellular technology used and the cellular telephone provider. There are vendors in which the BTS is a plain transreceiver which receives information from the MS (mobile station) through the Um air interface and then converts it to a TDM (PCM) based interface, the Abis interface, and sends it towards the BSC.

- The BTSs are equipped with radios that are able to modulate layer 1 of interface Um, for GSM 2G+ the modulation type is Gaussian minimum-shift keying (GMSK), while for EDGE-enabled networks it is GMSK and 8-PSK. This modulation is a kind of continuous-phase keying, the signal which is to be sent on carrier is smoothed with Gaussian low pass filter which in prior feed to frequency modulator, which reduces the interference of neighboring cells.
- Frequency hopping is used to increase the BTS performance, it involves the rapid switching of voice traffic between TRXs in a sector. A hopping sequence is followed by the TRXs handsets by using the sector. The hopping sequence is broadcasted on specific time of interval to intimate the handsets in that cell.

Transreceivers transmit and receive according to GSM standards, which specify eight TDMA timeslots per radio frequency. Transcreceivers may lose some of the capacity as certain messages are needed to be broadcasted in the network this signaling makes use of a channel known as the Broadcast control channel (BCCH).

- **Base Station Controller:** All base transreceivers are controlled by base station controller. It reserves radio frequencies, handles the handovers from one BTS to another within the BSS.
    - Base station controller is the intelligence behind BTSs one BSC has tens or even hundreds of BTSs under its control.
    - BSC manages the allocation of radio channels, receives measurements from the mobile phones and controls the handovers from BTS to BTS.
    - BSC acts as a concentrator that is different from low capacity connections to BTSs. It reduces to a smaller number of connections towards the mobile switching center (MSC) the network constitutes of many BTSs which are connected to the large centralized MSC.

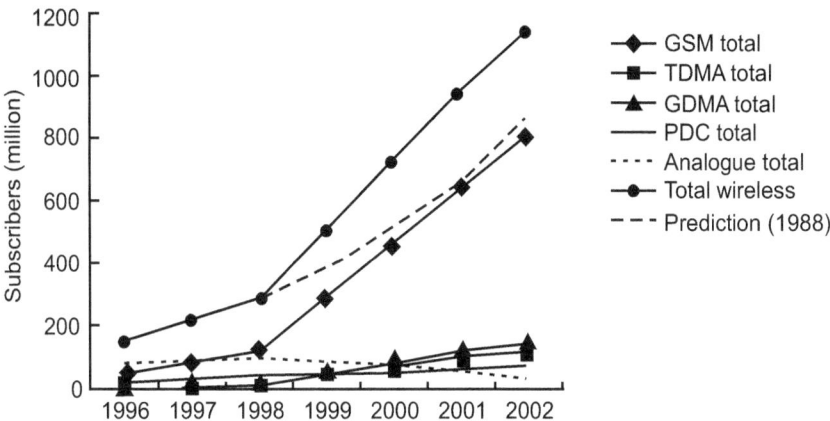

Fig. 3.3 : Worldwide subscribers of different mobile phone

- It is the robust component of BSS, it not only controls all BTSs but also it acts as a full switching center as well as an SS7 NODE WITH CONNECTIONS IS required to support serving GPRS support node. It also provides all the required data to the operation support subsystem (OSS) as well as to the performance measuring centers.
- BSC is based on distributed computing architecture, with redundancy applied to critical functional units to ensure availability in the event of fault conditions.
- BSC stores the huge database the information such as carrier frequencies, frequency hopping lists, power reduction levels, receiving levels for cell border calculation are stored into BSC. This data is obtained by radio planning engineering which involves the modeling of the signal propagation as well as traffic projections.
- **Mobile Stations:** A mobile station consists of independent hard, soft and subscriber identity module (SIM), which stores all user-specific data that is relevant to GSM.
    o International mobile equipment identity is used to recognize mobile station.
    o For any mobile station there are two types of mechanisms.
        (a) User-specific mechanism e.g. charging, authentication of SIM card.
        (b) Device specific mechanism – theft protection, use the device specific IMEI.
    o SIM card contains many identifiers/tables, card-type, serial number etc.
      Following is the list of subscribed services:
        (i) PIN (Personal Identity Number) which unlocks the MS.
        (ii) PIN Unlocking Key (PUK) to unlock the SIM.
        (iii) Authentication key Ki.
    o MS also supports the functions like display, loudspeaker, microphone, programmable soft keys.

Mobile station:
o Terminal for the use of GSM services
o A mobile station (MS) comprises several functional groups

MT (Mobile Terminal):
- It offers common functions used by all services that MS offers.
- It corresponds to the network termination (NT) of an ISDN access.
- It is the end-point of the radio interface (Um)

TA (Terminal Adapter):
- Terminal adaptation and it hides radio specific characteristics

TE (Terminal Equipment):
- Peripheral device of the MS, it offers services to a user
- It does not contain GSM specific functions

SIM (Subscriber Identity Module):
- Personalization of the mobile terminal, it stores all user parameters

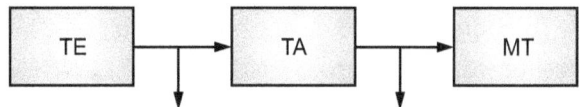

Fig. 3.4: Mobile terminals

3.1.2.2 Network and Switching Subsystem

Network switching subsystem (NSS) is the main component of a GSM system that performs call switching and mobility management functions for mobile roaming phones, which are the part of a network. It is handled by mobile phone operators which allow mobile phone to communicate with each other and also with the mobiles which are present in PSTN (Public Switched Telephone Network) the architecture have special features as mobile are not fixed in one location.

- This subsystem is the basis of core circuit switched GSM network, which is used for voice calls, SMS, circuit switched data calls. It is extended with special features to acquire the GPRS core network. This allows mobile service to have an access to WAP, MMS and the internet.
- It acts like a bridge between standard public networks with wireless network. The NSS made up of following switches and database :

(a) Mobile Services Switching Center (MSC):

It helps to form the backbone of GSM. These are high-performance digital ISDN switches. They set up connections to other MSCs and to the BSCs via 'A' interface.

- The networks like PSTN and ISDN are connected to gateway MSC. By using interworking functions (IWF), public data network (PDN) is connected to MSC, such as X.25.
- MSC uses standard signaling system No. 7 for connection setup, connection release and handover of connections to other MSC.

- The mobile switching centre server is switch variant of mobile switching centre, which provides circuit switched calling, mobility management, and GSM services to the mobile phone roaming within that area. NSS enables split between control and user plane (media gateway), which places network elements into the network.
- **Home Location Register (HCR):** It is used to store all user specific information such as mobile subscriber ISDN number (MSISDN) subscribed services. (e.g. call forwarding, roaming restrictions, GPRS) and the international mobile subscriber identity (IMSI).
- It also stores current location area of MS, mobile subscriber roaming number (MSRN), the current VLR and MSC.
- HLR keeps record of current location of the MS, this helps in locating the mobile station in GSM network and mobile stations are registered to only one HLR.
- HLR stores the central database that contains details of each mobile phone subscribers that are authorized to use GSM core network. There are several logical and physical HLRs per public land mobile network, included in one international mobile subscriber identity (IMSI) MSISDN.
- It can be associated with one HLR at a time. MSISDNs, which are the telephone numbers used by mobile phones to make and receive calls. The primary MSISDN is the number used for making and receiving voice calls and SMS, but it is possible for a SIM to have other secondary MSISDNs associated with it for fax and data calls. Each MSISDN is also a primary key to the HLR record.
- The HLR stores details of every SIM card issued by mobile phone operator. Each SIM has a unique identifier called an IMSI which is the primary key to each HLR record.
- HLR system directly receives and processes MAP transactions and messages from elements in the GSM network, e.g. the location update messages received as mobile phone roam around.

HLR also stores the other details against IMSI are:
1. GSM services that the subscriber has requested.
2. GPRS settings to allow the subscriber to access packed services.
3. Current location of subscriber (VLR and serving GPRS support nodes)
4. Call diverts settings applicable for each associated MSISDN.
- **Visitor Location Register (VLR):** When mobile station moves outside the HLR region, VLR keeps track on its location register associated with the MSC.

It takes all the relevant information about the mobile stations from HLR. VLRs are **enabling** to manage up to one million customers.

3.1.2.3 Operation Subsystem

This subsystem is used to control and monitor the components of GSM network. It is connected to the components of NSS and BSC. It is also responsible to handle the traffic of BSS as the number of BS increases with the scaling of subscriber population, some of the maintenance tasks are transferred to the BTS.

Operation subsystem contains necessary operation and maintenance. This system has following entities:

(1) Operation and Maintenance Center (OMC):

'O' interface helps OMC to monitor and control the other network entities. Following functions are performed by OMC:

(i) Traffic monitoring.

(ii) Status reports of network entities.

(iii) Subscriber and security management.

(iv) Accounting and billing.

(2) Authentication Center:

To protect the user identity and data transmission. ACIC contains algorithms for authentication as well as the keys for encryption and generates the values needed for user authentication in the HLR.

(3) Equipment Identity Register (EIR):

Equipment Identity Register or EIR is a database that identifies the devices that are permitted to access the network. This restricts on unauthorized access, it is used by second generation wireless services.

It is the database which stores all devices registered for network.

Functions of EIR:

(a) EIR blacklists the stolen devices i.e. it locks it.

(b) It has valid list of IMEI 'S' (white list), and a list of malfunctioning devices (gray list).

Before Mobile Services GSM Address and Identifiers:

GSM uses the following addresses and identifiers to make a difference between the user and device, subscriber and telephone number.

(1) International Mobile Station Equipment Identity (IMEI): This number is provided by device manufacturers and registered by the network operator in EIR.

(2) International Mobile Subscriber Identity (IMSI):

When mobile station gets registered with GSM network, each subscriber is assigned a unique identifier which resides in SIM to validate SIM card. It consists of following parts.

(i) Mobile Country Code – For India – 404.

(ii) Mobile Network Code – This uniquely identifies a mobile operator within the country.

(iii) Mobile Subscriber Identification Number – Home network identifies subscriber with this number.

(3) Mobile Subscriber ISDN Numbers:

MSISDN number which is a unique identification subscription in a GSM or UMTS mobile network, it is a telephone number to the SIM card in a mobile/cellular phone. The MSISDN together with IMSI are two important numbers used for identifying a mobile subscriber. IMSI is used as a key in the HLR and MSISDN is the number normally dialed to connect a call to the mobile phone. A SIM is uniquely associated to an IMSI, while the MSISDN can change in time, i.e. different MSISDNs can be associated to the SIM.

It is a real telephone number with which you operate. MSISDN is public information whereas IMSI is private to the operator. The MSISDN categories follow the international ISDN (Integrated Systems Data Network) numbering plan as the following.

(a) Country Code – One-to-three decimal digits of CC.

(b) National Destination Code – Typically 2 to 3 decimal digit.

(c) Subscriber Number (SN) – Maximum 10 decimal digit.

e.g. CC – India – 91

USA – 1

NDC – BSNL-94, 98 for rest.

SN – 8 digits in India.

3.1.3 Protocols

The layered model of the GSM architecture integrates and links the peer-to-peer communications between two different systems. The underlying layers satisfy the services of the upper-layer protocols. Notifications are passed from layer to layer to ensure that the information has been properly formatted, transmitted, and received.

- GSM is the layered architecture which integrates and links the peer to peer communication between two different systems. The underlying layers satisfy the services of the upper-layer protocols. Notifications are passed from layer to layer to ensure that the information has been properly formatted, transmitted, and received.

MS Protocols:

The signaling protocol in GSM is structured into three general layers, depending on the interface.

Layer1: The physical layer, which uses the channel structure over the air interface. Air interface which is nothing but Um interface which lies in between mobile station and base transreceiver station (BTS). It is called Um because it is mobile analog to the U interface of ISDN.

Physical layer of air interface is responsible to channel structure, coding.

- This handles radio specific functions. It creates the bursts according to format multiplexes it using TDMA, and then synchronizes with the BTS.

All mobile stations in one cell must be synchronized with respective to the BTS, as BTS generates different time structure frames and slots. Because of that every mobile station has different round trip times (RTT) which depends upon the distance of mobile station from BTS.

All bursts should reach BTS within their time limit, this can be done by using 'timing advance 'variable in which mobile station adjusts and controls their access.

The main task of physical layer is channel coding and error detection/correction.

Forward error correction techniques add redundancy to user data allowing for the detection and correction of selected errors. The performance of FEC depends on amount of redundancy, coding algorithm and further interleaving of data to minimize the errors. The interleaving of data to minimize the errors.

Layer 2: The data-link layer across the Um interface, the data-link layer is a modified version of the Link access protocol for the D channel (LAP-D) protocol used in ISDN, called Link access protocol on the Dm channel (LAP-Dm). Across the A interface, the Message Transfer Part (MTP), Layer 2 of SS7 is used.

- LAPDm is used protocol in the data link layer. It is derived from ISDN system. It is the link access procedure for the D-channel which is version of HDLC.
- It also offers reliable data transfer over connections, re-sequencing of data frames and flow control.
- It provides services like segmentation and reassembly of data and acknowledged/ unacknowledged data transfer.

Layer 3: The third layer of the GSM signaling protocol is divided into three sublayers:

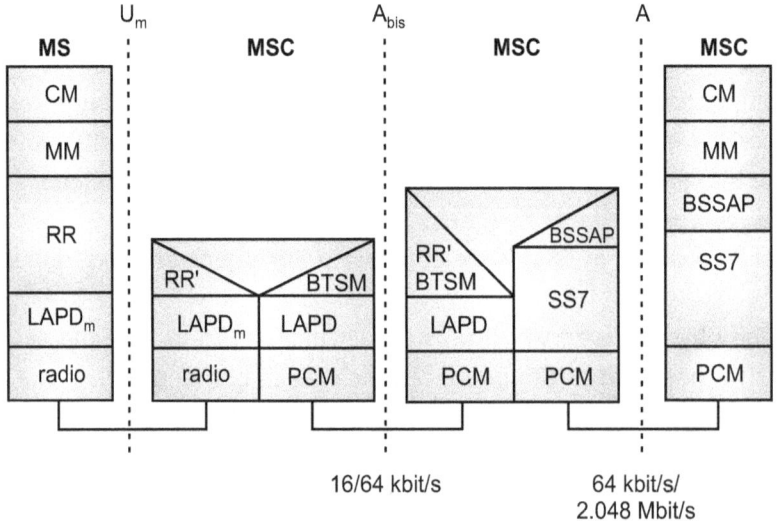

Fig. 3.5: Protocol architecture for signaling

- **Radio Resource management (RR):** It presents at the BTS. Its main task is setup, maintenance, release of radio channels. It access physical layer for radio information and forward it to higher layers.

- **Mobility Management (MM):** It performs the following functions: (i) Registration, (ii) Authentication, (iii) Identification, (iv) Location Updating, (v) Provision of temporary mobile subscriber identity (TMSI) that replaces IMSI.

- **Connection Management (CM):** It contains three elements:

    (i) call control, (ii) SMS, (iii) Supplementary services.

3.1.3.1 Localization and Calling
Localization and Calling

- GSM architecture enable the system to locate the user worldwide, it performs periodic location updates even if a user does not use the mobile station. The HLR always contains information about the current location and VLR is responsible for the MS which informs HLR about location changes. As soon as MS move into the range of a new VLR, the HLR sends all user data needed to new VLR.

- Roaming changes the position of services. To locate the MS and to address the MS following numbers are required :

1. Mobile Station International ISDN Number (MSISDN):

The only important number for a user of GSM in is the phone number. Phone no is associated with SIM, which is personalized for a user. This no consists of country code (CC) the National Destination Code (NDC), and subscriber number (SN).

2. International Mobile Subscriber Identity (IMSI):

GSM uses the IMSI for internal unique identification of a subscriber it consists of Mobile Country Code (MCC), the Mobile Network Code (MNC), and Mobile Subscriber Identification Identity (MSIN).

3. Temporary Mobile Subscriber Identity (TMSI):

Four byte TMSI number is local subscriber identification which is selected by the current VLR and which is temporary and within the location of VLR. It is used to hide the IMSI which gives exact identity of the user signaling over the air interface.

4. Mobile Station Roaming Number (MSRN):

Another temporary address that hides the location of a subscriber is MSRN. MSRN contains the current Visitor Country Code (VCC), the Visitor National Destination Code (VNDC).

The steps involve in calling from a fixed network to a MS (MTC), and from a MS to fixed network (MOC) is given below :

Mobile Terminated Call (MTC)

1: Calling a GSM subscriber
2: Forwarding call to GMSC
3: Signal call setup to HLR
4, 5: Request MSRN from VLR
6: Forward responsible MSC to GMSC
7: Forward call to current MSC
8, 9: Get current status of MS
10, 11: Paging of MS
12, 13: MS answers
14, 15: Security checks
16, 17: Set up connection

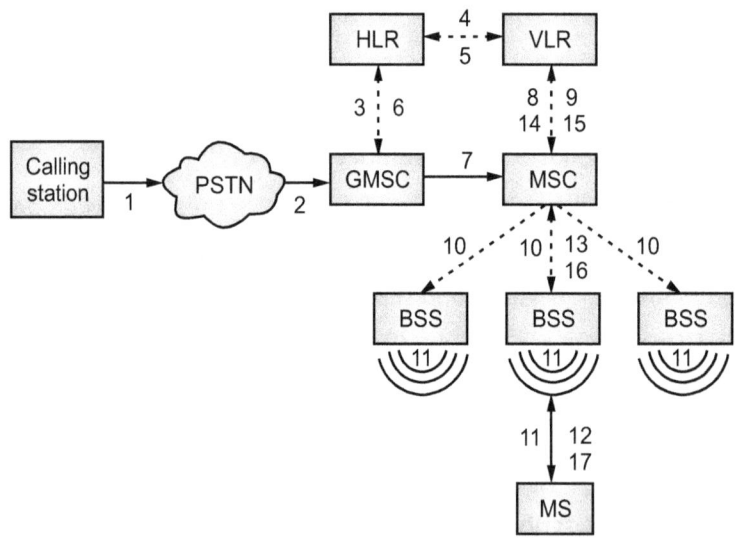

Fig. 3.6: Mobile Terminated Call (MTC)

Mobile Originated Call (MOC)

1, 2: Connection request
3, 4: Security check
5-8: Check resources (free circuit)
9-10: Set up call

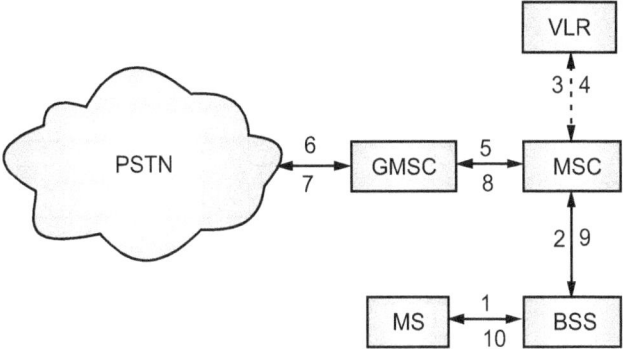

Fig. 3.7: Mobile Originated Call (MOC)

3.1.3.2 Handover   (April 2015)

The term handover or handoff in cellular telecommunications refers to the process of transferring an ongoing call or data session from one channel connected to the core network to another channel and in Satellite communication it is the process of transferring satellite control responsibility from one earth station to another without loss or interruption of service.

- Single cell structure does not cover the whole geographical area approximately the cell structure size is 35 Km at countryside and some hundred meters in the cities.
- There are two reasons for handover :
   (i) The MS moves out of range of BTS, so the strength of received signals decreases the error rate increases due to interference and may be due to distance of MS to BTS is more than 35 Km.
   (ii) Due to heavy traffic in one cell, MSC or BSC decided to shift some MS to another cell which is having lower load.
- The following are the situations when the handovers takes place.
   (i) **Intra-cell handover:** This happens within a cell, narrow band interference could make transmission at a certain frequency. BSC changes its frequency.
   (ii) **Inter-cell intra BSC handover:** Under the control of same BSC, mobile station moves from one cell to another cell.
   (iii) **Inter-BSC, intra MSC handover:** Less than one MSC is mobile station handovers from one BSC to another BSC.
   (iv) **Inter MSC handover:** In different MSCs, handover is required, in which both MSCs handovers together.

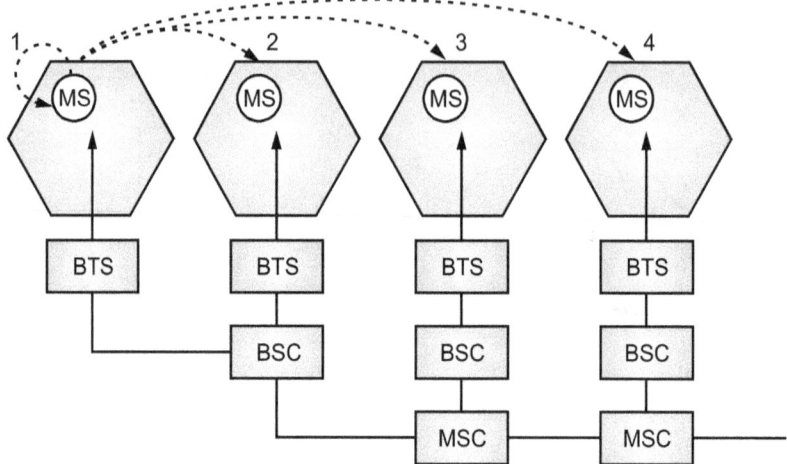

Fig. 3.8: Types of handover in GSM

- The first two handovers are called internal handovers. As it is managed by BSC, without MSCs, to save the signaling bandwidth and notify it to MSC.
- The last two handovers are called external handovers, handled by MSC.

1. SMS Short Message Service

The GSM Short message Service (SMS) provides a connectionless transfer of message with low-capacity and low-time performance.

- To allow message longer than 160 character concatenation of SMS and compression have been defined.
- SMS operates like a paging service with added capacity that can pass in both the directions. There are two types of GSM Short Message Service has been defined
    1. Cell broadcast service which periodically delivers short message to call subscriber in a given data.
    2. Point to point service which sends short message to a specific users.

A scientist named Neil Papworth in 1992 sends the first SMS to Vodafone GSM operator. On 3rd December, he sends "merry Christmas" massage to the director of Vodafone.

- SMS is popular data bearer services with on average billions of people transacted through it.
- It has 160 characters capacity.

Characteristics of SMS:

(i) **Omnibus Nature of SMS:** It is the only one bearer service that allows the user to send the data/SMS over a long distance.

(ii) **Stateless:** It is stateless and session less i.e. it is routed interdependently regardless of the context. It is good for notifications and alerts.

(iii) Asynchronous: SMS works differently than HTTP protocol. It doesn't have request response paradigm whereas SMS works for both synchronous as well as asynchronous messaging.

(iv) Self-configurable and last mile problem resistant: This service has no constraints as mobile station moves from one network to another. It gets self configured and subscriber is always connected to SMS bearer services.

(v) Always connected: As SMS using SS7 signaling mechanism, user cannot switch OFF, BAR or DIVERT any SMS message. If phone is busy in voice or fax still SMS gets delivered.

- Value added services through SMS:

Voice, SMS are the basic services offered by GSM system.

(ii) It can be an add-on basic service and as such, may be sold at a premium price.

(iii) It stands alone in terms of profitability and revenue generation potential.

(iv) It can sometimes stand-alone operationally.

Cell Broadcast Service:

It is also called as Short Message Service cell-broadcast SMS-(B). It is a mobile technology feature defined by the ETS's GSM committee and part of GSM standard.

- It is used to deliver the SMS to multiuser in the same area which is supported by UMTS.
- In 1997, this was introduced in Paris, cell broadcasting allows text or binary message.
- Cell broadcast messages reaches a huge number of terminals at a time. It is one of the 'PUSH' type services that are when sender sends the message to recipient's sender does not know who have received the messages.
- It is made up of 82 octets, which uses default character set of 93 characters. The Cell Broadcast (CB) identifier will be same for all the messages that are sent.

2. MMS:

The standard is developed by the Open Mobile Alliance (OMA), although during development it was part of the 3GPP and WAP groups.

In third generation messaging includes multimedia objects this is called as multimedia messaging service. Multimedia Messaging Service (MMS) is a standard way to send messages that include multimedia content to and from mobile phones. It extends the core SMS (Short Message Service) capability that allowed exchange of text messages only up to 160 characters in length.

- Camera equipped handsets have the facility to send the photographs to and from mobile devices, it is also used to deliver the entertainment content including videos, pictures, text pages and ringtones.

MMS Architecture:

The user of mobile station uses wireless or radio network to deliver MMS between each other. Multimedia message service environment is consisting of many elements required to deliver MMS.

(i) **MMS client:** This is an application on user's mobile and this entity interacts with the user.

(ii) **MMS relay:** MMS client interacts with MMS relay. It accesses the message storage services and responsible for messaging activities with other messaging systems.

(iii) **WAP gateway:** It provides standard WAP services needed to implement MMS.

(iv) **MMS server:** This is the content server, where the MMS content is generated.

(v) **Email server:** Email system integrates with MMS.

MMS client interacts with MMS relay through WAP gateway, the data is transferred by using WAP Session Protocol (WSP) between MMS client and WAP gateway. Data is transferred between the WAP gateway and MMS relay using HTTP.

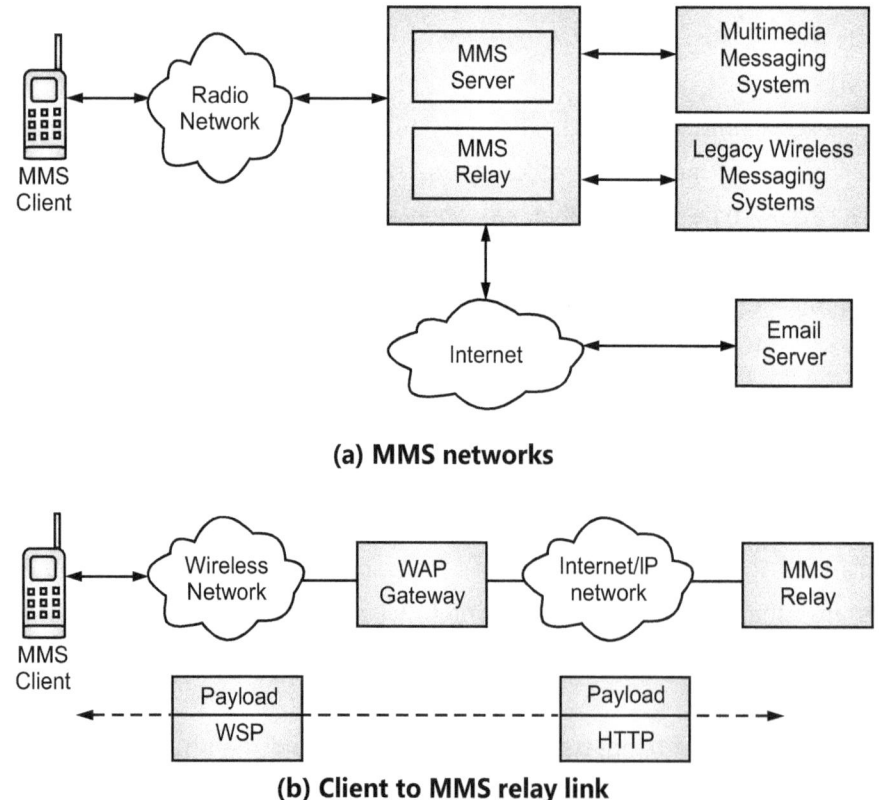

(a) MMS networks

(b) Client to MMS relay link

Fig. 3.9: MMS Environment

Location Services:

Location based services determines location and time data of the users. It is nowadays used in social networking.

- This service has various domains such as health, indoor objects search, entertainment, work, personal life etc.
- Location Based Service includes vehicle tracking services and mobile commerce, whether based services.
- The push mechanisms like SMS plays important role in Location Based Service. It can carry mobile advertisements schemes to mobile phones.
- In order to maintain security the location privacy protection act of 2012 is applied.
- While using location based services with mobile phones user must take care of the following:
    (a) Consider turning off feature while using social networking sites.
    (b) Share your location only then you trust.

3.2 WAP

Wireless Application Protocol (WAP)

WAP is introduced to improve the wireless data network.

It enables devices and many mobile operators to join the WAP forum.

- WAP forum is the set of global wireless protocol specifications for many wireless networks.
- It integrates a light weight web browser to handle the devices which has limited computing.
- WAP application protocol is implemented in both the WAP gateway and WAP handset to enable a mobile user to access internet web application.

WAP Model:

In WAP networks architecture, WAP handset communicates with the origin server through the mobile network.

The origin server is a standard Hypertext transfer protocol.

- As use of internet and its application widely spreads and much mobile communication led to avail these services in mobile phones.
- www is most important but it is mostly incompatible with mobile phones.
- To avail internet service through mobile phones in June 1997, companies like Erricsson, Motorola, Nokia and unwired planet developed wireless application protocol forum (WAP forum).
- Open Mobile Alliance (OMA) which constitutes of WAP forum and SYNCML which introduces standards such as 3GPP, IETF. It also introduces version of WAP 1.X

- The basic objective of WAP is to make available the internet services and other digital services to cellular phones and other wireless, mobile terminals. WAP integrates a light weight web browser to handle device with limited computing.
- The framework for WAP 1.X version and it should contain:

(i) **Interoperable:** It allows terminals and software from different provider to communicate with each other.

(ii) **Scalable:** Customers needs should meet the protocols and services.

(iii) **Efficient:** Provision of QOS suited to the characteristics of the wireless and mobile networks.

(iv) **Reliable:** To deploy services the reliable platform is needed.

(v) **Secure:** Protection of devices and services from security problem and to preserve integrity of data.

Networks for WAP:

WAP is accessible from the following networks :

1. GSM-900, GSM-1800, GSM-1900
2. GPRS
3. CDMA IS-95, CDMA 2000
4. TDMA IS-136.

3.2.1 Architecture of WAP

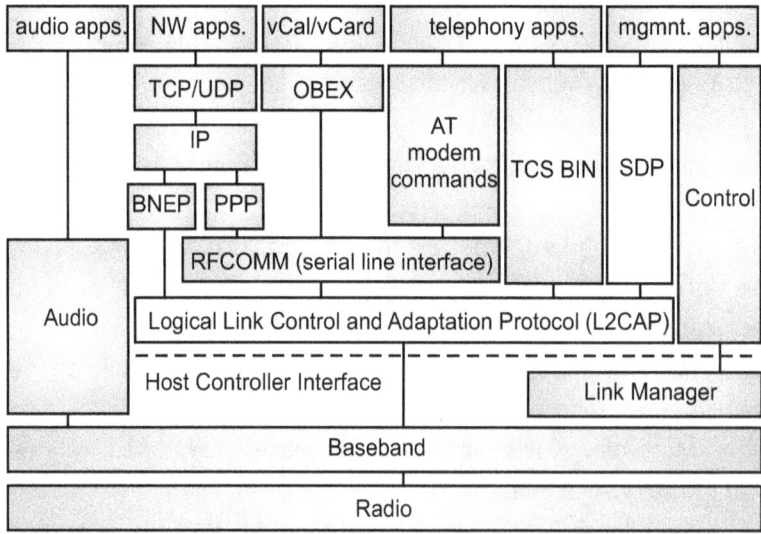

Fig. 3.10: Architecture of WAP

- WAP handset encodes the contents in a compact binary format of Wireless Markup Language (WML).
- WAP gateway is located between the Internet and the mobile network, it receive the WAP.
- Request form the handset and decode the request into text format and to origin server.

The origin server retrieves the file and return to the WAP gateway via HTTP.

Mobile Computing - Wireless Application Protocol (WAP)

WAP provides end to end security if handset and origin server communicates directly using WAP protocol.

The micro browser is used to optimize the web browser for the wireless environment. WML is an XML language is designed to handle mobile device. It describes the WAP content present in WAP handset. WML document is divided into set of cards each represent one unit of interaction between the user and user agent. User can navigate among cards from WML documents.

WAP defines a user-interface model for handheld device.

- WAP gateway is a middleware and which is developed by using UNIX and Windows NT both. The Motorola and Ericsson gateway is base on the Windows NT platform.
- WAP gateway utilizes web proxy technology to provide efficient wireless access to the Internet. A proxy plays the roles of both the server and client making request on behalf of the client. So the gateway server acts as a proxy to handle request form the WAP handset and passes the request to origin server.
- On the internet side the WAP gateway translates the request from WAP protocol to the internet protocol stack (HTTP) and (TCP/IP).
- WAP gateway supports the DNS service to resolve the domain name used in URLs.
- WAP gateway performs on demand transformation which effectively reduces the wireless traffic and protects the semantic content of documents .and allow user to quickly retrieve a simplified version of an object.

3.2.2 WAP Protocol Stack

- WAP specification is defined as a set of light weight protocol designed to operate over a variety of wireless bearer services.
- These services have different quality of services (QoS). WAP protocol compensate these.
- Qualities of services (QoS) requirements.

- These services are based on IP based or Non IP based mechanism.

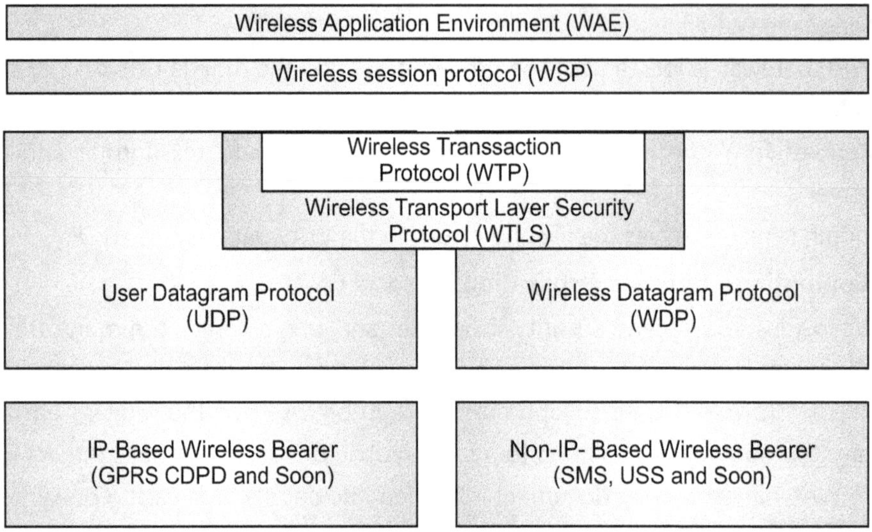

| Wireless Application Environment (WAE) |
| Wireless session protocol (WSP) |

Wireless Transsaction Protocol (WTP)	
Wireless Transport Layer Security Protocol (WTLS)	
User Datagram Protocol (UDP)	Wireless Datagram Protocol (WDP)

| IP-Based Wireless Bearer (GPRS CDPD and Soon) | Non-IP- Based Wireless Bearer (SMS, USS and Soon) |

Fig. 3.11: WAP Protocol Stack

Wireless Application Environment (WAE)

WAP forum has introduced this architecture and compares this with typical architecture of internet using www.

- WAP uses existing data services and integrates the data which is generated by all bearer services. E.g. SMS for GSM, GPRS is GSM, high-speed circuit switched data in GSM. It is bottom layer of WAP architecture.
- With transport layer service access point (T-SAP) which is a common interface between bearer services and transport layer. Transport layer has wireless data gram protocol and wireless control message protocol (WCMP). These protocols are bearer specific, which performs consistent datagram oriented service to the higher layers of WAP architecture.

Wireless Datagram Protocol (WDP)

WAP represents the WAP transport layer and it offers consistent services to the upper layer protocol of WAP.

In WDP the higher WAP layers can function independently of the underlying wireless network because of different function provides by bearers.

- For IP based bearer network, the user datagram protocol is used and it provides port based addressing and segmentation that is required by WAP connectionless datagram services.

For non IP based bearer adaptation is decreased with efficiency of the bearers.

- WDP sends the datagram TD unit Data request with destination address (DA), destination port (DP), source address (SA), source port (SP) to the higher layer.

T-Dunitdata.ind indicates the acknowledgement on reception of data. If higher layer didn't receive the datagram, T-D Error in datagram is sent back to the transport layer.
- WCMP provides error-handling mechanism for WDP.

Typical WCMP messages are:
(i) Parameter problem
(ii) Destination unreachable
(iii) Messages are too big to send
(iv) Reassembly failure.
- Adaptation to environment such as changes in configuration of device, available bearer services, processing and memory resources is done with the help of WDP management entity.
- **Security layer:** Next higher layer is security layer and offers its service to security SAP (SEC-SAP). It has wireless transport layer security (WTLS) which is based on transport security layer (secure socket layer). It provides authentication, privacy and integrity.

Wireless Transport Layer Security (WTLS)

This defines a WAP security layer which act according to industrial standard transport layer security protocol so that it can be used in narrowband communication channels.
- WTLS supports unchanged and uncorrupted data integrity delivery with encryption and authentication.
- WTLS uses low processing power and very limited memory of mobile devices for applying cryptographic algorithms.
- The secure session is created in between the peers who are communicating the following steps involved in establishing the session.

Wireless Transaction Protocol (WTP)

WAP defines the wireless transaction layer WTP acts same as a TCP, except WTP reduced the amount of information needed for transaction.
- WAP supports following three transactions in which the switches saves processing and memory cost in WAP handset.
    1. Unreliable one way request
    2. Reliable one way request
    3. Reliable two way request

(1) Session is created with SEC-create session id with source address (SA), source port (SP), destination address (DA), destination port (DP) parameters. The parameters needed for cryptographic algorithms such as cipher suite compression method. The sender also issues

SEC-Exchange primitive which indicates public key authentication. It is followed by client certificate from source port i.e. originator with this client certificate (cc), it performs handshake by sending SEC-commit request primitive.

- The WTLS layer of peer/receiver sends back confirmation to originator and ends with full handshake.
- The next higher layer is transaction layer, and it is having wireless transaction protocol. It offers transaction service at transaction SAP (TR-SAP). It offers reliable or unreliable requests asynchronous transactions.
- Wireless Transaction Protocol (WTP) runs on very thin client such as mobile phones.

Functions provided by wireless Transaction Protocol are as follows to higher layers:

(i) Reliability over datagram services.
(ii) Improved efficiency over connection oriented services.
(iii) Support for transaction oriented services.

- These features offered to the higher layer by WTP. It has three classes of transaction services. WTP class 0 provides unreliable message transfer without any result message. WTP classes 1 and 2 offers reliable services. Reliability is achieved by duplicate removal, retransmission acknowledgements and transaction identifiers. WTP provides three services TR-Invoke to initiate a new transaction, TR-Result to send back result, TR-Abort to terminate the transaction. The communication is held with the help of invoke PDU, ack PDU, result PDU.
- Next layer is session layer with wireless session protocol and it offers services at session SAP (S-SAP).

The features needed for wireless mobile access to the web:

(i) Long-lived session-state
(ii) Session suspend and resume
(iii) Session migration
(iv) WSP/B web browser that offers HTTP/1.1.

Wireless Session Protocol:

- WAP supports the WAP session layer which has optimized for low bandwidth bearer networks with relatively long latency.
- WSP supports content exchange for client/server application by establishing a session from client to server and releasing a session in order.
- WSP sometimes suspends the session to release network resources and save power consumption of WAP handset.

WSP have two types of session services:

1. **Connection-oriented services:** Connection-oriented services operate above WTP and connectionless operates above WDP.

2. Connection less services: The current version of WSP is suited for browsing application in which WAP gateway makes the connection between WSP client and HTTP servers

WSP offers a content exchange between client and server. WSP protocol tries the 'stateless' to be reduced from traditional internet architecture as it leads to overhead of storing.

The following features are needed for transferring data:

(i) Session Management: WSP manages sessions that are established from client to server. The sessions should be well managed for suspending and resuming the session's e.g. mobile device should resume its previous session where it is left.

(ii) Capability Negotiation: The common parameters are introduced and client, server should be agreeing on these Parameters. E.g. parameters such as client SDU size, maximum outstanding requests, Protocol options, server SDU size etc.

(iii) Content encoding: WSP defines the efficient binary encoding for the content it transfers.

WSP/B Offers Additional Features:

(i) Exchange of session headers: Clients and servers exchanges header with request/reply that remains constant throughout the session. These headers include content type, character sets, languages, device capabilities.

(ii) Push and pull data transfer: Pulling data from web is traditional mechanism. WSP also offers push services.
- Confirmed data push within an existing session context.
- A non-confirmed data push within an existing session context.
- Non-confirmed data push without an existing session context.

(iii) Asynchronous request: Multiple requests can be sent by client to the server. Latency also improved as each result can be sent to the client.

- The uppermost layer is application layers, wireless application environment (WAE) offers a framework for integration of mobile telephony applications and different www. This environment provides a way to approach different wireless platforms. These platforms are important for service providers, software manufacturers or hardware environment.
- WAE defines the WAP application which provides an environment to efficiently build applications on different wireless platforms.

It provides a set of content format including images, phone book records and calendar information.

It supports user Agent Profile and push technologies. It also defines micro browser for WML.

Following are the elements of WAE:
1. **WAE User Agent:** It interprets network content referenced by a URL.

WAE defines a set of user agent capabilities that is exchanged between client and server using WSP. There capabilities include global device characteristics as WML version.

- This environment is scripted by WML script wireless markup language which is based on HTML, JavaScript and handheld device markup language (HDML). It also includes Vcards which allows exchange of business cards.
- **How it works:** Client issues encoded request for operation on a remote server. Decoders in gateway translate this encoded request into a standard request as understood by the origin server. The origin server responds to the request and encodes response with the content of client. Several user agents can reside within a client e.g. browser, phone books, message editors etc. WML user agent supports WML and WML script.

WAP 2.0:

WAP form published the second version of WAP in July 2001. It supports WAP 1.X protocol but additionally supports IP, TCP, and TLS and HTTP. WAP 2.0 browser uses WML as well as XHTML, it is developed by W3C to replace current HTML.

The protocol architecture consists of following components.

(i) **Bearer services:** Same as WAP 1.X, many bearer services such as GPRS in GSM, SMS in push services are supported 3G network directly supports IP services.

(ii) **Transport services:** These services are both connection oriented and connection less and it offers end-to-end communication as an abstract of all bearer services. Connection oriented service uses TCP whereas connection less service uses WDP or UDP protocol.

(iii) **Transfers services:** The transfer protocols such as HTTP which is combined with WTP/WSP which are streaming and message transfer protocol. Hypermedia protocols are used for web browsing. Multimedia messages transfer's isochronous data (audio and video). This has become a basic service supported by all service providers.

(iv) **Session services:** The following are the session services:
   (a) **CC/PP:** Composite capabilities/preference profiles. It maintains user profiles and device capabilities. It has information about client, server, and proxy capabilities.
   (b) **Push OTA:** It offers reliable and unreliable push services.
   (c) **Cookie:** Cookie service maintains the state of client.
   (d) **Synchronization:** This is used for synchronizing replicated data.

Protocol stack for WAP 2.0:

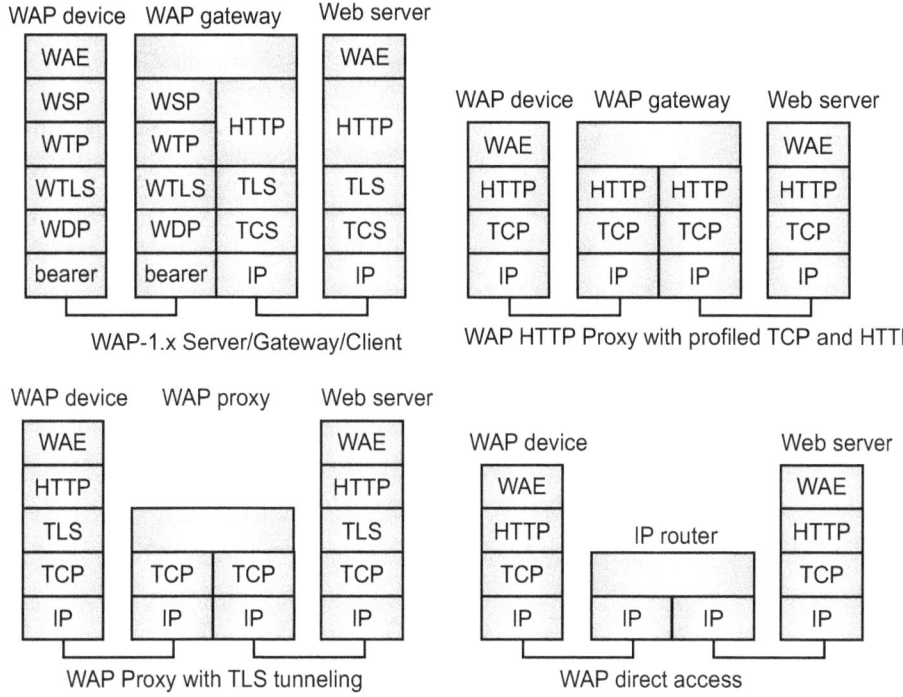

Fig. 3.12: WAP 2.0 protocol stack

- The classical WAP 1.X configured with a WAP gateway that translates between internet and WAP protocols is shown in upper left corner.
- Upper right corner shows protocol stack similar to imode. The WAP proxy translates the HTTP/TCP protocols in their profiled versions.
- Lower left corner defines the WAP proxy tunneling HTTP over TLS. This is to achieve end-to-end security.
- The right lower corner shows WAP device that can directly access to the internet. It does not need proxy but usually they are used to enhance the performance e.g. profiled TCP, profiled HTTP. These are four different examples of protocol stack according to WAP 2.0.
- WAP development Toolkit: the toolkit helps the WAP application monitors to test and debug the application on WAP origin server. It also provides the content environment.
- Several WAP development tools are available like Ericsson's WAP IDE (Integrated Developer's Environment) SDK (Software Developer's Kit) is an integrated development Environment for creating WAP service. It contains (a) WAP browser, (b) An application Designer, (c) Server tool set. Each WAP development tool provides a simulator. The simulator applications run in local mode which simulates WAP handset, WAP gateway and GSM network.

(a) WAP Simulates Environment:

In this vendor provides free access for their WAP gateway, so that WAP application Developers are able to test a complete set of WAP enabled services and APIs.

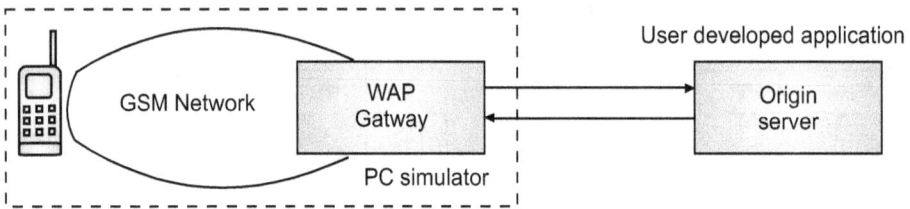

Fig. 3.13: WAP simulation environment

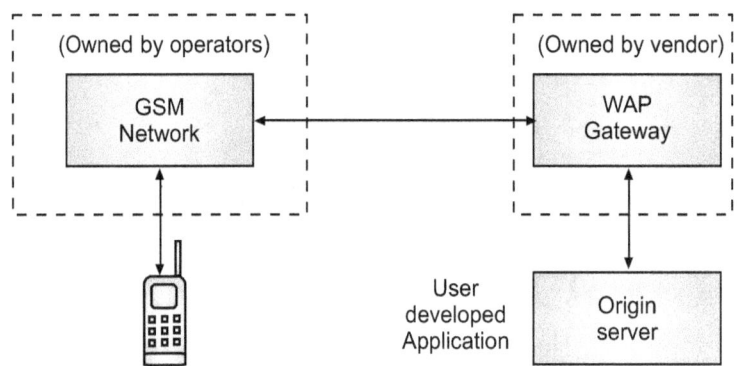

Fig. 3.14: WAP application trial environment

(b) WAP Application Trial Environment:

In this, developer can create a new application and actually test it with a WAP Handset by connecting the origin server of the new application to the vendor supported free WAP gateway.

Mobile Station Application Environment:

Mobile Station Application Execution Environment (MEXE) is a framework to ensure a predictable environment for third generation application in GSM or UMTS which provides standard execution environment for an MS to access the internet and internet server. MS have to undergo some of the tests such as by processing memory and displaying receiving MXME services to classify according to the standard capacities, that concept is called as "class mark".

- MEXE class mark 1 is based on WAP. In class mark 1, MS and the MEXE service Environment (MSE) interact via WSP.
- MEXE class mark 2, it is based on personal Java. It provides a run time system to support more powerful application and more flexible man-machine interfaces. Class mark 2 requires more storage for processing and display.

The personal Java APIs provide a standard execution environment from which it accesses.

The user interface using the java. AWT and allow internet / intranet connection by this package.

The java phone APIs supported by the Java MEXE MS that extends the Personal Java API to provide the telephone facility that also includes application installation and power management.

The services and application for java MEXE include WAP browser support and network Protocol support for HTTP.

Practice Questions

1. Write a note on:
   (a) History of GSM.
   (b) Wireless Application Environment.
   (c) WAP 2.0
2. State and explain the types of services provided by GSM.
3. Explain the entities in detail of GSM architecture.
4. Explain wireless Application Protocol in detail.
5. Explain all the protocols that used in WAP (Wireless Application Protocol).
6. List all the value added services of GSM.
7. Explain what is mean by Handover? And how it takes place between BSCs and MSCs.
8. Explain GSM architecture, entire in detail along with security issue.

Chapter 4...

ACCESS TECHNOLOGIES

4.1 Bluetooth
    4.1.1 Architecture
    4.1.2 Protocol Stack
    4.1.3 Applications of Bluetooth
4.2 GPRS – (General Packet Radio Service)
    4.2.1 GPRS Network Architecture
    4.2.2 Applications of GPRS
4.3 802.11
    4.3.1 Standards of 802.11
    4.3.2 802.11 Architecture
    4.3.3 Advantages of 802.11
- Practice Questions

4.1 Bluetooth

Bluetooth is a wireless technology standard which allows transfer of data over short distances from fixed or mobile devices, which helps in creating personal area networks with high end security. This helps devices to easily transfer data at speed of 720 kbps within 50 meters of range or beyond through the walls.

Bluetooth is managed by Bluetooth special interest groups which involve companies like telecommunication, computing, networking and electronics. These groups such as IEEE 8.2.11 started developing Wireless Personal Area Networks (WPAN) under following criteria.

    (1) Market Potential: How many applications, devices, vendors and customers are available for certain technology.

    (2) Technical Feasibility: Study groups need to be technically investigates the technology and should not rely on paper work.

    (3) Distinct Identity: Study groups does not want the versions of 802.11 whereas they want network to resolve the task.

    (4) Compatibility: Compatible with IEEE 802.11

    (5) Economic feasibility: It should be cheaper than the other networks.

4.1.1 Architecture

IEEE 802.11 b, bluetooth operates in the 2.4 GHz ISM band. It operates on 79 channels with 1 MHz carrier spacing. Each device performs frequency hopping with 1600 hops/s in pseudo random fashion.

- A piconet is column of bluetooth devices, in which all are synchronized with the same frequency hopping sequence.
- The Bluetooth architecture is made up of master and slave. All slaves talk to each other with the permission of a master node. This formation of network is called as piconet.
- The several piconets can be linked each other which forms a large network called as scatter net.
- The architecture of Bluetooth is based on different protocols. These are divided into Bluetooth core protocols and Bluetooth radio protocols.
- The base layer is a physical layer which uses spread spectrum techniques which may be a connection oriented or connectionless. The application oriented protocol is made up of cable replacement layer, the telephony control layer and adopted protocol layer.

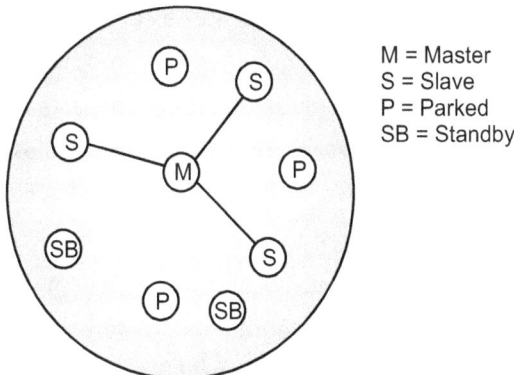

M = Master
S = Slave
P = Parked
SB = Standby

Fig. 4.1: Simple Bluetooth Piconet

Figure shows one device acts as a master whereas others are slaves.

4.1.2 Protocol Stack

The Fig. 4.2 shows, the bluetooth specification with the protocol stack.

- The protocol stack consists of core specification (bluetooth, 2001a), which describes the protocol from physical layer to data link control together with management functioning. And profile specification (Bluetooth, 2001b).
- Bluetooth Core Protocols : This include the Baseband and Link Manager Protocol (LMP)
- Logical Control and Application Protocol (L2CAP) and Service Discovery Protocol (SDP).

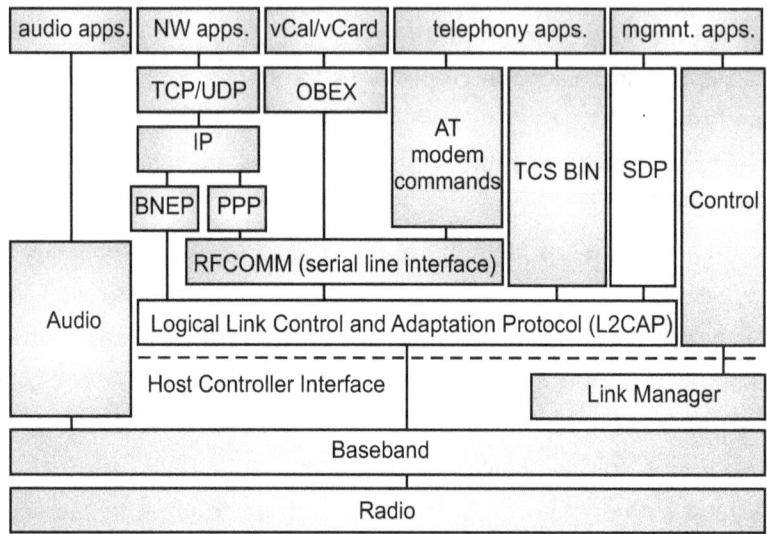

Fig. 4.2: Bluetooth protocol stack

(a) Baseband:
1. The following elements are considered to comprise core protocols of Bluetooth.
    - **(1) Radio:** It specifies the air interface i.e. frequencies, modulation and transmit power.
    - **(2) Baseband:** It gives Description of basic connection establishment, packet formats timing, and basic QoS parameters. The baseband enables the physical RF to link between Bluetooth devices which can form a piconet. This layer uses inquiry and paging procedures to synchronize the transmission with different Bluetooth devices.
    - **(3) Link Manager Protocol:** Link set-up and management between devices includes security function and parameter negotiation. When two Bluetooth devices come within each other radio range, link manger of either device discovers each other link manager then engages itself within devices.
    - **(4) Logical Link Control and Adaption Protocol (1.2 CAP):** This protocol is responsible for multiplexing of Bluetooth packets from different applications.
    - **(5) Service Discovery Protocol:** This protocol enables the devices to enquire about the availability of connection in a piconet with the help of these devices it enquire about the service which is available in a piconet and how to access it.
2. **Cable Replacement Protocol:** In this stack only one protocol is developed i.e. RFCOMM. It is a serial line protocol and is based on European Telecommunication Standard Institute (EISI 0.710) specification. On the top of 1.2 CAP is the cable replacement protocol RF communication which enables many legacy applications and protocols to run over bluetooth. It supports multiple serial ports over one single channel.

3. **The Telephony Control Protocol Specification Binary:** It is a bit oriented protocol which describes controls over voice and data calls between Bluetooth devices. It also supports mobility and group management functions.

   This protocol enables a set of AT commands to control mobile phones to be used or controlled modem as a fax and data transfer. It also can be used as a DCE (Data Circuit Terminating Equipment).
   - The Host Controller Interface (HCI) between baseband and 1.2 CAP provides a command interface to the baseband controller and link manager and access to the hardware status and control registers.
   - Audio application directly use baseband layer after encoding the audio signal.

4. **Adopted protocols:** This have many protocols included such as Point to Point Protocol (PPP), TCP/IP protocol, OBEX (Object Exchange Protocol), Wireless Application Protocol (WAP), and Vcard etc.

   (a) **PPP:** Bluetooth offers PPP over RFCOMM to accomplish point to point connection. It takes one packet from one PPP layer and places them onto the LAN.

   (b) **TCP/IP:** This protocol enables the communication over the internet bridge scenarios these are used in devices like computers, mobile handsets. To access such type of protocols socket programming is used.

   (c) **OBEX:** It is developed by the Infrared Data Association (IrDA) to exchange objects. It provides the functionality of HTTP in much higher fashion.

   (d) **Vcard:** It specifies the format of an electronic business card and personal Calender entries. It is used to exchange message and notes. It is defined in IrMC (IrDA Mobile Communication) specification.

   The following are the benefits and reasons to use bluetooth:

   (1) It is Wireless.
   (2) Bluetooth is inexpensive.
   (3) Bluetooth is automatic.
   (4) It is a standardized protocol.
   (5) It offers low interference.
   (6) Low energy consumption.
   (7) It establish instant PAN.
   (8) There are no versions to upgrade the bluetooth standard.
   (9) Sharing voice and data.
   (10) It is the wireless standard for ages.

4.1.3 Applications of Bluetooth

It supports the following applications:
1. **File transfer:** File transfer offers the ability to transfer data objects from device to another object types include Xls, ppt, wov, folder or directories etc.
2. **LAN Access:** It connects the multiple data terminals of LAN access points to the Ethernet LAN.
3. **Synchronization:** It offers synchronization in between device to device.
4. **Handset:** The handset can be wirelessly connected, for the purpose of acting as a remote device's audio input and output interface. This provide convenience for hands free cell phone.
5. **Internet Bridge:** It offers the mobile phone or cordless modem to act as modem to the PC, providing dial-up networking and fax capabilities without the need of physical connection to PC.

Bluetooth Security / Authentication
- In Bluetooth environment every bit is on air, so security is very important.
- It offers the security infrastructure starting from authentication, key exchange, to encryption.
- Frequency hopping scheme with 1600 hops/sec is employed for synchronization of data devices are like phone, PDA, computer etc. For example – Personal Information Management (PIM), phone book etc.
- It uses cipher algorithm called as SAFER to authenticate a device identity.
- In additionally at the application layer, it uses their own security infrastructure

4.2 GPRS – (General Packet Radio Service) (April 2015)

GPRS is a new revolution in terms of packet data network. It allows a new range of applications such as mobile e-commerce to mobile corporate VPN access.
- It works in burst traffic at data speed of 14.4 Kbps to 171.2 Kbps. It serves services such as e-mail, web browsing and large data.
- GPRS users are "always connected" or "always on".
- The GPRS system is an integrated part of the GSM network switching system.
- GPRS core network provides mobility management, session management and transport for Internet Protocol packet services in GSM and WCDMA networks, it also provides the other additional functions such as billing and lawful interception.
- General Packet Radio Service (GPRS) is needed where GSM system uses such a services which are not supported by easy access and high data rate.
- GPRS reuse the existing GSM infrastructure which provides end to end packet switched services and new radio channels are defined which are flexible in allocation.

- Radio resources can be shared dynamically between speech and data services such as a function of traffic load and operator preference.
- Mobile packet data applications are measured according to QoS (Quality of Service). GPRS defines QoS in terms of following parameters:

    (1) Service Precedence: It exists in three levels high, low, normal. It is priority of a service to another service.

    (2) Reliability: It defines three classes on the basis of loss or duplication of data, mis-sequencing and corruption of packets. GPRS security is equivalent to GSM where ciphering algorithm is used.

    (3) Delay: Parameters define maximum values for the mean delay. It is end-to-end transfer time between two communicating mobile stations, mobile station and signaling interface.

    (4) Throughput: It specifies the maximum/peak bit rate and the mean bit rate.

    The following are the functional groups in GPRS:

    1. Network access
    2. Packet routing and transfer
    3. Mobility management
    4. Logical link management
    5. Radio resource management
    6. Network management.

1. Network Access:

It supports standard point to point data transfer without authentication and ciphering. The function includes:

(a) Registration which associates the mobile station identity with the packet data protocols.

(b) Authentication and authorization.

(c) Admission control, which determines the radio and network resources to be used for communication of an MS.

(d) Message screening, which filters out unsolicitated message.

2. Packet Routing and Transfer:

It route the data between a MS and the destination through the serving and Gateway GPRS support node (GSNs). This group has the following functions:

(a) Destination of the packets can be determined by routing.

(b) Base station uses the reply function to forward packets between MS and serving GSN.

(c) Encapsulation and tunneling: It encapsulate packets at the source of tunnels and decapsulation packets at the destination.

(d) Compression and ciphering.

(e) Domain name service functions which resolve logical GSN names to their IP address.

3. Logical Link Management:

It maintains the communication channels between a MS and the GSM network across the radio interface. It includes

(a) Logical link establishment

(b) Logical link maintenance

(c) Logical line release.

4. Mobility Management:

It keeps track of the current location of an MS.

Three different scenario exists when MS enters a new cell and new routing. Scenarios are as follows:

(a) Cell update

(b) Routing area update

(c) Combined routing area and location area update.

Network management function provides mechanisms to support OAandM functions related to GPRS.

5. Radio Resource Management:

It allocates and maintains radio communication paths.

The function includes:

(a) Um interface management, which determines the amount of radio resources to be allocated for GPRS usage.

(b) Cell selection which enables the MS to select the optimal cell for radio communication.

(c) Path management, which maintains the communication path between the BSS and the serving GSNs.

4.2.1 GPRS Network Architecture

GPRS follows a traditional GSM architecture. GPRS operates in packet data network, so it needs additional nodes to support for delivery and routing of data packets between the mobile stations and external packet data network. For this support SGSN (Serving GSN) and GGSN (Gateway GSN) are added.

4.2.1.1 Serving GPRS Support Node (SGSN)

It is similar to MSC in GSM architecture. SGSN works for voice in packet data network. It is equivalent to the MSC / VLR in the current GSM network

Tasks of SGSN:

1. It connects the BSS to GSGN which provides ciphering, mobility management, charging and statistics collection.
2. It establishes the MM context that contains mobility and security information for the MS to provide services in GPRS and MS.
3. Packet Switching.
4. Routing and transfer the data.
5. Mobility management (attach/detach) and location management
6. Logical link management
7. Authentication and charging services
8. Registration of new subscriber to HLR. It's respective location register (current cell, current VLR).
9. Sends query to HLR to obtain subscriber's data.

4.2.1.2 Gateway GPRS Support Node (GGSN)

It is in between the GPRS backbone network and external packet data network. It is nothing but a router in LAN.

- GGSN stores current SGSN address of a user to readdress the packets.
- PDP sends and receives packets from data network and converts them to GSM address of destination user.
- It converts packets coming from SGSN to PDP format (Packet Data Protocol).
- It supports the traditional gateway functionality such as publishing subscriber address, mapping address, routing and tunneling packets, screening messages and counting packets.

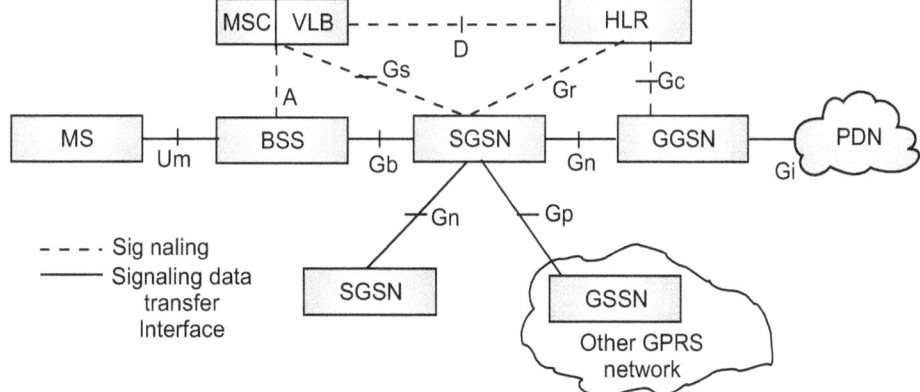

Fig. 4.3: GPRS architecture

- A GGSN may contain DNS functions to map routing area identifiers with serving SGSNs and Dynamic Host Configuration Protocol (DHCP) functions to allocate dynamic IP address to MSs.
- It maintains an activated PDP for tunneling the packet to the attached MS for the corresponding SGSN.
    - The following existing elements of GSM must be enhanced when used in each packet data network.
    - GPRS network nodes and corresponding interfaces although SMS related component and the equipment register are not shown in this architecture.
    - In this architecture MS, BSS, mobile switching centre or Visitor Location Register (MSC/VLR) and Home Location Register (HLR) in the existing GSM network are modified.

(1) Base Station System (BSS): It should be enhanced in order to send and receive packet data. Base Transreceiver Station allows transportation of user data to SGSN same as in between BTS and MS.

- The Base Transreceiver Station (BTS) and Base Station Controller (BSC) in the BSS are modified to the new component packet control unit (PCU) to accommodate the GPRS.
- The BSC forwards the circuit-switched call to MSC and the packet-switched data through PCU to the SGSN.
- A BSC can connect to one SGSN via Gb interface for providing function such as paging and mobility management for GPRS.
- BSS should also manage GPRS related radio resources such as allocation of packet data

(2) Home Location Register (HLR): It needs upgradation to register GPRS user profiles and respond to queries originating from GGSN.

- To accommodate subscriber and routing information new fields in the MS are introduced.
- In HLR the fields are accessed by SGSN and GGSN using IMSI International Mobile Subscribers Identity as an index key to map MS to one or more GGSN, update SGSN of MS at attach and detach and stored the fixed IP address.
- In MSC/VLR a new field, the SGSN number is added to indicate the SGSN currently serving the MS. It contact SGSN to request location information or paging for voice call.
- It also perform signaling coordination for class B mobile by Gs interface and suspends GPRS activities by class A and Gb interfaces.

(3) Mobile Station: (SMS nodes) – These nodes are upgraded to transmit via SGSN to enhance GPRS functionality MSC/VLR co-ordination.

The new fields are added to GPRS mobile station, that are mobile terminal (MT) and Terminal Equipment (TE). The MT is equipped with software for GPRS functionality to establish links to SGSN. The TE can be computer, attached to the MT.

There are three MS operation modes in GPRS.

(a) Class A (b) Class B (c) Class C

- **(a) Class A:** A mode of operation which allows simultaneous circuit-switched and packet switched services. There is a need of duplexer to support this mode.
- **(b) Class B:** B mode of operation provides automatic choice of circuit-switched as packet-switched service but only one at a time.
- **(c) Class C:** C mode of operation supports packet–switched data only.
- MS maintains MM and PDP context to support GPRS mobility management. Some of MM context field stored in GPRS aware SIM (Subscriber Identity Modular) are :
- (a) International Mobile Subscribers Identity (IMSI), which uniquely identifies the MS. IMSI is used to search the database in VLR, HLR and GSN.
- (b) Address of the routing area where the MS resides.
- (c) Packet Temporary Mobile Subscribes Identity (P-TMSI), which is the GPRS equivalent of TMSI in GSM.

4.2.1.3 GPRS Interfaces

There are number of interfaces and reference points (these are the logical points of connection which shares a common physical connection with the other reference points).

- The GPRS interfaces are as follows (1) Um Interface, (2) Gb Interface (3) Gn Interface, (4) Gs Interface, (5) Gi Interface

(1) Um Interface:

Um describes the radio interface between the MS (Mobile station) and BTS. (Base Transreceiver station)

- GPRS radio technology is based on GSM radio architecture which introduces a new logical channel structure to control the signaling and traffic flow over the Um radio interface that is Um channel.
- It dedicated to packet data traffic which is called as packet data channel (PDCH). It is used for data transfer.
- Packet Random Access Control (PRACH) is introduced for uplink of packet common control channel (PCCHS) to sent form MS to the BTS to initiate the uplink transfer for data or signaling.

(2) Gb Interface:

The Gb interface connects the BSS and the SGSN, allowing many users to be multiplexed over the same physical resources.

- GPRS Gb interface only allocate resources to the user during the periods when data is actually delivered.
- Gb interface protocol layers are from highest to lowest including the LLC (Logical Link Control) and SNDCP (Sub Network Dependent Convergence Protocol) LLC provides one or more logical link connections with sequence control, flow control, detection of transmission.
- SNDCP converts, encapsulates and segments external network formats (like Internet Protocol Datagram's) into sub-network formats (called SNDCPUs)
- SNDCP provides the function to improve the channel efficiently.

(3) Gn and Gp Interfaces

Both Gn and Gp interface utilizes the GPRS Tunneling Protocol (GTP). GTP is defined for the Gn interface, i.e. the interface between GSNs within a PLMN, and for the Gp interface between the GSNs in different PLMNs.

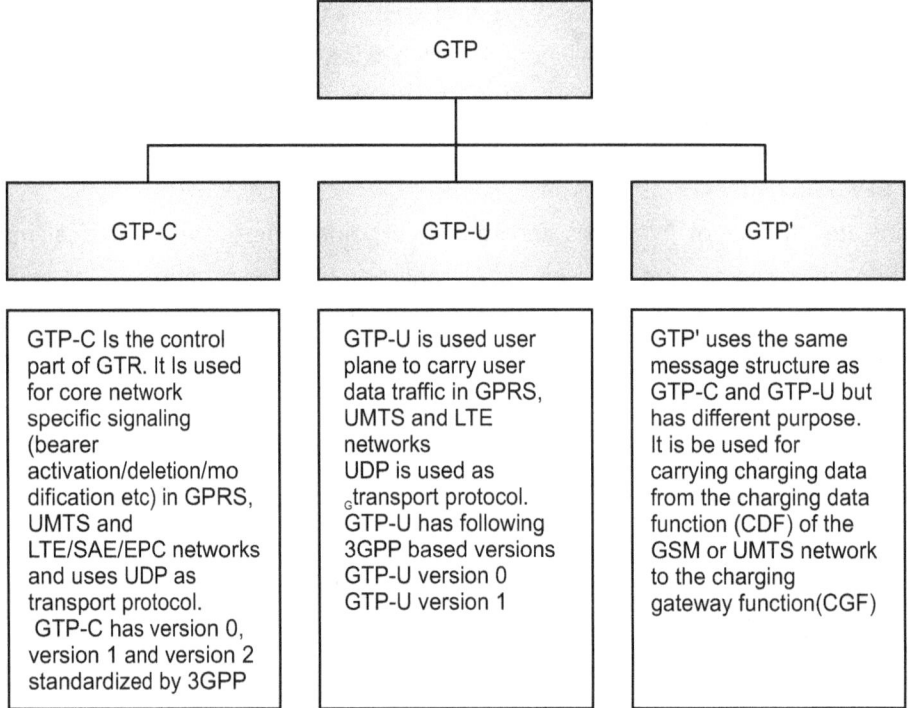

Fig. 4.4: GPRS Interfaces

- GTP tunnels the user data and signaling message between GSN.
- In Gn interfaces the GSN is within the same GPRS network. Whereas In GP it involve different GPRS network.

- Gp is same as Gn except that extra security functions are required over Gp interface to communicate.

(4) Gs Interface:

The Gs interface connects the databases in MSC/VLR and the SGSN, which does not involve under data transmission.

- Base station system application part + (BSSAP +) implement the function for Gs interface.
- It utilizes SS7 signaling connection control as a lower layer protocol.
- It coordinates the location, information of MS that are in both IMSI and GPRS attached.

(5) Gi Interface

GPRS interworks with the Public Switched Data Network (PSDN) and the Packet Data Network (PDN) through Gi interface.

- In Gi interface GGSN serves as the access point of the GPRS network to the external data network.

All the entities and nodes in GPRS core network of GSM are interconnected to each other by interfaces.

- The MS and BSS communicate via Um interface. The BSS and SGSN are connected by Gb interface using relay frame.
- The SGSN/GGSN is connected through Gn Interface.
- When SGSN and GGSN are in different GPRS networks they are connected by Gp interface.
- GGSN connect to external network through Gi interface.
- The MSC/VLR communicates with BSS by using existing GSM. 'A' interface, with SGSN using Gs interfaces are used in this communication.
- The HLR connects to the SGSN via the Gr interface and GGSN via the Gc interface.
- The HLR and VLR are connected through existing GSM D interface.
- Interface 'A, Gs, Gr, Gc' and D is used for signaling without involving user data transmission in GPRS.
- Interface Um, Gb, Gp and Gs are used for both signaling and transmission in GPRS.

GPRS Procedures

- GPRS procedures are attached / detach procedure and Packet Data Protocol (PDP) context manipulation.
- The GPRS attach procedure establish a logical link between MS and SGSN.
- The PDP context activation procedure allows data transmission between MS and the external data network.

GPRS Attach and Detach Procedure

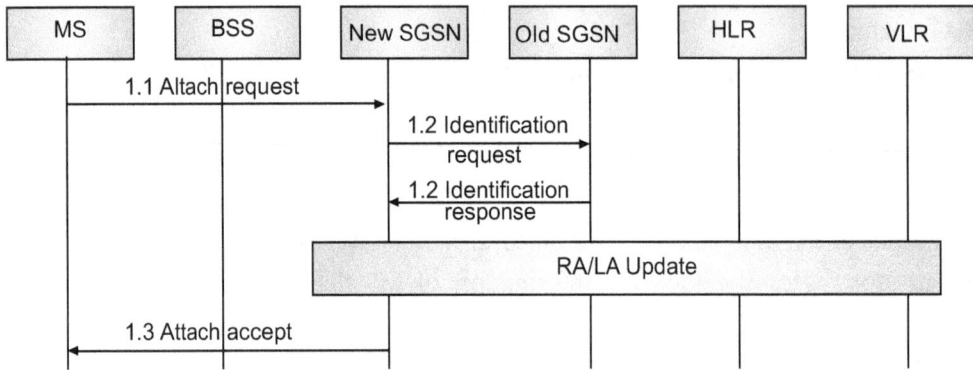

Fig. 4.5: GPRS Attach Procedure

GPRS Attach Process:

When a mobile subscriber turns on their handset, the following actions occur:

1. A handset attach request is sent to the new SGSN.
2. The new SGSN queries the old SGSN for the identity of this handset. The old SGSN responds with the identity of the handset.
3. The new SGSN requests more information from the MS. This information is used to authenticate the MS to the new SGSN.
4. The authentication process continues to the HLR. The HLR acts like a RADIUS server using a handset-level authentication based on IMSI and similar to the CHAP authentication process in PPP.
5. A check of the equipment ID with the EIR is initiated.
6. If the equipment ID is valid, the new SGSN sends a location update to the HLR indicating the change of location to a new SGSN. The HLR notifies the old SGSN to cancel the location process for this MS. The HLR sends an insert subscriber data request and other information associated with this mobile system and notifies the new SGSN that the update location has been performed.
7. The new SGSN initiates a location update request to the VLR. The VLR acts like a proxy RADIUS that queries the home HLR.
8. The new SGSN sends the Attach Accept message to the MS.
9. The MS sends the Attach Complete message to the new SGSN.
10. The new SGSN notifies the new VLR that the relocation process is complete.

GPRS Detach Procedure:

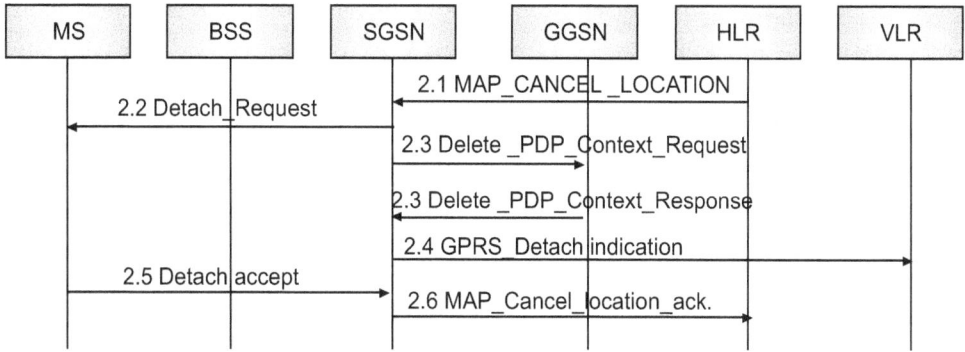

Fig. 4.6: GPRS detach procedure

Step 2.1: GSM MAP the HLR and sends the message to SGSN with cancellation.

Step 2.2: SGSN sends the detach request to MS. The message contain detach parameter. To show MS should not make new attach.

Step 2.3: SGSN and GGSN exchange the request and response, the message pair deactivate the MS PDP context in the GGSN.

Step 2.4: MS attached to SGSN and send message to VLR to remove the association with SGSN and update the location without going through SGSN.

Step 2.5: After the MS detach operation, the SGSN send the message to confirm the Deletion of the MM and PDP mobility management and Packet Data Protocol context.

PDP (Packet Data Protocol) CONTEXT PROCEDRES

This describes the activation, modification and deactivation of the PDP contexts. The message flow for these contexts is the messages. Before data can be sent or received a PDP context (a data address) must be activated (created for the MS). A GPRS subscription contains several PDP addresses and an individual PDP context is maintained in the MS, SGSN and GGSN for every PDP address.

It is possible to enquire/set the following parameters in PDP:

1. Requested QoS (peak bit rate, mean bit rate, delay requirements, reliability level expected).
2. Data compression or no data compression.
3. Whether or not to use TCP/IP header compression.
4. PDP address and type requested.
5. Each PDP context can be either active or inactive and three PDP context functions are (1) activate, (2) deactivate, (3) modify.
6. The MS is responsible for activation and deactivation.

7. GGSN is responsible for activation (for incoming packets) and deactivation.
8. SGSN is responsible for modification.
9. A MS in standby or ready state can initiate activation or deactivation at anytime to activate the PDP context in the MS, the SGSN or the GGSN.

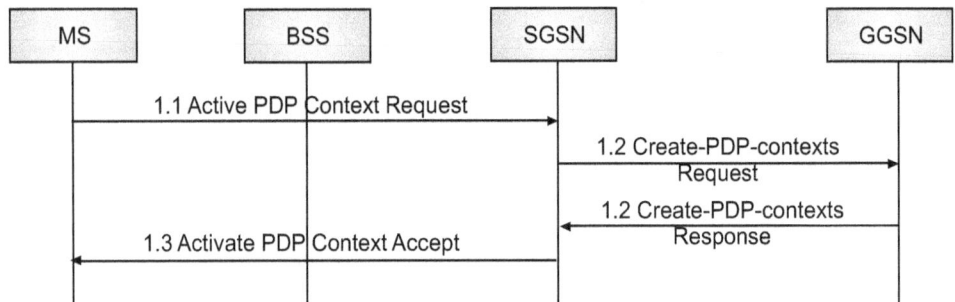

Fig. 4.7: Context Activation Message Flow

Step 1.1: The MS sends an activate PDP context request message to SGSN to indicate whether the MS will use a static or a dynamic PDP address.

Step 1.2: The SGSN send create –PDP-context-Request message to GGSN. It creates a tunnel between SGSN to GGSN.

Step 1.3: Based on the information received from the GGSN, the SGSN stores the GGSN address and the dynamic PDP address in the PDP context. The SGSN selects the radio priority based on QoS.

After the PDP context activation a connection between the MS and the external data network is established. The SGSN is ready to route and charge for packets delivered between GGSN and the MS. The message flow is used for the updation.

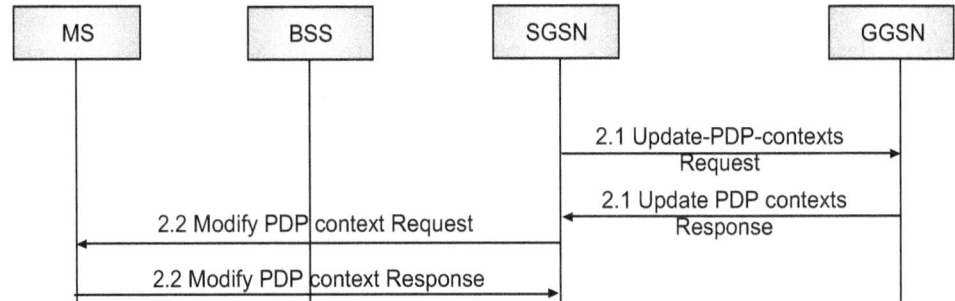

Fig. 4.8: PDP Context update message flow

Steps for the message flow of PDP context update are:

Step 2.1: The SGSN and the GGSN exchange the update PDP-context–Request and response message pair to update the PDP context.

Step 2.2: The SGSN and the MS, exchange the modify PDP context request and accept message pair to update the PDP context to the MS.

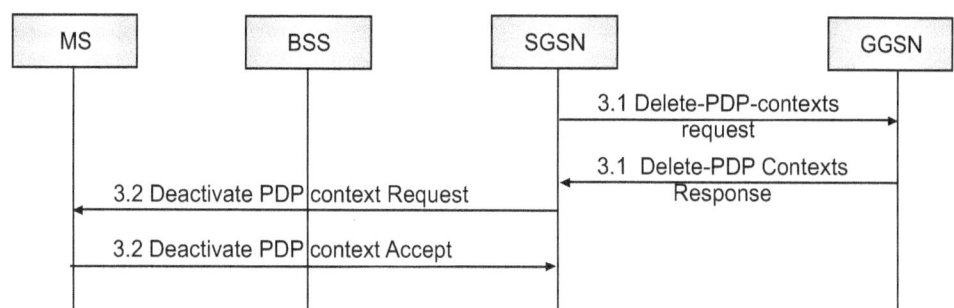

Fig. 4.9: Context deactivation message flow

The message flow for PDP context deactivation initiated by SGSN is:

Step 3.1: SGSN and the GGSN exchange the Delete-PDP-context request and Response message pair to deactivate the PDP context.

Step 3.2: The SGSN and the MS exchange the Deactivate PDP context Request and accept message pair. The MS removes the PDP context. That the SGSN may initiate this step immediately after the Delete-PDP-context Request in sent in step 3.1.

Additional Functionalities of GPRS in GSM Network

1. GPRS Billing:

In GPRS the charging information is collected by SGSNs and GGSNs. The SGSN collects charging information for radio resource usage by MS. Depending on the agreement between the GPRS operator and external network operator a charge for the external packet network usage may be collected in the external network or in GGSNs of the GPRS network. If the visited GPRS network assigns a dynamic address to MS, the charging of the GPRS and the external network is gathered and sent to the home GPRS network of that MS. Both SGSN and GGSN record the GPRS network resource usage.

Data Services in GPRS:

Wide range of applications is operated with the help of GPRS. A user can use two modes of GPRS network.

- **(1) Application Mode:** In this mode, the user will be using the GPRS mobile phone to access the application running on phone itself. All devices operating execution environments supported are Symbian and J2ME. Application can be developed in C/C++ or Java.

- **(2) Tunneling Mode:** This mode is for mobile computing to where user access to network. The mobile phones are connected to the devices like large laptops or small devices like PDAS through PC cable to GPRS capable phone terminals. GPRS handsets have unique form factor and terminals. GPRS are of three classes A, B, C.

    - **(a) Class A:** Involves simultaneous attach, activation, monitoring of traffic. It can make or receive calls on two services simultaneously.

- **(b) Class B:** Monitors GPRS and GSM simultaneously but supports one service at a time.
- **(c) Class C:** Supports only non-simultaneous attach. It can make and receive call to manually services.

4.2.2 Applications of GPRS

There is wide range of generic as well as GPRS specific applications. Generic applications involve information services, internet access, e-mail, web browsing, weather, news etc.

GPRS Specific Applications:

- **(1) Chat:** It is means of communication nowadays. It is integrated by wireless chat and internet that using WAP and SMS.
- **(2) Multimedia Services:** It provides multimedia services like photographs, postcards, greeting cards these all services are used by users like doctors, police, law enforcement agents, journalists.
- **(3) Virtual Private Network:** These networks are used in banking sector. It connects ATM system to bank offices.
- **(4) Personal Information Management:** It helps in maintaining personal info, address book; appointments, using J2ME and WTAI (Wireless Telephony Application Interface) the address book and diary is integrated to home and office.
- **(5) Job Sheet Dispatch:** It helps in communicating office based staff to mobile field staff. Job dispatch application is combined with vehicle dispatch application so that the nearest available personnel can be deployed to serve a customer.
- **(6) Unified Messaging:** It uses single mail box for all types of messages, voice, e-mail, fax, SMS, MMS, pager message. It helps in categorizing the types of messages.
- **(7) Vehicle Positioning:** GPS is free to use global network of 24 satellites run by US departs of defense. With GPS anyone can get the current location of user from satellites.
- **(8) Location Based Services and Telematics:** Intelligent Transportation System (ITS) is built around GPRS and GPS technology. It is used in vertical application such as workforce management or vehicle tracking also used for hotel or restaurant finding, city specific news and information.

Limitation of GPRS:

- **(1) Limited cell capacity for all users:** Voice and GPRS uses the same network resources. There are limited radio resources that can be deployed for different uses.
- **(2) Speed Lower in Reality:** To achieve the speed of 172.2 Kbps single user require overall eight time slots without any error protection, but practically GPRS terminals supports only one, two or max 3 time slots. It provides data speed of 56-114 Kbps in 2G system.

4.3 802.11

In the year 1997, the Institute of Electrical and Electronics Engineers (IEEE) specifies 802.11 specifications as a standard for wireless LANs. This version of 802.11 provides for 1 Mbps and 2 Mbps data rates and a set of fundamental signaling methods and other services.802.11 standard focuses on bottom layers of ISO model, physical layer and link layer.

- Any LAN based application, network operating system, protocol such as TCP/IP and novel NetWare are compatible to 802.11 WLAN standards.
- IEEE 802.11 standard specifies the time bounded and asynchronous services for the simple and robust WLAN.
- It has one MAC layer which operates with multiple physical layers, each of which has different medium sense and transmission characteristics.
- It is a famous family of WLANs in which many products are included such as 802.X LAN standard, 802.3 Ethernet or 802.5 token rings.
- 802.11a operates in 5 GHz frequency band and it uses Orthogonal Frequency Division Multiplexing for modulation 802.11b operates in 2.4 GHz. It is deployed as "Hot Spot" in hotels, airports and starbucks. 802.11g operates in 2.4 GHz. Its speed decreases as the distance increases.

	IEEE 802.11a	IEEE 802.11b	IEEE 802.11g
Std. Ratified	Sep. 99	Sep. 99	May 2003
Raw Data Rate	54 Mbps	Sep. 99	54
Avg. Actual	4-5 Mbps	27	20-25
Throughput Frequency	5 GHz	2.4	2.4
Available Spectrum	300 MHz	83.5 MHz	83.5
Modulation Encoding	OFDM	DSSS / CCK	DSSS / PBCC
Channels / Non-overlapping	12/8	11/3	11/5

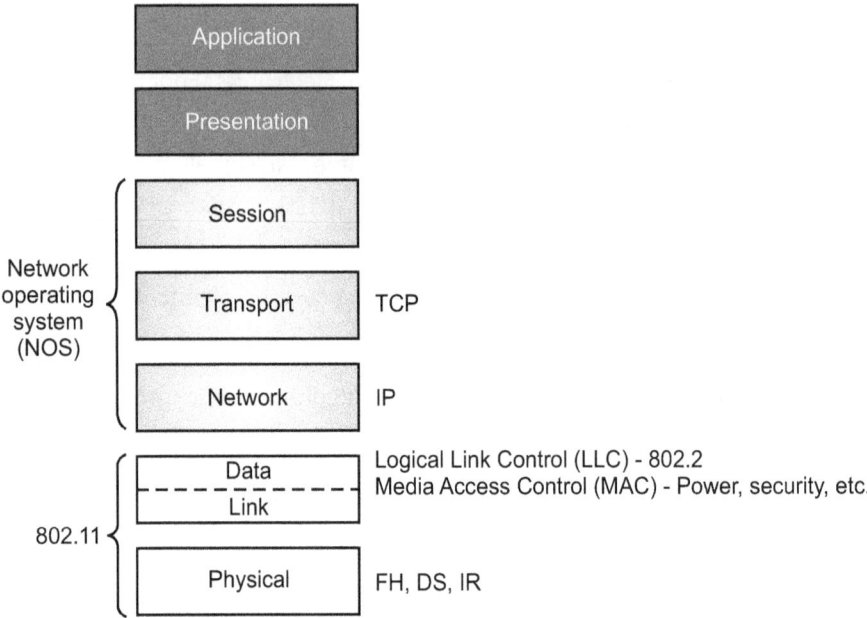

Fig. 4.10: Example of 802.11 in OSI model

History of 802.11

- In 1985, the U.S Federal Communications Commission releases the ISM band for unlicensed use, they brought up with the thought of 802.11 technology.
- NCR Corporation AT and T invented the preversion of 802.11 in the year 1991 in Nieuwegein (Dutlon) this technology previously invented for cashier system and the first wireless product called WaveLAN is developed with raw data rates of 1Mbit/s and 2 Mbit /s.
- "Father of Wi-Fi "Vic Haves, was involved in the initial release of IEEE 802.11 standards as 802.11 b and 802.11 a.
- In the year 1999, Wi-Fi Alliance was formed which is a trade association to hold the Wi-Fi frameworks.
- For the coming ten years the 802.11 standard served for transmission but the data rates supported by this standards are very slow according to the business requirements. To support higher data rate transmission up to the need IEEE ratified 802.11b for transmission of up to 11Mbps.
- In January 2002, one more standard 802.11 has been released till early 2003 802.11 g has been approved for higher data rate transmission.

4.3.1 Standards of 802.11

802.11 -1997

The IEEE 802.11 releases in 1997, it specifies the two net bit rates of 1 or 2 megabits per second (Mbps) added to it is forward errors correction code.

This also specifies physical layer with three alternative technologies such as

1. Infrared operation at the rate 1 Mbit /s.
2. Frequency hopping spread spectrum operating at 1 mbit /s or 2 mbit /s.
3. Direct sequence spread spectrum operating at 1 mbit /s or 2 mbit /s.

The next two standards uses microwave transmission over the Industrial scientific Medical frequency band at 2.4 GHz.

802.11a OFDM Waveform

- The data link layer protocol and frame format of the original standard remains same for this version, but OFDM based air interface is used at the physical layer. It operates in the 5 GHz band with maximum net data rate of 5mbit /s, with error correction code which increases the throughput.
- Using a band of 5 GHz gives advantage as 2.4 GHz band has a heavy traffic. The disadvantage of this standard is it has less range than the standards 802.11 b/g the fact is signals are absorbed by walls and many solid things when this standard is used, so signal is not able to penetrate as far as other standards are considered.

802.11b

- This standard operates at maximum data rate of 11 mbps and uses the same media access methods original standard, this standard operates in the range of 2.4 GHz band. This increases the throughput of the data transmission. This range includes the devices such as microwave ovens, Bluetooth devices etc.

802.11g

- In June 2003,the third standard 802.11 g was released which works at 2.4GHz band and uses OFDM based transmission rate as 802.11a.it operates at maximum physical layer bit rate 54 Mbit /s with forward error correction codes. This standard was hardware compatible with the 802.11 b.
- Like 802.11b, 802.11g devices suffer interference from other products operating in the 2.4 GHz band, for example wireless keyboards.

4.3.2 802.11 Architecture

When two or more nodes that may be fixed or portable, forms a network to communicate with each other, they form a Basic Service Set (BSS).one BSS must contain minimum two stations. 802.11 LANs use the BSS as the standard building block.

802.11 have two basic system architectures:

(1) Infrastructure Based
(2) Ad-hoc.

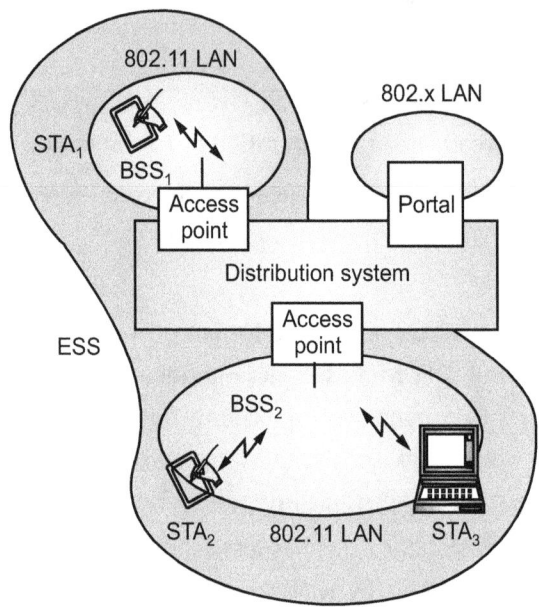

Fig. 4.11: Architecture of an infrastructure based IEE 802.11

Infrastructure Based IEEE 802.11:
- Many nodes called stations (STA1) are connected through access point (AP).
- BSS1 basic service set is formed with the help of stations and access points which are in the same radio coverage form.
- Distribution system connects one BSS1 to another BSS2 with the help of AP, which forms a network. It helps to extend wireless coverage area. This network is called as Extended Service Set (ESS) which is identified with the help of EESID number in wireless LAN.
- Distribution system consists of bridged IEEE LANs, i.e two stations may be from same BSS or different BSS can communicate to each other by using Distribution System (DS) wireless links or any other network.

The basic requirement of IEEE 802.11 is, it may be used with the wired network, the portals acts as a logical integration of wired LAN and 802.11 it also act as an access point to a distribution system it acts as a bridge between wired and wireless network.

- Stations selects their associative APs which supports roaming (i.e. changing access point) the distribution system manages data transfer, power management, and controls medium access.
- The implementation of distribution system is not mentioned in 802.11 standards. But the functionalities are divided into two sections:

(1) Station Services (SS)

Station services are:

1. **Authentication:** There are two types of authentication services offered by 802.11. The first is Open System Authentication. This means that anyone who attempts to authenticate will receive authentication. The second type is Shared Key Authentication. In this type of authentication user must have the secret key.
2. **Deauthentication:** Deauthentication is when either the station or AP wishes to terminate a stations authentication. When this happens the station is automatically disassociated.
3. **Privacy:** Privacy is an encryption algorithm, which is used so that other 802.11 users cannot overload on your LAN traffic. IEEE 802.11 specifies Wired Equivalent Privacy (WEP) as an optional algorithm to satisfy privacy. If WEP is not used then stations are "in the clear" or "in the red", meaning that their traffic is not encrypted.

(2) Distribution System Services (DSS)

There are five services provided by the DSS

1. **Association:** It supports no-transition mobility to the devices.
2. **Reassociation:** This service allows the station to switch its association from one AP to another. Both association and reassociation are initiated by the station.
3. **Disassociation:** Disassociation is when the association between the station and the AP is terminated; a disassociated station cannot send or receive data. ESS-transition is not supported. A station can move to a new ESS but will have to reinitiate connections.
4. **Distribution:** Distribution is simply getting the data from the sender to the intended receiver. The message is sent to the local AP (input AP), then distributed through the DS to the AP (output AP) that the recipient is associated with. If the sender and receiver are in the same BSS, the in and out AP's are the same.
5. **Integration:** Integration is when the output AP is a portal. Thus, 802.x LANs are integrated into the 802.11 DS.

Ad-hoc Network:

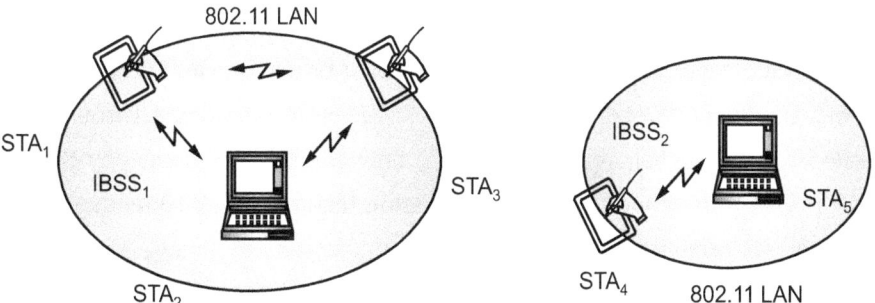

Fig. 4.12: Architecture of IEEE 802.11 ad-hoc wireless LANs

- Ad-hoc networks are formed as Independent Basic Service Set (IBSS). A group of stations which are using same frequency forms one IBSS. It has peer to peer communication directly as there is no base node.
- IBSS1 has STA1, STA2, STA3 and IBSS2 has STA4 and STA5. By using Ad-hoc architecture, STA2 can not communicate to STA4 as both stations are in different IBSSs.
- It does not specify the node which supports routing, forwarding of data or exchange of topology information. E.g. Hiperlan, Bluetooth.

Protocol Architecture:

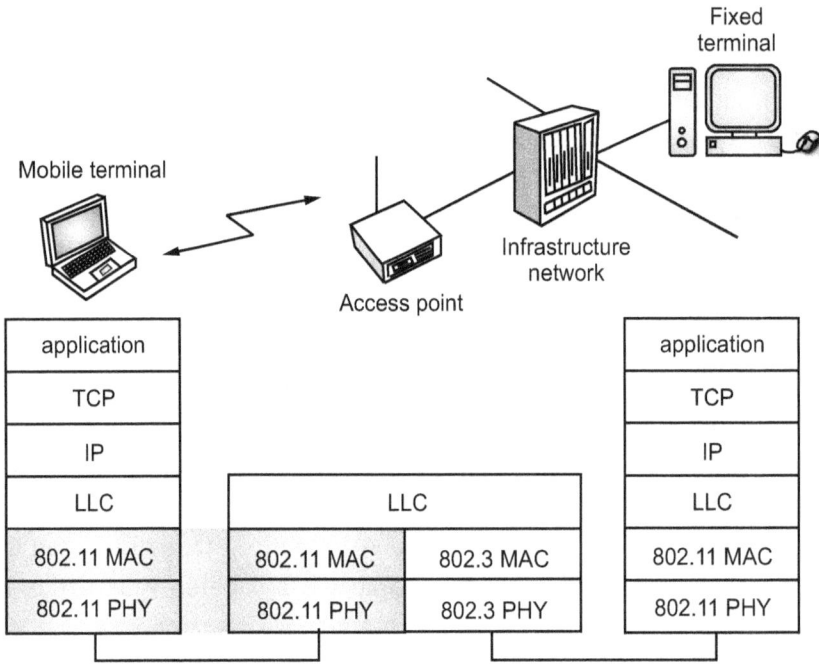

Fig. 4.13: IEEE 802.11 protocol architecture in bridging

- The Fig. 4.13 shows an IEEE 802.11 wireless LAN connected to the switched IEEE 802.13 Ethernet via a bridge.
- The physical layer is divided into Physical Layer Convergence Protocol (PLCP) and the Physical Medium Dependent Sublayer PMD. PLCP provides a carrier sense signal, called Clear Channel Assessment (CCA) and provides common phy Service Access Point (SAP) independent of the transmission technology. PMD manages modulation and encoding/decoding of signals.
- MAC layer is responsible for fragmentation of user data and encryption.
- The standard also specifies MAC management and station management.

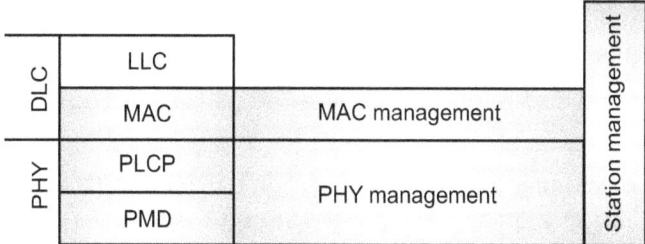

Fig. 4.14: Detailed IEEE 802.11 protocol architecture and management

- Association and reassociation of stations to the access points and roaming between different access points is possible with MAC management. It also controls authentication, encryption, synchronization of stations related to access point.
- Channel tuning and Phy MIB (i.e. MAC Management Information Base) is maintained by Phy mgmt.
- Both management layers communicate with each other with the help of station management and it also responsible for higher layer functions.

4.3.3 Advantages of 802.11

Wireless LAN increases the mobility. Users can move from one location to another location without any restriction and can access LAN everywhere.

It also offers the cost effective network for hard –to- wire locations such as historical places, old buildings.

WLAN offers roaming to the user which also gives added benefits to the variety of work environments it also supports the real time applications as following:

- Immediate bedside access to patient information for doctors and hospital staff.
- Easy, real-time network access for on-site consultants or auditors.
- Improved database access for supervisors such as production line managers, warehouse auditors, or construction engineers.
- Simplified network configuration with minimal MIS involvement for temporary setups such as trade shows or conference rooms.
- Faster access to customer information for service vendors and retailers, resulting in better service and improved customer satisfaction.
- Location-independent access for network administrators, for easier on-site troubleshooting and support.
- Real-time access to study group meetings and research links for students.
- In the year 1970, mobile phones and sites are linked with the help of digitalization of control links. By using analog technology first generation standard for cellular phones is developed.
- Japan NTT (Nippon Telegraph and Telephone) introduced the first ever commercial automated cellular network in 1979, initially in metropolitan area of Tokyo.
- USA also launched the 1G network in Chicago using Motorola DynaTac mobile phone. Several countries after that developed 1G network including UK, Mexico and Canada.

- **Nordiac Mobile Telephone System (NMT S450):** This is the first multinational cellular system was developed within the Scandinavian Countries of Denmark, Sweden, Finland and Norway. That time Europe was dealing with nine incompatible analog communication systems that were causing roaming difficulties. Strong support of government turns this difficulty in this 1G standard.
- **Advanced Mobile Phone Services (AMPS):** On Oct 1983, the regional bell operating company Ameritech started the first American commercial cellular service in Chicago. AMPS were developed along a higher 800 MHz frequency and used FDMA technology for transferring information.
- **Total Access Communication System (TACS):** Around 1985, the UK had developed TACS as a new national standard for its own region.
- AMPS, TACS use the frequency modulation (FM) technique for radio transmission and traffic is multiplexed onto an FDMA.
- On the 48th independence day of India, the first cellular service is introduced over Modi Testra's MobileNet GSM network of Kolkatta. Most operators' follows GSM mobile system operates under 900 MHz bandwidth. Few recent players started operating under which 1800 MHz bandwidth.
- It fulfilled the basic mobile voice.

1st Generation:
- In the year 1970, mobile phones and sites are linked with the help of digitalization of control links. By using analog technology first generation standard for cellular phones is developed.
- Japan NTT (Nippon Telegraph and Telephone) introduced the first ever commercial automated cellular network in 1979, initially in metropolitan area of Tokyo.
- USA also launched the 1G network in Chicago using Motorola DynaTac mobile phone. Several countries after that developed 1G network including UK, Mexico and Canada.

2nd Generation:
2G stands for Second Generation technology, it doesn't support to transfer the data such as email or software other than a digital voice call itself .It also supports the SMS messaging.
- In 1991, Finland, Radiolinja introduced the 2G cellular system that is based on GSM.
- Three benefits of 2G over 1G are:
    (1) Phone conversation was digitally encrypted.
    (2) It provides data services like SMS, picture MSG and MMS.
    (3) It is more efficient on the spectrum allowing for far greater mobile penetration levels.

- 2G technology used TDMA and CDMA based standards depending on the type of multiplexing.
- 2G technology using digital signals between handsets and towers. Digital voice is compressed and multiplexed through used of codecs. The less power is emitted from radio power cells, so cell towers and related equipment had become less expensive.
- On the type of multiplexing used in 2g technology can be divided into Time division multiplexing multiple access and code division multiple acc smaller than 1G units.ess.CODEC (Compression Decompression Algorithm) is used by 2 G to compress and multiplex digital voice data.

Benefits of 2G

1. The digital signal consumes less battery power than analog signals so it gives long lasting battery power.
2. The digital signaling controls the noise pollution on the channel and it enhances the voice quality, these are considered as ecofriendly transmissions.
3. Digital encryption offers the privacy and security of the data and voice calls.
   2G has 2.5 G and 2.7 G services which are mainly built for voice services.
4. 2.5 G (second and half generation) is implemented packet-switched domain in addition to the circuit switched domain. The evolution GPRS (General Packet Radio Service) in architecture of GSM and 1 XRTT in CDMA2000 network happens in 2.5 G era. It supports bidirectional peak data rates up to 153.6 Kbit/s. It gives 80-100 Kbit/s data throughput in commercial network. It is also in WAP (Wireless Application Protocol), SMS and MMS Multimedia Messaging services as well as internet access.
5. 2.5 G was informal standard, in which GPRS should provide the data rates from 56 kbit /s up to 115 kbit /s.
6. This standard is also used for internet communication services such as email and World Wide Web access. GPRS data transfer is charged per megabyte which is transferred on the channel.

2.7G (EDGE):

It is firstly used by AT and T Company in United States and deployed on GSM network in the year 2003. As the need of sending messages in air-interface increases enhanced data rate for GSM evolution (EDGE), Enhanced GPRS (EGPRS) or IMT single carrier (IMT-SC) supports as backward compatible digital mobile phone technology. It allows faster data transmission rate.

- Second generation has introduced capacity and coverage.

- EDGE technology is considered as an extended version of GSM .which provides a fast noiseless transmission of data and information. It is termed as IMT SC or single carrier medium which has flexibility to carry packet switched data and circuit switched data.
- Edge technology is used in smart phones specifically BlackBerry family N95,N97 mobile phones, which transfers the data at higher speed as compared to GPRS.

3rd Generation (3G):

The first commercial 3G network was launched by NTT Docomo in Japan based on IDMA and W-CDMA technology.

- In EDGE high volume of data was possible but as messages are sent through air-interface which behaves like a circuit switches call. Thus, part of this packet connection efficiency is lost in circuit switched network. Thus, to define the standards that are shame globally has to be defined and 3G was born.
- The data transmission rate has capability at speed of 14.4 Mbps on downlink and 5.8 mbps on the uplink.
- It opens doors for truly mobile broadband era.
- Services defined under 3G are based on IMT-2000 technical standards. It should provide a peak data rate of 200 Kbit/s. Recent 3G services such as 3.5G and 3.7G are used for mobile broadband access to smart phones and laptops.

3.5G – HSDPA (High-Speed Downlink Packet Access)

High-Speed Downlink Packet Access (HSDPA) is a mobile telephony protocol, also called 3.5G (or "3½G"), which provides a smooth evolutionary path for UMTS-based 3G networks allowing for higher data transfer speeds.

- HSDPA is a packet-based data service in W-CDMA downlink with data transmission up to 8-10 Mbit /s (and 20 Mbit /s for MIMO systems) over a 5MHzbandwidth in WCDMA downlink. HSDPA implementations includes Adaptive Modulation and Coding (AMC), Multiple-Input Multiple-Output (MIMO), Hybrid Automatic Request (HARQ), fast cell search, and advanced receiver design.

3.5G – HSDPA (High-Speed Downlink Packet Access)

It is high speed packet based transmission protocol which is called as 3.5 G, which offers a smooth revolutionary path for UMTS based 3G network. It is a W-CDMA downlink transmission up to 8-10 Mbit/s over 5MHz bandwidth in W-CDMA downlink. The implementation involves adaptive modulation and coding (AMC), Multiple input multiple output, hybrid automatic request, fast cell search, advanced receiver design.

3.7 G (High Speed Uplink Packet Access):

It refers to a high speed uplink packet data transfer for UMTS W-CDMA uplink transmission this mobile communication technology is related to HSDPA and these two are complimentary to each other. It provides the improvements in person to person data application with higher and symmetric data rates like email or games it provides a data rate of 1.4 Mbps and releases 5.8 Mbps.

Advantages:

(1) Data Rates: It is expected to provide a data rate for stationary device as 2 Mbit /s and for mobile user 384 Kbit/s.

(2) Security: It provides the user equipment to authenticate the network it is attaching.

Some of the applications of 3G:

(1) Location Based Services.

(2) Global Positioning System (GPS).

(3) Video Conferencing.

(4) Video on Demand.

(5) Mobile TV.

(6) Telemedicine.

CDMA 3

CDMA stands for Code Division Multiple Access which is used by many radio communication technologies for the channel access method.

- CDMA uses a single communication channel which provides multiple accesses that means several transmitters can send information simultaneously in such a way all transmitters shares the same bandwidth. To avoid the interference into the transmission, CDMA uses the spread spectrum technology and a special coding scheme.

- Many mobile phone standards such as cdmaOne, CDMA2000 (the 3G evolution of cdmaOne) and WCDMA uses CDMA as the access method.

- Global system for Mobile Communication (GSM) and Code Division Multiple Access (CDMA) are very popular technologies in cellular networks. When GSM is used with 3G technology which is known as Universal Mobile Telecommunication (UMTS) and when 3G is used with CDMA it is known as CDMA2000 are competing with each other depending upon (1) coverage area, (2) data access, (3) data transfer speed and (4) hardware used for the technologies.

What is CDMA 3G:

There are two popular terms 3G and CDMA which are used in wireless internet and data access. When these two are phrased together i.e. "3G CDMA", 3G signifies a specific group of standards for the third generation of cellular phones. And cdma offers the multiple access network type. These together has the capability to provide the high speed access to a variety of data access on wireless devices.

Revolutions in CDMA 3G

3g technology had become the superior in wireless network for speed and capabilities by the year 2010 it provides high speed data access for various smart phones and similar devices. CDMA network are utilized by the mobile phones radios, computers and similar technologies cdma networks requires the phones that are activated via the mobile provider.

The users who are availing the CDMA network do not need to use a subscriber identity module card(SIM card)which can easily interchange amongst the devices whereas on GSM mobile network having 2G second generation models SIM cards are necessary.

CDMA 2000

The first 3G CDMA network is known as CDMA 2000 1xEV-DO, which provides the speed of up to 3.1 megabytes per second (Mbps) this technology is first used by Monet Mobile networks, after it Verizon wireless started using the network in 2003.

- CDMA2000 (also known as C2K or IMT Multi-Carrier (IMT-MC)) is a family of 3G mobile technology standards, which use CDMA channel access, to send voice, data, and signaling data between mobile phones and cell sites. The name CDMA2000 actually denotes a family of standards that represent the successive, evolutionary stages II of the underlying technology.

- All approved radio interfaces for the ITU's IMT-2000. CDMA2000 has a relatively long technical history and is backward-compatible with its previous2G iteration IS-95 (cdmaOne). In the United States, CDMA2000 is a registered trademark II of the Telecommunications Industry Association (TIA-USA).

- CDMA 2000 is multi carrier 3G mobile technology which uses the CDMA technique for accessing a data channel which is used to send voice, data. It also provides the signaling between the mobile phones and cell structure. The following are the successors of the CDMA 3 G technology.

CDMA2000 1xRTT

- It is known as core CDMA 2000 wireless air interface standard. 1x signifies that 1 times radio transmission technology which provides a duplex pair of transmission technology which indicated the same radio frequency. It supports the transmission of packet data speed up to 153 kbit /s .it provides the best effort delivery for data over circuit switched channel for voice.

- **CDMA2000 1xEV-DO: Release 0, Revision A, Revision B:** The first 3G CDMA network is known as CDMA 2000 1xEV-DO, which provides the speed of up to 3.1 megabytes per second (Mbps).
- **CDMA2000 1xEV-DO Revision C or Ultra Mobile Broadband (UMB):** The next release known as ultra mobile broadband, which uses radio transmission for internet broadcast access. It uses Code Division Multiplexing Access (CDMA) as well as Time Division Multiplexing Access (TDMA) to maximise user's as well as system's throughput.
- **CDMA2000 1xEVDV:** 1X Advanced is the evolution of CDMA2000 1X. It provides up to four times the capacity and 70% more coverage.

Practice Questions

1. Explain the architecture of Bluetooth.
2. Write a short notes on :
   (a) First generation.
   (b) Second generation.
   (c) 802.11.
3. Explain GPRS architecture in detail.
4. Discuss functional groups of GPRS.
5. Explain different interfaces used in GPRS.
6. State the various applications of GPRS.
7. State the various applications of Bluetooth.

Chapter 5...

DATABASE ISSUES

5.1 Hoarding Techniques
5.2 Data Caching
5.3 Client Server Computing
    5.3.1 Client Server Computing with Adaption
5.4 Power Aware and Context Aware Computing
    5.4.1 Context Aware Computing
5.5 Transactional Models, Query Processing, Recovery, and Quality of Service Issues
    5.5.1 Transactional Models
- Practice Questions

- A Database is a collection of systematic and formatted data or information. Database can be stored on all types of devices such as desktop, mobile phones and tabs etc. A data base can be retrieved data from a server or network. Device cannot retrieve data from a network for each computation. The devices are enhanced and they caches specific data which may be required for future computations, during the interval in which the device is connected to the server or network.
- A cache is a list or database of items or records stored at the device. The databases are hoarded at the application or enterprise tier. The application layer allows the direct user interaction so that the database server uses the business logic and connectivity for retrieving the data and then it transmits it to the device.
- The copies of the databases that are hoarded at the server are distributed or transmitted to the mobile devices from the enterprise servers or application databases. The copies that are stored at the device are similar to the cache memories at the processor in a multiprocessor system with a shared main memory and copies of the main memory data stored at different locations.

5.1 Hoarding Techniques   (April 2015)

The database hoarding may be done at the application tier itself, Fig. 5.1 shows.
- The mobile device APIs are used to retrieve the data from a database. The following figure has the two ways of retrieving data from the database server.

- Fig. 5.1 (a) shows mobile device database API that sends the queries and retrieves the data from the database server and Fig. 5.1 (b) shows the data from the server is fetched through a program for e.g. IBM DB2 Everyplace (DB2e).

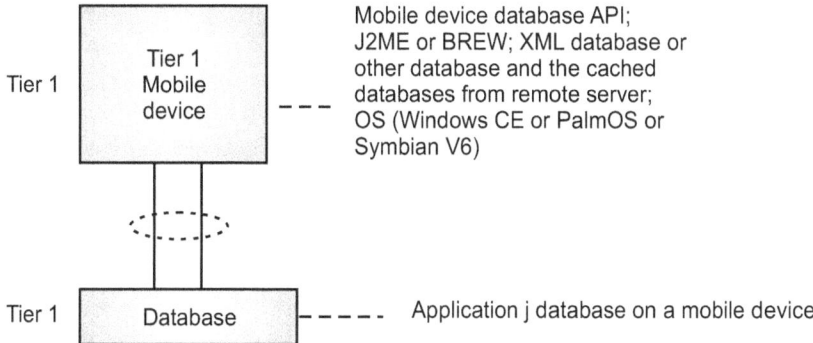

(a) API at mobile device sending quires and retrieving data from local database

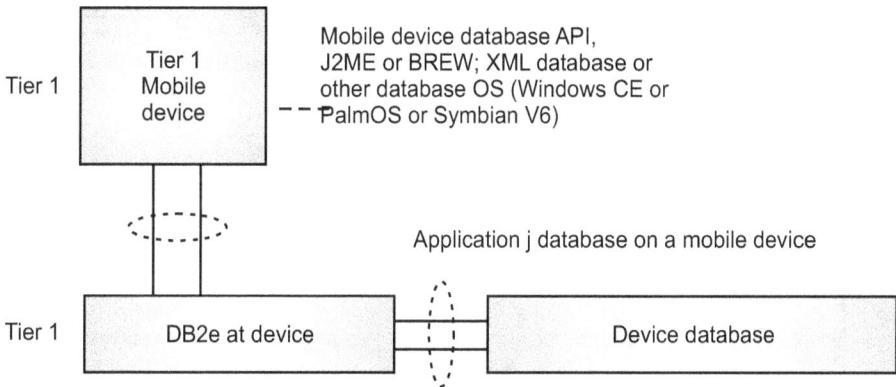

(b) API at mobile device retrieving data from database using DB2e

Fig. 5.1

- The database that is applicable to mobile devices is not distributed to multiple devices. Both the architectures belong to the class of one tier database architecture because the databases are specific to a mobile device it is not synchronized with the new updates that are stored at the device itself. Examples are downloaded ringtones, music etc.
- IBM DB 2 Everyplace (DB2e) it is a relational database engine which has been designed to reside at the device it supports J2ME and most of the mobile operating systems. DB2e synchronizes with DB2 databases at the synchronization, application or enterprise server.

- The data base architecture figure shows a two tier (c) or multi tier (d) databases. The database resides at the remote servers and the copies of these databases are cached at the client tiers.
- This is known as client server computing architecture.

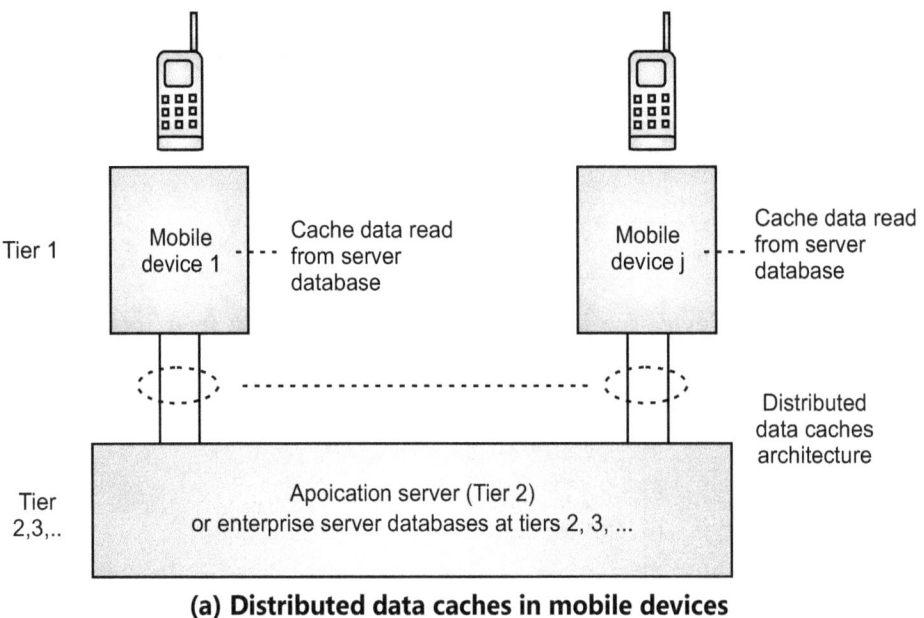

(a) **Distributed data caches in mobile devices**

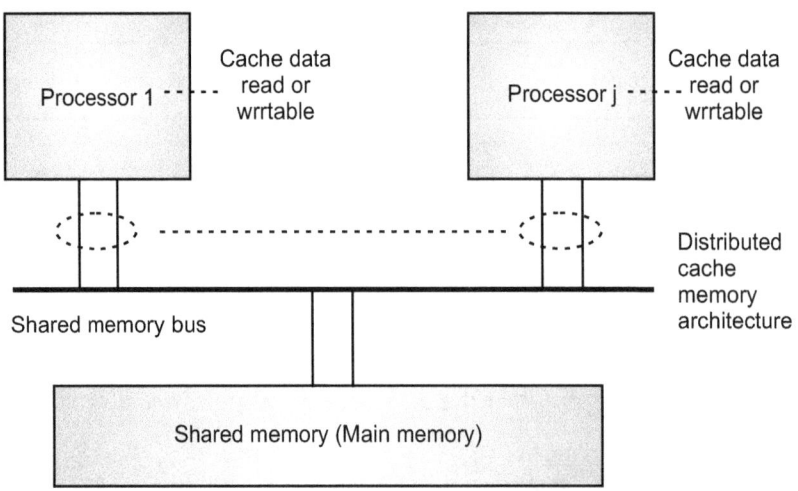

(b) **Similar architecture for a distributed cache memory in multiprocessor system**

Fig. 5.2

- In two (or three) tier client server computing architecture first tier is nothing but the cache data read by mobile APIs. A cache data is nothing but the list or database of items or records. Stored at the device. And cache data resides at the application tier.
- The local and updated copies of the database are modified by the server at the mobile device which are connected to the computing API (first tier) at the mobile devices which uses the cached data records i.e. the local copy of it. And from tier 2 or 3 the server retrieves and transmits the data records to tier 1 using business logic and synchronizes the local copies at the device. These local copies function as device caches.
- The **advantage of hoarding** is that there is no access latency it does not introduce any delay in retrieving the queried record from the server over a wireless medium. The client device API has rapid data access to hoarded or cached data.
- The client device API has instantaneous data access to hoarded or cached data. When a device caches the data distributed by the server, the data is hoarded at the device
- The disadvantage of hoarding is that the consistency of the cached data with the database at the server needs to be maintained.
- Hoarded copies of the database resides at the mobile devices which are transmitted by application database servers or enterprise servers the copies of the cached data are stored in the same manner how the processor of the multiprocessor system stores it in main memory in which data can be stored at different locations.

5.2 Data Caching (April 2015)

- **Cache access protocol:** Pulling and pushing data from cache database.
    - Data fetching from the cache database which resides at the mobile device i.e. at client side is done by data pushing and pulling methods. Caching leads to a reduced access interval as compared to the pull (on demand) mode of data fetching. And it also reduces the precedence of the pushing mode at the server. This method is called as cost-based data replacement or caching.
    - **Caching can be based on ratio of two parameters:**
      (1) Access portability (at the device),
      (2) Pushing rates (from the server) for each record.
    - This method uses the average time of access which is in between the two successive instances of the access to the record and pushing rates to the record.
    - Caching of data records can be based on 'hot record'.
    - The database records which are least frequently fetched and the records with larger access time are placed in a database.

- **Prefetching** is another alternative of fetching the data.
    1. This process considers the future view of the need instead of caching from the pushed records.
    2. It reduces the server load as the process requests for the data by considering the future need and pulls the data as required.
    3. The time is taken in accessing the record, which is required by the device API. If in case the record is not found in the device database, then this instance is termed as "Cost of cache misses". The cost of cache misses get reduced in this processing.
- **Cache consistency:** This factor is used for the cache maintenance. This mechanism is used for validation of the record i.e. the process which is validate the data, this record is fetched at the server is valid and that records are used for caching computations.

Cache access protocols based on cache Invalidation mechanism:
- The access protocols which are fetching the records that may be invalidated. This is may be the case of expiry or modification of the record at the database server.
- Cache invalidation is a process in which a cached data record becomes invalid and it is not further usable due to modification, expiry or invalidation by another computing server or system.
- With the help of this process server communicates about data invalidation to all client devices.
- Cache invalidation mechanism are used to synchronize the data at the other processors whenever the cache data is written by a processor in a multiprocessor system, this process is also active in mobile devices having distributed copies from the server.
- A cache is nothing but the group of the records. Each record is called as cache line, copies of which can be stored at the devices or servers.
- The records which are to be cached at a given point of time may have the following states Modified, Exclusive, Shared and Invalidated. These four states are denoted by letters as M, E, and S, I respectively. These states indicates instances that are mentioned below.
    - **E (Exclusive):** This state indicates that the exclusive state of the record is for the internal use of the record and which is not available for other device.
    - **S (Shared):** This tag indicates the shared state indicates that the data record can be used by other devices also.
    - **M (Modified):** This state indicates that the data is modified at the server.
    - **I (Invalidated):** The tag states that the server database is no longer having a copy of the record which was shared and used for computations earlier.

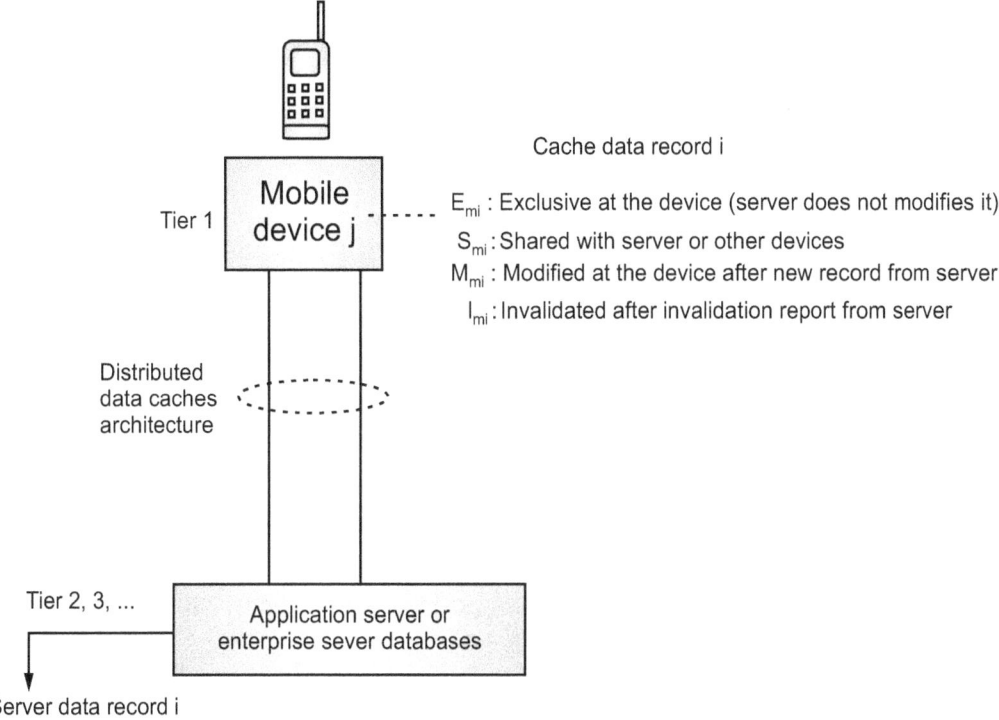

Cache data record i
E_{mi} : Exclusive at the device (server does not modifies it)
S_{mi} : Shared with server or other devices
M_{mi} : Modified at the device after new record from server
I_{mi} : Invalidated after invalidation report from server

Server data record i
E_{Si} : Exclusive at server and the device record does not affect it
S_{Si} : Shared with other devices or server
I_{Si} : Invalidated at server, report is sent to the devices
M_{Si} : Modified at the server

Fig. 5.3: Four possible states of data record

The above figure shows the four possible states of the data item or a record i at an instance in the server database and its copy at the cache of the mobile device j.

Server instantiates the mechanism of cache Invalidation in mobile devices .there are four possible invalidation mechanisms:

- Stateless asynchronous
- Stateless synchronous
- Stateful asynchronous
- Stateful synchronous

1. Stateless Asynchronous:

This is the mechanism that describes broadcasting of the invalidation of the cache to all the clients of the server. The client device keeps the track of the all records stored whereas server does not keep the record of stored data at the device cache.

- The server keeps uniformly updated to all the devices irrespective of the knowledge that particular device has that records or not.

- Term asynchronous means the invalidation information for an item is sent as soon as its value changes. The server does not keep the information for current state. (Emi, Mmi, Smi or Imi) of a data record in cache for broadcasting later.
- The server's responsibility is to advertise the invalidation information. The client can either request for a modified copy of the record or cache the relevant record when data is pushed from the server.
- The server advertises as and when the corresponding data record at the server is invalidated and modified(deleted and replaced)
- The advantage of the asynchronous approach is that there are no frequent, unnecessary transfers of data reports, thus making the mechanism more bandwidth efficient.
- The disadvantages are listed below:
- Every client device gets an invalidation report, whether that client requires that copy or not.
- Client devices assume that if there is no invalidation report from server, the data records are taken as a valid copy of it.
- If link failure happens and if server fails to update the invalidation report to the data then client device uses that data for computation.

2. **Stateless Synchronous:**

This is also a stateless mode in which the server has no information about the present instance of the client devices. But it keeps on updating about the invalidation of the records periodically.

- The difference of stateless synchronous mechanism is the server advertises the reports of data invalidation periodically as well as it publishes when the particular data gets invalidated or modified.
- This mechanism ensures the synchronization because if the client devices failed in receiving about the periodically published advertisements, due to any link failure. The client devices receive the updation regarding the data at the end of the period or client devices send the request to the server for the same.
- The advantage of the synchronous approach is that the client devices receive periodic updation regarding the data which is stored in cache. The periodic invalidation reports lead to greater reliability of cached data as updates requests for invalid data, which can be sent from server to all client devices.
- Following are the disadvantages of the stateless synchronous mechanism:
  1. Unnecessary transfers of data invalidation reports take place.
  2. Every client devices gets an advertised invalidation report periodically irrespective of whether that client has a copy of the invalidated data or not.

- Each client device got updated periodically and when invalidation report is not validated during a specific time interval. Client device request for it before using the invalidated data record from a cache database.

3. **Stateful Asynchronous:**

   Stateful asynchronous mechanism which applies the 'Stateful' scheme for updating the client devices. In this scheme the Stateful term indicates that the server will notify the invalidation report to only those clients who are affected that means users that data instead of broadcasting it to all clients.
   - The server keeps updating the current instance of each record (Emi, Mmi, Smi or Imi) in data cache at the home location cache. Home Location Cache (HLC) is updated by using the Home Agent (HA).
   - The client devices intimates the HA of the current state of the data records which also be stored by the server at the HLC. The server gets the information about clients which are using the specific data .in case such a data gets invalidated or modified then, the server intimates the only affected client devices.
   - Once the client gets updated with the advertisement, the client device requests to the server to replace the invalidated data with the modified data .after that it updates the cache database with the current state for each data record.
   - The advantage of this updation is that the server keeps the track for each data record; this helps the server to keep on updating the data cache and updation of the HLC.
   - One more advantage of this scheme that only affected clients are intimated about the data updation and other devices are not flooded with this irregular updation.
   - Major disadvantage is that client devices assumes that as these are not updated with the invalidation report, the data is valid for computation. So if there is link failure the device uses the invalidated data.

4. **Stateful Synchronous:**

   The server keeps the information of the current state (Emi, Mmi, Smi and Imi) of data records at the client cache. The server keeps all the current state of copies at the Home Location Cache (HLC) using the Home Agent (HA).
   - The server also keeps on updating the client devices about the invalidation of records periodically and in between if the data got invalidated or modified it also intimate to the client devices.
   - The advantage of this approach is that the reports related to the invalidation of the data records are updated periodically at the server and also server updates the Home Location Cache on regular time intervals.

- The server synchronizes whenever the data gets modified or considered as a valid data records.
- If the client devices does not receive any invalidation report from the server it does not use the copy of that data instead of this it requests the server to update the information related to the invalidation of that data.
- The disadvantage is that this mechanism requires the higher bandwidth for updating all the client devices periodically and updation in home location cache.

Data cache maintenance in Mobile environment:
Importance of data cache in a Mobile Environment?
- Whenever the client devices need the data records to be fetched from the cache database at the server, it sends the request to the server, this mechanism is called as pulling.
- Whenever the application which is running at the client devices requests for the data records. Then the server starts processing the request. The time taken for the application to access a particular record in known as access Latency. Caching and hoarding the record at the device reduces access latency to zero. Therefore the data cache maintenance is important in Mobile Environment.
- Data cache inconsistency means that data records cached for applications are not validated at the device; these are modified at the server but not modified at the device.
- The consistency in the data cache should be maintained as the client device request for runtime demands of the data records from database cache. It can be maintained by the three methods given below:
    - **Cache Invalidation Mechanism (Server initiated case):** The server sends the invalidation reports on invalidation of records (asynchronous) or at regular intervals (synchronous)
    - **Polling Mechanism (Client initiated case):** In Polling mechanism the server information is checked for the state of data record whether the record is in (1) valid, (2) invalid, (3) modified, (4) exclusive state. Each cached data record copy is polled whenever required by the application software during computation. If that record is found to be modified or invalidated then device requests for the modified data and replaces the earlier cached record copy.
    - **Time–to-live Mechanism (client initiated case):** The "Time-to-live" (TTL) term indicates the end of the session, it is applied on each data record. i.e. Each data record is assigned "time-to-live", which is adjusted according to the previous update intervals of that record. After the end of the TTL, the cached copy is polled and if it is modified then the devices requests server to replace the copy of that data with the modified data. When TTL is set to 0, the TTL mechanism acts as similar to polling mechanism.

Web Cache Maintenance in Mobile Environment:

All the client devices and servers are connected to the web server that is responsible to provide web contents on demand. The client's device also has the web cache as it have for server .client devices also updates the web server data. If an application running at the devices needs a data record from the web, which is not available at web cache then it is known as access latency.

- Web cache maintenance is important in mobile environment to overcome the access latency from downloading the data from the websites due to disconnection.
- Web cache consistency can be maintained by two methods:
  - **Time-to-Live Mechanism (Client initiated case):** Each data record from the web cache is assigned "Time-to-live" which is adjusted according to the previous update of the record. Once the time exceeds to the cached copy it is polled for checking the updation of that record .if it is updated it is replaced by modified data.
  - **Power aware computing mechanism (Client initiated case):** Each web cache stored at the device is maintained by CRC (Cyclic Redundancy Check) bits. Assume that there are N cached bits and n CRC bits (N > n) at the server n CRC bits are stored.
- Whenever the data records are modified at the server the CRC bits are also modified.
- After the TTL expires or on demand the client API demands for the web cache records then CRC is polled and obtained from the server.

5.3 Client Server Computing

Client server computing is a distributed architecture in which there are two modes:

1. **Client:** A client is a computing system which requests the server for resources or for computing the tasks.
2. **Server:** It is a system which responds to the one or more client requests.

- The client devices fetch the data records from the server or cache at itself.
- The data records can be accessed on demand from the client device or broadcasted or distributed by the server.
- In client server computing architecture client and server may reside on same computing system it may be on different computing systems.
- Client server can have N tier architecture (N = 1, 2, 3, 4), when N = 1, the client and server resides at the same computing device and when client and server are on different computing devices then N = 2. Client and server has request response paradigm and they communicate to each other on command interchange (HTTP) basis.
- For any application, specifically 2, 3 or n tier architecture is applied. The tiers are connected to each other with a connecting, synchronizing, data or command interchange protocol.

1. **Two tier architecture:**

   The following architecture shows the application server at the second tier. The data records are retrieved using business logic and synchronized with the local copies at the devices. When the copies of the database are modified at the server then the copies cached at the client devices also modified. There are no restrictions on hardware and software platforms on designing the APIs.

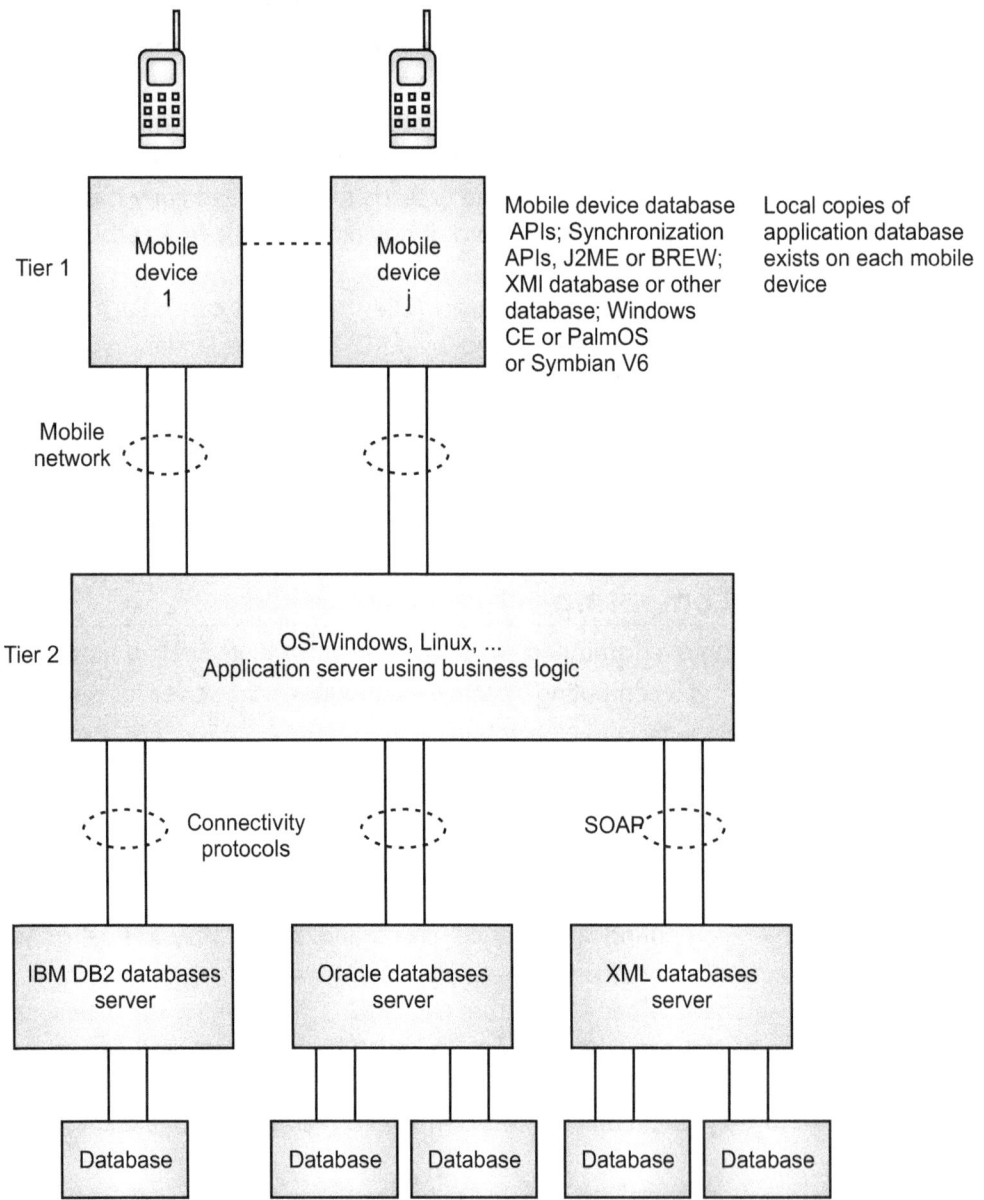

Fig. 5.4: Multimedia file server in two-tier client-server computing architecture

2. Three-tier Architecture:

In three-tier architecture application interface, business logic and database resides at the different layers. The database is associated with the enterprise server tier and only local copies of the database reside at the mobile devices. The database connects to the enterprise server by connecting protocol. The enterprise server connects the databases on different platforms such as oracle, XML and IBM DB2.

The following figure shows the three tier architecture, tier 3 are communicates to tier 1 with synchronization of Tier 2 this architecture has in between server called as synchronization server which sends and synchronizes the copies at the multiple devices. It retrieves the data records at the enterprise tier (Tier 3) using business logic. In diagram the local copies of 1 to k databases are hoarded at the mobile devices for the applications 1 to k.

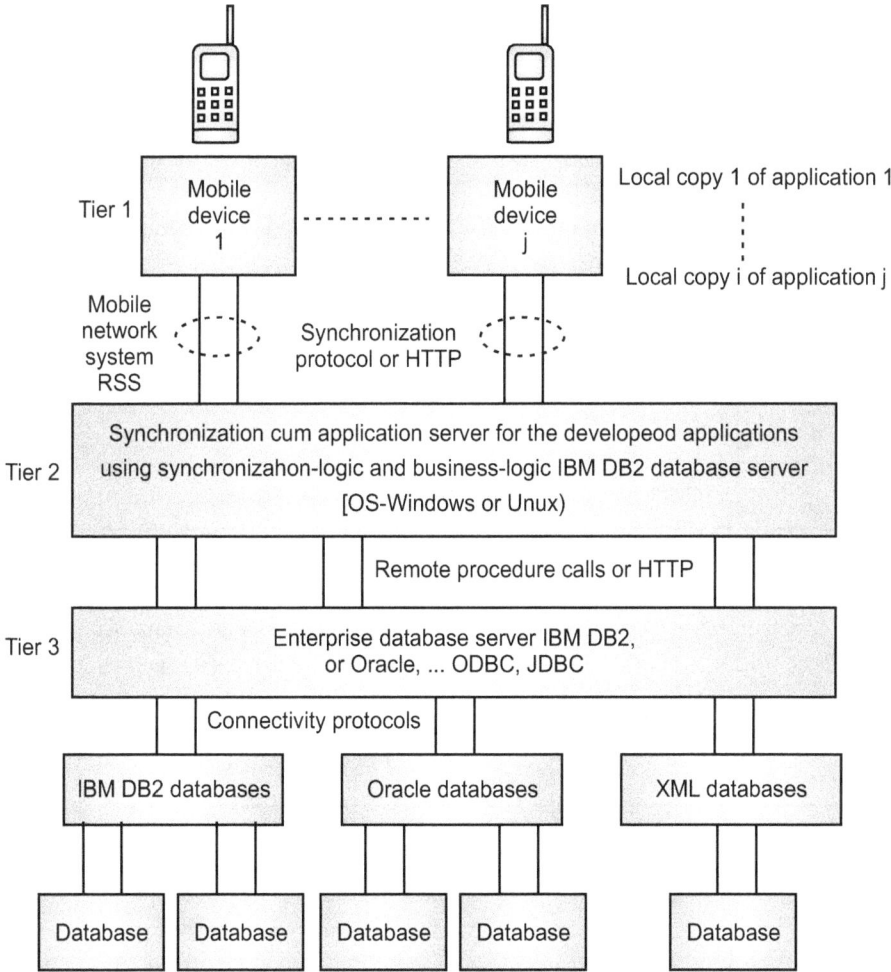

(a) Local copies 1 to j of database horded at the mobile device using an enterprise database

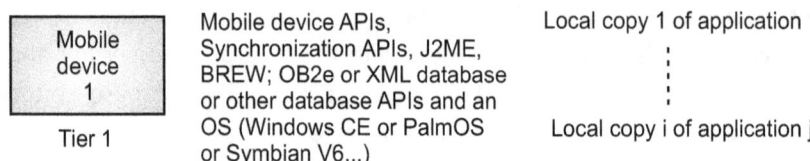

(b) Mobile device with J2ME or BREW platform

Fig. 5.5

3. N tier architecture:

This architecture is designed when N>3 .In this architecture I between the client devices and enterprise sever there is a presentation server.

The following figure shows the 4 tier architecture in which client device connects to the data presentation server at a tier 2.

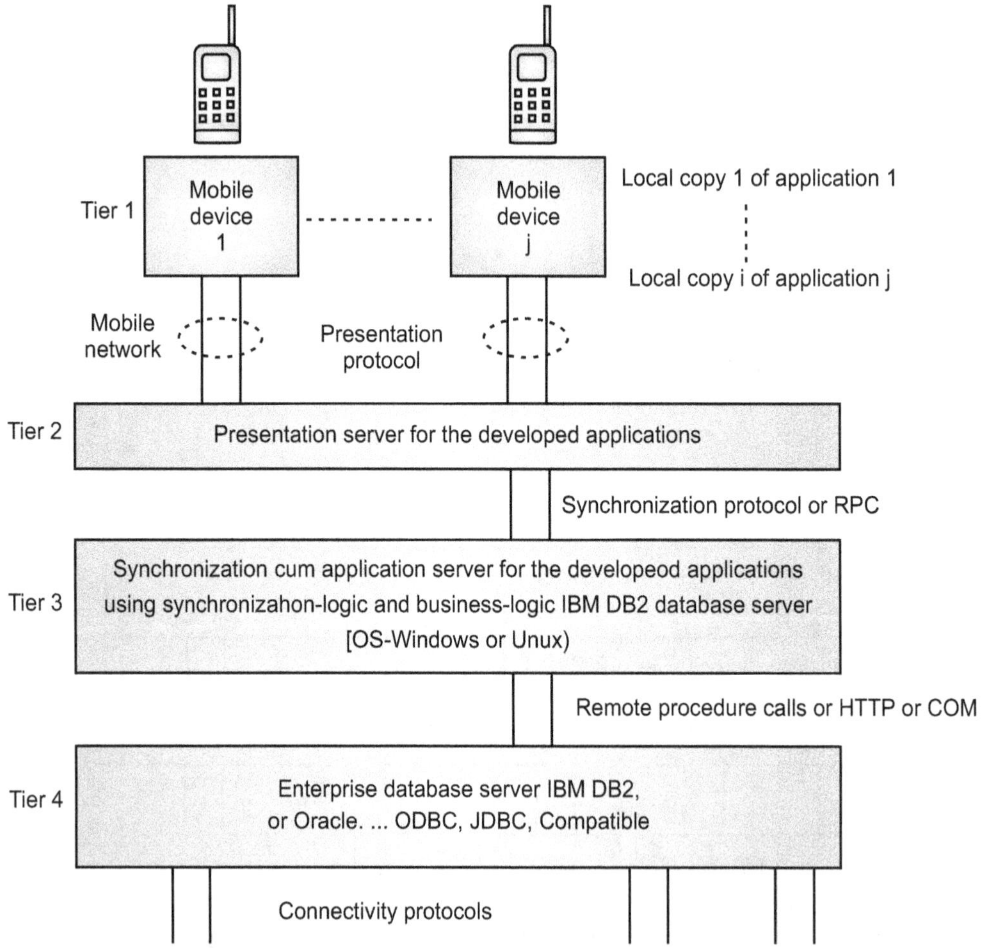

Fig. 5.6: Architecture in which a client device connects to a data-presentation server

- The presentation server is connected to the application server (tier 3). The application server is connected to database server by connecting protocol and multimedia server using Java or XML API at Tier 4.
- The presentation, application and enterprise servers can be connected using RPC, Java RMI, JNDI or HOP. These servers may also use HTTP or HTTPs in case the server at a tier j connects to a tier j + 1 using the internet.

5.3.1 Client Server Computing with Adaption

The communication of data exchange is in between the synchronization server and database server, the device APIs may be different than the data which is sent from the synchronization server. To synchronize the data the two adapters are used at a mobile device

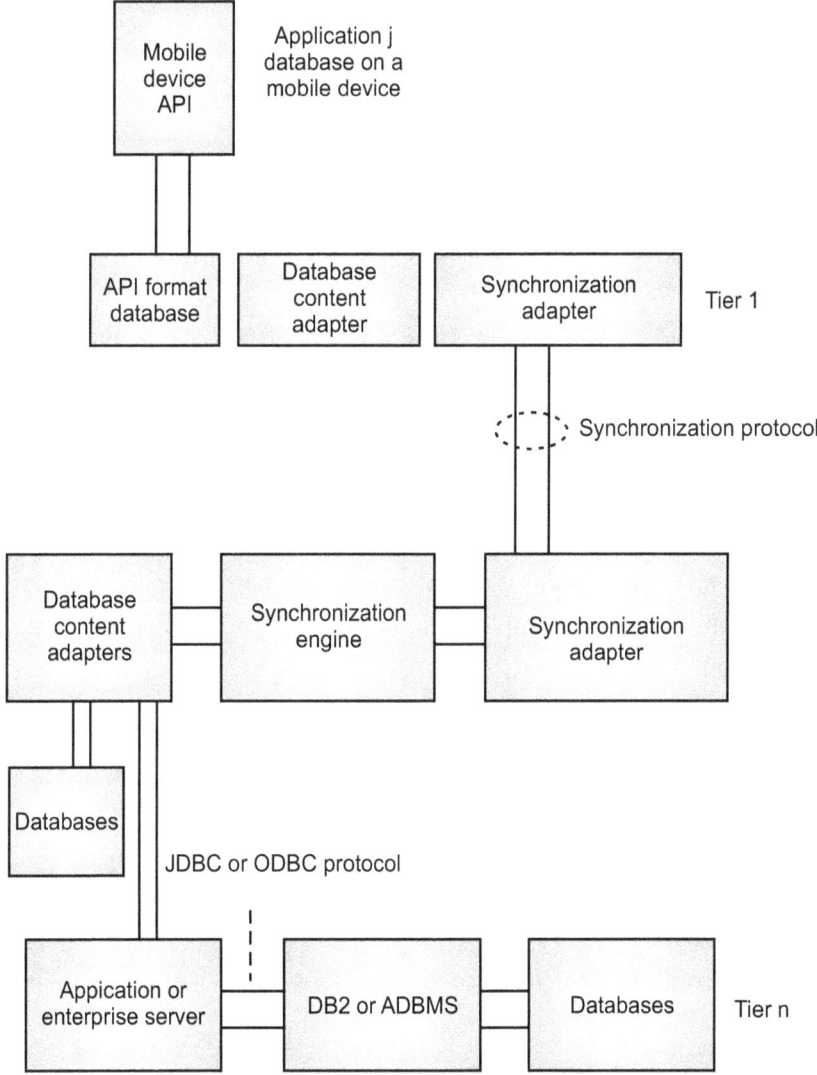

Fig. 5.7: Client server computing with adaptation

- One adapter is used for responding to the standard format data for synchronization at the mobile device. And second adapter is used for backend that is database copy which may be in different data format for the API at the mobile device.
- An adapter is used to convert the data from one format to another format. It also converts the data under one protocol to the data under another protocol. That is converted the data from one format or data under one protocol to the data in another format or data under another protocol.
- The following figure shows the API, database and adapters at the mobile devices and also adapters at application, presentation and enterprise servers. Adapters are used for interchange of the data in between a standard format to API's data format.

5.4 Power Aware and Context Aware Computing

5.4.1 Context Aware Computing

The context of a mobile device, is used for mobile devices which are under certain circumstances, situations, applications or physical environment.

- The device itself learns how to handle the physical environment context e.g. if the mobile device is been used in crowded area and if device is aware of the surrounding noise then it itself increases the speaker volume, and as device moves from that area it will decreases the volume.
- A context aware computing system has user, device and application interface which keeps track of past and present situations, circumstances or actions at the present mobile network.
- The circumstances such as present time of the day, presently available connectivity to the network, presently remaining memory or battery power, previously cached data, previous track of an application. All these circumstances are considered while computation.

What is Context?

The term 'context' is referred as interrelated situations in which a collection of elements, records, components or entities exists or not. All the elements, components and entities have their own functionalities, but if there is some circumstance then these will communicate with each other and perform for the better performance. e.g. Contacts

Categories of the Context

1. Structural context: Structural context is considered regarding to the structural arrangement of the data. The collection of fields forms one record and arrangement of records is done for a specific purpose.

e.g. The fields such as name, address and 10 digit mobile number have the individual specification. These fields are arranged in such a way that, it will form one records and all records together considered as a telephone directory which is a context.

2. Implicit and Explicit context: A context may be an Implicit or Explicit. Implicit context omits the specific data by considering the history tasks. It deletes the unimportant data it takes independent world view and performs certain alterations .the purpose of omitting the unwanted data is to make the device compatible with protocols, interfaces and APIs by changing the messages.

- Implicit context uses the history to examine the call history, to manage the omission or to determine the recipient and performs the contextual interactions.

  Example of implicit context is placing a call by using a context as 'Contacts'. The name, email-id, and address these fields are implicit in a contact in the context 'Contacts'.

  A computing device may uses the context 'Contacts ' in different way that means by using it, device may place a call or send an email.

  1. For placing a call device uses name records and an independent view is taken on it and deploys the CDMA or GSM protocols to be connected to a mobile network. Context CDMA is implicit in defining the records of 'Contacts'.
  2. For sending an email, the use of emailed field is implicit to a system and use of SMTP (Simple Mail transfer Protocol) or other mail sending protocols is implicit.

  In this case implicit contexts also get compatible with the data which may be in different formats. Consider the context 'Document', name or personal information is extrinsic.

  The information such as 'document author' is extrinsic while processing the document context.

  The 'contacts' context is imported in 'document' context to establish interrelationship between the two contexts.

- Explicit contexts are to be defined by the user itself for example the current location of the device may be considered as a context .once the current location is fetched the standard mobile applications such as clock, tone dialing are adapted into a mobile device.

Context Aware Computing:

Context aware computing leads to application aware computing. Applications are also aware of the context environment. The APIs are the part of a context(Implicit or Explicit).for example in 'Contact' context the phone calling application adapts the phone number list and places the call by using 'contacts 'and also GSM and CDMA communication.

The benefits of using context in computation:
- It reduces the possibility of the errors.
- It also reduces the ambiguity in the actions.
- It helps in awaring the performance of the execution of computation .and also the expected system is the response of the computation.

- There are two different contexts one is resume and another which is already discussed earlier is telephone directory.
- Name, address, qualification and achievements are the fields of the records which constitute the resume context and name address and telephone number together forms the records for telephone Directory context. In both the context the other fields are associated to the Name field. But as we consider these two contexts for the computation the name field and the other associated field have different actions while computations.

Context types in context aware computing:

There are five types of contexts that are important in context aware computing
1. Physical context
2. Computing context
3. User context
4. Temporal context
5. Structural context

(1) Physical context: A context may be of physical environments. The parameters for defining a physical context are service disconnection, light level, noise level and signal strength. The device is able to sense the physical conditions and enhances the performance e.g. mobile device may sense the light levels and increases the brightness of the mobile during the day time and during night time or poor light it reduces the device display brightness. The physical context is changed and the device display is adjusted accordingly.

(2) Computing Context: In context aware computing the context may be a computing context. Computing context is defined as interrelationships or conditions of the network connectivity Protocols that uses (Bluetooth, GSM, CDMA or GPRS) bandwidth and available resources such as keypad, display unit e.g. When a mobile device is on with Bluetooth interface it detects the other computing context resources and uses the Bluetooth connectivity to connect to a computer.

(3) User context: The user context defines the user's location, user's profiles and persons near the user. User Context is defined as a computation of (1) all user interface components, (2) condition of the user, (3) primary intent of the system and (4) all the other elements that allow other users and computing system.

(4) Temporal Context: Temporal context defines the interrelation between the time and the occurrence of the event or actions. A group of interfaces has intrinsic or extrinsic temporal context. The mobile devices are performing different actions at each time interval e.g. assume that user is dialing a number and places a call in the next instance of time user press add new contact button for adding new contact. Then device seeks the name as an input in the contact.

(5) Structural Context: It is the structure or sequence formed by the elements or records. Graphical user Interface (GUI) elements have structural context. Structural context may be as extrinsic to other context. The interaction among all GUI elements depends upon the display screen.

When time is context, then the hour and minute are the elements.

e.g. Consider "Time" as a context.

5.5 Transactional Models, Query Processing, Recovery, and Quality of Service Issues

5.5.1 Transactional Models

A Transaction is the execution of the interrelated instructions in a sequence for a specific operation on a database. To maintain the integrity of the data transaction, it should follow its ACID properties to enhance the performance.

1. **Automicity:** Atomicity of a transaction is nothing but the each transaction is "all or nothing": i.e. all actions of a transaction are performed completely or not at all if one part of the transaction fails, the entire transaction fails, and the database state is left unchanged. In such a case the transaction must be undone (rolled back).the operations of one transaction are considered as one indivisible unit (atomic).

2. **Consistency:** A transaction must preserve the integrity constraint and follows the declared consistency rules. Consistency means after the execution of transaction it will be expected to be in consistent state.

3. **Isolation:** If two transactions are executed concurrently there should be an interaction between the two. Further intermediate results in a transaction should be invisible or any other transaction.

4. **Durability:** Once the transaction is completed it should be consistent that is it should not be aborted or discarded.

Every transaction has the life cycle that begins with BEGIN TRANSACTION command. If some failure happens transaction is ABORTED or ROLLED BACK .on successful completion of a transaction it gets COMMITTED.

- **Example:** Consider a base class 'library' included in Microsoft.NET. There are ActiveX data objects which are computer software components. These ADO.NET ActiveX data objects which are used to access and modify the data from a relational database.
- ADO.NET transaction model permits three transaction commands:
  1. **Begin Transaction:** It is used to begin transaction. This command used to begin a transaction .this command is executed as follows:
     Connection A .open ();
     Trans A = Connection A. Begin Transaction ();
     Connection A and Trans A are distinct objects.
  2. **Commit:** This command gets executed after the transaction gets completed successfully.
     All statements between BEGIN TRANSACTION and COMMIT are executed properly.
     Trans A. Commit ();
  3. **Rollback:** Rollback action is performed after the BEGIN TRANSACTION command is executed.

Query Processing:

Query processing means constructing the efficient execution strategy by query decomposition and query optimization.

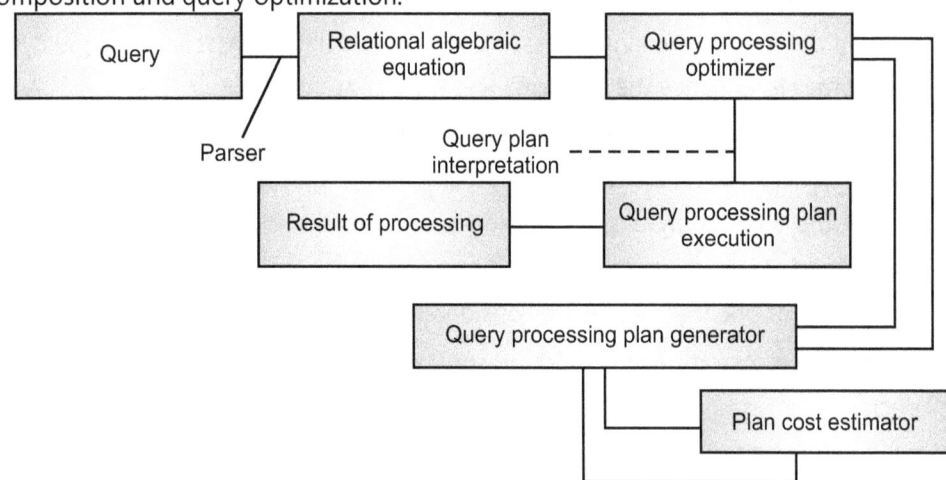

Fig. 5.8: Query Processing Architecture

- Relational algebraic equation defines a set of operations needed during query processing.
- It represents the projection operation ,selection operation and AND operation
- It is clear that second set of operations in Query processing is less efficient than the first. Query decomposition of the first set gives efficiency. Decomposition is done by
  1. Analysis
  2. Conjunctive or Disjunctive normalization
  3. Semantic analysis.

- Optimization of the query can be based on cost (number of micro operations in processing) by evaluating the costs of sets of equivalent expression.

  It follows the selection steps and projection steps as early as possible and eliminates duplicate operations.

  The Query optimizer employs
  1. Query processor plan generator
  2. Query processor cost estimation to provide an efficient plan for Query processing.

  The following two relational algebraic equations are used to select the number from context 'contacts' and place the call.

- The query is written to crosscheck and match the records of a column in contacts with all dialed number. It will work as follows:

  cTelNum (Phone numbers in contact) and dTelNum (dialed number in contact) are two columns of 'contact' context. The inner query will match this values of this two columns as contact. cTelNum = contact dTelNum.

Data Recovery Process:

Data is recoverable in case of media failure, intentional attack on the database and transactions logging data, or physical media destruction. However data recovery is possible in other cases.

- Fig. 5.9 shows data recoverability management architecture. The recovery manager is responsible for atomicity and durability.
- Atomicity ensures that an uncommitted but started transaction aborts on failure and aborted transactions are logged into a log file.
- Durability takes care of that a transaction is not affected by failure and is recovered.
- The secondary storage keeps the track of stable state database. That is stable state database are stored in secondary storage at the start and at the end. Transaction commands are sent to the recovery manager.
- Recovery manager forwards the fetch command to database manager the database manager processes the queries during the transactions and it uses a database buffer.
- The recovery manager also sends the flush commands to transfer the committed transactions and database buffer data to the secondary storage.
- The recovery manager detects the result of operation. It also recovers the lost operations from secondary storage.
- The recovery manager keeps the track of all operations of transaction by keeping the log file.

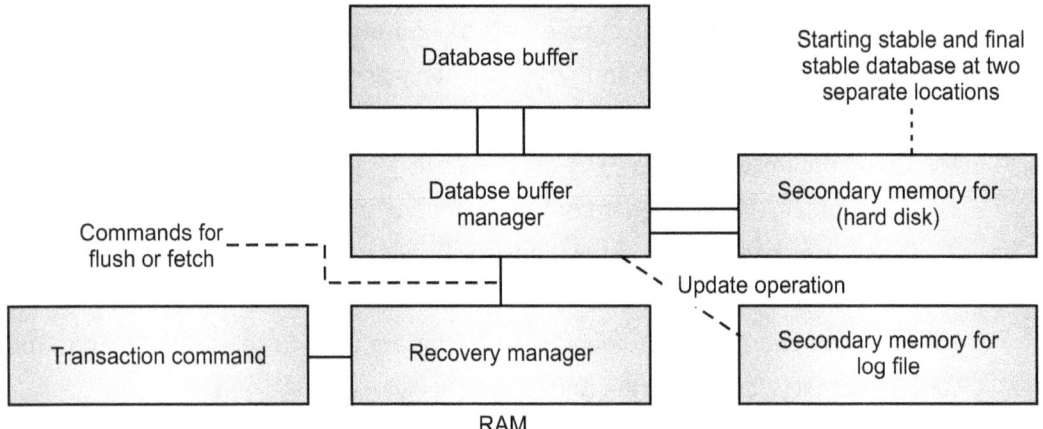

Fig. 5.9: Recovery management architecture

- Log file is maintained by recovery manager in the following manner:
    1. Each instruction of transaction for update (insertion, deletion and updation) must be logged.
    2. Database read instructions are not logged.
    3. Log files stored at a different storage medium.
    4. Log entries are flushed out of the final stable state when database is stored.
- Each logged entry contains the following:
    1. Transaction type (begin, commit and rollback)
    2. Transaction ID
    3. Operation type
    4. Object on which operation is performed.
    5. The values of the objects before operation and after operation.
- The procedure called the Aries algorithm is also used for recovering lost data .The basic types of algorithm are:
    1. Analyse from last checkpoint and identify all dirty records (written again after operation restarted) in the buffer.
    2. REDO all buffered operation in the update log to finish and make final pages.
    3. Undo all write operations and restore pre transaction values.
- The recovery models used in data recovery processes are as follows:
    1. **Full Recovery model:** It creates the backup of the database and incremental backup of the changes. All the transactions are logged from the last backup taken for the database.

2. **Bulk logged Recovery model:** This model takes the logging and backup of bulk data records the size of bulk records are kept to minimum, as it does not take the full logging and backup of the data record so there is need to enhance the performance the database can be recovered from the point of failure by restoring it with the bulk transaction log file backup.
3. **Simple recovery model:** This model is used for full backup but the incremental changes are not logged and by using this model the database is recovered from the recent backup.

Practice Questions

1. Explain Data Recovery process in detail.
2. Explain three-tier architecture.
3. What is Query Processing ? Explain in detail.
4. Explain Power Awaring Computing.
5. Explain the database transaction models and the ACID rules.
6. What are the advantages of hoarding the data at the mobile device.
7. What are the hoarding techniques and explain in detail.

Chapter 6...

PLATFORM/OPERATING SYSTEMS FOR APPLICATION DEVELOPMENT

6.1 Introduction
6.2 Programming for the Palm OS
    6.2.1 Palm OS Architecture
    6.2.2 Application Development
6.3 Windows CE
    6.3.1 Windows CE Architecture
6.4 Embedded Linux
6.5 J2ME
    6.5.1 Introduction to Java2 Micro Edition (J2ME)
    6.5.2 Connected Device Configuration
    6.5.3 CLDC Configuration
    6.5.4 Latest in J2ME
6.6 Symbian
    6.6.1 Features
    6.6.2 Application Development
    6.6.3 Symbian Kernel
- Practice Question

6.1 Introduction

There is a wide and rapid growth observed in the field of mobile communication.

In early days, mobile phones have several groups such as phones, pagers, Personal Digital Assistants (PDAs). Initially each group was having the fixed assignment of the task such as phones offers calling, pagers are used for text messaging and PDA's are mentioned for maintaining contacts, calendars, events and notes.

- On rapid evolution Nokia introduces NOKIA 9000 as all-in-one communicator in 1996.
- PDA's role replaced by not only maintaining contacts, calendars, events but also it supports for multimedia messages. As from Fig. 6.1 (b) PDA has evolution from 1970 to till date and they are changed into mobile phones.

1983	1995	2001	2002	2007 onwards
Circuit based analog systems	Digital circuit switched systems	Digital systems	High capacity digital systems, packet switched networks	Ultra broadband, Internet access, seamless roaming and ubiquitous net access, digital convergence
800-900 MHz bandwidth	1800-1900 MHz, 800 = 900 MHz Data 10 Kbps	1800-1900 MHz Data 56.6 Kbps	Data 144 Kbps 2 mbps	
AMPS NMT TACS.	GSM 2G TDMA CDMA PDC	GPRS CDMA	WCDMA UTRA TDD	Data rate upto 100 Mbps
Voice-only	Simple data access, SMS, email, wap	Multimedia, MMS fax	Web browsing capabilities	IMS, HSPA+, LTE Advanced, Mobile WiMAX

(a) Evolution of cellular technology

Time	1970s-1987	1988-1992	1993	1994-1996	1997-1999	2000-2005	2005 onwards
Devices	Pison organizer	Grid Pad, Atari, Sharp	Message Pad, Zoomer, PenPad, Envoy	Palm, Marco, MagicLinc	Sharp, Palm VII	Nokia 9210, iPaq	Nokia E72, Nokia N97, Nokia N 900, Blackberry, Treo Pro, i-mate ULTIMATE 8502
Key features	Stand alone data organizer	Handwriting recognition	Telephony application	Synchronization	Wireless link	Personal organizer cum wireless data communicator	Could run almost all desktop applications while being connected to internet 24 × 7. Great multimedia capabilities.

(b) Evolution of PDA

Fig. 6.1

- To access, store and manipulate the data on mobile phones there is a need of applications to run on them. Programming with mobile phones is a tedious job. So we need some level of abstraction on hardware. This is called as device operating system.

- The mobile phone architecture is shown in Fig. 6.2, which constitutes of three layers application, operating system and hardware, operating system communicates and relates the functionalities of both remaining layers.
- There are many device operating systems such as Palm OS (C, C++) Symbian (C++, Java and Win CE) Pocket PC (VB, embedded VC).

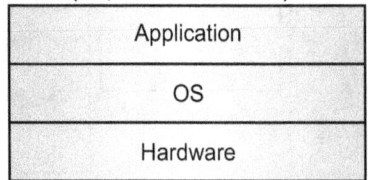

Fig. 6.2: Mobile phone architecture

6.2 Programming for the Palm OS (April 2015)

Palm OS license decide which applications are included on their Palm OS devices. License can also customize the applications.

History:
- The first release was near about 1994.
- In the year 1996, Palm Inc. developed a palm operating system for the Personal Digital Assistance (PDA) it is developed for easy implementation on touch screen based Graphical User Interface (GUI). It has the basic applications for personal information management. But several later versions are upgraded to be used in smart phones.
- In 1996, U.S. Robotics supported the OS and released the next version i.e. Palm Pilot 1000. Then the company is takeover by Com3 and released the third version Palm Pilot III in 1998. The device is doubled with RAM, infrared supported, character recognition algorithms are enhanced. The next to that Palm OS 3.0 has added more fonts and stylish design.
- The year 2000 begins with a competition as Win CE entered market, company releases next versions of OS as Palm OS 4.0. It supports secure flash card displays, new batteries with longer life and color display.
- Company introduces Palm one device and Palm source which is working on licensing the Palm OS. As a result, Palm OS 6.0 (cobalt) are emphasizes more on wireless capabilities, built-in camera, integrated keyboard, longer battery life.
- The success of any OS is the environment that supports application to be run. Palm OS serving at its best and facing the competition with new Web OS Symbian in 2004. Palm OS overcomes with spread sheets, documents presentations, business tools like CRM, messaging application like e-mail, SMS, EMS, instant messengers etc.

- The later versions of palm OS are named as Garnet OS by ACCESS. In the year 2007 access introduced the successor of garnet OS as Access Linux Platform and in 2009 the main license of palm OS ,Palm Inc. switched from palm OS to Web Os for the upcoming devices.
- Jeff Hawkins designed Palm OS by considering the feedback from the previous product zoomed. He has drawn three principles.

(i) Handwriting recognition should be simplified to hieroglyphics.
(ii) Pocket fit handheld device.
(iii) Cradle to synchronize data with a PC.

- Companies using Palm OS for mobile phones are Samsung, SONY, Lenovo, IBM etc. and Palm OS cell phones range.

The key features of the current Palm OS Garnet are:

- It is a simple single tasking environment which allows full screen applications with basic and common Graphical User Interface (GUI).
- The devices have monochrome or color screens with resolution up to 480X320 pixels.
- It enables the environment for handwriting recognition input system (Graffiti 2).
- HotSync technology for data synchronization with desktop computers.
- It has Sound playback and record capabilities.
- Device can be locked by password, arbitrary application records can be made private TCP/IP network access, Serial port/USB, Infrared, Bluetooth and Wi-Fi connections.
- Expandable memory card support.
- It defined standard data format for personal information management applications to store calendar, address, and task and note entries, which are accessible by third-party applications.
- The version history given below enlist the details of different licensed versions of Palm source/ACCESS. All the manufacturers of the devices are free to enhance different features of the OS in their devices and even add new features to it.

Palm OS 1.0

This is the original version of Palm OS on the pilot 1000 and 5000.

- It has personal information management features such as address, date book, memo pad and to do list .it is enhanced with the calculator and security tool.
- It specifically does not differentiate between RAM and file system storage.
- Applications are: Installed directly into RAM,
  - File system is not supported,
  - Operation system depends on RAM refresh cycles to keep it memory.

- 160 × 160 monochrome output display is supported by this OS. The system also supports the data synchronization to another PC via its HotSync technology. It also has virtual keyboard for handwriting recognition.

Palm OS 2.0

On March 10, 1997 palm OS 2.0 version was introduced. For palm pilot Personal and professional versions. This version adds TCP/IP network HotSync and displays the backlight support.

- It is enhanced with two new applications Mail and Expenses and it upgraded with Personal Information management application.

Palm OS 3.0

On March 9, 1998 palm OS 3.0 was introduced with Palm III series. This version adds IrDA infrared and enhanced font support to it. This was upgraded with PIM application and an application launcher.

- The minor new feature network HotSync upgraded to palm OS 3.1 .It was introduced with the Palm IIIX and Palm V.
- Palm OS 3.2 adds Web Clipping support, which brought the web contents to a small PDA screen.
- Palm OS 3.3 adds faster HotSync speeds and the ability to do infrared HotSync. It was introduced with Palm VX organizer.
- Palm OS 3.5 was the first version which has native 8 bit color support the datebook application is supported by the release of this version on Palm IIIC.

Palm OS 4.0

Palm OS 4.0 was released with the new Palm m500 series on March 19, 2001. This was added with standard interface for external file system access. Application code and data need to be loaded into the device's RAM, similar to desktop operating system. Universal connector with USB is supported in this version. To coordinate with the different application, attention manager was introduced in Palm OS 4.0.

- It enhanced with sound LED blinking or vibration to get the user's attention.16 bit color screens and different time zones are also supported. It was upgraded with the security and UI enhancements.
- Palm Os 4.1 was introduced with the launch of the Palm i705 it was considered as bug fix release.
- Palm OS 4.2 was developed specifically to target the Chinese market therefore it was named as simplified Chinese edition. The co release was Palm OS 5.3
- In June 2002 the Palm subsidiary Palm Source introduces palm OS 5 which implemented on the Plam Tungsten T. It was the first version to support ARM devices, with the support of dragon ball application through the Palm Application Compatibility Environments (PACE) emulator.

- In this version palm OS was enhanced for multimedia features. High density screens 320X320 are supported together with a full digital sound playback and records API. Palm OS has its separate Bluetooth tack which is added together to an IEEE 802.Mb Wi-Fi stack.
- Secure network connections over SSI are supported.
- For palm OS 5, Palm Source developed and licensed a web browser called palm source, web browser which is based on ACCESS net front 3.0 browsers.
- Palm OS 5.2 is a bug fix release, it was first implemented on Samsung SGH-i500. It provides the support to the 480X320 resolution screens. Which has new handwriting input system called graffiti 2.

Palm OS5

Palm OS 5.3 was simplified Chinese Edition which provides full simplified Chinese support. It adds support to the QVGA resolution and a standard API. This version was introduced with Lenovo's P100 and P300 handhelds.

- Palm OS Garnet (5.4) provides a support for multiple screen resolutions ranging from 160X160 up to 480X320. It supports the Bluetooth libraries.
- Garnet OS 5.5 is the version developed by ACCESS this version run on Garnet VM (Virtual Machine). It is the core part of Access Linux Platform and also available in NOKIA Internet Tablets.

Palm OS Cobalt 6.0

Palm OS 6.0 was named as Cobalt which was introduced on February 10,2004. It was enhanced with modern operating system features to an embedded operating system based on a new kernel with multitasking and memory protection. Multimedia and graphic framework, new security features and an adjustment to PIM files was corporate with the Microsoft outlook.

- Palm Os Cobalt 6.1 presented standard communication libraries for telecommunication, Wi-Fi and Bluetooth connectivity.

6.2.1 Palm OS Architecture

Palm OS architecture consist of three main parts:
(i) Kernel, (ii) Memory, (iii) System Manager.

6.2.1.1 Kernel

Kernel is the most important part of Palm OS. Kernel interface through the hardware abstraction layer. On the top kernel have application services such as messaging with e-mail, constructing notes.

- Each service is managed with the help of service manager. Service managers are such as event manager, graffiti manager, resource manager, sound manager. These are mapped in ROM.

- There are system libraries and independent third party libraries. The applications from top most layers use these libraries to perform the task.

Features of Kernel:

(1) Multitasking: It supports multitasking including semaphores.

(2) Interrupts: It traps the error and handles hardware interrupts.

(3) Time slicing and scheduling: Execution of several tasks should be done according to time slices. It has three triggers:
  (i) Context switching
  (ii) Hardware interrupts
  (iii) Timer expiration.

6.2.1.2 Memory

- A Palm device has ROM and RAM. There is no hard disk. OS and other static data resides on ROM, new models uses flash ROM. Hence, OS needs an update. OS supports extended memory in the form of memory cards.
- Memory is divided into three heaps: Dynamic heap, storage heap and ROM heap. Each one of the heaps has following:
  (1) A header containing the unique heap ID, status flags, heap size.
  (2) A master pointer table i.e. functionally similar to page table and holds pointers at the beginning.
  (3) A variable size chunk.
  (4) Terminator indicating the end of the chunk.
  (5) Additional reserved space for global variables.

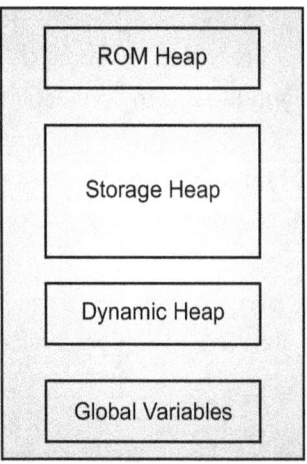

Fig. 6.3: Memory architecture

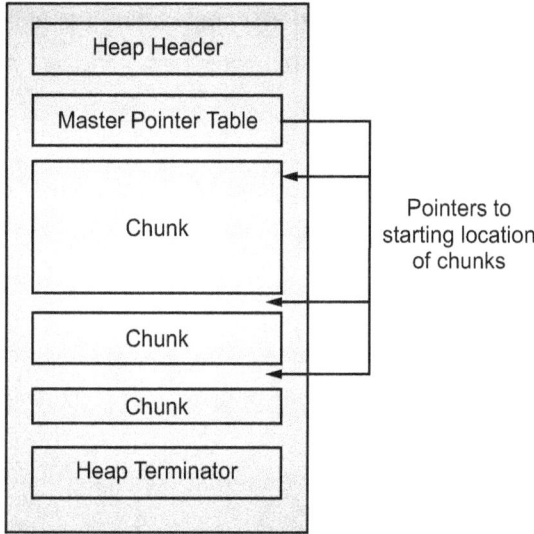

Fig. 6.4: Heap Architecture

- The uppermost part of heap is ROM, which holds operating system Kernel. Storage heap holds all the application its data, system patches, other persistent data in the system and dynamic heap contains OS's global variable and data objects, user interface, buffers, components, application stack.

Database

There are two types of database:

(1) Resource db: Stores all applications and free form data 200 trillion records.

(2) Record db: Stores user data upto 64 K records.

- Memory manager handles the logical and physical memory segmentation. Indexing is used to locate and retrieve the data.

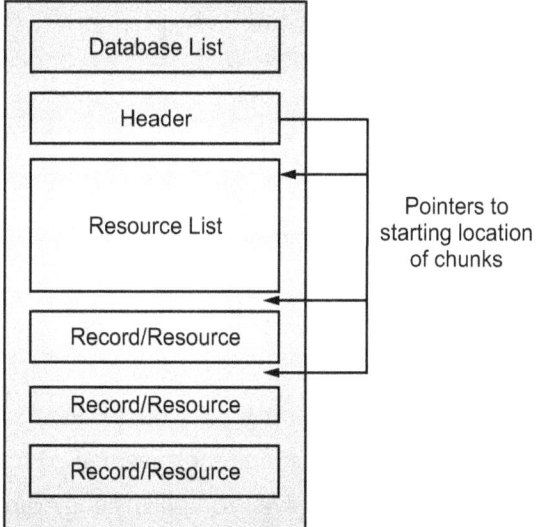

Fig. 6.5: Database Memory Architecture

It is also responsible for memory allocation, manipulating the main data structure.
- It provides programming APIS that ensures standard memory access across different versions of OS.

6.2.1.3 System Managers

The Palm OS is developed with programming language 'C'. Respective manager's accesses system service through programming.

(1) Event Manager: It is responsible for handling events or else it should enter sleep mode.

(2) Attention Manager: It handles all the alarms that set in system.

(3) Data and Resource Manager: Responsible for record and resource creation, modification and deletion.

(4) Exchange Manager: It handles all data that are shared in several Palm OS devices includes IR, TCP/IP and Bluetooth.

(5) Feature Manager: It manages memory of different features i.e. tasks.

(6) Graffiti Manager: All graffiti is handled via this manager.

(7) Memory Manager: It manages user data as well as application data.

(8) Sound Manager: It allows synchronous and asynchronous sound.

(9) Telephony Manager: It is added in version 4.0 and it manages telephony API.

(10) VFS Manager: It is added in 4.0.

6.2.2 Application Development

- Palm operating system is event-based. Some of events like button presses, menu selections, pen taps and so on.
- Actions are generated according to user and arranged in FIFO manner.

6.2.2.1 Event Loop

It shows flow chart for typical Palm event loop.

- Each application has its own event queue which receives events which are to be performed from operating system.

The event loop has following steps:

(1) Fetch an event from EvtGetEvent () queue

(2) An optional Preprocess Event.

(3) It will check the event is system event or not, if yes it calls SysHandleEvent. Else go to step (4).

(4) It will check for the event as user event, it calls MenuHandleEvent else calls (5).

(5) If the event loaded it will call ApplicationHandleEvent. If (5) fails go to (6).

(6) Call FrmDispatchEvent it sends the even to applications event handler for the active form.

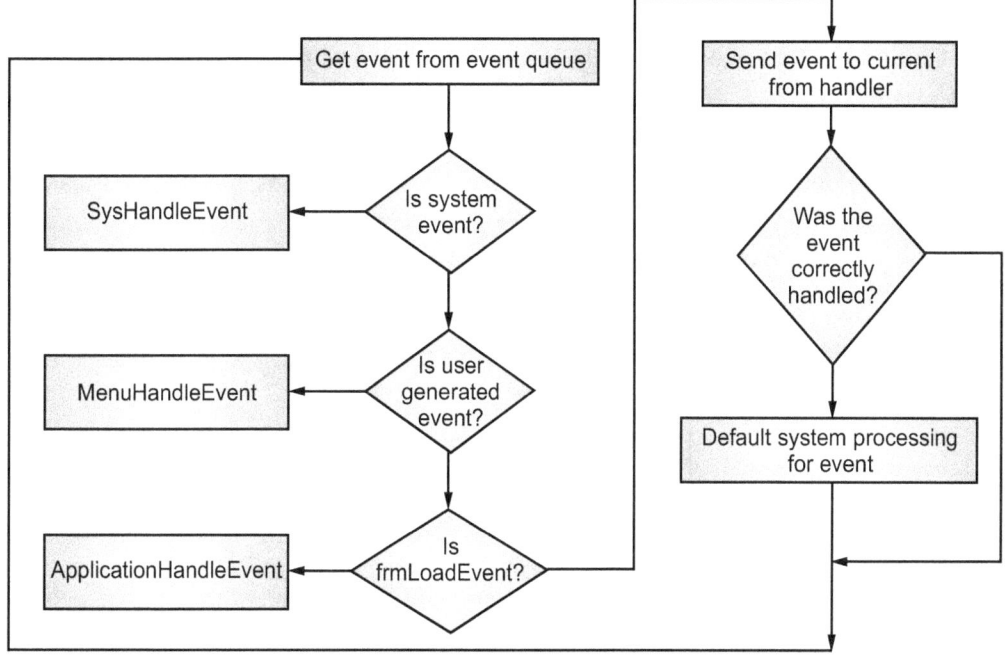

Fig. 6.6: Event Handling

The system handles events such as power on/power off, Graffiti® or Graffiti® 2 input, tapping input area icons or pressing buttons.

- MenuHandleEvent handles two types of events :
  (1) Bringus up the menu.
  (2) Puts the events that result from the command on the event queue.
- FrmDispatchEvent: sends the event to the application's event handler for the active form. If it processes and successful else will give a call FrmHandleEvent to provide system's default processing.
- ApplicationHandleEvent: Handles FrmLoadEvent it loads and activates application form resources and sets event Handler for the active form.

Standard Palm OS Applications

The following are standard PIM applications: (1) "Address", (2) "Date Book", (3) "Memo Pad" and (4) "ToDos" which are replaced by their improved counterparts "Contacts", "Calendar" "Memos" and "Tasks".

Following are some of the applications of palm OS:

1. Contact:

The Palm's Address program stores contact information. Entries are displayed and sorted in last name, first name order (this can be changed only to Company, Last Name order).

There are five slots for phone or e-mail, each of which may be designated Work, Home, Fax, Other, E-mail, Main, Pager or Mobile (the slot designations cannot be changed).

The newer Contacts app adds the following features: several addresses, nine new fields: Website, Birthday, More phone numbers, Instant Messaging with quick connects etc..

2. Calculator:

Calc turns the Palm into a standard 4-function pocket calculator with three shades of purple and blue buttons contrasting with the two red clear buttons. It supports square root and percent keys and has one memory.

It also has an option to display a running history of the calculations, much like the paper-tape calculators that were once common.

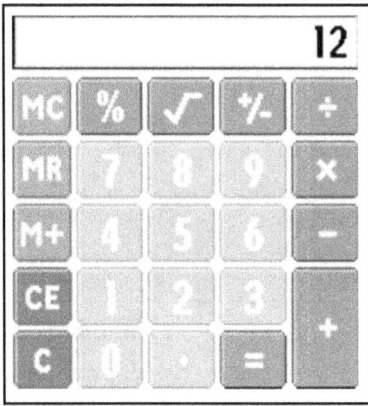

Fig. 6.7: Calculator Palm OS 4.1

3. Date Book:

Date Book shows a daily or weekly schedule, or a simple monthly view. The daily schedule has one line per hour, between user-selected begin and end times. Clicking on an empty line creates a new event. Empty lines are crowded out by actual events, whose start and stop times are shown by default bracketed in the left margin.

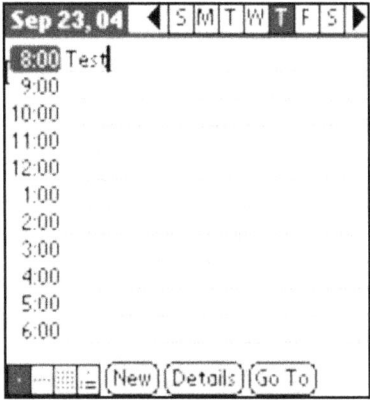

Fig. 6.8: Date Book

4. Calendar:

The Calendar app adds the following features: New Day view, use of categories for events, event location, and event can span midnight, event details, and birthdays as timeless events. It supports time zone designation for events, a feature lacking in some more recent competitors.

An event, or appointment, can be handled by an alarm, any number of minutes, hours or days before it begins. These alarms sound even when the unit is switched off.

Appointments can occur in a specified number of days, weeks, months or years and can contain notes.

5. Expense Tracker:

Expense tracks common business expenses. No totals are calculated on the Palm. The user must sync with a host computer and view the expense data in a worksheet (templates for Microsoft Excel are supplied).

- HotSync integrates with the user's PC. Usually activated by a press of the physical HotSync button on the Palm's cradle (a dock station), this application communicates with various conduits on the desktop PC to install software, backup databases, or merge changes made on the PC or the handheld to both devices. It can communicate with the PC through a physical connection (USB on newer models; although drivers for Windows x64 based platforms are still unavailable, 32 bit editions work well), Bluetooth or IrDA wireless connections, and direct network connections on devices with networking capability.

Fig. 6.9: HotSync

6.3 Windows CE

Microsoft Windows CE is an operating system developed by Microsoft for embedded systems. Windows CE is a distinct operating system and kernel, it is a trimmed version of windows Embedded Standard which is an NT based version of desktop Microsoft Windows.

- The current version of Windows Embedded compact supports Intel x86 which is compatible with ARM processors with Board Support Packages (BSP) directly.

- All windows mobile was based on windows CE kernel and it was implemented as a Pocket PC 2000 operating system Microsoft windows API appears same as their desktop version of windows. Third parties also can develop the applications for the mobile without any restrictions. The applications are available in Windows marketplace for mobile.

Windows CE

Windows CE operating system is developed from scratch and it ranges from smaller handled devices to PDA and pocket PCs. It categorizes the devices as handheld device and embedded device.

Different types of windows CE are mentioned below:

(1) Windows mobile for Pocket PC: It is a miniature of a personal computer. This version is used in pocket PC which is developed by Microsoft with windows CE 5.2 Kernel. It has basic windows APIS and it enables applications to run for small devices by using user interface, application size and corresponding features set. It enables user to store and retrieve e-mail, contacts, and appointments, play media files, games, exchange of data, browse the web and so on.

(2) Windows CE.NET: Windows CE.NET and Windows XP are embedded belong to the Microsoft family of embedded OS. It combines advanced real time OS with tools that grows rapidly. It is basically embedded in devices such as digital camera, voice over internet service and so on.

(3) Windows for Mobile Phones: This OS is categorizes into pocket PC and smart phones. We have seen PDA's are combined with phone features whereas smart phones are phone combined with PDA features.

Brief History of Versions of Windows CE:

Version	Changes
1.0	Released in Nov., 1996 "Alder" * Handheld PC.
2.0	Released in Sep., 1997 "Birch" * Palm sized PC 32-bit color screen SSL 2.0 and SSL 3.0 * Real time task scheduling.
3.0	Released in June 2000 "Cedar" * Pocket PC 2000 * Priority levels increased from 8 to 256. * Object store was increased from 65,536 to 4, 19 million allowed objects.
4.X	Released in January 2002 "Talisker" * Bluetooth support * TLS (SSL 3.1)
5.X	Released in August 2004 "Mccallan" * Automatic report of bug * Remote desktop protocol support * Direct draw for 2D graphics and Direct show for camera.
6.0	Released in September 2006 :Yamazaki: * Process address space from 32 MB to 1 GB * Number of processes has been increased * User mode and Kernel mode are possible * System call performance improved.

1. The research projects were began on portable devices by Microsoft in the year 1990.Windows CE official name given to this research project in 1992.In initial stage the operating system and user interface were separated .

Windows CE is based on previous code of Windows 95 and "win pad", this was the team working on user interface.

2. During development of Win Pad a separate team worked on a project called Pulsar; designed to be a mobile communications version of Win Pad, described as a "pager on Steroids"

3. Windows CE works on any device with minimum storing capacity. Kernel may run under a megabyte of memory. It is considered as a real time operating system, with deterministic interrupt latency. The working depends on thread which helps to simplify the interface and improves the execution time.

4. In Windows CE, CE stands for Consumer Electronics or Compact Edition. Also Microsoft defines the meaning of including CE that is the system is "Compact, Connectable, Compatible, Companion, and Efficient. "The first version is known as Pegasus which has windows GUI and many Microsoft applications, which were later trimmed down for minimal storage, memory and speed of palmtops.

5. The windows CE is different from other Microsoft operating system because it is more compatible with the hardware in which it is installed .source code was offered well in advance to adjust with the hardware devices to many vendors.

6.3.1 Windows CE Architecture

Windows CE is a layered architecture. Hardware layer is the bottom most layer of architecture. Next layer to that is OEM layer followed by the OS. At the top of this stack is the application layer, which interacts with the user.

6.3.1.1 OEM Layer

This layer helps windows CE based OS to run on a new hardware platform.

- This layer acts as an interface in between hardware of the device and windows CE Kernel.
- It provides a path to operating system communicate with target device and includes a code to handle interrupts, timers generic IOCTLs (I/O control codes).
- Different hardware interacts with the Kernel through respective device drivers.
- Boot loader which resides in a non-volatile memory required to boot the device. The updates to boot loader are handled by it and it provides user a menu to set the configuration.

6.3.1.2 Operating System Layer

Operating system layer has all softwares supplied by Microsoft. Components make operating system to be compact in size using minimum ROM and RAM.

The main component is Kernel.

(1) Kernel:

Kernel in Windows CE is represented by coredll.dll

Window CE is responsible for memory management, process management, and file management. It also handles virtual memory, scheduling, multitasking, multithreading, exception handling, graphics etc.

- Windows CE occupies 4 GB of space in 32-bit machine. 2 GB of memory is used by operating system itself, which includes hardware, object store and ROM, the bottom 2 GB address space is used for processes and application shared space.

Other components are listed below:

(1) Graphic windowing and Event System (GWES): It is the graphical user interface which managers user input/output by providing controls, menus, dialog boxes and resources for devices that requires a graphical display.

(2) Device manager: Device manager are loaded and used according to the need in Windows CE operating system.

It provides functions like:

(a) Loads drivers by reading and updating register keys.

(b) Uploads drivers when a device no longer needs them.

(c) Manages device interfaces and its notification.

(d) Manages resources relevant to device drivers such as I/P space and interrupt requests.

(3) Windows CE Storage:

Storage in Windows CE is managed with the help of registry, file system, object store and databases.

- Object store is only available in Windows CE.
- These storage are RAM-based so it is kept alive by using internal battery of the device.

(4) Registry: Coredll.dll is a registry and it is managed by DLL. It also includes coredll.lib library file to it.

(5) File System: File system is known for persistent storage. In Windows CE, it is RAM based, all drives are under the root directory. Different API's are used to handle file system.

(6) Object Store: This is the unique component to Windows CE, which acts as a database and stores PIM (Personal Information Manager).

It performs following tasks:

(i) Mounting of DB volume.

(ii) To create or open existing database by calling functions ceCreateDatabase () and CeOpenDatabase ().

(iii) Read or write a record ceSeekDatabase() and ceReadRecordPropsEx() for reading a record. CeWriteDatabasePropsEX() for writing a record.

(7) Database: These are database that are based on ADO (Active Data Object) technology. ADO is a middleware and offers a complete datastore abstraction. The ADO CE version is used for Windows CE. It accesses SQL data store, non SQL data store, and mainframe and legacy data.

6.3.1.3 Communication Services and Networking

This layer includes components that are responsible for accessing media.

- The communication is performed by using serial port and infrared. There is a support of internet and remote access.
- It connects Local Area Network using Ethernet and WiFi wireless LAN.
- Windows CE supports voice, SMS and other telephony services.
- Communication hardware and data protocols are mentioned below:
  (1) Serial I/P support
  (2) RAS
  (3) TCP/IP
  (4) LAN
  (5) Wireless services for Windows CE
  (6) Telephony API (TAPI)

6.3.1.4 Application Layer

This is the last layer of Windows CE. It includes the applications developed by OEM or developed by third parties.

- The development environment of Window CE is built using desktop environment and it is tested through simulator.
- Window CE OS can be developed by using Windows 2000, Visual C++ or VB toolkit.

6.4 Embedded Linux

It is an embedded computer system such as mobile phones, Personal Digital Assistance (PDA), Media palyers, set top boxes other consumer electronics devices, networking equipment machine control and industrial automation navigation equipment.

History:

- Linux has been ported a variety of CPUs which are not primarily used as the processor of a desktop or server computer. All of the embedded Linux-based systems contain Linux as their kernel.
- Due to its low cost and end of customization, Linux has all the devices like PDAs, TOmTOmm GPS navigation devices, residential gateways and smart phones. The Motorola exz series, theOpenMoKo handsets, the Nokia N900 and Nokia N9 cell phones were all using the Linux Kernel.
- On June 4 2012, the website "LinuxForDevices" has many devices with an embedded Linux as the operating system. It also facilitates to machine control system, Industrial automation, and medical instruments.

Different types of Embedded Linux Systems:
- There are different types of Linux systems. Linux can be safely run on any computer that executes code. The ELKS (Embedded Linux Kernel Subset) project plans to put Linux onto a Palm Pilot.

Embedded Linux versions are mentioned below:
1. **ETLinux:** A complete Linux distribution designed to run on small industrial computers, especially C/104 modules.
2. **LEM** - a small (<8 MB) multi-user, networked Linux version that runs on 386s.
3. **LOAF** -- "Linux on a Floppy" distribution that runs on 386s.
4. **UClinux** - Linux for systems without MMUs. Currently supports Motorola 68K, MCF5206, and MFC5207 Cold Fire microprocessors.
5. **uLinux** -- tiny Linux distribution that runs on 386s.
6. **ThinLinux** -- a minimized Linux distribution for dedicated camera servers, X-10 controllers, MP3. Players and other such embedded applications.

Software and Hardware requirements:

1. Several User-interface tools and programs enhance the versatility of the Linux basic Kernel. Linux has microkernel with memory management, task switching and timer services to a full blown server, supporting a complete range of file system and network services.

A minimal Embedded Linux system needs three essential elements:
1. A boot utility
2. The Linux micro-kernel, composed of memory management, process management and timing services
3. An initialization process

Additional requirements are listed below:
1. A file system (perhaps in ROM or RAM)
2. TCP/IP network stack
3. A disk for storing semi-transient data and swap capability
4. A 32-bit internal CPU (required by all complete Linux systems)

1. Linux Kernel requires about 1 MB memory and Micro Kernel consumes a little of this memory, only 100 k on a Pentium CPU, it includes the virtual memory and core operating system functions. A Linux system can actually be adapted to work with as little as 256 KB ROM and 512 KB RAM. So it's a lightweight operating system to bring to the embedded market.

2. The benefit of using Linux over the Real Time Operating System (RTOS) is the Linux development community tends to support new IP and other protocols faster than RTOS vendors do.

3. Networking and file systems are layered on top of the microkernel and drivers and other functions are included to the kernel, this provides a highly modular building block for constructing custom embedded system.

4. Linux is also well-suited for embedded Internet devices, because of its support of multiprocessor systems, which lends its scalability.

6.5 J2ME

J2ME is a Java technology available for mobile applications.

Java Platform Micro Edition is a Java Platform designed for embedded systems. The target for J2ME system was ranging from mobile phones to set top box. Sun provides a reference implementation of the specification, but it doesn't provide binary implementation of its Java ME runtime environments.

- Procedural and object oriented approach has deficiency regarding its platform. Java has overcome this problem as it is a cross between compiled and interpreted language. It first compiles and then generates intermediate codes called byte codes which are interpreted by virtual machine in second step.
- It is the four E's "Everyone, Everything, Everywhere, Every time". Pull and push services can be performed whenever it is required.

There are two types of mobile application:

(i) **Device Resident:** It utilizes device resources and do not interact with the application outside. e.g. Games.

(ii) **Network-Enabled Applications:**
- Revolution of Java starts with Java till Java2 released in between 1992 to 1998.
- In 1999, Sun announces J2EE, J2SE, J2ME as J2EE Java 2 Enterprise Edition for server side, JVM powered J2SE to virtual machine and J2ME for handheld devices and set-top boxes.
- After that consecutive evolution of Java is Sun community process or JCP is established to define functionality of Java. It specified technical Java specifications.

6.5.1 Introduction to Java2 Micro Edition (J2ME)

There was a wide range of devices that needs to have computing environment as they were having different configuration in terms of resources and capabilities. Examples of wide range of devices are as follows. The low-end PDA offers offline data storage sync with serial cable with PC, microcomputers, mobile phones and set-top boxes.

- J2ME should define the platform which supports all these devices, but that was a challenge in front of J2ME developers. They introduces configuration as follows to resolve this gap up to some extent.

Configuration defines minimum capabilities across a range of devices:

(i) A JVM (Java Virtual Machine).

(ii) A set of core Java runtime classes.

(iii) A set of supported API (Application Programming Interface).

- J2ME defines two configuration and these are applied to two different devices:

(i) The devices which are having excellent UI facilities and which needs higher computing power and should be always connected, for these devices there is defined connected device configuration (CDC) is given e.g. Set-top boxes, internet TVs, internet enabled screen phones, car entertainment/navigation system.

(ii) The second category of devices is personal mobile information devices. These are implemented using Connected Limited Device Configuration (CLDC) e.g. mobile phones, two-way pager, PDAs.

- A 'profile' concept configuration little further as applying configuration is broad and still incomplete. Profiles make libraries available to create applications. It utilizes J2ME configuration.
- Profile contains event handling input functions, user interface, APIs, application lifecycle management. It makes possible interoperability in between all the devices.

6.5.2 Connected Device Configuration (CDC)

CDC is applied to high-end devices with memory of 2 MB or more (at least 512 K for runtime environment plus another 256 K for applications) providing connectivity through some UI.

- CDC is a superset of the connected limited device configurations.
- CDC specification:
- Full-featured JVM, called CUM
- A subset of J2SE 1.3 classes
- APIs introduced in CDLC: It should form generic connection framework.

CDC defines three profiles:

(1) Foundation Profile: It does not support user interface whereas it provides stronger support to other profiles. It has following requirements. Memory minimum 1024 KB ROM and 512 KB RAM. Stable network connectivity.

(2) Personal Basis Profile: J2ME personal basis profile is modified from personal Java application environment to fit into J2ME environment.

(3) J2ME RMI Profile: It provides support for RMI applications. It uses TCP/IP as the connection protocol.

6.5.3 CLDC Configuration

Connected Limited Device Configuration (CLDC) is applied to low-end, battery operated device which has specification as follows:

- A minimum of 128 to 512 KB for platform.
- 16-bit or 32-bit low-end processor.
- A low bandwidth network with intermediate connectivity.
- It uses KVM, which is optimized than JVM. It includes basic classes from Java, package, java.lang, java.io, java.util
- CDC and CLDC configuration can not be defined on single platform, CLDC is a subset of CDC.

CLDC Configuration has Two Profiles:

(1) MIDP:

Mobile Information Device Profile which is very popular and used in wide range of devices.

- It provides cluster of downloading applications and services.
- It is applicable to devices having following capabilities.
- A minimum of 512 KB for the platform.
- Intermittent connectivity to some type of wireless network.
- Limited UI.
- Some kind of input mechanism.

(2) PDAP:

Personal Digital Assistant Profile. It is released for PDA market. It provides UI and user interface and data storage APIs for devices with following device capabilities:

- Minimum 1000 KB for platform.
- Battery powered, low power devices.
- Good UI capabilities with resolution 128×128 pixels.
- An intermittent input mechanism in the form of 'T' keypad.

6.5.4 Latest in J2ME

J2ME offers JavaME 3.0 SDK, which is highly integral with third party application and framework.

- One of the recent capability of J2ME is the integration with Android.
- Availability of JavaFX application platform is a recent add-on. This provides to access capabilities of file system, camera GPS, Bluetooth of handheld devices using JavaFX script.

6.6 Symbian

Symbian is a mobile operating system (OS) and computing platform designed for smart phones and currently maintained by Accenture. It was originally developed by Symbian Ltd. as a descendent of Psion's EPOC.

- Symbian is an open source platform developed by symbian foundation in the year 2009. Samsung, Motorola, Sony Ericsson and Nokia mobile brands uses this operating system.
- Until the end of 2010 symbian was the popular among the smartphones after it is overtaken by Android.
- In the year 2002 Symbian rose that is used with S60 (Series 60) platform developed by Nokia was released are at the same time UIQ another symbian platform released, both were ran in parallel, according to observation these two platforms were not compatible with each other.
- Different manufacturers of mobile phones developed different software platforms such as Series 60(Nokia, Samsung and LG), UIQ (iccson and Motorola) and MQAP (Japanese Fujitsu, sharp).
- The third party applications were introduced into the operating system which restricts the Foundation from releasing the full source code under the norm EPL (Eclipse Public License). The code was published under the Symbian Foundation License (SFL) and accesses the full source code which was limited to its member companies.
- Symbian 3 was released in 2010 which is the successor of S60 and UIQ.first used in Nokia N8. In May 2011 symbian Anna was officially announced followed by Nokia Belle.
- In November 2010, due to lack of support of members of Samsung and Sony Ericsson, Nokia announces it would take over the stewardship of the symbain platform. On February 2011, Nokia announced the partnership with Microsoft and it would be adopted the windows phone market.
- Due to changes in Global economic and market conditions, the use of symbian as a platform was rapidly dropped in June 2011 research marks that only 39% of global market was used by Symbian mobile developers.
- On 11 Feb 2011, Microsoft Windows Phone OS was declared as primary smart phones platform by Nokia. Later times On June 22, 2011 nokia made an agreement with Accenture for outsourcing the symbian operating system for their smart phones.

- Accenture will provide Symbian based operating system and support services to Nokia through 2016. Nokia 808 Pure View is officially the last symbian smart phones.

By the year 2011, nokia collaborated with a small group preselected partners and ceased to open source of the system.

6.6.1 Features

User Interface:

1. Series 60 (S60) was designed to be manipulated by a keyboard like interface metaphor such as 15 key augmented telephone keypad. Symbian had a native toolkit for its inception known as AVKON.
2. Symbian 3 includes the Qt framework, which is considered as user interface toolkit for new applications.
3. Symbian 4 introduces a new GUI library frame work which was specifically designed for touch based interface which is known as "UI Extensions for Mobile" (Orbit) which was developed on the basis of QT widgets. But due to some circumstances Nokia announced that UIEMO(orbit) has been cancelled.
4. Currently the developers uses QT Quick with QML, which is high declarative UI and scripting network which creates a descent touch screen user interface.
5. Browser: Symbian 3 have a built in webkit based browser. It was known as a first webkit user in June 2005. Before that opera mobile browser was the default browser. Nokia released a new browser with the release of Symbian Anna with improved speed and an improved user interface
6. Multiple Language Support: On demand of Global economic and Market conditions Symbian was stand by a strong localizing support for the manufacturers and third party applications. Current Symbian release (Symbian Belle) has support for 48 languages, which was made available by Nokia device packages.

6.6.2 Application Development

- In the year 2010 symbian started using standard C++ with Qt as the main SDK which also supports Symbian series S60 Symbian series S60 is a fifth edition release it also supports Windows, Linux and MAC OS.
- Application development can be done using python, Adobe Lite or Java ME.
- A phone simulator allows testing of Qt apps. Apps compiled for the simulator are compiled to native code for the development platform, rather than having to be emulated. Application development can either use C++ or QML.
- Symbian OS has C++ version and Integrated Development Environments (IDE) as the native application development environments. Before the release of the Qt SDK, this

was the standard development environment. There were multiple platforms based on Symbian OS that provides Software Development Kits (SDKs) for application developers wishing to target Symbian OS devices, the main ones being UIQ and S60 series.

- Symbian OS 9 and the Symbian platform uses a new Application Binary Interface (ABI) and needed a different compiler. Symbian C++ requires the use of special techniques such as descriptors, active objects and the cleanup stack. This can make even relatively simple programs initially harder to implement than in other environments.
- The widgets can be created by using Web Run Time (WRT) portable application .it is an extension to the S60 webKit based browser that allows launching multiple browser instances.

Other Languages:
- All Symbian devices are able to run the programs for other languages such as Python, Java ME, Flash Lite,Ruby,.NET,Web Runtime(WRT) and standard C/C++.Ns basic helps the Visual Basic developers to develop the apps for S60 Edition and UIQ 3 devices.
- Symbian OS development is also possible with Linux and Mac OSX using the tools and methods which is published in source code of the system. Java ME application for Symbian OS are developed using standard techniques and tools such as Sun Java Wireless Toolkit.
- Symbian 7 OS was build with the tools such as SuperWaba using Java.
- The deployment of the Symbian application into the targeted devices such as mobile phones can be done by packaging them in SIS files which are installed over via internet, via PC connect, Bluetooth or on memory card. Or other way out to have partnership with manufacturers and avail the software that runs on those devices.
- Symbian Operating system is subdivided into technology domains. Each domain has its own software packages. Symbian Foundation has the managers to manage the journey of each technology.
- A Package is categorized according to the technology domain and categorization depends upon the functionality of that package into an influence of the technology.
- Symbian Foundation strongly believes to form a technology groups to support the releases of Symbian. The Symbian System Model illustrates the scope of each of the technology domains across the platform packages.
- Packages are owned and maintained by a package owner that is who accepts the code contributions from the wider Symbian community.

6.6.3 Symbian Kernel

Symbian kernel supports a single core phone processor that executes all the user applications and signaling stack. It is very fast real time response processor. It has the micro kernel architecture containing minimum and basic functionalities and offers maximum robustness availability and performance.

- Nano kernel has supportive services such as scheduler, memory management and all device drivers. With supportive files and telephony. Operating system services layer has Base Service layer in which all the drivers are included

Design

Symbian operating system has the features as pre emptive multitasking and memory protection it is based on asynchronous server based events.

- Symbian Operating System has the following three design principles:
    1. The integrity and security of user data is paramount.
    2. User time must not be wasted.
    3. All resources are scarce.
- To follow these principles Symbian uses microkernel which has request and callback approach to services and it maintains separation between user interface and engine.
- The operating system is mounted on devices low power battery based devices and ROM based systems. Applications and the OS follow the object oriented design.
- The enhancement of operating system is done by using conservation of resources, it uses the programming idioms descriptors and clean up stack. All Symbian programs are event based the current central processing Unit is switched into a low power mode when applications are not running and handling any event. This is done by using active objects.

Latest in Symbian:

Being the popular mobile phone operating system and having the support for 2G, 2.5G and 3G technologies, symbian OS walls through various versions, latest one being symbian 9.5.

- Symbian OS includes symbian OS source code with documentation, documentation includes : (1) Tech view: It is GUI framework for testing OS. (2) Middleware components. (3) Symbian OS emulator supports prompt development and debugging of all symbian based OS.

Symbian 9.5:

It is the most recent symbian OS update with following mentioned features:

1. Support for OMA device management.
2. Improved memory management.
3. Support for WiFi and High Speed Downlink Packet Access (HSDPA).
4. Demand paging.
5. Various digital television format.
6. SQL support for handling database.

Practice Questions

1. Explain the architecture of palm OS.
2. Explain the architecture of Windows CE.
3. Explain the architecture of J2ME.
4. Explain in brief about LINUX operating system.
5. Write short notes on :
   (a) Application development of palm OS.
   (b) Latest in J2ME.
   (c) System Kernel.

Chapter 7...

ANDROID APPLICATION DEVELOPMENT

7.1 Overview of Android
    7.1.1 History
    7.1.2 Android Operating System
    7.1.3 User Interface of Android
    7.1.4 Memory Management
7.2 Devices Running Android
    7.2.1 Android device Supports Different Languages
    7.2.2 Android Devices Supports Different Screens
7.3 Why Develop for Android?
7.4 Android
    7.4.1 Features in Android
7.5 Android Architecture
    7.5.1 Linux Kernel
    7.5.2 Native Libraries
    7.5.3 Applications and Widgets
7.6 Software Development Kit
7.7 Creating Application and Activity
    7.7.1 Introducing the Application Manifest File
    7.7.2 Creating Resources
    7.7.3 Simple Values Strings, Colors, Dimensions
- Practice Questions

7.1 Overview of Android   (April 2015)

    Android is milestone and becomes leading operating system in today's era. Android is a Linux based operating system which is designed for touch screen mobile devices such as smart phones and tablet computers.

    Android is an open source operating system which is released by Google under the Apache license. This software system is open to freely modified and distributed by device manufacturers, wireless carriers and enthusiastic developers.

It is enhanced with the number of applications written by huge number of developers that is used to extend the functionality of devices which is written in Java Programming language. Currently there are more than 7000,000 apps available for android and all these apps are available to be downloaded from Google Play.

Following are the factors that are contributed towards making Android the world's widely spread smart phone platform.

1. It has overtaken the Symbian operating system in the year 2010 due to its customizable, low cost, lightweight operating behaviour.
2. It was developed from the scratch, so it operates suitably for televisions, games and digital cameras along with the targeted devices such as smart phones and tablets.
3. It inspires a large number of developers which enhances the existing applications with advanced features.
4. By 2013, the android's Global market led by Samsung mobiles was 64%. In July 2013 the Android was populated with 11,868 models of Android devices, huge number of screen sizes and eight OS versions simultaneously in use.
5. It is competing and almost leaded the smart phone wars. As of May 2013, 48 billion apps have been installed from the Google Play store and as of September 3, 2013, 1 billion Android devices have been activated.

7.1.1 History

- In the year 2003, Andy Rubin (co-founder of Danger), Rich Miner (co-founder of Wildfire Communications, Inc.) Nick Sears (once VP at T-Mobile), and Chris White (headed design and interface development at WebTV) founded an Android Inc. operating system.
- They started with the vision for developing a software system for digital cameras. As they realized the market for the system they were thinking was not big enough, so they change their direction of efforts towards the operating system for smart phones.
- At that time Symbian and windows mobile were used rapidly. By considering the rivals the founders were secretly reveling that they were working on an operating system for mobile phones.
- Running through the development android was taken over by Google on August 17, 2005. The key employees of Android Inc. Rubin, Miner and White, stayed at the company after the acquisition A team led by Rubin developed a mobile device platform powered by the Linux Kernel. Google published this platform to mobile device manufacturers and promised them of providing a flexible and upgraded user friendly system.

- Till the end of December 2006, Google tried best to get into the mobile phone markets, the sources like BBC and Wall Street Journal witnessed these efforts of Google to introduce their search and applications on mobile phones.
- In September 2007, Information Week covered the EValue Serve study and announced that Google had a several patent applications in the mobile telephony area.
- On November 5, 2007 Android reveals as it's a first product, a mobile device platform built on Linux Kernel Version 2.6 till that date the many organizations supported Google and comes together. Open handset Alliance, a consortium of technology companies including Google, device manufacturers such as HTC, Sony and Samsung wireless carriers such as Sprint Nextel and T mobile, and chipset makers such as Quacomm and Texas instruments were the organization involved in development of open standard for mobile phones. The first commercial device to run Android was HTC dream released on October 22, 2008.
- HTC collaborated with the Android to release the first Nexus series of devices in 2010, the series was upgraded from their to Nexus 4 and Nexus 10 tablet which is made by LG and Samsung respectively.
- On March 2013 Andy Rubin the founder of Android moved ahead from Google to handle their upcoming projects. He was replaced by Sundar Pichai who also continues his role as the Head of Google's Chrome division, which develops Chrome OS.
- Numerous updates have been seen in Android to improve the operating system, which was added with a new features and fixing the relative bugs of previous release. The major releases of the versions are named in an alphabetical order as desert or sugary treat. For example version 1.5 cupcake was followed by 1.6 Donut. The released version is 4.3 jelly Bean and version 4.4 Kit Kat was announced on September 3, 2013. Then latest release version is 5.0 lollipop and upcoming version is 6.0 Marshmallous

7.1.2 Android Operating System

Basically Android operating system is a combination of:
1. A free open source operating system for embedded devices
2. An open source development platform for creating applications
3. Devices, particularly mobile phones that run in the android operating system and the applications created for it.

- Android is made up of several necessary and interdependent parts which are listed below:

1. The two compatibility documents such as Compatibility Definition Document (CDD) and Compatibility Test suite (CTS). This describes the capabilities required to device to support software.

2. A Linux operating system that provides a low level interface with the hardware memory management and process control.
3. Open source Libraries for application development including SQLite, WebKit, OpenGL and a media manager.
4. A run time used to execute and host Android applications, including Dalvik Virtual Machine (DVM) and the core libraries that provide Android specific functionality.
5. An application framework that exposes system services to the application layer, including the window manager and location manager databases, Telephony and sensors.
6. A user interface framework used to host and launch applications.
7. A set of core pre installed applications.
8. A Software Development Kit (SDK) and to create applications, including the related tools, plug INS and documentation.

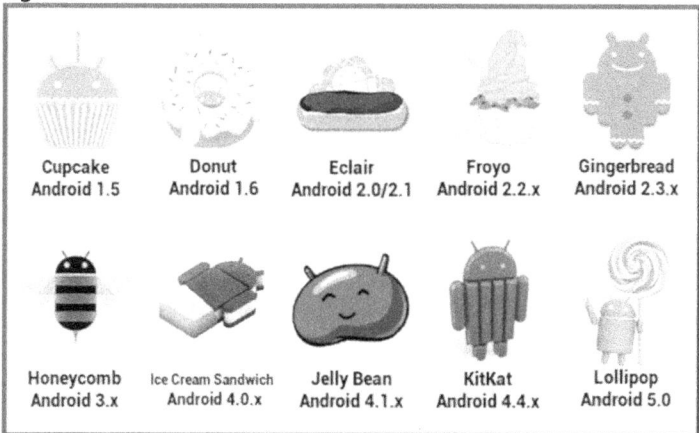

Fig. 7.1: Android operating systems versions

Versions of Android

Versions and Image	Release Date	Features
1.0 Android 1.0 (API level 1)	23 September 2008	1. Web browser to show, zoom and pan full HTML and XHTML web pages – multiple pages show as windows ("cards") 2. Camera support – however, this version lacked the option to change the camera's resolution, white balance, quality, etc. 3. Folders allowing the grouping of a number of application icons into a single folder icon on the Home screen. 4. Access to web email servers, supporting POP3, IMAP4, and SMTP. 5. Gmail synchronization with the Gmail application. 6. Google Contacts synchronization with the People application

		7. Android Market application downloads and updates through the Market application. 8. Google Calendar synchronization with the Calendar application. 9. Google Maps with Street View to view maps and satellite imagery, as well as find local business and obtain driving directions using. 10. Google Sync, allowing management of over-the-air synchronization of Gmail, People, and Calendar. 11. Google Search, allowing users to search the Internet and phone applications, contacts, calendar, etc. 12. Google Talk instant messaging. 13. Instant messaging, text messaging, and MMS. 14. Media Player, enabling management, importing, and playback of media files – however, this version lacked video and stereo Bluetooth support. 15. Notifications appear in the Status bar, with options to set ringtone, LED or vibration alerts. 16. Voice Dialer allows dialing and placing of phone calls without typing a name or number. 17. Wallpaper allows the user to set the background image or photo behind the Home screen icons and widgets. 18. YouTube video player. 19. Other applications include: Alarm Clock, Calculator, Dialer (Phone), Home screen (Launcher), Pictures (Gallery), and Settings. 20. Wi-Fi and Bluetooth support.
Android 1.1 (API level 2)	9 February 2009	1. Details and reviews available when a user searches for businesses on Maps. 2. Ability to save attachments in messages. 3. It gives added support for marquee in system layouts. 4. Longer in-call screen timeout default when using the speakerphone, plus ability to show/hide dial pad.
Android 1.5 Cupcake (API level 3)	30 April 2009	1. Integration of home screen widgets. 2. Support for folders on home screen. 3. Stereo Bluetooth support. 4. Copy/paste in web browser. 5. Video recording and playback.

Android 1.6 Donut (API level 4)	15 September 2009	1. Quick search box. 2. Updated interface for camera. 3. Cam recorder and Gallery. 4. Updated Google Play (Android Market). 5. Battery usage indicator. 67. Text-to-speech engine.
Android 2.0 Eclair (API level 5)	26 October 2009	1. Google Maps Navigator (beta). 2. Updated browser. 3. Support for multiple accounts. 4. Improved keyboard. 5. SMS search. 6. Exchange support.
Android 2.0.1 Eclair (API level 6)	3 December 2009	1. Minor API changes, bug fixes and framework behavioral changes.
Android 2.1 Eclair (API level 7)	12 January 2010	1. Minor amendments to the API and bug fixes.
Android 2.2–2.2.3 Froyo (API level 8)	20 May 2010	1. Support for Adobe Flash. 2. Portable hotspots. 3. Multiple keyboard languages. 4. Speed and performance improvements. 5. Enhanced Microsoft Exchange support
2.2.1	18 January 2011	1. Bug fixes, security updates and performance improvements.
2.2.2	22 January 2011	1. Minor bug fixes, including SMS routing issues that affected the Nexus One.
2.2.3	21 November 2011	1. Two security patches.
Android 2.3-2.3.2 (API level 9)	6 December 2010	1. Updated user interface design with increased simplicity and speed. 2. Enhanced copy/paste functionality, allowing users to select a word by press-hold, copy, and paste.
2.3.1 2.3.2	December 2010 January 2011	1. Improvements and bug fixes for the Google Nexus S.

Android 2.3.3–2.3.7 Gingerbread (API level 10)		1. Several improvements and API fixes.
2.3.3	9 February 2011	1. UI refinements. 2. NFC support. 3. Native support for SIP VOIP. 4. Faster/more intuitive text input. 5. Enhanced copy and paste
2.3.4	28 April 2011	1. Support for voice or video chat using Google Talk. 2. Switched the default encryption for SSL from AES256-SHA to RC4-MD5.
2.3.5	25 July 2011	1. Fixed Bluetooth bug on Samsung Galaxy S. 2. Improved Gmail application.
2.3.6	2 September 2011	1. Fixed a voice search bug.
2.3.7	21 September 2011	1. Google Wallet support for the Nexus S 4G.
Android 3.0 Honeycomb (API level 11)	22 February 2011	1. Revamped (holographic) UI designed specifically for tablets. 2. Action bar. 3. Improved multi-tasking. 4. Updated standard Android apps. 5. Battery usage indicator. 6. Copy/paste in web browser, 7. Redesigned keyboard
Android 3.1 Honeycomb (API level 12)	10 May 2011	1. UI refinements 2. Connectivity for USB accessories
Android 3.2 Honeycomb (API level 13)	15 July 2011	1. Increased ability of applications to access files on the SD card, e.g. for synchronization

3.2.1	20 September 2011	1. Update to Google Books
3.2.2	30 August 2011	1. Bug fixes and other minor improvements for the Motorola Xoom 4G
Android 4.0–4.0.2 Ice Cream Sandwich (API level 14)	19 October 2011	1. Improved multi-tasking. 2. Face unlocks. 3. Resizable widgets. 4. Android beam. 5. Enhanced email options. 6. Improved text and voice input. 7. Soft buttons can replace hard keys
4.0.1	21 October 2011	1. Fixed minor bugs for the Samsung Galaxy Nexus.
4.0.2	28 November 2011	1. Fixed minor bugs on the Verizon Galaxy Nexus, the US launch of which was later delayed until December 2011
Android 4.0.3–4.0.4 Ice Cream Sandwich (API level 15)	16 December 2011	1. Numerous bug fixes and optimizations
4.0.4	29 March 2012	1. Stability improvements 2. Smoother screen rotation 3. Better camera performance 4. Improved phone number recognition
Android 4.1 Jelly Bean (API level 16)	9 July 2012	1. Larger, rich, and actionable notifications. 2. Offline voice dictation. 3. Streamlined UI. 4. Performance improvements "Project Butter". 5. Smart widget placement. 6. Multi-user profiles for tablets (4.2). 7. Lock screen widgets (4.2). 8. Daydream (4.2). 9. OpenGL ES 3.0 (4.3). 10. Bluetooth Smart Ready (4.3). 11. Restricted user profiles for tablets (4.3)

4.1.1	23 July 2012	1. Fixed a bug on the Nexus 7 regarding the inability to change screen orientation in any application
4.1.2	9 October 2012	1. Lock/home screen rotation support for the Nexus 7 2. Bug fixes and performance enhancements 3. One-finger gestures to expand/collapse notifications
Android 4.2 Jelly Bean (API level 17)	13 November 2012	1. Lock screen improvements, including widget support and the ability to swipe directly to camera 2. Multiple user accounts (tablets only) 3. Support for wireless display (Miracast)
4.2.1	27 November 2012	1. Fixed a bug in the People application where December was not displayed on the date selector when adding an event to a contact.
4.2.2	11 February 2013	1. Fixed Bluetooth audio streaming bugs 2. New download notifications, which now shows the percentage and estimated time remaining for active application downloads.
Android 4.4 KitKat (API level 19)	31 October 2013	1. Refreshed interface with white elements instead of blue. 2. Ability for applications to trigger translucency in the navigation and status bars. 3. Web Views now based on Chromium engine (feature parity with Chrome for Android 30). 4. Applications can now use "immersive mode" to keep the navigation and status bars hidden while maintaining user interaction. 5. Optimizations for performance on devices with lower specifications, including zRAM support and "low RAM" device API.
Android 6 Marhs-mallow	2015	1. USB Type-C support 2. Fingerprint Authentication support 3. Better battery life with "deep sleep" 4. Permissions dashboard 5. Android Pay 6. Google Now improvements
Android 5.1.1 Lollipop	21 April 2015	1. Speed improvement 2. Bug fixes

Android 5.1 Lollipop	9 March 2015	1. Multiple SIM cards support. 2. Quick settings shortcuts to join Wi-Fi networks or control Bluetooth devices. 3. Lock protection if lost or stolen. 4. High Definition voice call. 5. Stability and performance enhancements.
Android 5.0.2 Lollipop	19 December 2014 Lollipop	Performance improvements and bug fixes.
Android 5.0.1 Lollipop	2 December 2014	Bug fixes, fix issues with video playback and password failures.
Android 5.0 Lollipop		1. New design (Material design). 2. Speed improvement. 3. Battery consumption improvement.

7.1.3 User Interface of Android

- The user interface of Android is based on direct manipulation using touch inputs these actions resembles to real world actions such as tapping, pinching, swiping etc. to manipulate the on screen objects, the device is also enriched with vibration capabilities which response with haptic feedback to a user.
- The internal hardware such as accelometer, proximity sensors are used by some of the application to respond with the additional user actions. E.g. adjusting screen from portrait to landscape and it depends upon how the device is oriented. It is also used in games.
- The home screen is made up of several pages which user swipes. The Android user can adjust the look of the display screens that is home screen which is customizable. The home screens are made up of Widgets, which are nothing but the app icons. The third party apps are available on Google Play.
- The home screen is available with the status bar that is pulled, which show the device information and its connectivity. This status bar also updates the new incoming emails are SMS text messages. In a way it does not interrupt the user in between the current scenario.

- **Applications**

Fig. 7.2: Play Store on the Nexus 4

- The third party applications are available in Google play or Amazon Appstore or also available by downloading and installing the applications APK files from a third party site.
- The users can browse, download and update the apps which are published by Google and third party developers these are pre installed on devices that comply with Google's compatible requirements. The app filters all the applications and displays those which are compatible with the user's device. The developers may restrict their applications in specific country or carriers.
- Some applications are paid and some are free of cost unwanted applications can be refunded within 15 minutes of time of download and the cost of application is added into the phone's monthly bill.
- As of September 2012, there were more than 6,75,000 apps available for Android, and the estimated number of applications downloaded from the play store was 25 billion.
- Applications are developed in the Java language using the Android Software Development Kit (SDK). It includes the development tools such as debugger, software libraries, a handset emulator based on QEMU, documentation, software libraries, and sample code.
- The officially supported Integrated Development Environment (IDE) is provided using the Android Development Tools (ADT) plug-in.
- Primarily Android is developed by Google in private and when it is ready to release in public platform it ran on selected devices only without any modification. The green Android logo was designed by graphic designer Irina Block.

- Android consists of Kernel based on Linux kernel version 3.x (version 2.6 prior to Android 4.0 Ice cream sandwich) with middleware libraries and API written in C and application software running on an application framework which includes Java compatible libraries based on Apache harmony.
- Android uses Dalvik virtual machine with just in time compilation to run Dalvik "dex-code' (Dalvik Executable), which is usually translated from Java byte code.
- The main hardware platform for Android is the ARM architecture. There is support for x86 from the Android-x86 project.

7.1.4 Memory Management

- Android devices are usually battery powered, android is designed to manage RAM to keep power consumption at a minimum. When android app is no longer in use, the system will automatically suspend in memory while the app is technically open in background.
- The resources are no more to the app which resides in background, it has double benefit of increasing the general responsiveness of Android device since app does not need to be closed and reopened from the scratch. But also it ensures background apps don't waste power.
- There is automatic management of the memory that means when memory is low the system will begin killing apps and processes that are inactive for a while. This service is invisible to user, such that users need not to manage the memory or kill the process.

Security and Privacy

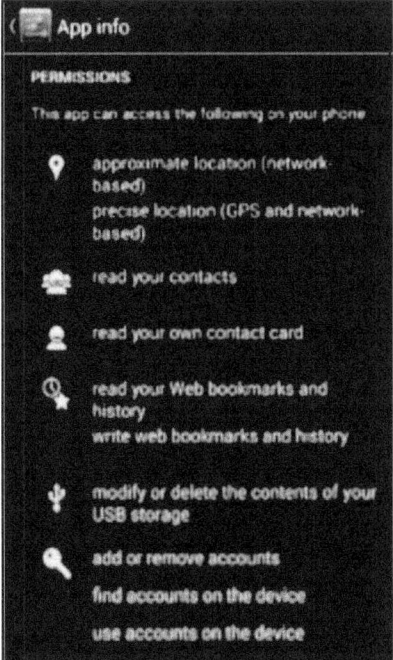

Fig. 7.3: Security and Privacy in Android

- Permissions are used to control a particular apps access to system functions.
- The sandbox is the area, where the system does not have access to the rest of system's resources, Unless access permissions are explicitly granted by the user when app is installed.
- Before installing the app play store shows all the permissions. After reviewing these permissions the user can choose to accept or discard them, installing the app only if they accept.
- Some of the companies such as Lookout Mobile Security, AVG technologies, Macafee and Quick heal have released antivirus software for Android devices.
- Google currently uses Google Bouncer malware scanner to watch over and scan the Google Play store apps. It is intended to flag up suspicious apps and warn users of any potential issues with an app.
- The latest version of Android 4.2 Jelly Beans was released in 2012 was released with enhanced security features including a malware scanner built into the system, which works in combination with Google Play but can scan apps installed from third party sources as well and an alert system which notifies the user when an app tries to send a premium rate text message.
- Android smart phones have the ability to report the location of Wi-Fi access points, encountered as phone users move around, to build database containing the physical locations of hundreds of millions of such access points.
- In August 2013, Google released the Android Device Manager, a component that allows users to remotely track, locate, and wipe their Android device through an online interface

7.2 Devices Running Android

Mobile devices have restrictions as limited power, small-form factor and restricted memory. The application will not run same as for desktop or web, as it also has hardware limitations such as devices are on the move, so the need is that your application should run fast, responsive and easy to use.

- The primary goal of mobiles is for calling, second SMS and e-mail communicator, third is camera, media player comes under fourth part and fifth part is management of mobile tools.
- The huge and wide range of mobile devices is embedded with operating system. Mobile devices have different languages, screen sizes and versions of the Android platform.
- Android devices come in all shapes and sizes, as of from November 2010 Android OS can be seen on following devices.
- Smart phones such as :
    1. Tablets
    2. E-reader devices
    3. Net books
    4. MP4 players
    5. Internet TVs

Fig. 7.4: Android devices

- The devices such as Samsung GALAXY, HTC Desire HD, LG optimistic smart phones the another category of devices like tablets which typically starts at size of 7 inches Samsung Galaxy Tab, Dell streak etc are shown in Fig. 7.4.
- E-book readers are the dedicated devices for specific purpose. Besides smart phones and tablets android also run on E-book readers (diagram shows the Barnes and noble's Nook color, which is color e-book reader running on Android OS).
- A Swedish company brings android to a living room it has developed an Android based TV, called Scandinavia Internet Android TV set.
- Google also developed a smart TV platform based on Android and co developed with companies such as Intel, Sony and Logitech.

7.2.1 Android device Supports Different Languages

- The resource directory '/res' is used to interact with all types of languages i.e. UI is extracted and save into resource directory.
- To support more languages, add hyphen (–) and ISO country code at the end of directory name 'values', Values directory is created under resource directory.

e.g.   myproject/
        res.
            values/
                strings.xml
            values-es/   → it is used for Spanish language.
                strings.xml
            values-fr/   → it is used for French language.
                strings.xml

7.2.2 Android Devices Supports Different Screens

- The mobile devices are categorized on the basis of size and density.
- Four generalized sizes of device are: small, normal, large, xlarge and four generalized densities: low (ldpi), medium (mdpi), high (hdpi), extra high (xdpi).
- The different layout and bitmaps are created according to the size and density of a mobile device and these must be stored in different directories.
- To create appropriate screen layouts, the orientation (landscape or portrait) also should be taken into consideration.

- An unique layout .xml file needs to be created for each screen size and density. Android takes care of optimizing the scales to layouts. This directory is also included in resource directory:

    myproject/
      res/
        layout/
          main.xml
        layout-large
          main.xml

The file contains exactly the same as main.xml but the code should be run to satisfy. The constrain it to run on device which fits to its size.

    myproject/
      res/
        layout/
          main.xml
        layout-land/
          main.xml

layout/main.xml is used for portrait and layout-land/main.xml is used for landscape.

7.3 Why Develop for Android?

It provides a more agile environment, which helps developer to test application and introduces best marketing channels.

1. Biggest Addressable Smart phone Market: iOS and Android are the two platforms that are growing faster in mobile industry. The research says that Android platform is larger and growing faster as compared to iOS. As compared to other operation system. Android is a huge and filled with opportunities. Recent research Nielson adds that 48.5% of market is using Android. NPD group releases that 60% of us market are under android activation. According to Google 850,000 android devices are activating every day.

2. Discoverability: It provides a robust search capability. Google play has efficiency to reach prospective users. For mobile applications, the Apple App store and Google Play environments provides search engines. As a comparison, the search capabilities of iOS are limited, whereas Google Play provides robust search capabilities, making it easier for the users. A study by Fiksu shows that mobile users mostly search from Google Play rather than the Google for searching the different applications.

Marketers also have access to tools that provide keyword insight. This lets them optimize the app titles, descriptors and helps prioritize product features. Google Play's search capabilities level the playing field, allowing less well known apps and brands additional opportunities to reach prospective users.

3. Lower User Acquisition Costs: Android provides a platform for the promotion and marketing resources. Significantly it is cheaper to acquire a new customer on Google play. Recently Fiksu conducted an analysis and declared Android is 12% more inventory and estimated cost of that inventory was 40% lower than iOS

4. Reduced Privacy Concerns: In recent months, the scrutiny advertisement raised by the press and governments on privacy of user to the device. The long lasting industry standard for marketing attribution on iOS platforms, the unique Device Identifier has been cited for coupling and tracking to an identifier that many consider being the digital equivalent of a social security number.

In contrast android has a standard mechanism for marketing attribution. This mechanism is well understood and is consistent with how marketers have been executing on the desktop for more than 15 years.

5. Highly Reliable Ad Attribution: Marketing attribution on iOS several methods that require database matching of user data between Ad networks and marketer's. Because of the way this process works, it is prone to inconsistencies in the data. Android's referrer based mechanism is unambiguous and provides a consistent mechanism for marketing attribution.

6. Agility Fast Turnaround: The ability to quickly adapt to changes according to feedback of users is necessary for the consistent market. Google play provides a quick update for an application in few hours. Developers can react to feedback quickly and have an app update available on Google Play literally in few hours. These delays and the added uncertainty can be a significant headache in the development process.

7. Shared Learning: Android implementation allow user to test an application and design.accordingly it provides enhancement towards the skills of development. The android development environment will allow you to perfect and test your app design, so you can leverage your learning for development and rollout of iOS apps with an increased probability of success.

8. The Early Bird: Google Play and iOS have very different methods to determine rank. In IOS raw downloads are very important in achieving high ranks. Apps can not sustain large numbers of downloads. Google's ranking algorithm works very differently.

Getting an app into Google Play first and building a steady user base is rewarded, presenting an early more advantage for apps debuting on Google Play.

9. The research conducted by Fiksu determined that Android users convert from installs to loyal users at about the same or a higher rate than on iOS.

App research firm Distimo indicates 80 percent improvement in average daily revenues for the top 200 US apps between December 2011 and March 2012. Furthermore, it is mentioned in a post titled. Treat Android as a first-class citizen... it'll pay off!.

Game developer TinyCo noted that Average Revenue Per Paying User (ARPPU) for Google Play and iTunes is about the same as iOS, and found that Amazon performance surpassed that of iOS by a significant margin.

10. Easier Transition to Amazon's Store: Amazon's app store is based on Android. Therefore it allows developers to easily submit a build to Amazon for approval. What is particularly interesting here is that recent research shows the Amazon store users monetize better than the App Store and Google Play.

Conclusion
- The discussion above mentioned why there is need to develop for Android. It provides developers with testing ground with lower cost and accesses largest smart phones.
- The barrier entry for new Android developers is minimal:
  (a) No certification is required to become an Android developer.
  (b) There is no approval process for application distribution.
  (c) Google play provides free, up-front purchase and in-app billing options for distribution and monetization of user's application.

7.4 Android (April 2015)

Android is an open source for mobile phones that is developed by Google and open handheld alliance.

Android is getting more attention and introduces the "wow" factor to range of Smart phones as compared to Symbian, iphone, Windows mobile, Blackberry, Java mobile edition, Linux mobile (Limo) and more.

7.4.1 Features in Android

1. **Handset Layouts:** The platform is adaptable to larger, VGA, 2D graphics library, 3D graphics library based on Open GL ES 2.0 specification, and traditional Smart phone layout.
2. **A Component-Based Architecture:** The architecture of this platform is component based parts of one component i.e. application can be embedded in an application. Built-in components can be replaced by customized versions.
3. **Tons of Built-In Services Out of the Box:** Built in capabilities are embedded in an application. E.g. Location based services use GPS, browser and map views can be embedded directly in your application.
4. **Automatic Management of the Application Life Cycle:** There is an isolation of programs from each other by multiple layers of security. This environment offers low power, low memory devices. So, end user needs not to bother which applications are running and to be closed to run another application.
5. **High Quality Graphics and Sound:** To run new kinds of games and business application 2D graphics and animation is inspired by Flash with 3D openly graphics. It also has codec's for most common industry standard audio and video formats including H.264 (AVC), mp3 and AAC.
6. **Portability Across a Wide Range of Current and Future Hardware:** As all the programs are written in Java and it is executed by Android's Dalvik virtual machine, so code gets portable across ARM, X86 and other architectures.

7. **Storage:** SQLite a lightweight relational database is used for data storage purposes.
8. **Connectivity:** Android supports connectivity technologies including GSM/EDGE, IDEN, CDMA, EVDO, UMTS, Bluetooth, Wi-Fi, LTE, NFC, and WiMAX.
9. **Messaging:** SMS and MMS are available forms of messaging, including threaded text messaging and Android Cloud to Device Messaging (C2DM) and now enhanced version of C2DM, Android Google Cloud Messaging is a part of Android Push Messaging service.
10. **Multiple Language Support:** Android supports multiple languages.
11. **Web Browser:** The web browser available in Android is based on the open source WebKit layout engine, coupled with Chrome's V8 JavaScript engine. This browser scores 100% on the Acid 3 test on Android 4.0
12. **Java Support:** Most of the Android applications are written in Java. There is no Java Virtual Machine in the platform. Neither Java byte code is executed nor. Java classes are complied into Dalvik executables and run on Dalvik, a specialized virtual machine designed specifically for Android and optimized for battery powered mobile devices with limited memory CPU.
13. **Media Support:** Android supports the following audio/video/still media formats: WebM, H.263, AAC, HE-AAC, MPEG-4 SP, AMR, AMR-WB, MP3etc.
14. **Streaming Media Support:** RTP/RTSP streaming (3GPP,PSS) HTML progressive download, Adobe Flash Streaming (RTMP) and HTTP Dynamic streaming are supported by the Flash plug-in.
    Apple HTTP Live streaming is supported by Real Player for Android and by the operating system in Android 3.0(Honeycomb).
15. **Additional Hardware Support:** Android can use video/still cameras, touch screen, GPS, accelometers, gyroscopes, barometers, nanometers, dedicated gaming controls, proximity and pressure sensors, thermometer, accelerated 2D bit and accelerated 3D formats.
16. **Multitouch:** The previous handsets such as HTC hero have some native android application which supports multi touch. The feature was disabled at kernel at initial stage. But Google releases the updates for the Nexus one and Motorola Droid which enables multi touch natively.
17. **Bluetooth:** It supports A2DP, sending files (OPP), accessing phone book (PBAp), voice dialing and sending contacts between phones. Keyboard, mouse and joystick (HID) support is available in Android 3.

18. **Video Calling:** Android does not support native video calling. But some handsets have a customized version of the operating system that supports it, either via UMTS network or over IP. Video calling in Android is available through Google Talk which is available in 2.3.4 and later. Gingerbread allows Nexus S to place internet calls with a SIP account. Skype 2.1 the Google + android app can have video chat with other google+ users through hangouts.

19. **Multitasking:** Multitasking of applications, with unique handling of memory allocation, is available.

20. **Accessibility:** Text to speech is built facility is provided by Talk back for people with low or no vision. Enhancements for people with hearing disabilities are also available.

21. **Voice Based Features:** Google search through voice has been available since initial release. Voice actions for calling, texting, navigation, etc. are supported on Android 2.2 onwards. As android 4.1 Google has expanded Voice Actions with the ability to talk back and read answers from Google's knowledge Graph when queried with specific commands.

22. **Tethering:** Android supports tethering which allows a phone to be used as a wireless/wired Wi-Fi hotspot. Before Android 2.2 was supported by third party applications or manufacturers customization.

23. **Screen Capture:** Android supports capturing a screenshot by pressing the power and volume down button at the same time. Prior to Android 4.0 the only method of capturing a screenshot were through manufacturers and third party customization or otherwise by using a PC connection.

24. **External Storage:** Most Android devices include microSD slot and can read microSD cards formatted with FAT 32, EXT3 and EXT4 file system. To allow use of high capacity storage media such as USB flash drives and USB HDDs. Many Android tablets also include USB's' receptacle.

7.5 Android Architecture (April 2015)

The Android architecture contains many layers and its components are represented as a stack. Each bottom layer provides the services to its upper layer.

Android operating system is a stack of software components which is roughly divided into five sections and four main layers are shown below in the architecture diagram.

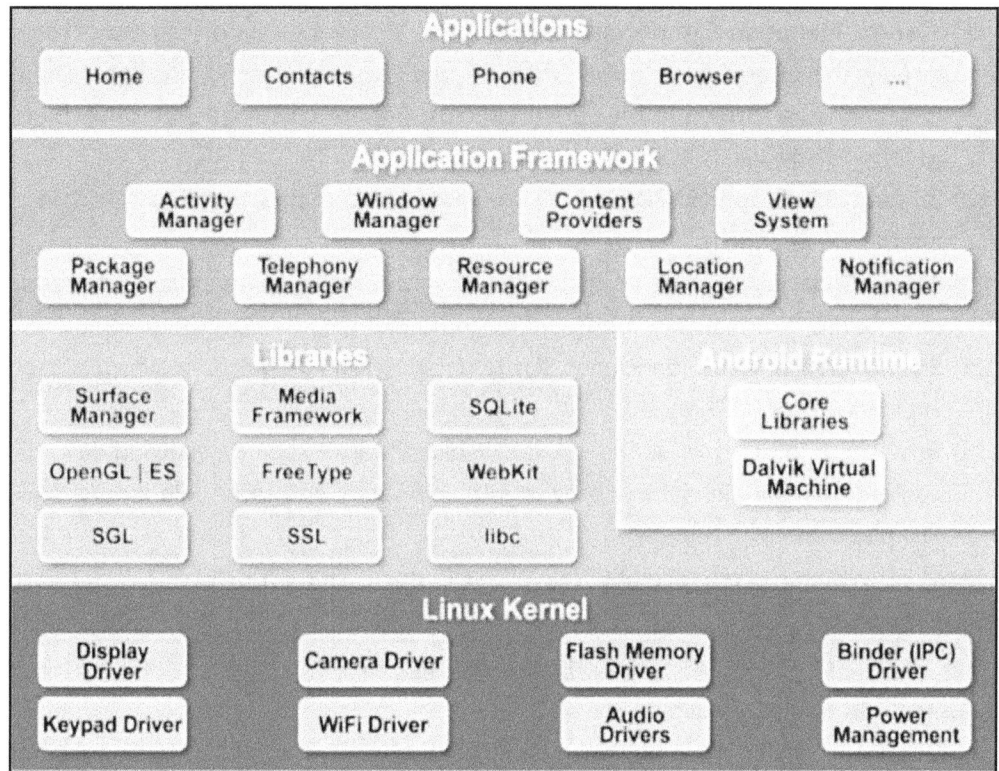

Fig. 7.5: Android Architecture

7.5.1 Linux Kernel

This is the bottom layer in architecture. Linux Kernel is developed by Linux Torvalds in 1991 and it occupies by all ranges of devices. It allows Android to interact with the hardware with the help of various platforms.

Linux provides the memory management, process management networking and other operating system services. It includes the device drivers for various applications display, Bluetooth, camera, keypad, USB, audio etc. This layer facilitates with the functionality like process management, memory management, device management like camera, keypad, display it.

Linux Kernel handles networking and a vast array of device drivers.

7.5.2 Native Libraries

It is the next layer above Kernel. It is set of android native libraries, which are coded in C++. Libraries include open source web browser engine webkit, library lbc, SQLite database. Libraries for storing and sharing of application libraries to play and record audio and video.

The following are the important native libraries:

(1) **Surface Manager:** Surface manager works as similar to vista or compiz. It helps to display the effects such as see-through windows and fancy transitions. Drawing commands are copied to off-screen bitmaps that are combined with other bitmaps to form the display.

(2) **2D and 3D Graphics:** 2D and 3D elements are grouped together in single user interface with android.

(3) **Media Codecs:** AAC, AVC (H.264) H.263, advanced video compression, video coding, mp3, MPEG-4 formats are supported by android. It records videos and audios.

(4) **SQL Database:** Android includes SQLite database engine the same which is used in Firefox and Apple iPhone.

(5) **Browser Engine:** This is the similar webkit library used for showing fast HTML contents, as Google chrome browser, Apple's safari, and the Apple iphone Nokia's S60 platform.

These native libraries are called by Native Development Kit (NDK).

Android Runtime

The second last layer also contains the Android runtime, which includes core Java libraries and Dalvik virtual machine.

- Dalvik is a virtual machine which is developed by Dan Bornstein at Google. Dalvik machine executes the byte code (byte code is generated when code is compiled into machine independent instructions). It is Java virtual machine with low memory requirements. Multiple VM instances ran at once. In android, code is written in Java and run with the help of VM Dalvik.
- Dalvik VM run.dex file which are converted at compile time from jar and class filler.dex files are more compact and efficient than class files.
- The core Java library of android is different from Java standard edition (SE) libraries and Java mobile edition (ME).

Application Framework

This layer is above the native libraries and Dalvik virtual machine. It provides high-level building block to create the application. This framework is preinstalled in an android. The following are the most important parts of application framework:

(1) **Activity Manager:** It controls the life cycle of an application and maintains back stack for user navigation.

(2) **Content Providers:** Data is encapsulated within these objects and used by applications.

E.g. contacts.

(3) **Resource Manager:** All the resources are provided that are needed for applications to run.

(4) **Location Manager:** Locating and sensing where the particular device is the main task of this component.

(5) **Notification Manager:** Events such as arriving messages, appointments, proximity alerts, and alien invasions are notified with the help of this manager.

Types of Android Applications:

(a) **Foreground Activity:** The application which gets suspended, when it is not visible in its foreground. E.g. games, map mashups.

(b) **Background Activity:** The applications which are most of the time hidden and has limited interaction. E.g. SMS auto-responders, call screening applications.

(c) **Intermittent Activity:** The applications run most of the time in background. They are setup and run silently in the background. E.g. media player.

Advanced android APIS offers better functionality, but at the same time android is widely used in wide range of mobiles. So, compatibility of these APIS with different devices is different.

(1) **Android Location:** Location based services API gives your application access to device's current physical location.

(2) **Android Media:** It provides support for playback and recording of audio and video media files, including streamed media.

(3) **android.opengl :** To develop dynamic 3D user-interface android offers powerful 3D rendering engine which uses openGL ES API.

(4) **Android.hardware:** It includes hardware APIS, sensor hardware is included like camera, accelometer, compass sensors.

(5) **android.bluetooth, android.net.wifi, android.telephony:** Android offers low level access to hardware platform, it includes Bluetooth, WI-Fi, telephony hardware.

7.5.3 Applications and Widgets

This is the higher most layer of android architecture, in other language. This layer interacts with the user. Applications that run on screen take over the control and interact with the user. Widgets are the small rectangles that are present on home screen.

Android Libraries.

Top layer of Linux kernel is a set of libraries including open source Web browser engine WebKit, well known library libc, SQLite database which is a useful repository for storage and sharing of application data, libraries to play and record audio and video, SSL libraries responsible for Internet security.

Android offers a wide range of APIS for development of an application. The following list is of core APIs and all android devices supports these APIs.

- **(1) android.util:** This utility package contains low-level calls like containers, string formatters, XML parsing utilities.
- **(2) android.os :** This utility acts as controller and provides an access to basic operating system services like message passing, interposes communication, clock function, debugging.
- **(3) android.graphics:** These APIS supports graphics classes, like canvases, colors and drawing primitives.
- **(4) android.txt :** The text processing tools for displaying and parsing text.
- **(5) android.database:** It supports low level classes like for handling cursors which works with a database.
- **(6) android.content:** These APIS are used to manage data access and publishing by providing services for dealing with resources, content providers, packages.
- **(7) android.view:** All user interface contents are constructed using these APIS.
- **(8) android.widget:** It built on view packages, it includes lists, buttons and layouts.
- **(9) com.google.android.maps:** Map view control, overlay and map controller classes are used to control and provides access to native maps.
- **(10) android.app:** It is a high-level API. It provides access to application model, which constitutes of activity and service APIS.
- **(11) android.provider:** It provides access to some standard content providers (e.g. contact database).
- **(12) android.telephony:** The telephony APIS provides you an ability to directly interact with device's phone stack. It monitors phone calls, phone status, SMS messages.
- **(13) android.webkit:** It supports APIS for working with web-based content, including a web view control for embedding browsers.

Android also includes the libraries from C/C++ that are accessed by an application framework.

These Libraries Includes:

- **(1) OpenGL:** It is used to support 3D graphical based on the openGL ES 1.0 API.
- **(2) Free Type:** It supports bitmap and vector font rendering.
- **(3) SGL:** It provides a 2D graphics engine.
- **(4) libc:** It is a standard C library optimized for Linux based embedded services.
- **(5) SQLite:** It is database engine used to store application data.
- **(6) SSL:** It supports and uses SECURE sockets layer cryptographic protocol for secure internet communications.

7.6 Software Development Kit

Requirements to Learn Android

1. As we gone through Android operating system overview and its features, the following are the tools that are required for the development of android application.
2. Knowledge of any object oriented language like Java in spite of prior knowledge of any development in mobile application.
3. Android learning includes four parts:
   (1) First part is introduction to Android, Android emulator is installed and it is integrated with Integrated Development Environment (IDE). It also contains android's life cycle.
   (2) Second part is user interface for this platform, 2D graphics, multimedia components and simple data access.
   (3) Third part connects android with outside world, location based services, built-in SQLite database and 3D graphics.
   (4) Fourth part is advanced features with multi-touch including widgets lives wallpaper to home screen making application with multiple devices using androids and versions and publishing it to Android market.

The development of Android is supported by Windows, Mac OS, and Linux with the SDK available from the android website.

For developing android application, the environment needs to download android SDK libraries, developer tools, Java Development Kit. Developer may install Eclipse and Android developer tool plug-ins for the ease. Android runs under Dalvik virtual machine. It runs on following platforms.

(a) Windows (XP or Vista)
(b) Mac OS X 10.4.8 or later (Intel Chips Only)
(c) Linux

Download and Install:

(a) Android SDK
(b) Java Development Kit (JDK) 5 or 6.

(a) Android SDK

SDK includes an emulator for all above mentioned operating systems. As android applications runs on virtual machines.

- All Android libraries, documentation and sample applications are included in SDK. SDK helps to write and debug the application. Emulator helps in running and Dalvik Debug Monitoring Service (DDMS) helps in debugging them.
- Java is used to write an android application core libraries of Android core Java APIS.

- Downloading and Installing the SDK: It is an open source and you can download it from the android home page and used as a platform for the development of an application.
- You can download the Android SDK from http://developer.android.com/sdk/index.html
- SDK is presented as ZIP file which contains API libraries, developer tools, documentations and several sample programs. Install it in new folder without unzipping the SDK. API demos highlight the use of particular API features.
- The development tools for android applications are included in the Android software development kit(SDK) these include, a debugger, libraries, a handset emulator based on QEMU, documentation, sample code and tutorials.
- The currently supporting operating systems are Linux, MacOS X 10.5.8, and WindowsXP. The developer can develop Android software by using android only i.e. AIDE Android IDE –Java++ app and Android java editor app.
- The officially supported Integrated Development Environment (IDE) is Eclipse using the Android Development tools.
- Developers can also use any text editor to edit Java and XML files, then use command line tools Java Development kit (JDK) and Apache Ant are required to create, build and debug Android applications as well as control attached Android devices.
- Android platform development is relative to enhancements to Android's SDK. The SDK also supports older versions of Android platform in case developers wish to target their applications at older devices.
- Development tools are downloadable components, so one has downloaded the latest version and platform, older platform and tools can also be downloaded for compatibility testing.
- '.apk' is the format where all android applications are stored and these are stored under '/data/app' folder on the Android OS '.APK' package contains .dex files (complied byte code files called Dalvik executables).

Android Debug Bridge

The Android Debug Bridge (ADB) is a toolkit included in the Android SDK package .it consists of both client and server side programs that communicate with one another. The ADB is typically accessed through the command line interface.

adb [-d|-e|-s <serialNumber>] <command>

Fast boot is a protocol included in SDK package used primarily to modify the flash file system via a USB connection from host computer.

This protocol is added to android SDK to modify the flash file system via USB connection from host computer. The requirement that is the device should be started in a boot loader or second program loader mode where the basic initialization of hardware is done.

The following are the fast boot commands:

- Flash - Rewrites a partition with a binary image stored on the host computer.
- Erase - Erases a specific partition.
- Reboot - Reboots the device into the main operating system, the system recovery partition or back into its boot loader.
- Devices - Displays a list of all devices (with the serial number) connected to the host computer.
- Format - Format a specific partition. The file system of the partition must be recognized by the device.

(b) Eclipse:

The first step towards the developing any application is obtaining the Integrated Development Environment (IDE). For Android development, you should download the Eclipse IDE for Java EE developers(www.eclipse.org/downloads/packages/eclipse-ide-java-ee-developers/ heliossr1)

- Once the Eclipse IDE is downloaded, unzip its contents into folder e.g.:\Android.\

- **Native Development Kit**

All libraries written in C and other languages can be compiled to ARM, MIPS or X86 native code and installed using the Android Native development kit. Native classes can be called from Java code running under the Dalvik VM using the system load library call, which is part of the standard Android Java classes.

- Traditional Development tools are used to compile and install the complete applications. The native ARM, MIPS or x 86 codes can be uploaded and executed under the emulator which is provided by the ADB debugger. The graphics library Android's uses to arbitrate and control access to this device is called the Skia Graphics Library (SGL) for both Win32 and UNIX which allows the cross platform applications and it is the graphics Google chrome web browser.
- NDK is bases on command line tools and requires invoking them manually build, deploy and debug the apps. Several third party tools allow integrating the NDK into Eclipse and Visual studio.

Android Open Accessory Development Kit:

The Android 3.1 platform introduces Android Open Accessory support, which allows external USB hardware. To interact with an Android powered device in a special 'accessory' mode, Andoroid USB accessories are specifically designed to attach to Android powered devices.

When an android powered device is in accessory mode the connected accessory acts as the USB host and Android powered device acts as the USB device.

- **App Inventor for Android**

The App Inventor was introduced by Google on July 12 2010.A web based visual development environment for novice programmers is based on MIT's Open Block Java library and providing access to Android device's GPS, accelometer, orientation data, phone functions, text messaging, speech to text conversion, contact data, persistent storage and web services.

- **Hypertext Android Creator**

Hypertext Android Creator is a software development system aimed at beginner programmers that can help to create their own Android apps without knowing java and the Android SDK.

  - This is based on HyperCard which is a stack of software and only one card is visible at one time and it suits to mobile applications that have only one window visible at one time. Hypertext Android creator's main programming languages. Hypertext is loosely based on HyperCard's hyper talk language.
  - It supports growing subset of the Android SDK including its own background service, so app can continue to run and process information while in the background.

- **SDL**

The SDL library offers a development possibility besides Java, allowing the development with C and the simple porting of existing and native C applications.

- **Android Development Tool (ADT)**

  - This tool is an extension to the Eclipse IDE that supports the creation and debugging of Android application.

Using ADT the following tasks are possible to be followed:

1. Create new android application project.
2. Access the tools for accessing your android emulators and devices.
3. Compile and debug Android Application.

4. Export Android applications into Android packages (APK)
5. Create digital certificates for code-signing your APK.

- The steps to install the ADT:

1. To install ADT, first launch Eclipse by double clicking on the eclipse.exe file located in the eclipse folder.
2. When Eclipse is first started, it will display a folder to use as your workspace .the workspace is a folder where you store all the projects.
3. Once Eclipse is up and running, select HELP->Install new software.
4. In install window type http://dl.ssl.google.com/android/eclipse in the text box.
5. After this step, the Developer tool item appear in the middle of the window, as the menu expanded the contents such as Android DDMS, Android Development tools, and Android hierarchy viewer. After checking this contents click on NEXT.
6. The installation details are flashed click on NEXT.
7. You will be asked to review the licenses for the tools-check the option to accept the license agreement .and click FINISH to continue.
8. Once the AT installed, you will be prompted to restart the Eclipse. After this go to Windows->preferences.
9. In the preferences window there appears, Select Android you will see an error message saying that the SDK has not been set up .Click OK to dismiss it.
10. The location of the android SDK folder is to be selected. For example:

    C: \Android\android-sdk-windows .click OK.

Creating Android Virtual Device (AVDs)

The android applications are tested by using the AVD. The following are the steps for creating the AVD.

1. An AVD is an emulator instance that enables you to model an actual device, it consists of a hardware profile, a mapping to a system image, as well as emulated storage such as a secure digital card (SD).
2. You can create the several AVDs with different configuration to test the application. This testing is important to confirm the behavior of your application when it is run on different devices.
3. To create AVD, go to Windows->Android SDK and AVD manager.

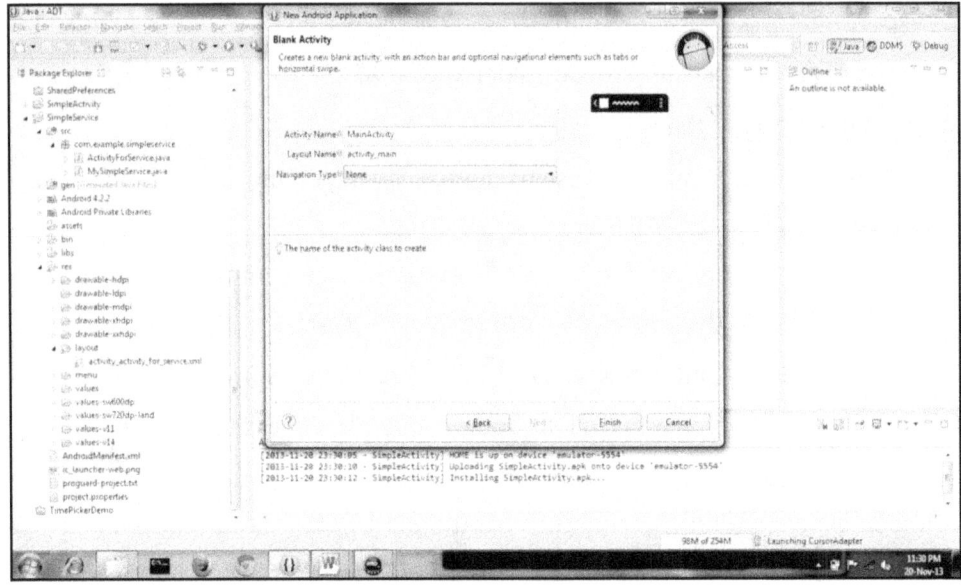

Fig. 7.6: Creating Android Virtual Device

4. Select the available packages option in the left pane and expand the package name shown in the right pane. The various packages are available to create AVDs to emulate the different versions of an Android device.
5. You have to check the relevant tools, documentation and platforms what is needed for the project.
6. Once you have selected the items you want, click on Install selected button to download them. Because it takes a while to download from Google's server.
7. Each version of the Android OS is identified by an API level number. for example; Android 2.3 is level 9, while Android 2.2 is level 8 and so on. For each level, two platforms are available.

   Level 9 offers the following:
   1. SDK Platform Android 2.3
   2. Google API by Google Inc.
8. The difference between the two is that the Google API platform contains the Google Maps if the application where you require Google Maps; you need to create an AVD using the Google. APIs platform.
9. Click the virtual Devices item in the left pane of the window. Then click the new button located in the right pane of the window.
10. In the create new Android Virtual Device (AVD) window, enter the items, click the create AVD button when you are done

Here by following the above steps, you have created an AVD that emulates an Android device running version 2.3 of the OS. In addition to this you also have the option to emulate the device with an SD card and different screen densities and resolutions.

Build the First Application

The android application requires various components, while starting with the application development of android the following steps are taken into consideration:

1. Using Eclipse, crate new project by selecting File→New→Project.

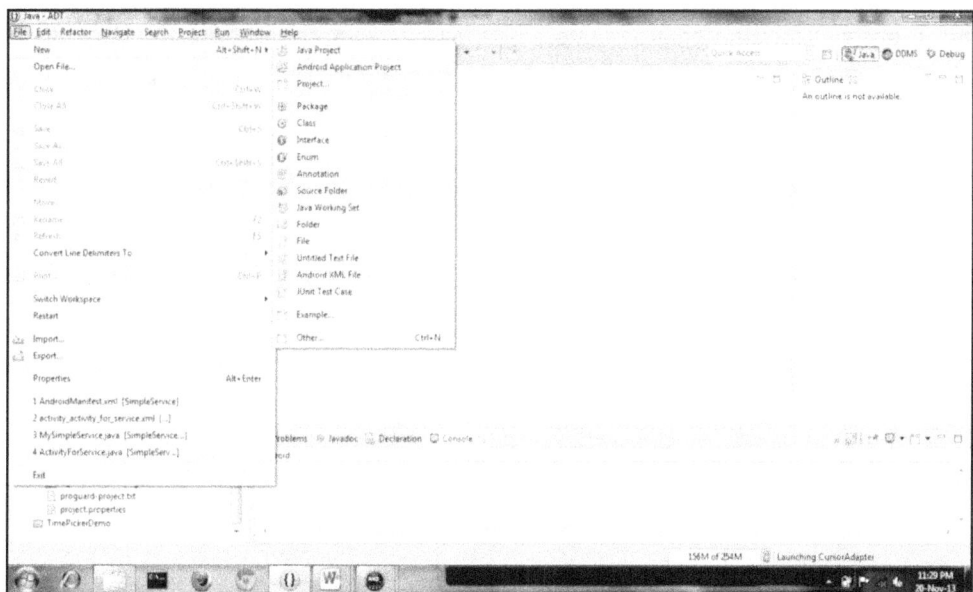

Screen Shot 7.1: Creating New Project

2. Expand the android folder and select Android project.
3. Name the android project and click on Finish.

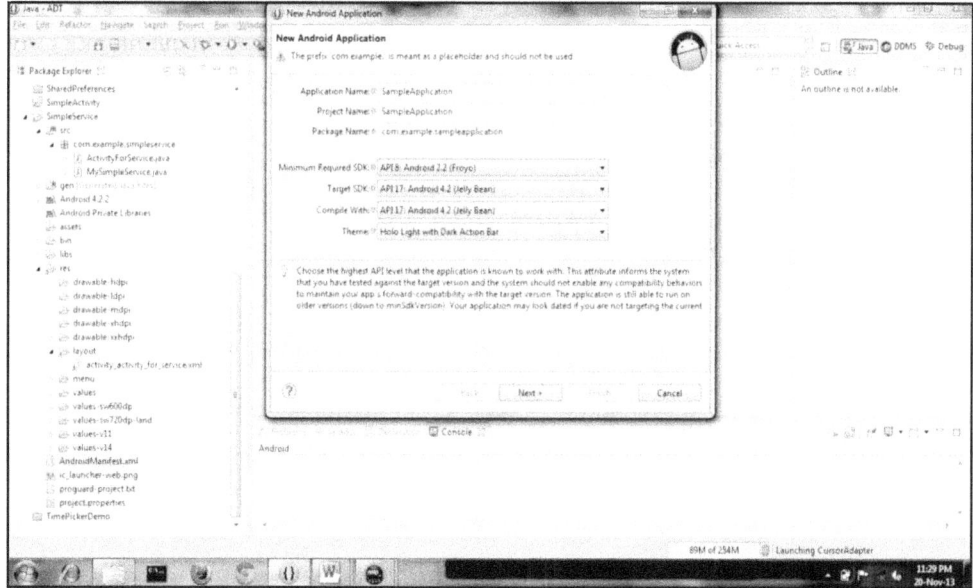

Screen Shot 7.2: Creating New Android Application

4. The Eclipse IDE should look like which contains the details of project, and minimum required SDK with target SDK.
5. In the package Explorer (left side of an Eclipse IDE), expand the Hello World project by clicking various arrows displayed to the left of each item in the project. In the res/layout Folder, double click the main.xml file.
6. The main.xml file defines the user interface of your application. The default view is the Layout view, which lays out the activity graphically. The main.xml file is used to modify the user interface.

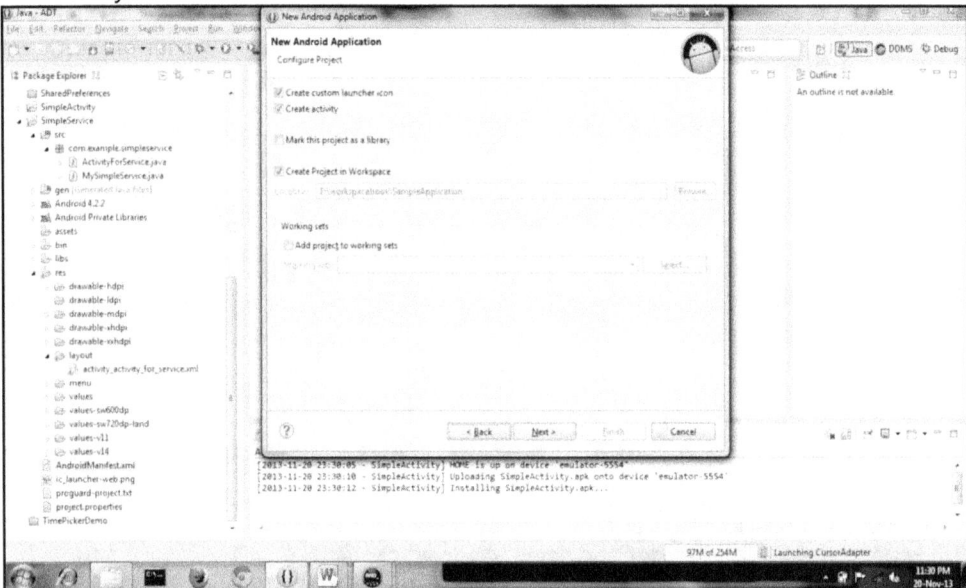

Screen Shot 7.3: Configure Project

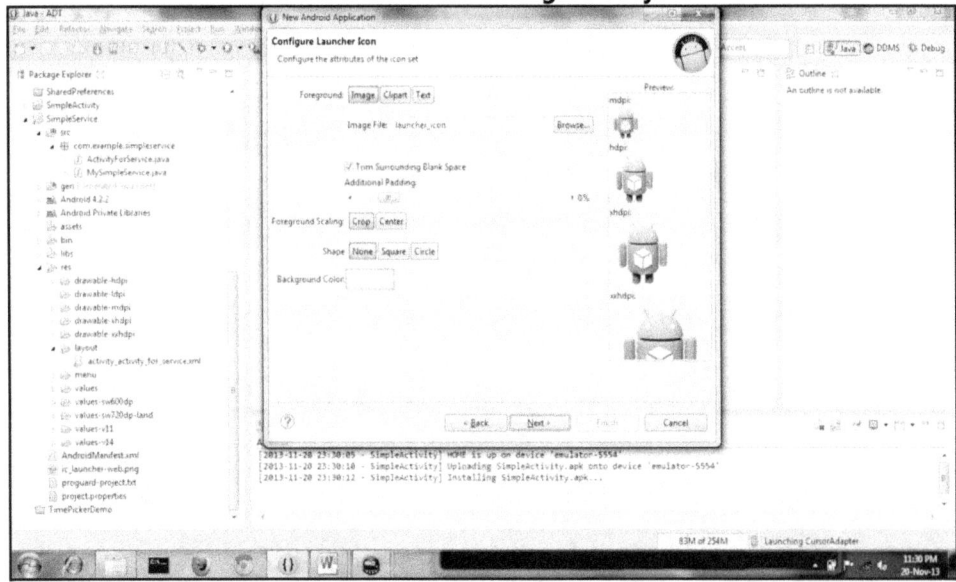

Screen Shot 7.4: Configure Launcher Icon

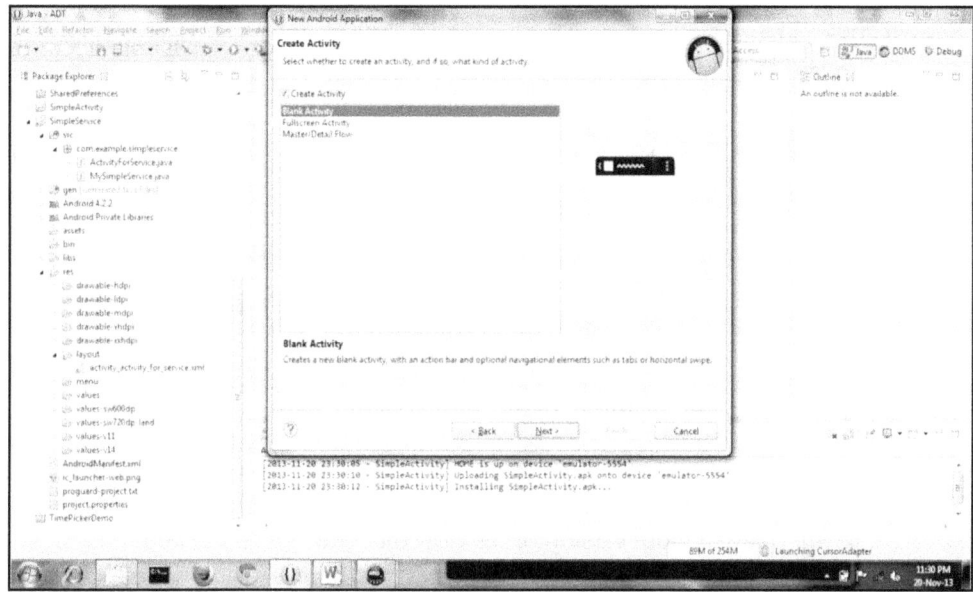

Screen Shot 7.5: Create Activity

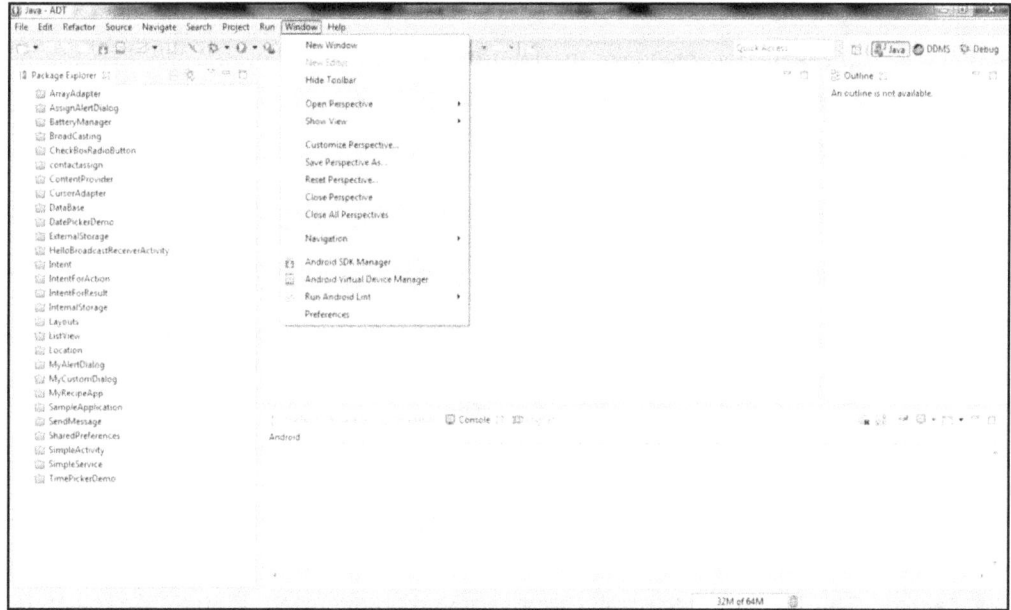

Screen Shot 7.6: Create New Window

7. The application can be tested by using an emulator. Select the project name in Eclipse and press F11.
8. The android Emulator will now be started (if the emulator is locked you need to slide the unlock button to unlock it first.

9. Click the HOME button (the house icon in the lower left corner above the keyboard) so it shows in home screen.
10. Creating launch configuration.

How it works?

The following information needs to be filled while starting with building the android application.

Properties	Description
Project name	The name of project
Application name	A user friendly name for your application
Package name	The name of the package. You should use a reverse domain name for this.
Create activity	The name of the first activity in your application
Min SDK Version	The minimum version of the SDK that your project is targeting

In android the activity is the window that contains the user interface of your applications. An application can have zero or more activities. The application contains one activity: MainActivity. This MainActivity is the entry point of the application.

The main.xml file contains the user interface of the activity, which is displayed when MainActivity is loaded.

Anatomy of an Android Application:

Various files and folders are created when you create the application of the android. The following are the files and folders created:

1. **src:** It contains .java files for your project. MainActivity.java is the source file for your activity. The application code is written in this file.
2. **Android 2.3 libaray:** This item contains one file, android.jar, which contains all the class libraries needed for an application.
3. **gen:** contains R.java file, a compiler generated file that references all the resources found in your project.
4. **assets:** This folder contains all the assets used by your application, such as HTML, text files, databases.
5. **Res:** This folder contains all the resources used in your application .It also contains subfolders drawable<resolution>, layout and values.
6. **Android manifest.xml:** This is the manifest file for Android application. The permissions needed to run the application are specified in this file.

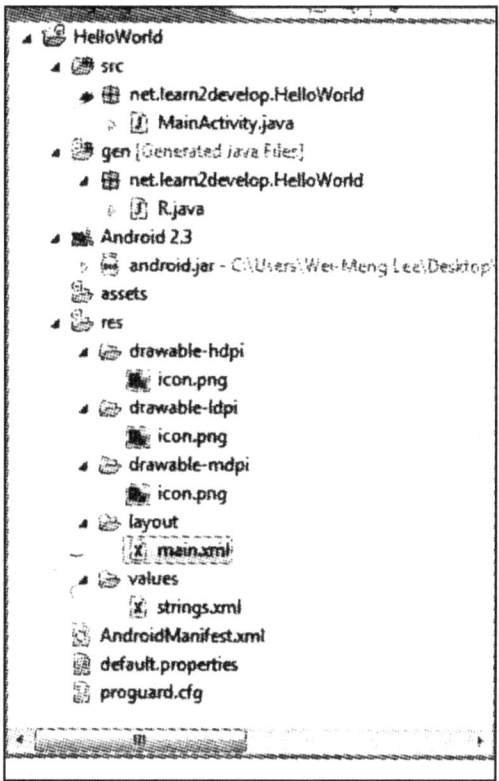

Fig. 7.7: Anatomy of Android Application

7.7 Creating Application and Activity

An Activity is an application component that provides a screen with which users can interact in order to do something, such as dial the phone, take a photo, send an email, or view a map. Each activity in window is used to draw its user interface. The window fills the screen, but may be smaller than the screen and float on top of other windows.

An application usually consists of multiple activities that are loosely bound to each other. The main activity is treated as application launcher each activity can start another Activity which performs the actions. Each time the new activity starts, then the previous activity is stopped but the system preserves the activity in a stack.

The call-back methods that an activity might receive due to change in its state, whether the system is creating it, stopping it, resuming it or destroying it. When stopped your activity should release any large objects, such as network or database connection.

Android Application Life Cycle

- Each android application runs in its own process, each of which is running a separate instance of Dalvik. Memory and processes are handled separately at run time.

- Application's Process State: Application has multiple processes and that are defined by using android process attribute. Processes are killed sometimes without warning so that gets freed for higher priority application.
- Process priorities affected by interpose dependency as processes are shared by multiple applications. Because of process priority the application goes through different states.
    1. **OnCreate():** The system calls for these methods are implemented when you start the activity. You should initialize the essential components of your activity. It calls setContentView() defines the layout for the activity's user interface.
    2. **OnPause():** The system calls this method as the indication that user is leaving your activity. This is usually where you should commit any changes that should persist beyond the current user session.

Implementing a User Interface

- The user interface for an activity is provided by a hierarchy of views–objects derived from the view class. The view object responds to the user interactions.

    For example a view can be a button which initiates some action.
- Android provides a set of readymade views that are used to design and organize the layout. "Widgets "are the view that provides a visual element for the screen, such as button, text field, checkbox or an image.
- "Layouts" are views derived from ViewGroup that provides a unique layout model for all children views, such as a linear layout, a grid layout or relative layout.
- The layouts are defined by XML layout file which saved in application resources. You can set the layout as the UI for your activity with setContentView(), passing the resource ID for the layout. However, you can also create new Views in your activity code and build a view hierarchy by inserting new Views into a ViewGroup, then use that layout by passing the root ViewGroup to setContentView().

Declaring the Activity in the Manifest File:

You must declare your activity in the manifest file in order for it to be accessible to the system. To declare your activity, open your manifest file and add an <activity> element as a child of the <application> element. For example:

```
<manifest ... >
  <application ... >
    <activity android:name=".demoActivity" />
    ...
  </application ... >
  ...
</manifest >
```

- The other attributes are used to define the properties for the activity, an icon for the activity or theme of activity. The android name attribute gives the class name of the activity. Once the application published the android name cannot be changed because it may break some functionality such as application shortcut.
- When a new application is created by using Android SDK tools, the stub activity created which includes an intent filter that declares the activity responds to the main action and should be placed in the launcher category. <activity> element specifies the various intent filters using the <intent filter> element which declares how other application components may activate it.
- The <action> element specifies that, this is the "main" entry point to the application. <category> element specifies that this activity should be listed in the system's application launcher.
- Activities that you don't want to make available to other applications should have no intent filters and you can start them yourself using explicit intents
- However, if you want your activity to respond to implicit intents that are delivered from other applications (and your own), then you must define additional intent filters for your activity. For each type of intent to which you want to respond, you must include an <intent-filter> that includes an <action> element and, optionally, a <category> element and/or a <data> element. These elements specify the type of intent to which your activity can respond.

Starting an Activity

- By calling start Activity() and passing an intent to it which describes the activity you want to start or describes the type of action you want to perform.
- Intent can have small amount of data to be used by the activity that is started.
- An intents specifies either you are starting with an activity or describes the type of action you want to perform.
- When working with own application simply launch a known activity .this is done by creating an intent explicitly which describes which activity you want to start by specifying the class name.
- One activity that starts another activity is given as below:

  Intent = new Intent(this, SignInActivity.class); start Activity(intent);

  Intent intent = new Intent(this, SignInActivity.class); start Activity(intent);

  However, your application might also want to perform some action, such as send an email, text message, or status update, using data from your activity. In this case, your application might not have its own activities to perform such actions,

  So you can instead leverage the activities provided by other applications on the device, which can perform the actions for you. This is where intents are really valuable.

You can create an intent that describes an action you want to perform and the system launches the appropriate activity from another application. If there are multiple activities that can handle the intent, then the user can select which one to use.

For example, if you want to allow the user to send an email message, you can create the following intent:

Intent intent = new Intent(Intent.ACTION_SEND); intent.putExtra(Intent.EXTRA_EMAIL, recipientArray); start Activity(intent);

Shutting Down an Activity

You can shut down an activity by calling its finish() method. You can also shut down a separate activity that you previously started by calling finishActivity().

Managing the Activity Lifecycle

By using call-back methods, it is crucial to handle the lifecycle of your activities the lifecycle of an activity is also affected by it association with other ativities, its stack.

An activity can exist in essentially three states:

1. **Resumed:** The activity is in the foreground of the screen and has user focus. (This state is also sometimes referred to as "running".)
2. **Paused:** A paused activity is completely alive that an activity remains in memory and maintains all state and member information and remains attached to the window manager. But the activity which is in paused state can be killed by the system in extremely low memory situations.

Stopped: A stopped activity is also still alive that means the activity object is retained in memory, it maintains all state and member information, but is *not* attached to the window manager. However, it is no longer visible to the user and it can be killed by the system when memory is needed elsewhere.

If an activity is paused or stopped, the system can drop it from memory either by asking it to finish, by calling finish() method. When activity is opened again it started all over

Implementing the lifecycle callbacks

When an activity transitions into and out of the different states described above, it is notified through various call-back methods. All of the call-back methods are hooks that you can override to do appropriate work when the state of your activity changes. The following skeleton activity includes each of the fundamental lifecycle methods:

```java
public class DemoActivity extends Activity {
    @Override
    public void onCreate(Bundle savedInstanceState) {
        super.onCreate(savedInstanceState);
        // The activity is being created.
    }
```

```
@Override
protected void onStart() {
    super.onStart();
    // The activity is about to become visible.
}
@Override
protected void onResume() {
    super.onResume();
    // The activity has become visible (it is now "resumed").
}
@Override
protected void onPause() {
    super.onPause();
    // Another activity is taking focus (this activity is about to be "paused").
}
@Override
protected void onStop() {
    super.onStop();
    // The activity is no longer visible (it is now "stopped")
}
@Override
protected void onDestroy() {
    super.onDestroy();
    // The activity is about to be destroyed.
}
}
```

- The activity lifecycle may follow the three nested loops and these methods define overall the entire lifecycle of an activity.
- The entire lifetime of an activity happens between the call to onCreate() and the call to onDestroy(). Your activity should perform setup of "global" state (such as defining layout) in onCreate(), and release all remaining resources in onDestroy(). For example, if your activity has a thread running in the background to download data from the network, it might create that thread in onCreate() and then stop the thread inonDestroy().

- The visible lifetime of an activity happens between the call to onStart() and the call to onStop(). During this time, the user can see the activity on-screen and interact with it. For example, onStop() is called when a new activity starts and this one is no longer visible. Between these two methods, you can maintain resources that are needed to show the activity to the user.
- The foreground lifetime of an activity happens between the call to onResume() and the call to onPause(). During this time, the activity is in front of all other activities on screen and has user input focus. An activity can frequently have transition in and out of the foreground—for example, onPause() is called when the device goes to sleep or when a dialog appears.

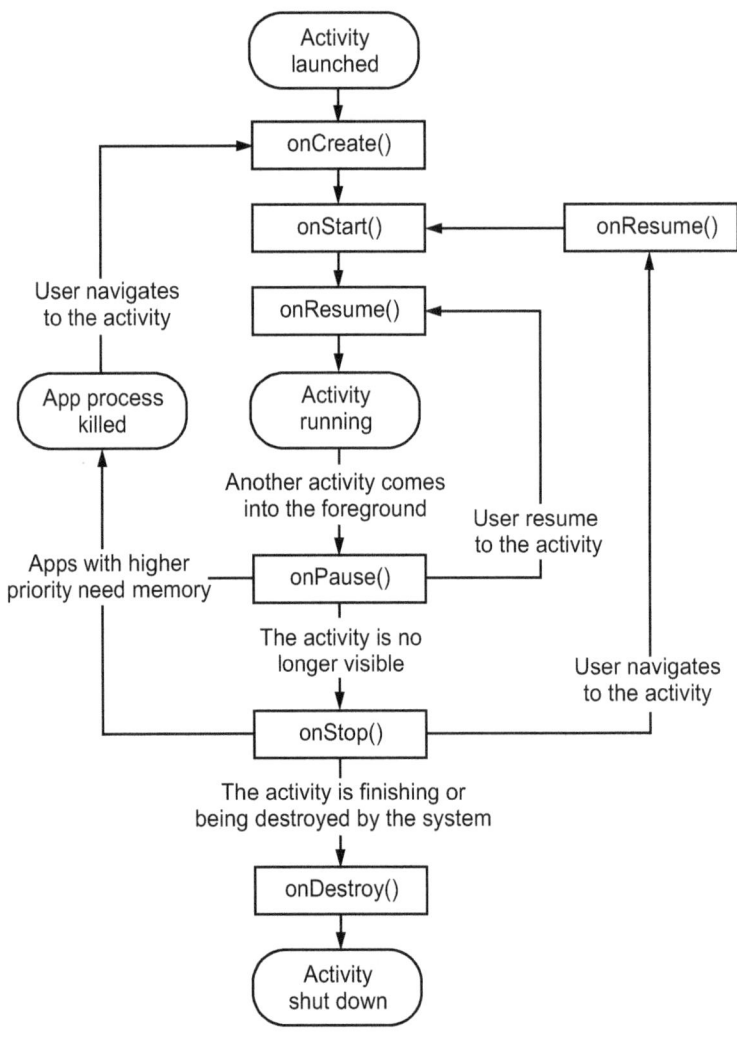

Fig. 7.8: The activity lifecycle

Table 7.1: A summary of the activity lifecycle's call-back methods

Method	Description	Killable after?	Next
onRestart()	Called after the activity has been stopped, just prior to it being started again. Always followed by onStart()	No	onStart()
onStart()	Called just before the activity becomes visible to the user. Followed by onResume() if the activity comes to the foreground, or onStop() if it becomes hidden.	No	onResume() or onStop()
onResume()	Called just before the activity starts interacting with the user. At this point the activity is at the top of the activity stack, with user input going to it. Always followed by onPause().	No	onPause()
onPause()	Called when the system is about to start resuming another activity. This method is typically used to commit unsaved changes to persistent data, stop animations and other things that may be consuming CPU, and so on. It should do whatever it does very quickly, because the next activity will not be resumed until it returns. Followed either by onResume() if the activity returns back to the front, or by onStop() if it becomes invisible to the user.	**Yes**	onResume() or onStop()
onStop()	Called when the activity is no longer visible to the user. This may happen because it is being	**Yes**	onRestart() or onDestroy()

Method	Description	Killable after?	Next
	destroyed, or because another activity (either an existing one or a new one) has been resumed and is covering it. Followed either by onRestart() if the activity is coming back to interact with the user, or byonDestroy() if this activity is going away.		
onDestroy()	Called before the activity is destroyed. This is the final call that the activity will receive. It could be called either because the activity is finishing (someone called finish() on it), or because the system is temporarily destroying this instance of the activity to save space. You can distinguish between these two scenarios with theisFinishing() method.	**Yes**	*nothing*

- The three methods (onPause(), onStop(), and onDestroy() are marked"yes" for this column.
- OnPause() is called once the activity is created and it might be called before the process can be killed. OnStop() and onDestroy() might not be called, therefore, onPause() should be used to write crucial persistent data
- The no marked columns specifies that these are protected the process hosting the activity from being killed from the moment they are called. Thus the activity is killable from the time onPause() returns to the time onResume() is called. It will not again be killable until onPause() it is again called and returns.
- Some device configuration can be changed at run time (screen orientation, keyboard availability and language). When such situation occurs android recreates the running activity, the system calls on Destroy() and immediately calls onCreate() method. This way the application can grasp the new configurations.

- If you properly design your activity to handle a restart due to a screen orientation change and restore the activity state as described above, your application will be more resilient to other unexpected events in the activity lifecycle.

- The best way to handle such a restart is to save and restore the state of your activity usingonSaveInstanceState() and onRestoreInstanceState() [or onCreate()]

Coordinating Activities

When one activity starts another, they both experience lifecycle transitions. The first activity pauses and stops (though, it won't stop if it's still visible in the background), while the other activity is created. In case these activities share data saved to disc or elsewhere, it's important to understand that the first activity is not completely stopped before the second one is created. Rather, the process of starting the second one overlaps with the process of stopping the first one.

The order of lifecycle callbacks is well defined, particularly when the two activities are in the same process and one is starting the other. Here's the order of operations that occur when Activity A starts Activity B:

1. Activity A's onPause() method executes.
2. Activity B's onCreate(), onStart(), and onResume() methods execute in sequence. (Activity B now has user focus.)
3. Then, if Activity A is no longer visible on screen, its onStop() method executes.

7.7.1 Introducing the Application Manifest File

(1) This file, AndroidManifest.xml is included in each android project and it is stored in the root of its project hierarchy. This file defines structure and metadata about an application, its components and its requirements.

(2) This file includes nodes for each activities, services, content providers and broadcast receivers that makes up the application and using intent filters and permissions, that determines how the nodes should interact with each other.

(3) It also have the details about application such as icons, version number, or theme additionally required permissions, unit tests and define hardware, screen or platform requirements.

(4) The manifest is made up of root manifest tag with a package attribute set to the project's package. It includes xmlns: android attribute that supplies several system attributes used within the file.

(5) The current application version is defined by version code attribute, version name attribute is used to specify public version that is displayed to users.

(6) Install location attribute is used to allow on external storage (SD Card) rather than internal storage. If install location attribute is not set to preferExternal or auto the application, it will be stored in an internal storage and later it is not possible to move it to the external storage. Internal storage is limited so better to store it to an external storage.

The following is typical manifest code:

```
<manifest xmlns: android=http://schemas.android.com/apk/res/android
→ Package= "com./
Android:versioncode="1"
Android:versionname="0.9 Beta"
Android:installLocation="PreferExternal">
[… manifest nodes …]
</manifest>
```

The manifest tag includes nodes that define the application components, security settings, test classes and requirements.

The following are the sub-node tags and provides xml snippet how each tag is used.

(1) Uses-sdk: This node defines a minimum and maximum SDK version that must be available on a device for the application to work properly on the device. MinSDKVersion, maxSDKVersion and targetSDKVersion attributes are set properly.

- Minimum SDK version indicates the lowest version of SDK that includes APIS that are to be used in the application, by default it takes 1. Application crashes when it attempts to access unavailable APIS. The target SDK version attribute enables you to specify the platform against which application is developed and tested. It supports the maximum SDK which defines an upper limit, that willing to support your application.
- In our examples which are mentioned in this book, following configuration is used. i.e. minimum required SDK version as API8 (Android 2.2) and target (maximum) SDK version as API17 (Android 4.2).

  `<uses-sdk android: minSDKVersion="8"android: targetSDKVersion="17"/>`

(2) Uses-configuration: Each node specifies combination of input mechanisms are supported by an application. This is used for games to install particular input controls.

(3) Uses-feature: uses-feature node is used to specify which hardware features are required by an application. The set of optional features that are supports for any hardware on a compatible device are mentioned as follows.

    (i) Audio: It is used for applications that require a low latency audio pipeline.

    (ii) Bluetooth: Where Bluetooth radio is required.

    (iii) Camera: For applications that requires a camera auto focus, flash or a front-facing camera.

    (iv) Location: If application requires location based services, it specifies either network or GPS support explicitly.

    (v) Microphone: For application that requires audio point.

    (vi) NFC: It requires NFC (Near-Field Communication) support.

    (vii) Sensors: It enables you to specify a requirement for any potentially available hardware sensors.

    (viii) Telephony: Either telephony is general or a specific telephony radio (GSM or CDMA) is required.

    (ix) Touchscreen: The type of touch screen that application requires.

    (x) USB: For application that requires USB host or accessory mode support.

    (xi) Wi-Fi: Where Wi-Fi network support is required.

E.g.

<uses-featureandroid:name="android.hardware.microphoneandroid:required="false"/>

E.g. Camera hardware where required attribute is added to the tag.

<uses-featureandroid:name=android.hardware.camera"/>

<usesfeatureandroid:name="android.hardware.camera.autofocus"android:required="false"/>

(4) Supports-Screen: This node specifies the screen sizes the application is designed and tested. The two sets of attributes are used to define screen support. The first set is used primarily for devices running Android version prior to Honey Comb MR2 (API level 13). The default value for each attribute is true.

    (i) Small Screen: Screens with a resolution smaller than traditional HVGA.

    (ii) Normal Screens: It is used to specify typical mobile phones screens of at least HVGA including WVGA and WQVGA.

    (iii) Large Screen: Screens larger than normal.

    (iv) Large Screens: Screen larger than typically tablet services.

E.g.

<support-screensandroid: smallscreens="false"android: normalscreen="true"android: largescreen="true" Android"xlargescreen="true"/>

(5) **Uses-permission:** This defines the user permissions for the application. Each permission which is specified will be presented to the user before application is installed. The APIS and methods that are generally have cost or security implication requires permission.

<uses-permissionandroid:name=android.permission.ACCESS_FINE_LOCATION/>

(6) **Application:** A manifest can contain only one application node. It uses attributes to specify the metadata for the application. To enable debugging, set the debuggable attribute to "true" and for release built remove it.

It acts as a container for activity, service, content provider, broadcast receiver node that specify the application components.

<applicationandroid:icon="drawable/icon"android:logo="drawable/logo"android:theme="android:style/Theme.Light"android:name=".MyApplicationClass"android:debuggable="true">

<Application node...>

</application>

(7) **Activity:** Activity tag is used in each and every application. Use the 'android: name' attribute to specify the activity class name. The main activity tag and other activities must be included in the application.

Each activity tag supports intent-filter as a child tags that specify the intents that can be used to start the activity.

<activity android: name=".MyActivity"android: label="string/app-name">

<Intent-filter>

<Action android: name="android.intent.action.MAIN"/>

<category android: name=>>android.intent.category.LAUNCHER"/>

<lintent-filter>

</activity>

(8) **Service:** Service tag is added for each service class of the application. It also supports intent-filter child tags for late runtime binding.

<service android: name=".MyService">

</service>

(9) **Provider:** This tag specifies each of the application's content providers. It used to manage database access and sharing.

<Provider android:name=".MyContentProvider"android:authrorities="com.paad.myapp.mycontentprovider"/>

(10) Receiver : By adding receiver tag to manifest xml file, the process of registering of an application becomes autonomous. Broadcast receiver is global listeners and acts when application get registered by matching the intents. Each receiver node supports intent filter child tags that define the intents that can be used to trigger the receiver.

<receiver android: name=".MyIntentReceiver">
<intent-filter>
</receiver>

(11) Uses-library: It is used to define the shared library that the application requires.

<uses-library android: name="com.google.android.maps" android: required="false"/>

7.7.2 Creating Resources

Non-Code resources such as images, string constants, and external codes are kept separated. Android supports all resources ranging from strings, colures to more complex structure as images, themes and layouts.

- Android dynamically allows selecting resources from resource trees that has different values for different hardware configuration, languages, locations android itself selects the resources when application starts.
  Where the resources are stored:
- Application resources are stored under res folder in the project hierarchy. Each of the available resource types is stored in subfolders, grouped by resource type.
- ADT Wizard, creates a res folder that contains subfolders for the values, drawable-hdpl, layout resources that contain the default string resource definition. Application icon and layouts. Drawables resource folder contains three different icons: (a) Low, (b) Medium, (c) High density respectively.
- Resource type is stored in different folders such as simple values, drawables, colures, layouts, animations, styles, menus, xml files and raw resources.
- This process generates R class that has references to each of the resources that are included in project.
- Resource filename should contain only lowercase letters, numbers, and period such as (.), underscore (_)

7.7.3 Simple Values Strings, Colors, Dimensions

Drawables all are stored in different location under res resource.

(1) Strings: These tags help in maintaining consistency of the application. It is defined with the help of string tag.

<string name="stop_message">stop</string>

Android supports the font related HTML tags such as <b>, <I>, <U> to the parts of the string.

<string name="stop_message"><b>stop</b> </string>

(2) Colors: Color tag is used to define new color resources. The following are the few notations i.e. hexadecimal number prefixed with # symbol.

#RGB
#RRGGBB
#ARGB
#AARRGGBB

e.g.
<color name="opaque_blue">#OOF</color>

(3) Dimensions: These are referred in regards of styling and layouts. They are used for creating layout constants such as borders and font sizes.

<dimen> tag is used to specify dimension tag, which is followed by scale as follows:

(i)   px (Screen Pixels)
(ii) in (Physical Inches)
(iii) pt (Physical Points)
(iv) pm (Physical Millimeters)
(v)   dp (Density-Independent Pixels)
(vi) sp (Scale-Independent Pixels)

Scale independent pixels are used for font sized whereas dp pixels are used for drawable resources.

(4) Styles and Themes: Style resources allow the application to maintain consistent look. <style> tag is used to create styles and has attributes such as name contain one or more item tag.

```
<?xml version="1.0" encoding="UTF-8"?>
<resources>
<style name="base_text">
<item_name="android:textsize">14sp</item>
<item_name="android:color">#111</item>
</style>
</resources>
```

It supports inheritence also

```
<?xml version="1.0" encoding="UTF-8"?>
<resources>
<style name="small_text" parent="base_text">
<item name="android:textsize">8sp </item>
</style>
</resources>
```

(5) Drawables : Drawables resource includes bitmaps and nine patches (PNG). More complex drawable from xml such as Level List Drawables and State List Drawables also included here.

All drawables are stored in res/drawable folder. Bitmap images are stored in –ldpi, -mdpi, -hdpi and –xhdpi folders.

Practice Questions

1. What is an Android Operating System ?
2. State the features of Android Operating System.
3. Explain the architecture of an Android Operating System.
4. What are the software development tools used for developing Android application.
5. Write short notes on :
    (a) Version history of Android Operating System.
    (b) User Interface of Android.
    (c) Devices Running Android.
    (d) Linux Kernel.

Chapter 8...

DESIGNING THE USER INTERFACE

8.1 Graphical User Interface
8.2 Introduction to Views and View Groups
    8.2.1 Fundamentals of Android UI
    8.2.2 Creating New Views
    8.2.3 Different Views in Android
8.3 Introducing layouts, Creating New Views
    8.3.1 Linear Layout
    8.3.2 Absolute Layout
    8.3.3 Table Layout
    8.3.4 Relative Layout
    8.3.5 Frame Layout
    8.3.6 ScrollView
8.4 Creating and Using Menus
    8.4.1 Introduction
    8.4.2 Menu Types
    8.4.3 Menu Item
    8.4.4 Creating Submenus
    • Practice Questions

8.1 Graphical User Interface

- In computing environment graphical User Interface (GUI) is a type of user interface that permits the user to interact with electronic devices through graphical icons and visual indicators. This is not like just a text based interface i.e. typed command labels or text navigation. GUI introduced from learning curve of command line interface (CLI) which requires commands on the keyboard.
- The actions in GUI are usually performed through direct manipulation of the graphical elements. GUIs can be found in hand held devices such as MP3 players, portable media players, gaming devices, household appliances, office and industry equipment. The GUI related to low resolution types of interface with display resolutions such as video games

are not considered as the specific term of Graphical User Interface. Or it is not restricted to flat screens, like volumetric displays because the term is restricted to the scope of two dimensional display screens that are able to describe generic information, in the tradition of computer science research at the PARC. (Palo Alto Research Center)
- To develop an application, it is mandatory to create a stylish and user friendly interface for the display on a screen. Increasing screen sizes, display resolutions and mobile processor power has seen in mobile application. These are used to develop UI elements. This uses new approach which is compatible with touch-screen devices.
    - The UI interface elements are arranged on the screen using a wide range of layout managers which are derived from view Group.
    - For creating a good user interface several native standard classes are used and developer also can create its own native classes.

User interface and interaction design
- The visual composition and temporal behavior of GUI is an important part of software application programming in the area of human computer integration. Designing the graphical user interface enhances the efficiency and ease of use for the underlying design of a stored program. This property of GUI is called as usability.
- The applications such as "chrome" or GUI (Goo-ee) are the graphical user interface where user interacts directly with information by manipulating visual widgets that allows for interactions appropriate to the kind of data they hold. All the widgets are well designed interface that are selected to support the actions necessary to achieve the goal of the user. A model view controller allows for a flexible structure in which the interface is independent from the user to select or design different screens. Good user interface design relates to the user, not the system architecture.
- Large widgets such as windows, which provides a frame or container for the main presentation content such as a web page, email message or drawing. Smaller one act as a user input tool.
- A GUI must satisfy the demand of vertical market as an application specific graphical user interfaces.
- Examples of application specific GUIs are:
    1. Automated teller machines (ATM).
    2. Point-Of-Sale touch screens at restaurants.
    3. Self service checkout used in a retail store.
    4. Airline self-ticketing and check-in.

5. Information kiosks in a public space, like a train station or a museum.
6. Monitors or control screens in an embedded industrial application which employ a Real Time Operating System (RTOS).

- The application specific touch screen GUI is implemented in latest smart phones and handheld games. GUI newer automobiles are GUIs in their navigation systems and touch screen multimedia centers.

8.2 Introduction to Views and View Groups

8.2.1 Fundamentals of Android UI

Fundamentals of android UI design which are the pillars of user interface designing:

(1) Views: Views are basic user interface class for visual interface elements (e.g. controls or widgets) views are used for user interface controls and layout classes.

(2) View Groups: These are the extensions of views. It contains multiple child views. Compound controls are combines together the various interconnected child views. Layout manager such as linear layout extends the view groups that help to constitute user interface.

(3) Activity: It is a screen or window that is displayed to the user. These are equivalent to form, to display the user interface, views or layouts are assigned to an activity.

Understanding the components of a screen:

- The basic unit of Android application is an activity. An activity displays the user interface of your application, which may contain widgets like buttons, labels, and text boxes and so on.
- The graphical user interface is coded in XML file.main.xml file located in the res/layout folder which may look like the following.
- A new activity starts with an empty screen where you places user interface. The following steps should be followed to create a user interface.
- By using layout resources developer, we can separate out presentation layer from the application logic, which provides flexibility of changing presentation layer with the same application code that is optimized to different layouts and different hardware devices.
- User interfaces can be developed in two ways. One is procedural and another is declarative. Android is implemented using both approaches procedural such as swing which is developed by using objects Jframe and JButton so on and declarative for example HTML which emphasized on contents.
- All visual elements are developed by using views control is an extension of view widgets are nothing but both compound controls and complex extension of views.

```xml
<?xml version="1.0" encoding="utf-8"?>
<LinearLayout xmlns:android="http://schemas.android.com/apk/res/android"
android: orientation="vertical"
android: layout_width="fill_parent"
android: layout_height="fill_parent"
>
<TextView
android: layout_ width="fill_parent"
android: layout_height="wrap_content"
android: text ="string/hello"
/>
/ LinearLayout>
```

- During the run time, load the XML UI in the onCreate() event handler in the Activity class, using setContentView() method of the Activity class.
  Public void onCreate (Bundle savedInstanceState)
  Super. OnCreate (savedInstanceState);
  SetContentView (R.layout.main);
- During compilation, each element in the XML file is compiled into its equivalent Android GUI class, with attributes represented by methods. The Android system then creates the UI of the activity when it is loaded.

8.2.2 Creating New Views

Android provides developer with the facility of creating new unique controls. Create composite widgets. It also facilitates with modifying existing view. There are three situations, in that developer feels a need of creating a new view.

(1) Modify or extend the existing control when it already supplies the basic functionality. Developer can customize the control and onDraw() method is override and it is reimplemented.

(2) It combines control to create atomic, reusable widgets that leverage the functionality of several interconnected controls. E.g. TextView and Button are combined together to create dropdown box, which displays ListView when clicked on it.

(3) Create a new control which is different from other interfaces.

(1) Modifying Existing Views:

- To create new widget based on an existing control, create a new class that extends it.
  Public class myTextView extends TextView
- Event handlers associated with it need to be override.

Public MyTextView (context context, AttributeSetattrs, int style) //attrs is the attribute to be set.
{
   super (context, attrs, style);
}
   Public MyTextView(context context)
{
   Super (context);
}

(2) Creating Compound Controls:

Compound control contains many child controls. These are atomic, reusable too.
- Interaction of views, layout is shown in compound controls.
- These are created by extending ViewGroup (usually layout manager).

Public class MyCompoundView extends LinearLayout.

(3) Creating Custom Widgets and Controls:
- It is basically customized that mean it can be developed according to requirements. It will be displayed by adding new controls to it which are unique.
- To create new views from blank canvas, extend it with view or SurfaceViewClasses.
- To create a view with graphics view class is loaded with a canvas object and series of draw methods and paint classes. SurfaceView provides a canvas that supports drawing from a background thread and using openGL for 3D graphics.

The following various tasks are to be performed for creating a new view:

(4) Creating a New Visual Interface: To change the size and visual display of a control, OnMeasure() and OnDraw() methods are overridden.

OnMeasure() – With this you can edit height and width of a control.

OnDraw() – It is used to draw on canvas to create a visual interface.

Various Paint objects are used to draw a new visual interface on canvas. Canvas class has circles, lines, rectangles, texts, drawable (images). It also supports transformations to rotate, translate, and scale the canvas.

- OnMeasure() method used for creating child controls, these are drawn on parent layout. It passes two parameters WidthMeasureSpec and HeightMeasureSpec. Parent control sets the size of child control by using above parameters. In returns view's height and width into SetMeasureDimension method.
- Handling User Interaction Events:

  (1) OnKeyDown() : Any device key is pressed includes D-pad, keyboard, hang-up, call, back and camera buttons.

  (2) One-up() : Called when a user releases a pressed key.

  (3) OnTrackballEvent() : Called when a device's trackball is moved.

  (4) OnTouchEvent() : Called when touch screen is pressed or released, or it detects movement.

```
public boolean OnKeyDown (int Keycode, KeyEvent KeyEvent)
   {
       return true;
   }
public boolean OnKeyUp (int KeyCode, KeyEvent KeyEvent)
   {
       return true;
   }
public boolean OnTrackballEvent(MotionEvent event)
   {
int actionPerformed=event.getAction();
       return true;
   }
public boolean OnTouchEvent(MotionEvent event)
   {
int actionPerformed=event.getAction();
   }
```

8.2.3 Different Views in Android

The following are the different views which are included in android widget toolbox:

(1) Text View: It is a standard read only text label. It supports multiline display, string formatting, automatic word wrapping.

(2) Edit Text: An editable text entry box. It accepts multiline entry and word wrapping.

(3) List View: This view group that creates and manages a group of views used to display the items in a list. The standard list view displays the string value of an array of objects using a Text View for each item.

(4) Spinner: Spinner is nothing but composition of Text View and List View. It displays the current selection combined with button. It displays the current selection dialog.

(5) Button: Standard push button.

(6) Check Box: It shows checked or unchecked, two states of button.

(7) Radio Button: Two state group button from group only one of the button got selected. Android also supports more view implementations by using date-time pickers, input boxes, maps, galleries and tab sheets.

- **Using Views Create Activity User Interface:**
    (1) SetContentView is used to display the user interface on an empty screen of a new activity. It is passed into the View instance.
    (2) The method accepts either layout resource ID or a single view instance. It helps in defining user interface either in code or a technique of external layout resources.
    (3) There are two approaches used for calling SetContentViewMethod.

- Traditional approach of accepting a View instance public void OnCreate (Bundle icicle)
  {
  ```
  super.onCreate (icicle);
  Textview myTextView = new TextView (this);
  SetContentView (myTextView);
  myTextView.SetText=("Hello, Android");
  ```
  }
- Another approach by setting user interface for an activity by using an external layout resource. FindViewById method helps to reference to the views used within a layout. Following code main.xml exist in res/layout folder.
  Public void onCreate (Bundle icicle)
  ```
  {   super.onCreate (icicle);
      SetContentView (R.layout.main);
      TextView myTextView=(TextView) findViewById (R.id.myTextVia),
      myTextView.SetText=("Hello, Android");
  }
  ```
- Another approach by setting user interface for an activity by using an external layout resource. FindViewById method helps to reference to the views used within a layout.
  Public void onCreate (Bundle icicle)
  ```
  {
      super.onCreate (icicle);
      SetContentView (R.layout.main);
      TextView myTextView=(TextView) findViewById (R.id.myTextVia),
      myTextView.SetText=("Hello, Android");
  }
  ```
- This onCreate() method is called when activity starts or restarts. An Activity contains View and View Groups. A view is widget that has an appearance on screen. The views in an android application are buttons, labels, and text boxes. A view drives from the base class android.View.
- A ViewGroup contains one or more Views. A ViewGroup provides the layout in which you can order the appearance and sequence of Views. Examples of View Groups are LinearLayout, FrameLayout.etc. A ViewGroup derives from the base class android.view.ViewGroup.

8.3 Introducing layouts, Creating New Views

- A Layout specifies the visual structure for a user interface, such as UI for an activity or any app widget.
- Layout can be declared in the following two ways:
  1. Declare UI elements in XML: the XML vocabulary of Android that corresponds to the View classes and subclasses, such as those for widgets and applications.
  2. Instantiate layout elements at runtime. Your application can create View and ViewGroup objects (and manipulate their properties) programmatically.
- Android supports the following ViewGroups:
  1. LinearLayout.
  2. AbsoluteLayout.
  3. TableLayout.
  4. RelativeLayout.
  5. FrameLayout.
  6. ScrollView.

Layout Parameters

- The layout parameters for the View that resides in any specific ViewGroup are specified by Layout_something which are XML attributes.
- Every ViewGroup class implements a nested class that extends ViewGroup. LayoutParams. This subclass contains property types that define the size and position for each child view, as appropriate for the view group. As you can see in Fig. 8.1, the parent view group defines layout parameters for each child view (including the child view group).

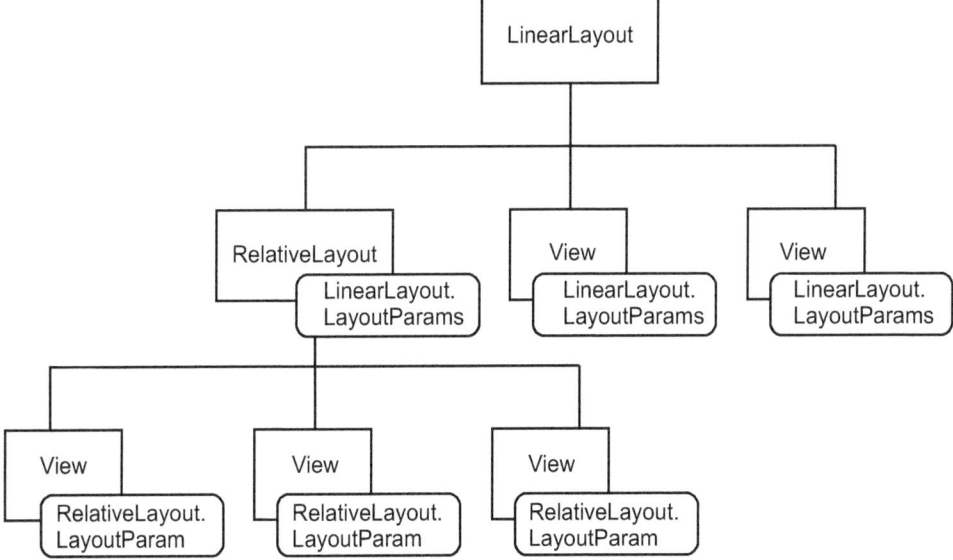

Fig. 8.1: Linear layout

- Every ViewGroup class implements a nested class that extends ViewGroup. LayoutParams. This subclass contains property types that define the size and position for each child view, as appropriate for the ViewGroup.
- The following figure shows the relative layout parameters are set to individual View.

8.3.1 Linear Layout

- The LinearLayout displays the views in a single column or single row. And the child views can be arranged vertically or horizontally.
- Each View and ViewGroup has a set of common attributes, some of which are shown in following table. <LinearLayout> is the root element which has the attributes.
- **Units of measurement:** When specifying the size of an element on an Android UI, the following units are used.
    1. dp:Density Independent pixel.160 dp is equivalent to one inch of physical screen size. This is a standard unit of measurement when views are specified in the layout.
    2. Spscale independent: This is similar to dp and is recommended for specifying font size.
    3. Pt:point: A point is defined to be 1/72 of an inch, based on the physical screen size.
    4. Px:pixel it corresponds to the actual pixel on the screen this unir is not recommended as UI not render it correctly.

Table 1: Common attributes of views and viewgroups

Attribute	Description
layout_width	Specifies the width of the View or ViewGroup the android:layout_width of each view to "0dp" (for a horizontal layout).
layout_height	Specifies the height of the View or ViewGroup. To create a linear layout in which each child uses the same amount of space on the screen, set the android:layout_height of each view to "0dp" (for a vertical layout)
layout_marginTop	Specifies extra space on the top side of the View or ViewGroup
layout_marginBottom	Specifies extra space on the bottom side of the View or ViewGroup
layout_marginLeft	Specifies extra space on the left side of the View or ViewGroup
layout_marginRight	Specifies extra space on the right side of the View or ViewGroup
layout_gravity	Specifies how child Views are positioned
layout_weight	Specifies how much of the extra space in the layout to be allocated to the View
layout_x	Specifies the x-coordinate of the View or ViewGroup
layout_y	Specifies the y-coordinate of the View or ViewGroup

- Note that some of these attributes are only applicable when a View is in certain specific ViewGroup(s).
- For example, The layout_weight and layout_gravity attributes are only applicable if a View is either in a LinearLayout or TableLayout.
- A LinearLayout allows *margins* between children View and the *gravity* (right, center, or left alignment) of each child.

Working Mechanism:

The main.xml is updated by adding following snippet to it.

```xml
<?xml version="1.0" encoding="utf-8"?>
<LinearLayout xmlns:android="http://schemas.android.com/apk/res/android"
android:orientation="vertical"
android:layout_width="fill_parent"
android:layout_height="fill_parent"
>
<TextView
android:layout_width="fill_parent"
android:layout_height="wrap_content"
android:text="@string/hello"
/>
</LinearLayout>
```

- In the above snippet the <LinearLayout > element is oriented vertically and <TextView> element has its width filling up with the width of its parent using fill_parent constant.
- And its height is set by using wrap_content constant that means the height is the height of its content.
- Many views are displayed by using the LinearLayout for example
    1. TextView
    2. EditText
    3. Button
    4. Checkbox, RadioButton
    5. ListView etc.

1. **TextView:**

For demonstrating a TextView element, we created a new android application namedas TextViewDemo with single activity TextViewDemo.java having UI file - activity_text_view_demo.xml as follows –

```xml
<LinearLayout xmlns:android="http://schemas.android.com/apk/res/android"
    xmlns:tools="http://schemas.android.com/tools"
    android:id="@+id/LinearLayout1"
```

```xml
    android:layout_width="match_parent"
    android:layout_height="match_parent"
    android:orientation="vertical"
    tools:context=".TextViewDemo" >

    <TextView
        android:id="@+id/tvlarge"
        android:layout_width="wrap_content"
        android:layout_height="wrap_content"
        android:layout_gravity="left"
        android:text="Welcome To Android World"
        android:textAppearance="?android:attr/textAppearanceLarge"
        android:textColor="#ff0000" />

    <TextView
        android:id="@+id/tvmedium"
        android:layout_width="wrap_content"
        android:layout_height="wrap_content"
        android:layout_gravity="right"
        android:text="Welcome To Android World"
        android:textAppearance="?android:attr/textAppearanceMedium"
        android:textColor="#00ff00" />

    <TextView
        android:id="@+id/tvsmall"
        android:layout_width="wrap_content"
        android:layout_height="wrap_content"
        android:layout_gravity="center"
        android:text="Welcome To Android World"
        android:textAppearance="?android:attr/textAppearanceSmall"
        android:textColor="#0000ff" />

    <TextView
        android:id="@+id/tvsimple"
        android:layout_width="match_parent"
        android:layout_height="35dp"
        android:background="#000000"
        android:text="Welcome To Android World"
        android:textColor="#ffffff" />
</LinearLayout>
```

```java
package com.example.textview;

import android.app.Activity;
import android.os.Bundle;
```

```java
public class TextViewDemo extends Activity {
    protected void onCreate(Bundle savedInstanceState) {
        super.onCreate(savedInstanceState);
        setContentView(R.layout.activity_text_view_demo);
    }
}
```

Working Mechanism:

In given snippet, we have created four TextView elements. Here we set many properties of TextView such as layout_width, layout_height, layout_gravity, layout_text i.e. text to be displayed. Also we set color of text using property textColor and background using background property. One of property we used is textAppearance which can be large, medium, or small.

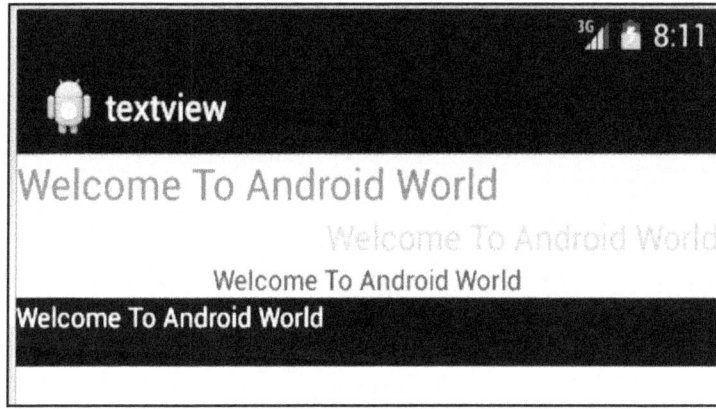

Fig. 8.2: Text View

2. EditText:

Here, we created android application of name EditTextDemo and activity files are – EditTextDemo.java, activity_edit_text_demo.xml as follows-

```xml
<LinearLayout xmlns:android="http://schemas.android.com/apk/res/android"
    xmlns:tools="http://schemas.android.com/tools"
    android:id="@+id/LinearLayout1"
    android:layout_width="match_parent"
    android:layout_height="match_parent"
    android:orientation="vertical"
    tools:context=".EditTextDemo" >

    <TextView
        android:id="@+id/tvlogin"
        android:layout_width="wrap_content"
        android:layout_height="wrap_content"
        android:text="@string/loginstr" />
```

```xml
<EditText
    android:id="@+id/etuser"
    android:layout_width="match_parent"
    android:layout_height="wrap_content"
    android:ems="10"
    android:hint="Enter your username here" >

    <requestFocus />
</EditText>

<EditText
    android:id="@+id/etpassword"
    android:layout_width="match_parent"
    android:layout_height="wrap_content"
    android:ems="10"
    android:hint="alphanumeric"
    android:inputType="textPassword" />

<EditText
    android:id="@+id/etnumericpassword"
    android:layout_width="match_parent"
    android:layout_height="wrap_content"
    android:ems="10"
    android:hint="numeric only"
    android:inputType="numberPassword" />

</LinearLayout>
```

```java
package com.example.edittext;

import android.os.Bundle;
import android.app.Activity;


public class EditTextDemo extends Activity {

    protected void onCreate(Bundle savedInstanceState) {
        super.onCreate(savedInstanceState);
        setContentView(R.layout.activity_edit_text_demo);
    }
}
```

Working Mechanism:

We can enter text in given different types EditText elements. First priority to type text in EditText is given by <requestFocus/>. Also using property hint, we can define text as a hint to user which will disappear when user enters text in EditText. For EditTextetpassword, we set property inputType to textPassword. Hence, entered text will appear in password format where password can be any text. And for EditTextetnumericpassword, inputType is set to numberPassword, hence it will accept only numbers as a password.

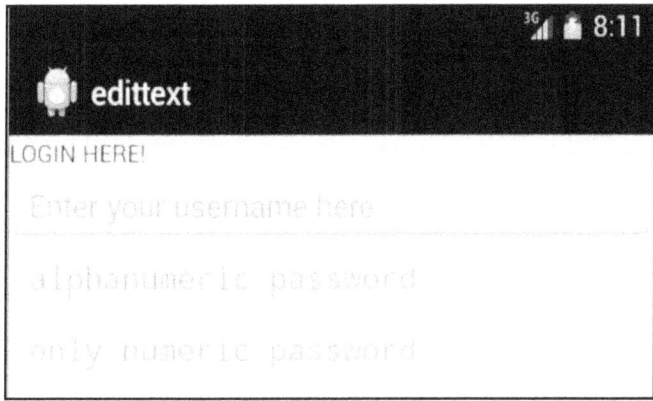

Fig. 8.3: Edit Text

3. Button:

We can handle button click event in 2 ways-
1. Using property of Button element 'android:onClick' in xml file
2. Using onClickListener interface and it's method onClick() in class file
   Following example show the first way to handle button click event. In which, we created application with name ButtonDemo and containing activity of class file- ButtonDemo.java and UI file -activity_button_demo.xml as follows -

```
<LinearLayout xmlns:android="http://schemas.android.com/apk/res/android"
    xmlns:tools="http://schemas.android.com/tools"
    android:id="@+id/LinearLayout1"
    android:layout_width="match_parent"
    android:layout_height="match_parent"
    android:orientation="vertical"
    android:paddingBottom="@dimen/activity_vertical_margin"
    android:paddingLeft="@dimen/activity_horizontal_margin"
    android:paddingRight="@dimen/activity_horizontal_margin"
    android:paddingTop="@dimen/activity_vertical_margin"
    tools:context=".ButtonDemo" >
```

```xml
<Button
    android:id="@+id/btndisplay"
    android:layout_width="wrap_content"
    android:layout_height="wrap_content"
    android:layout_gravity="center"
    android:onClick="functiondisplay"
    android:text="Click Me" />
```

```xml
</LinearLayout>
```

```java
package com.example.button;

import android.app.Activity;
import android.os.Bundle;
import android.view.View;
import android.widget.Toast;

public class ButtonDemo extends Activity {
    protected void onCreate(Bundle savedInstanceState) {
        super.onCreate(savedInstanceState);
        setContentView(R.layout.activity_button_demo);
    }
    public void functiondisplay(View v)
    {
        int xoffset=0;
        int yoffset=0;
        Toast tobj=Toast.makeText(getApplicationContext(), "You clicked Me", Toast.LENGTH_LONG);
        tobj.setGravity(Gravity.TOP, xoffset, yoffset);
        tobj.show();
    }
}
```

Working Mechansim:

In given example, as we set property of Button android:onClick="functiondisplay" which means when button is clicked, activity will call method functiondisplay(). In this method, we created 'tobj' i.e. object of Toast class with setting gravity properties and toast message will be shown using its method tobj.show().In short, when we click on the button, it will show you a toast message.

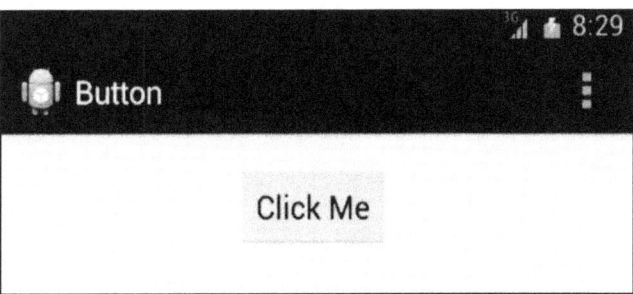

(a) Button

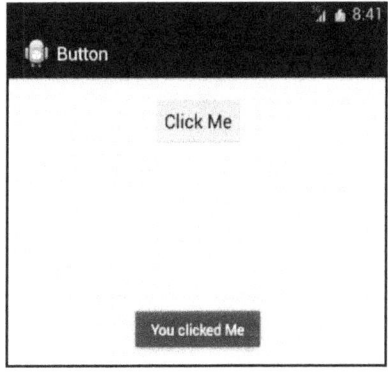

(b) Button click event

Fig. 8.4

4. **Screen Shot of Checkbox and Radiobox:**

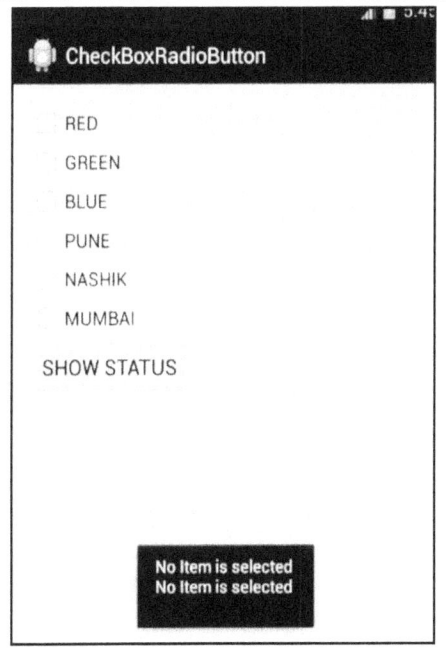

(a)   (b)

Fig. 8.5: Checkbox and Radiobox

5. **Screen Shot of ListView:**

Fig. 8.6: ListView

8.3.2 Absolute Layout

- This layout enables to specify the exact location of the child view.
- That is the x and y co-ordinates of the child views. Absolute layouts are less flexible and harder to maintain than other types of layouts without absolute positioning.
- There is a problem with Absolute Layout when the activity is viewed on a high resolution screen, for this reason android deprecated since Android 1.5 .to avoid AbsoluteLayout is the better option as it is not guaranteed to be supported in future version.

AbsoluteLayout Example :
```
<?xml version="1.0" encoding="utf-8"?>
<AbsoluteLayout xmlns:android="http://schemas.android.com/apk/res/android"
    android:id="@+id/AbsoluteLayout1"
    android:layout_width="match_parent"
    android:layout_height="match_parent" >

    <TextView
        android:id="@+id/displaytext1"
        android:layout_width="wrap_content"
        android:layout_height="wrap_content"
```

```
        android:layout_x="10dp"
        android:layout_y="80dp"
        android:text="This Is Absolute Layout"
        android:textAppearance="?android:attr/textAppearanceLarge" />

    <TextView
        android:id="@+id/displaytext2"
        android:layout_width="match_parent"
        android:layout_height="wrap_content"
        android:layout_x="30dp"
        android:layout_y="330dp"
        android:text="Position Values Are Specified Here"
        android:textAppearance="?android:attr/textAppearanceLarge" />

</AbsoluteLayout>
```

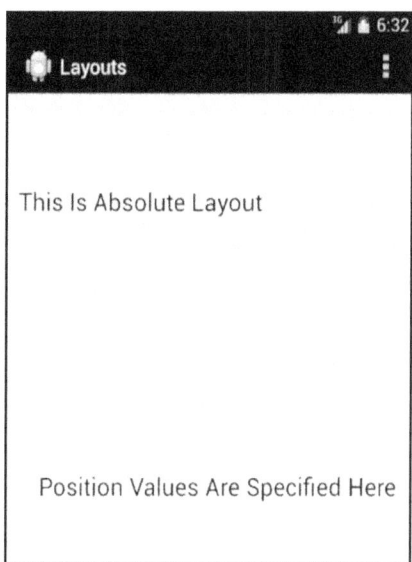

Fig. 8.7: Absolute Layout

8.3.3 Table Layout

- A layout that arranges its children into rows and columns. A TableLayout consists of a number of TableRow objects, each defining a row (actually, you can have other children, which will be explained below). TableLayout containers do not display border lines for their rows, columns, or cells. Each row has zero or more cells; each cell can hold one View object. The table has as many columns as the row with the most cells. A table can leave cells empty. Cells can span columns, as they can in HTML.

- A layout that displays its children views into rows and columns. A TableLayout consists of a number of TableRow objects each defines a row.
- TableLayout containers do not display the borders for their rows, columns or cells.
- Each row may consist of zero or more cells. Each cell can hold one view object; the table has as many columns as the row with the most cells. A table can leave cells empty.
- The <TableRow> element is used to designate a row in the table.

TableLayout Example :

```xml
<?xml version="1.0" encoding="utf-8"?>
<TableLayout xmlns:android="http://schemas.android.com/apk/res/android"
    android:id="@+id/TableLayout1"
    android:layout_width="match_parent"
    android:layout_height="match_parent" >

    <TableRow
        android:id="@+id/tableRow1"
        android:layout_width="wrap_content"
        android:layout_height="wrap_content" >

        <TextView
            android:id="@+id/textView1"
            android:layout_width="wrap_content"
            android:layout_height="wrap_content"
            android:text="Medium Text"
            android:textAppearance="?android:attr/textAppearanceMedium" />

        <TextView
            android:id="@+id/textView2"
            android:layout_width="wrap_content"
            android:layout_height="wrap_content"
            android:text="Medium Text"
            android:textAppearance="?android:attr/textAppearanceMedium" />

    </TableRow>

    <TableRow
        android:id="@+id/tableRow2"
        android:layout_width="wrap_content"
        android:layout_height="wrap_content" >
```

```xml
<Button
    android:id="@+id/button1"
    android:layout_width="200dp"
    android:layout_height="wrap_content"
    android:text="Button" />

<Button
    android:id="@+id/button2"
    android:layout_width="wrap_content"
    android:layout_height="wrap_content"
    android:text="Button" />

    </TableRow>

</TableLayout>
```

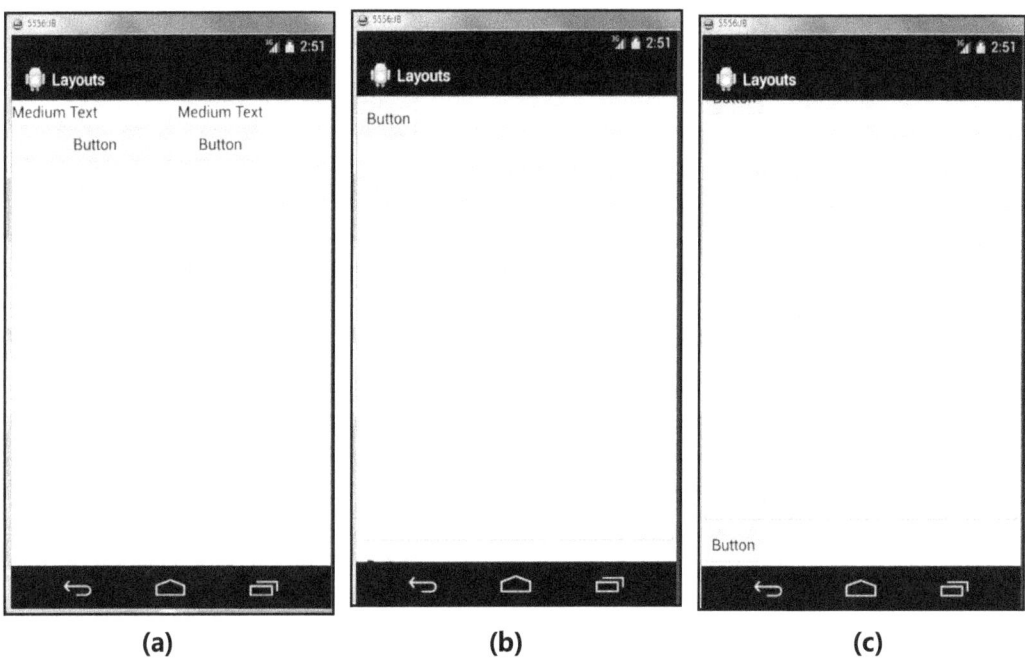

Fig. 8.8: Table Layouts

8.3.4 Relative Layout

- Relative Layout is a ViewGroup that displays child views in relative position. The position of each view can be specified by considering to sibling elements or in position relative to the parent relative layout area. (Such as aligned to the bottom, left of center).

- For improving the performance the nested View groups should be eliminated and a flat layout hierarchy should be maintained for this purpose the RealtiveLayout is used. The nested Linear Layout can be replaced with one RelativeLayout.
- Lets child views specify their position relative to the parent view or to each other (specified by ID). So you can align two elements by right border, or make one below another, centered in the screen, centered left, and so on. By default, all child views are drawn at the top-left of the layout, so you must define the position of each view using the various layout properties available from RelativeLayout.LayoutParams.
- Relative Layout specifies the each child view relative to their position to the parent view or to each other. So two elements can be aligned by right border or make one below another, centered in the screen, centered left, and so on. By default, all child views are drawn at the top left of the layout, so you must define the position of each view using various layout properties available .
- Each view embedded within the Relative Layout has attributes that allow them to align with another view. These attributes are:
    1. **layout_alignParentTop:** If "true", makes the top edge of this view match the top edge of the parent.
    2. **layout_alignLeft:** Positions the left edge of this view to the right of the view specified with a resource ID.
    3. **layout_alignRight:** Positions the right edge of this view to the right of the view specified with a resource ID.
    4. **layout_below:** Positions the top edge of this view below the view specified with a resource ID.

RelativeLayout Example :

```xml
<?xml version="1.0" encoding="utf-8"?>
<RelativeLayout xmlns:android="http://schemas.android.com/apk/res/android"
    android:id="@+id/RelativeLayout1"
    android:layout_width="match_parent"
    android:layout_height="match_parent"
    android:orientation="vertical" >

    <Button
        android:id="@+id/cancelbtn"
        android:layout_width="wrap_content"
        android:layout_height="wrap_content"
        android:layout_alignBottom="@+id/savebtn"
        android:layout_marginLeft="50dp"
        android:layout_toRightOf="@+id/savebtn"
        android:text="CANCEL" />
```

```xml
<EditText
    android:id="@+id/name"
    android:layout_width="wrap_content"
    android:layout_height="wrap_content"
    android:layout_alignBaseline="@+id/nametxt"
    android:layout_alignBottom="@+id/nametxt"
    android:layout_toRightOf="@+id/savebtn"
    android:ems="10" />

<EditText
    android:id="@+id/phone"
    android:layout_width="wrap_content"
    android:layout_height="wrap_content"
    android:layout_alignTop="@+id/phonetxt"
    android:layout_toRightOf="@+id/savebtn"
    android:ems="10"
    android:inputType="phone" />

<TextView
    android:id="@+id/heading"
    android:layout_width="wrap_content"
    android:layout_height="wrap_content"
    android:layout_above="@+id/name"
    android:layout_centerHorizontal="true"
    android:layout_marginBottom="16dp"
    android:text="ADD_CONTACT"
    android:textAppearance="?android:attr/textAppearanceLarge" />

<Button
    android:id="@+id/savebtn"
    android:layout_width="wrap_content"
    android:layout_height="wrap_content"
    android:layout_below="@+id/phone"
    android:layout_marginTop="75dp"
    android:layout_toRightOf="@+id/phonetxt"
    android:text="SAVE" />

<TextView
    android:id="@+id/nametxt"
    android:layout_width="wrap_content"
    android:layout_height="wrap_content"
    android:layout_alignParentTop="true"
```

```
            android:layout_marginTop="84dp"
            android:layout_toLeftOf="@+id/heading"
            android:text="Name :"
            android:textAppearance="?android:attr/textAppearanceMedium" />

    <TextView
            android:id="@+id/phonetxt"
            android:layout_width="wrap_content"
            android:layout_height="wrap_content"
            android:layout_alignLeft="@+id/nametxt"
            android:layout_below="@+id/name"
            android:layout_marginTop="38dp"
            android:text="Phone No"
            android:textAppearance="?android:attr/textAppearanceMedium" />
</RelativeLayout>
```

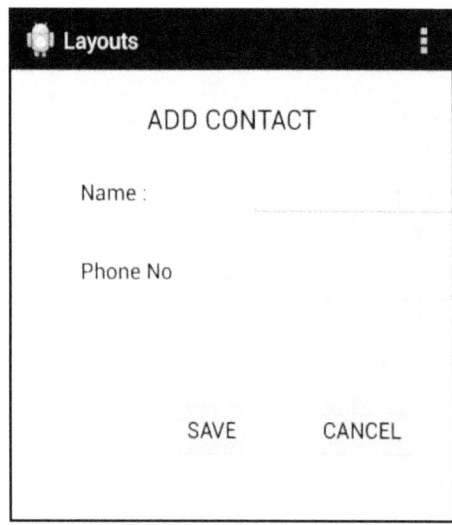

Fig. 8.9: Relative Layout

8.3.5 Frame Layout

- FrameLayout is designed to block out an area on the screen to display a single item. Generally, FrameLayout should be used to hold a single child view, because it can be difficult to organize child views in a way that's scalable to different screen sizes without the children overlapping each other.
- You can, however, add multiple children to a FrameLayout and control their position within the FrameLayout by assigning gravity to each child, using the android:layout_gravity attribute.

Fig. 8.10: Frame Layout

8.3.6 ScrollView
- The framelayout has a special type as of layout as scrollView, which allows users to scroll through list of child views that that occupy more space than the physical display. The scrollView can contain only one child view or ViewGroup, which normally is a linearlayout.
- The listview can not be used with scrollview. The listView is designed for showing a list of related information and is optimized for dealing with large lists.

8.4 Creating and Using Menus
8.4.1 Introduction
Menus are the common user interface component which is used in many applications. You should use the Menu APIs to present user actions and other options in your activities.

With Android 3.0 (API level 11), Android powered devices are no longer required to provide a dedicated the Menu button. With this change Android apps should migrate away from a dependence on the traditional 6 item menu panel and instead provide an action bar to present common user actions.

The design and user experience for some menu item have changed, the rules to define a set of actions and options is still based on the MENU APIs.

When device's menu button is pressed, each activity's menu id displayed in such a way that all activities are exposed

8.4.2 Menu Types
Android has three stage menu system to get optimized usability of application menus:

(1) Icon Menu : When menu button is pressed, it appears at the bottom of the screen. It displays the icons and texts up to six menus (or submenus).

(2) Expanded Menu : When user selects more menu item from icon menu, expanded menu gets generated. This specifically doesn't include any icons it displays scrollable list of only the menu item that weren't present in icon menu. It displays full text shortcut keys, check boxes/radio buttons.

(3) Submenu: When user selects any submenu android gives alternative of creating a floating window which has heading as a submenu, it doesn't support any icons whereas each menu item is displayed as full text, check boxes and shortcut keys.

Pressing back from submenu, it navigates without moving back to extend or icon menu.

8.4.3 Menu Item

- Menu Item is composed of various buttons on the screen such as shortcuts, checkboxes radio buttons and so on.
- Checkboxes and radio buttons: These buttons are visible in expanded menu and submenu. It is created by using setcheckable method and its state is maintained using setchecked.
- Radio buttons are always added within a group which is having group identifier. This identifier is passed to menu.SetGroupCheckable and the exclusive clicked button is set to true. Following code shows how checkboxes and radio buttons are added.

```
//create new checkbox
menu.add(0,CHECK_ITEM, Menu.NONE,"checkbox".setcheckable(true);
//create a group of radio button
menu.add(RB_GROUP, RADIOBUTTON_1, Menu.NONE,"Radiobutton1");
menu.add(RB_GROUP, RADIOBUTTON_2,Menu.NONE,"Radiobutton2");
menu.add(RB_GROUP,RADIOBUTTON_3, Menu.NONE,"Radiobutton3").SetCheckable(true);
menu.SetGroupCheckable(RB_GROUP, true, true);
```

(2) Shortcut keys : Keypad shortcut is created of menu item by using set shortcut Method. Two shortcut keys are required one is for numeric keypad and another is for full keyboard. '0' is used for numeric and 'b' is used for full keyboard inspite of case-sensitive.

menuItem.SetShortcut('0', 'b');

(3) Condensed Tiles : The icon menu does not have shortcuts, checkboxes, so to display the state of menu in the form of text these are used.

menuItem.SetTitleCondensed("Title");

(4) Icons : These are displayed only in an icon menu. These are absent in expanded and submenus. It is drawable resource identifier.

menuItem.SetIcon(R.drawable.menu_item_icon);

(5) menuItem click listner : This event is executed when menu item is selected. The following code shows how click listner is applied to menu item.

menuItem.SetOnMenuItemClickListner(NewOnMenuItemClickListner()
{
public boolean OnMenuItemClick(MenuItem_menuItem)
}
[... click handling, true if handled]
return true;
}
});

(6) Intents : When menu item is selected, it neither handled by MenuItemClickListner nor by OnOptionsItemSelected handler. The intent is assigned to menu item. Android executes StartActivity, passing in the specified intent.

menuItem.SetIntent(new Intent(this, MyotherActivityclass));

8.4.4 Creating Submenus

- Submenus are always displayed in single floating window, android uses different approaches for different screen devices.
- AddSubMenu method is used to add the menus. It has the parameters such as : (i) Unique identifier, (ii) Text string for each submenu.
- SetHeaderIcon() : To display the header of submenu and SetIcon() to add menus into the list.

SubMenu sub=menu.addSubMenu(0,0,menu.NONE,"submenu");
SubHeaderIcon(R.drawable.icon);
Set.SetIcon(R.drawable.icon);
MenuItem SubMenuItem=sub.add(0, 0, menu.NONE,"SubmenuItem");

1. **Options Menu :**

Creating an Activity Menu.

- By overriding OnCreateOption menu method the menu for an activity is created. This method gets triggered when first time activity's menu is displayed.
- The method accepts menu object as a parameter. This menu reference is stored and used else where in code until next time this method is called.
- For each menu item:
    (1) Specify a group value to separate Menu items for batch processing and ordering.
    (2) Unique identifier for each menu, menu item selections are generally handled by the OnOptionItem. Selected event handler, which is important to determine which menu item, was pressed.
    (3) An order value that defines the order in which the menu items are displayed.
    (4) The menu text, either as a character string or as a string resource.

Add method is used to populate menu object.

```
public boolean OnCreateOptionMenu (Menu menu)
{
super.on(createOptionsMenu(menu);
    #Groupid int groupid=0;
//unique menu item identifier used for event handling.
    int menuItemId=MENU_ITEM;
//The order position of the item
    int menuItemorder=menu.NONE;
//Text to be displayed for this menu item
    int menuItemText=R.string.menu_item;
//create the menu item and keep a reference to it.
MenuItem MenuItem=menu.add(groupId, menu Itemid, menuItemOrder, menuItemText);
    return true;
}
```

2. **Contextual Menu:**
   - A contextual menu is associated with a view on an activity and it is displayed when the user long clicks an item. For example if the user taps on a button view and hold it for a few seconds, a context menu can be displayed.
   - In contextual menu specific items generally has the options that affects only that particular item. The contextual menu in Android appears when a user presses and holds on a specific item. The contextual menu will be presented to the user, and the user may chooses the option from an array.
   - If user wants associate a context menu with a view on an activity, user should call setonCreateContextMenuListener() method of that particular view.

Registering the View for Contextual Menus
   - Here is the basic example that creates a contextual menu on one single item. A contextual menu is created within a view, so we will register that view for the contextual menu first and then move on to the menu itself.

Creating the Contextual Menu
   - Once we have registered the view for a contextual menu, we will create a menu in XML for our contextual menu. To create a menu in XML format, create a contextual.xml file in the menu folder of your resources. Add the following code to your contextual.xml file:
   - These are displayed in current view. It is triggered when trackball, middle D-pad button, or the view for around 3 seconds.
   - To create a context menu there are two different ways.

(1) Create a generic Context Menu for a View class by overriding OnCreateContextMenu handler

```
public void OnCreateContextMenu(Context Menu menu)
    {   super.OnCreateContextMenu(menu);
        menu.add("ContextMenuItem1";
    }
```

(2) Activity centric context menus by overriding the OnCreateContextMenu method and registering the views.

```
public void OnCreate(Bundle icicle)
    {   super.OnCreate(icicle);
        EditText view=new EditText(this);
        SetContentView(view);
        registerForContextMenu(view);
    }
```

The registerForContextMenu is used for registering views.

- Context menu item selection are handled by overriding the OnContextItemSelected method on the activity.

```
public boolean OnContextItemSelected(MenuItem item)
{
Super.OnContextItemSelected(item);
return false;
}
```

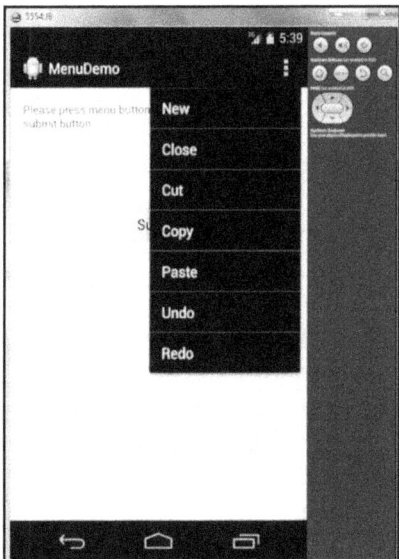

Fig. 8.11: Creating context menu

3. Popup Menu :

- A popup menu displays a list of items in a vertical list that's anchored to the view that invoked the menu. It's good for providing an overflow of actions that relate to specific content or to provide options for a second part of a command. Actions in a popup menu should not directly affect the corresponding content—that's what contextual actions are for. Rather, the popup menu is for extended actions that relate to regions of content in your activity.
- Android also supports the popup menu. A popup menu is a modal menu that can be programmed to appear when a button is clicked.

Defining a Popup Menu in XML

- For all menu types, Android provides a standard XML format to define menu items .Instead of building a menu in user's code; user should define a menu and all items in a XML menu resource.

Using a menu resource is a good practice for a few reasons:

- It's easier to visualize the menu structure in XML.
- It separates the content for the menu from your application's behavioral code.
- It allows you to create alternative menu configurations for different platform versions, screen sizes, and other configurations by leveraging the app resources framework.
- To define the menu, create an XML file inside your projects res/menu/ directory and build the menu with the following elements:

`<menu>`:defines a Menu, which is a container for menu items. A `<menu>` element must be the root node for the file and can hold one or more `<item>` and `<group>` elements.

`<item>`:Creates a MenuItem, which represents a single item in a menu. This element may contain a nested `<menu>`element in order to create a submenu.

`<group>`:An optional, invisible container for `<item>` elements. It allows you to categorize menu items so they share properties such as active state and visibility. For more information, see the section about Creating Menu Groups.

```xml
<?xml version="1.0" encoding="utf-8"?>
<menu
    xmlns:android="http://schemas.android.com/apk/res/android">
        <item android:id="@+id/new_game"
            android:icon="@drawable/ic_new_game"
            android:title="@string/new_game"
            android:showAsAction="ifRoom"/>
        <item android:id="@+id/help"
            android:icon="@drawable/ic_help"
            android:title="@string/help" />
</menu>
```

- The <item> element supports several attributes you can use to define an item's appearance and behavior. The items in the above menu include the following attributes:

    android: id
- A resource ID that's unique to the item, which allows the application, can recognize the item when the user selects it.

    android:icon

A reference to a drawable to use as the item's icon.

    android:title

A reference to a string to use as the item's title.

    android:showAsAction

Specifies when and how this item should appear as an action item in the action bar.

To use the menu in your activity, you need to inflate the menu resource (convert the XML resource into a programmable object) using MenuInflater.inflate(). In the following sections, you'll see how to inflate a menu for each menu type

- If you define your menu in XML, here's how you can show the popup menu:
    1. Instantate a PopupMenu with its constructor, which takes the current application Context and the View to which the menu should be anchored.
    2. Use MenuInflater to inflate your menu resource into the Menu object returned by PopupMenu.getMenu(). On API level 14 and above, you can use PopupMenu.inflate() instead.
    3. Call PopupMenu.show().

    Note: PopupMenu is available with API level 11 and higher.

Popup Menu Example :

```
<menu xmlns:android="http://schemas.android.com/apk/res/android" >

    <item android:id="@+id/m1" android:title="Developer" />
    <item android:id="@+id/m2" android:title="Tester" />
    <item android:id="@+id/m3" android:title="Manager" />
    <item android:id="@+id/m4" android:title="Supplier" />
    <item android:id="@+id/m5" android:title="Customer" />
    <item android:id="@+id/m6" android:title="User" />

</menu>
```

```xml
<LinearLayout xmlns:android="http://schemas.android.com/apk/res/android"
    xmlns:tools="http://schemas.android.com/tools"
    android:id="@+id/LinearLayout1"
    android:layout_width="match_parent"
    android:layout_height="match_parent"
    android:orientation="vertical"
    android:paddingBottom="@dimen/activity_vertical_margin"
    android:paddingLeft="@dimen/activity_horizontal_margin"
    android:paddingRight="@dimen/activity_horizontal_margin"
    android:paddingTop="@dimen/activity_vertical_margin"
    tools:context=".PopupMenuDemo" >

    <Button
        android:id="@+id/button1"
        android:layout_width="wrap_content"
        android:layout_height="wrap_content"
        android:text="Click button to see popup menu" />

</LinearLayout>
```

```java
package com.example.popupmenudemo;

import android.annotation.SuppressLint;
import android.app.Activity;
import android.os.Bundle;
import android.view.Menu;
import android.view.MenuItem;
import android.view.View;
import android.view.View.OnClickListener;
import android.widget.Button;
import android.widget.PopupMenu;
import android.widget.Toast;

public class PopupMenuDemo extends Activity implements OnClickListener {

    Button btn;
```

```java
@Override
protected void onCreate(Bundle savedInstanceState) {
    super.onCreate(savedInstanceState);
    setContentView(R.layout.activity_popup_menu_demo);
    btn=(Button) findViewById(R.id.button1);
    btn.setOnClickListener(this);
}

@Override
public boolean onCreateOptionsMenu(Menu menu) {
    // Inflate the menu; this adds items to the action bar if it is present.
    getMenuInflater().inflate(R.menu.popup_menu_demo, menu);
    return true;
}

@SuppressLint("NewApi")
@Override
public void onClick(View arg0) {

    PopupMenu popup = new PopupMenu(PopupMenuDemo.this, btn);
     popup.getMenuInflater().inflate(R.menu.popup_menu_demo, popup.getMenu());

    popup.setOnMenuItemClickListener(new PopupMenu.OnMenuItemClickListener() {
        public boolean onMenuItemClick(MenuItem item) {
        Toast.makeText(PopupMenuDemo.this,"You       Clicked     :     "     + item.getTitle(),Toast.LENGTH_SHORT).show();
        return true;
        }
    });
    popup.show();
    }
}
```

Fig. 8.12: Popup menu

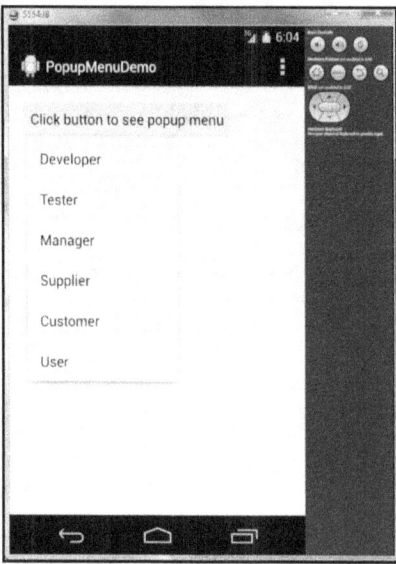
Fig. 8.13: Open popup menu

Fig. 8.14: Click event of popup menu

Practice Questions

1. What is view in Android Operating System ?
2. Explain the view Groups in Android Operating System ?
3. State and explain different types of layout.
4. List down the menus that can be used in Android Operating System.
5. Write short notes on :
   (a) Graphical user Interface
   (b) Linear layout
   (c) Table layout
   (d) Relative layout
   (e) Contextual menu
   (f) Pop-up menu.

Chapter 9...

STARTING WITH APPLICATION CODING

9.1 Introduction
    9.1.1 Application Components
9.2 Introduction to Intents
    9.2.1 Using SimpleCursorAdaptor
9.3 Using Internet Resources
    9.3.1 Connecting to an Internet Resource
9.4 Introducing Dialogs
    9.4.1 Introduction of Dialog Class
    9.4.2 Alter Dialog Class
    9.4.3 Specialist Input Dialogs
9.5 Example of Date Picker Control
9.6 Example of Time Picker Control
    • Practice Questions

9.1 Introduction

- Android applications are written by using Java Programming Language. The code is compiled with SDK compile tools by referring the data and resource files into an android package, an archive fill with an .apk suffix.
- The code in .apk file is considered to be one application and is the file that Android powered devices use to install the application.
  The application resides in own security sandbox when it is installed on a device.
- The Android operating system is a multi-user Linux system in which each application is a different user.
- A unique Linux user ID (Id which is used by system and unknown to the application) is assigned to the application by the system by default. The system sets the permission for all the files in an application so that only the userID assigned to that application can access them.
- Each process has its own virtual machine (VM), so an application's code runs in isolation from other applications.

- Every application runs in its own Linux process. Android starts the process when any of the application's components needed, to be executed, then shut down the process when it's no longer needed or when the system recover memory for other applications.
- The android system implements the principle of least privilege i.e. each application has access only to the components that it requires to do its work the secure environment is created in which the application cannot access parts of the system for which it is not given permission.
- In the following specified ways the application can share the data with the other application and for an application to access system services.
    1. The Linux user ID can be shared by two applications so that they can access each others files. To conserve system resources, applications with the same user ID can also arrange to run in the same Linux process and share the same.
    2. An application can request permission to access device data such as the user's contacts, SMS messages, the mountable storage (SD card), camera, Bluetooth and more. All application permissions must be granted by the user at install time.
    3. An application that resides in the sandbox and having unique Linux user ID has the following components:
        (i) The core framework components that define your application.
        (ii) The manifest file in which you declare components and required device features for your application.
        (iii) Resources that are separate from the application code and allow your application to gracefully optimize its behavior for a variety of device configurations.

9.1.1 Application Components

- The components of the application are the basic building blocks. Each component is a different point through which the system can enter your application. All components are the actual entry points for the user and some depend on each other, but each component exists its own entity and plays a specific role.
- There are four different types of application components. Each type serves a distinct purpose and has a distinct lifecycle that defines how the component is created and destroyed.
    (1) Activity, (2) Service, (3) Content Provider, (4) Broadcast Receiver.

Three of the four component types—activities, services, and broadcast receivers—are activated by an asynchronous message called an *intent*. Intents bind individual components to each other at runtime (you can think of them as the messengers that request an action from other components), whether the component belongs to your application or another.

Intent is created with an Intent object, which defines a message to activate either a specific component or a specific *type* of component—intent can be either explicit or implicit, respectively.

For activities and services, the actions to be performed are defined by intent, and it may specify the URI of the data to act on. For example, intent might convey a request for an activity to show an image or to open a web page. In some cases, you can start an activity to receive a result, in which case, the activity also returns the result in an Intent

For broadcast receivers, the intent simply defines the announcement being broadcast (for example, a broadcast to indicate the device battery is low includes only a known action string that indicates "battery is low").

The component type Content provider is not activated by intents .rather it is activated when targeted by a request from a Content Resolver. The content resolver handles all direct transactions with the content provider so that the component that's performing transactions with the provider doesn't need to and instead call methods on content resolver object. This creates a layer of abstraction between the content provider and the component requesting information.

There are separate methods for activating each type of component:
- You can start an activity (or give it something new to do) by passing an Intent to startActivity() orstartActivityForResult() (when you want the activity to return a result).
- You can start a service (or give new instructions to an ongoing service) by passing an Intent tostartService (). Or you can bind to the service by passing an Intent to bindService ().
- You can initiate a broadcast by passing an Intent to methods like sendBroadcast(), sendOrderedBroadcast(), or sendStickyBroadcast().
- You can perform a query to a content provider by calling query() on a ContentResolver.

(1) Activity
- An activity represents a single screen with a user interface. For example consider the application e-mail, which has several activities with different tasks. One activity with list of new emails, another activity with to compose an email and another activity for reading emails.
- Each activity is independent of each other the different activities may work together to form a cohesive user experience. For example, in email application different application such as a camera can start the activity that composes new email in order to share picture.

For creating a single activity, we have to create a java file and xml file. Also, every activity in our application must be declared in our AndroidManiFast.xml file. Here, we create a simple android application of name Simpleactivity using previous steps. And write a code for life cycle stages of activity using the methods onCreate(), onStop() etc. in java file of Name MainActivity.java. We set UI components which are declared in xml file using statement – SetContentView (R.layout.activity_main);

We add log statements such as –

Log.d (String tugname, String message);

```xml
<RelativeLayoutxmlns:android="http://schemas.android.com/apk/res/android"
xmlns:tools="http://schemas.android.com/tools"
android:layout_width="match_parent"
android:layout_height="match_parent"
tools:context=".MainActivity">

<TextView
android:layout_width="wrap_content"
android:layout_height="wrap_content"
android:text="@string/hello_world"/>

</RelativeLayout>
```

```java
package com.example.simpleactivity;

import android.os.Bundle;
import android.app.Activity;
import android.util.Log;

public class MainActivity extends Activity {
    @Override
    protectedvoid onCreate(Bundle savedInstanceState) {
        super.onCreate(savedInstanceState);
        setContentView(R.layout.activity_main);

        Log.d("Activity Events","Currently activity is in onCreate");
    }

    @Override
    protectedvoid onDestroy() {
        super.onDestroy();
        Log.d("Activity Events","Currently activity is in onDestroy");
    }
    @Override
    protectedvoid onPause() {
        super.onPause();
        Log.d("Activity Events","Currently activity is in onPause");
    }
```

```
    @Override
    protectedvoid onRestart() {
        super.onRestart();
        Log.d("Activity Events","Currently activity is in onRestart");
    }
    @Override
    protectedvoid onResume() {
        super.onResume();
        Log.d("Activity Events","Currently activity is in onResume");
    }

    protectedvoid onStart() {
        super.onStart();
        Log.d("Activity Events","Currently activity is in onStart");
    }

    @Override
    protectedvoid onStop() {
        super.onStop();
        Log.d("Activity Events","Currently activity is in onStop");
    }
}
```

Working Mechanism :

We run our application using 'F11' button. Now, you can see various logs in logCat Window of eclipse. When we load activity press back button or home button, logs are added

Fig. 9.1: Simple activity

(2) Service
- A service component that runs in the background to perform long running operations or to perform work remote processes. A service doesn't provide user interface.
- Example of service component, play music in background while the user in a different application, or it might fetch data over the network without blocking user interaction with an activity can start the service and let it run or bind to it in order to interact with it.

For creating our own service, first we create simple application of name SimpleService. And activity of name class file – ActivityForService.java and xmlfile of name activity_activity_for_service.xml. Then, we add new java class file MySimpleService.java with override methods onBind(...), onStartCommand() and onDestroy().

Also, we add service details in AndroidManifest.xml file as –

    <service android:name=".MySimpleService">

    </service>

```xml
<?xmlversion="1.0"encoding="utf-8"?>
<manifestxmlns:android="http://schemas.android.com/apk/res/android"
package="com.example.simpleservice"
android:versionCode="1"
android:versionName="1.0">

<uses-sdk
android:minSdkVersion="8"
android:targetSdkVersion="17"/>

<application
android:allowBackup="true"
android:icon="@drawable/ic_launcher"
android:label="@string/app_name"
android:theme="@style/AppTheme">
<activity
android:name="com.example.simpleservice.ActivityForService"
android:label="@string/app_name">
<intent-filter>
<actionandroid:name="android.intent.action.MAIN"/>
```

```xml
<categoryandroid:name="android.intent.category.LAUNCHER"/>
</intent-filter>
</activity>
<serviceandroid:name=".MySimpleService"></service>

</application>

</manifest>
```

```xml
<LinearLayoutxmlns:android="http://schemas.android.com/apk/res/android"
xmlns:tools="http://schemas.android.com/tools"
android:id="@+id/LinearLayout1"
android:layout_width="match_parent"
android:layout_height="match_parent"
android:orientation="vertical"
tools:context=".ActivityForService">

<Button
android:id="@+id/startbtn"
android:layout_width="wrap_content"
android:layout_height="wrap_content"
android:text="Click Here To Start Service"/>

<Button
android:id="@+id/stopbtn"
android:layout_width="wrap_content"
android:layout_height="wrap_content"
android:text="Click Here To Stop Service"/>

</LinearLayout>
```

```java
package com.example.simpleservice;

import android.app.Activity;
import android.content.Intent;
import android.os.Bundle;
import android.view.View;
import android.view.View.OnClickListener;
import android.widget.Button;
```

```java
public class ActivityForService extends Activity {

    Button start,stop;
    Intent i;

    @Override
    protected void onCreate(Bundle savedInstanceState) {
        super.onCreate(savedInstanceState);
        setContentView(R.layout.activity_activity_for_service);

        i=newIntent(getBaseContext(), MySimpleService.class);

        start=(Button) findViewById(R.id.startbtn);
        stop=(Button) findViewById(R.id.stopbtn);

        start.setOnClickListener(new OnClickListener() {
            @Override
            publicvoid onClick(View v) {
                                    startService(i);
            }
        });

        stop.setOnClickListener(new OnClickListener() {
            @Override
            publicvoid onClick(View v) {
                                    stopService(i);
            }
        });
    }
}

package com.example.simpleservice;

import android.app.Service;
import android.content.Intent;
import android.os.IBinder;
import android.widget.Toast;

public class MySimpleService extends Service {

    @Override
    public IBinder onBind(Intent arg0) {
    return null;
    }
```

```
@Override
public int onStartCommand(Intent intent, int flags, int startId) {
    Toast.makeText(this, "Service is started",Toast.LENGTH_LONG).show();
    return super.onStartCommand(intent, flags, startId);
}

@Override
public void onDestroy() {
    super.onDestroy();
    Toast.makeText(this, "Service is stopped",Toast.LENGTH_LONG).show();
    }
}
```

Working Mechanism :

When, we start our application, by clicking on StartService() startbtn' activity will raise onClickListener and we start service with created intent i by calling StartService(); method. Here, in our service, we just shown a single toast message, where you can write code for doing some task. When, we click on stop btn, it will stop service by calling StopService();

Here, onDestroy() is called and Toast is shown.

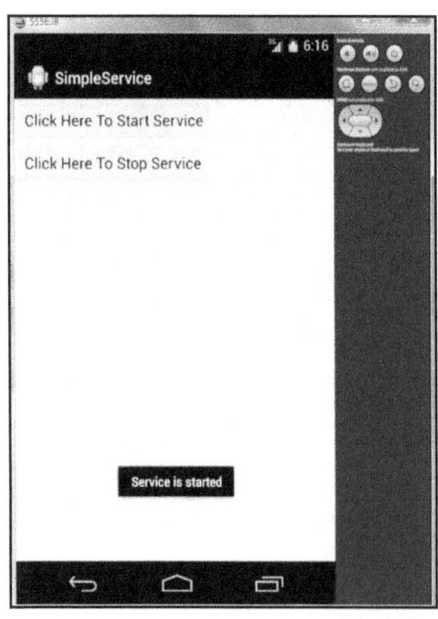
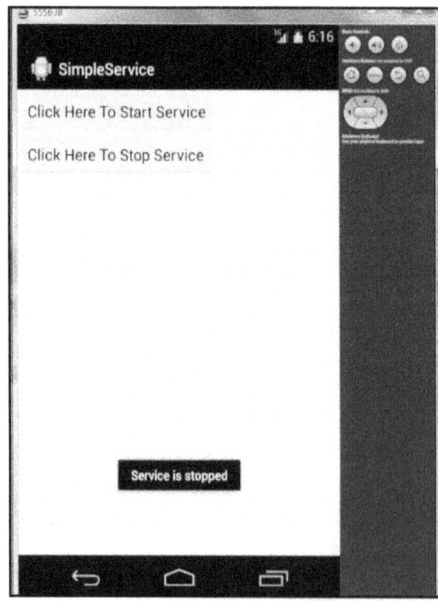

Fig. 9.2: Service start event   **Fig. 9.3: Service stop event**

(3) Content Provider

- A content provider manages a shared set of application data. Data can be stored in the file system, in a SQLite database, on the web, or any other persistent storage location that your application can access.
- By using the content provider other applications can query or even modify the data (if content provider allows it) for example, the Android's system provides a content provider that manages the user's contact information. That means any application with proper permissions can query part of the content provider to read and write the information about a particular person.
- Content providers are also useful for reading and writing data that is private to your application and not shared. For example, the Note Pad sample application uses a content provider to save notes.
- A content provider is implemented as a subclass of ContentProvider and must implement a standard set of APIs that enable other applications to perform transactions.

We create an application with name content provider, activity with name – DisplayContactActivity.java and activity_display_contact.xml file. Also we need permission for reading contacts from phone. Hence, add following line in AndroidManifest.xml file –

<uses-permission android:name="android.permission.READ_CONTACTS"/>

In our XML file, we have taken list view for displaying name contactlist.

In java file, create uri object as name contacturi and get cursor 'c' to read contacts. Read all contacts from cursor and add it in ArrayList contactrecords. Create array adapter object as ad and set adapter to listview using contactlist.SetAdapter(ad);

```xml
<?xmlversion="1.0"encoding="utf-8"?>
<manifestxmlns:android="http://schemas.android.com/apk/res/android"
package="com.example.contentprovider"
android:versionCode="1"
android:versionName="1.0">

<uses-sdk
android:minSdkVersion="8"
android:targetSdkVersion="17"/>
<uses-permissionandroid:name="android.permission.READ_CONTACTS"/>

<application
android:allowBackup="true"
android:icon="@drawable/ic_launcher"
android:label="@string/app_name"
```

```xml
android:theme="@style/AppTheme">
<activity
android:name="com.example.contentprovider.DisplayContactsAcivity"
android:label="@string/app_name">
<intent-filter>
<actionandroid:name="android.intent.action.MAIN"/>

<categoryandroid:name="android.intent.category.LAUNCHER"/>
</intent-filter>
</activity>
</application>
</manifest>

<LinearLayoutxmlns:android="http://schemas.android.com/apk/res/android"
xmlns:tools="http://schemas.android.com/tools"
android:id="@+id/LinearLayout1"
android:layout_width="match_parent"
android:layout_height="match_parent"
android:orientation="vertical"
tools:context=".DisplayContactsAcivity">

<TextView
android:id="@+id/textView1"
android:layout_width="wrap_content"
android:layout_height="wrap_content"
android:text="Contact List In Your Phone Is :"
android:textAppearance="?android:attr/textAppearanceLarge"/>

<ListView
android:id="@+id/contactlist"
android:layout_width="match_parent"
android:layout_height="419dp"
android:background="#ff0000">
</ListView>
</LinearLayout>
```

```java
package com.example.contentprovider;

import java.util.ArrayList;

import android.app.Activity;
import android.database.Cursor;
import android.net.Uri;
import android.os.Bundle;
import android.provider.ContactsContract;
import android.widget.ArrayAdapter;
import android.widget.ListView;
import android.widget.TextView;
import android.widget.Toast;

public class DisplayContactsAcivity extends Activity {

    String nameofcoulmn=ContactsContract.Contacts.DISPLAY_NAME;
    ArrayList<String> contactrecords=new ArrayList<String>();
    Cursor c;
    Uri contacturi;
    ListView contactlist;
    TextView tv;

    @Override
    protected void onCreate(Bundle savedInstanceState) {
        super.onCreate(savedInstanceState);
        setContentView(R.layout.activity_display_contacts);
        contactlist=(ListView) findViewById(R.id.contactlist);
        tv=(TextView) findViewById(R.id.textView1);

        contacturi=ContactsContract.Contacts.CONTENT_URI;

        c=getContentResolver().query(contacturi,null, null, null, null);

        if(c.moveToFirst())
        {
            do {
            contactrecords.add(c.getString(c.getColumnIndex(nameofcoulmn)));
            } while (c.moveToNext());
        }
```

```
        if(contactrecords.isEmpty())
        {
        tv.setText("No Contacts Found!!\nAdd Some Contacts In Your Phone");
        Toast.makeText(this,"No Contacts Found!!\nAdd Some Contacts In Your Phone", Toast.LENGTH_LONG).show();
        }
        else
        {
        ArrayAdapter<String> ad=new
        ArrayAdapter<String>(getApplicationContext(),
        android.R.layout.simple_list_item_activated_1, contactrecords);
        contactlist.setAdapter(ad);
        tv.setText("Contact List In Your Phone Is :");
        }
    }
}
```

Working Mechanism :

When we run application, if on emulator or on device, not a single contact is stored, then it will show you a toast message. Hence, add some contacts in phone and again run application, it will show you the name of all contacts stored in phone.

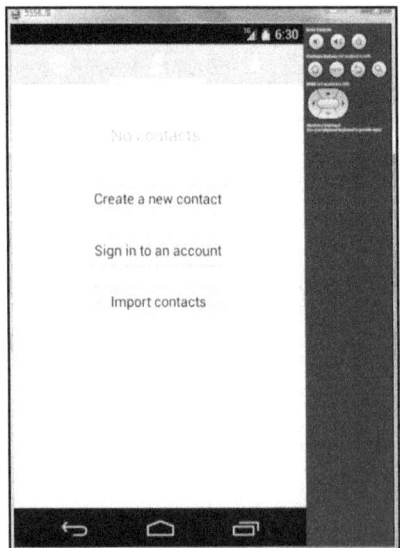

Fig. 9.4: Content provider   **Fig. 9.5: Creating new contact**

Fig. 9.6: Display contact in phone

(4) Broadcast Receiver

- Broadcast receiver is a component that responds to system wide broadcast announcements. Many broadcasts originate from the system. For example a broadcast announcing that the screen has turned off, the battery is low or a picture was captured.
- Application that resides on a device, these also can broadcast the messages, to let the other application knows that some data has been downloaded to the device and is available for them to use. These components don't display the user interface, they may create a status bar notification to alert the user when a broadcast event occurs.
- Broadcast receiver is just a gateway to other components and is intended to do a very minimal amount of work. For instance it might initiate a service to perform some work based on event.
- A broadcast receiver is implemented as a subclass of BroadcastReceiver and each broadcast is delivered as an Intent object.
- Android allows a unique system design specification that is any application can start another application's component .for example if you want the user to capture a photo with the device camera, the application completes one task and that may be used by another application. When camera application is used in another application, when camera finishes its task then it returns to its original application where it has been used.

- When the system starts a component, it starts the process for that application. And instant the classes needed for the component. For example, if your application starts the activity in the camera application that captures a photo, that activity runs in the process that belongs to the camera application, not in your application's process. Therefore, unlike applications on most other systems, Android applications don't have a single entry point (there's no main() function).
- The application runs in separate process handled by the system. It has the file permissions that restrict access to other applications, your application cannot directly activate components from another application. The Android system however can activate a component in another application, you must deliver a message to the system that specifies your intent to start a particular component. The system activities the component for you.

Here, we create application broadcasting with activity name of java file – RegisterActivity.java and XML file – activity_register. Here we register our broadcast Receiver dynamically in our program.

(Other option is you can register receiver in AndroidManiFest.xml file which we can unregister dynamically). Create a class file of name MyBroadcastReceiver.java with override method onReceive (). Here, we check for action: ACTION_TIME_TICK and show a toast of current time. In our activity, for startbtn onClick() method, we create object of MyBroadcastReceiver of name mbr and registerReceiver for action 'ACTION_TIME_TICK' and for stopbtn, we unregister receiver mbr by calling as – unregisterReceiver (mbr);

activity_register xml

```
<LinearLayoutxmlns:android="http://schemas.android.com/apk/res/android"
xmlns:tools="http://schemas.android.com/tools"
android:id="@+id/LinearLayout1"
android:layout_width="match_parent"
android:layout_height="match_parent"
android:orientation="vertical"
android:paddingBottom="@dimen/activity_vertical_margin"
android:paddingLeft="@dimen/activity_horizontal_margin"
android:paddingRight="@dimen/activity_horizontal_margin"
android:paddingTop="@dimen/activity_vertical_margin"
tools:context=".RegisterActivity">

<Button
android:id="@+id/startbtn"
android:layout_width="wrap_content"
android:layout_height="wrap_content"
android:text="Click To Register Receiver"/>
```

```xml
<Button
android:id="@+id/stopbtn"
android:layout_width="wrap_content"
android:layout_height="wrap_content"
android:text="Click To UnRegister Receiver"/>

</LinearLayout>
```

Register Activity.java
```java
package com.example.broadcasting;

import android.app.Activity;
import android.content.Intent;
import android.content.IntentFilter;
import android.os.Bundle;
import android.view.View;
import android.view.View.OnClickListener;
import android.widget.Button;
import android.widget.Toast;

public class RegisterActivity extends Activity {

    Button start,stop;
    MyBroadcastReceiver mbr;
    @Override
    protected void onCreate(Bundle savedInstanceState) {
        super.onCreate(savedInstanceState);
        setContentView(R.layout.activity_register);

        start=(Button) findViewById(R.id.startbtn);

        start.setOnClickListener(new OnClickListener() {

            @Override
            public void onClick(View v) {
                        mbr=new MyBroadcastReceiver();
            registerReceiver(mbr, new IntentFilter(Intent.ACTION_TIME_TICK));
            Toast.makeText(getApplicationContext(),  "Broadcast   Receiver   is
registered\nIt Will Show You Time At Each Minute", Toast.LENGTH_LONG).show();
            }
        });
stop=(Button) findViewById(R.id.stopbtn);

        stop.setOnClickListener(new OnClickListener() {
```

```java
            @Override
            public void onClick(View v) {
    unregisterReceiver(mbr);
    Toast.makeText(getApplicationContext(), "Broadcast    Receiver    is    Un registered", Toast.LENGTH_LONG).show();
            }
        });
    }
}

MyBroadcastReceiver.java
package com.example.broadcasting;

import java.util.Calendar;

import android.content.BroadcastReceiver;
import android.content.Context;
import android.content.Intent;
import android.widget.Toast;

public class MyBroadcastReceiver extends BroadcastReceiver {
    @Override
    public void onReceive(Context currentcontext, Intent currentintent) {
    if(currentintent.getAction().equalsIgnoreCase(Intent.ACTION_TIME_TICK))
        {
                        String format;
            int hr=Calendar.getInstance().get(Calendar.HOUR_OF_DAY);
            int min=Calendar.getInstance().get(Calendar.MINUTE);
            int type=Calendar.getInstance().get(Calendar.AM_PM);
                        if(type==0)
                            format="AM";
                        else
                            format="PM";
            Toast.makeText(currentcontext, "Time Is  "+hr+" : "+min+"
                            "+format, Toast.LENGTH_LONG).show();
        }
    }
}
```

Working Mechanism:

When we start application, by clicking on register receiver, it will register our BroadcastReceiver, and after every minute, it will show you a toast message of current time. It will continue till we unregister our receiver.

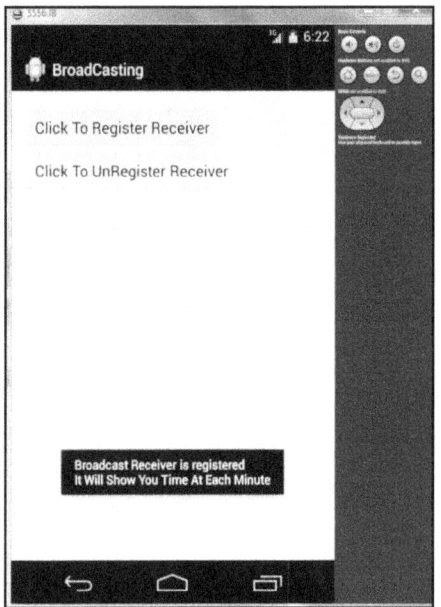

Fig. 9.7: Broadcasting

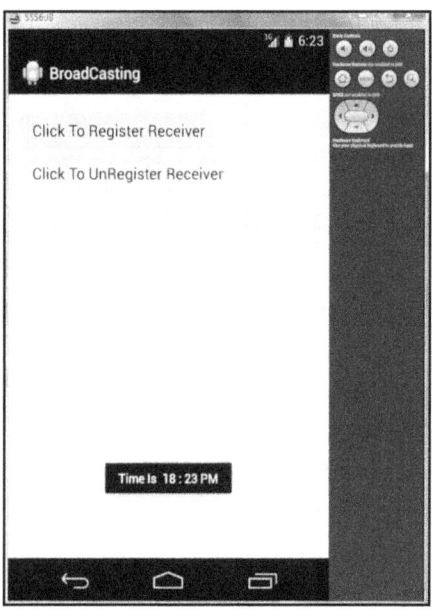

Fig. 9.8: Register in Broadcasting

Fig. 9.9: Unregistered Broadcasting

9.2 Introduction to Intents

- There are three core components of an application : (i) Activities, (ii) Services (iii) Broadcast receivers, which communicates through messages. In these components, intents are used as message-passing mechanism.
- The intent messaging is used for binding between components which are in same or different applications.
- Intent is a data structure that holds the description of the action to be performed. Each type of component is handled by different types of intent messages.
- An intent object holds the information such as component that receives the object also the category of a component that is significant to action to be taken or how to launch the target activity. Intent objects are used in Start Activity to launch an Activity Broadcast Intent to send it to any interested broadcast receiver components, and start service (Intent) or bindservice (Intent, ServiceConnection, into) to communicate with background service.
- Intent has action to be performed and data on which it should be performed is listed below by intents.

Android Intents

What is Intent?

- Intent is a specific command that allows user to send a command to the Android OS to do something specific. There are many actions that can be done such as sending an email or attaching a photo to an email or even launching an application.
- The logical workflow of creating intent is usually as follows:
  (a) Create the Intent
  (b) Add Intent options -> Ex. what type of intent we are sending to the OS or any attributes associated with that intent, such as a text string or something being passed along with the intent
  (c) RUN the Intent
- Real Life Example: Let's say I wake up in the morning and I "INTEND" to go to work. I will first have to THINK about going to get ready, but that DOESN'T really happen. I will then have to tell my brain to get out of bed first, then getting ready for work. Once I know where I'm going I SEND the command to begin and my body takes action.

Pending Intents

- Continuing from the real life example, let's say I want to take a shower but I want to shower, AFTER I brush my teeth and eat breakfast. So I know I won't be showering until at least 30-40 minutes. I still have in my head that I need to prepare my clothes, however this will not happen until 30-40 minutes have passed. I now have a PENDING intent to shower. It is PENDING for 30-40 minutes.

- That is pretty much the difference between a Pending Intent and a Regular Intent. Regular Intents can be created without a Pending Intent, however in order to create a Pending Intent you need to have a Regular Intent setup first.
- Regular Intent -> DOES NOT REQUIRE PENDING INTENT TO BE MADE
- Pending Intent -> REQUIRES A REGULAR INTENT TO BE CREATED

<intent-filter>

SYNTAX:

<intent-filter android:icon="drawable resource"
      android:label="string resource"
      android:priority="integer" >
        . . .
</intent-filter>

    CONTAINED IN:

    <activity>

    <activity-alias>

    <service>

    <receiver>

    MUST CONTAIN:

    <action>

    CAN CONTAIN:

    <category>

    <data>

- It specifies the types of intents that an activity, service or broadcast receiver can respond to. An intent filter declares the capabilities of its parent component –what an activity or service can do and what types of broadcast a receiver can handle.
- Most of the contents of the filter are described by its <action>, <category>, and <data> sub elements.

ATTRIBUTES:

1. android:icon
- An icon that represents the parent activity, service, or broadcast receiver when that component is presented to the user as having the capability described by the filter.
- This attribute must be set as a reference to a drawable resource containing the image definition. The default value is the icon set by the parent component's icon attribute. If the parent does not specify an icon, the default is the icon set by the <application> element.

2. android:label

- A user readable label is given for the parent component .this label is set by parent component that is presented to the user as having the capability described by the filter.
- The label should be set as a reference to a string resource, so that it can be localized like other strings in the user interface. However, as a convenience while you're developing the application, it can also be set as a raw string.
- The default value is the label set by the parent component. If the parent does not specify a label, the default is the label set by the <application> element's label attribute.

3. android:priority

- The priority that should be given to the parent component with regard to handling intents of the type described by the filter. This attribute has meaning for both activities and broadcast receivers:
- It provides information how able an activity is to respond to an intent that matches the filter, relative to other activities that could respond to the intent. When an intent could be handled by multiple activities with different priorities, here android will consider with higher priority values as potential targets for the intent.
- It controls the order in which broadcast receivers are executed to receive broadcast messages. The messages with higher priority are called first than the lower priority messages.
- Use this attribute only if you really need to impose a specific order in which the broadcasts are received, or want to force Android to prefer one activity over others.

(1) Action: A string that contains action to be performed or in case of broadcast intents, the action that took place and is being reported. Action class has following actions to be performed in the constants.

(i) Action_Call_Activity – Initiate a phone call
(ii) Action_EDIT_Activity – Display data for the user to edit.
(iii) ACTION_MAIN_Activity – Start up the initial activity of a task, with no data input and no returned output.
(iv) ACTION_SYNC_Activity – Synchronize data on a server with data on the mobile device.
(v) ACTION_BATTERY_Low_broadcast receiver – A warning that is receiver battery low
(vi) ACTION_HEADSET-PLUG_broadcast receiver – A headset has been plugged into the device, or unplugged from it.
(vii) ACTION_SCREEN_ON_Broadcast – The screen has been turned on.
(viii) ACTION_TIMEZONE_CHANGED_Broadcast receiver – The setting for the time zone has changed.

- Developer can use its own action constants to send to the components. The action in intent is set with the help of SetAction() and read by getAction().

(2) Data : URI of the data or MIME type of data acts on the action is to be performed.
- The type of data (MIME) with the URI helps to match the intent with corresponding component.
- ACTION_CALL needs to be performed on data that would contain tel:URI with the number to call.
- ACTION_VIEW on data field which is http:URI, the receiving activity which is called upon to download or display whatever data of the URI.

(3) Category: Any number of category descriptions can be placed in an intent object. The following category constants are defined in intent class.
  (i) Category_BROWSABLE – Browser displays the content data which is referenced by link. E.g. image, e-mail message.
  (ii) CATEGORY_GADGET – The activity which is embedded within another activity that hosts gadgets.
  (iii) CATEGORY_HOME – This activity displays the home screen, the first screen when user pressed HOME button.
  (iv) CATEGORY_LAUNCHER – This activity can be initial activity of a task and it is listed in top-level application launcher.
  (v) CATEGORY_PREFERENCE – The target activity is a preference panel.
      Add category(), which adds new category, removecategory() is used to remove the category. getcategory() gives the current categories that are set to an object.

(4) Extras: Some of the extra key-value pair values are to be set with data URI. e.g. ACTION_HEADSET_PLUG has a "state" extra indicating whether the headset in now plugged in or unplugged, as well as "name" extra for the type of headset.

The intent objects has a series of put() methods for inserting various types of extra data and similar set of get () methods for reading the data.

(5) Flags: Flag instructs Android system how to launch an activity and how to treat it after it's launch (whether it belongs in the list of recent activities). All these flags are defined in the intent class.

Data Continued:
- The following attributes supports to specify the data that your component supports.
  (1) android: Host – Specifies_valid host name.
  (2) Android: Mimetype – It specifies the type of data component handles.
     e.g. <type android:value="vnd.android.cursor.dir/*">.
     It would match to any android cursor.
  (3) android: Path – Valid path values for URI.

- **(4) android: Port** – Valid ports for the host.
- **(5) android: Scheme** – Requires a particular scheme.
- There are two primary types of intents:
  - **(1) Implicit:** It does not specify any component. It includes information according system can determine the components that are needed to run the intents.
  - **(2) Explicit:** It has specified component which provides exact class to run. These will not contain any other information.
- The activity starts with StartActivity and intent passed to it which resolves for only one single activity. If there are many activities which are capable of performing a given action on the specified data. Then best out of it is selected which is called as "Intent Resolution".
- Using intents to launch activity following method is used:
  StartActivity (myIntent);

This searches and starts the single activity that matches to your intent. Explicitly starting newly activity.

  Intent intent=new Intent(MyActivity.this, MyOtherActivity.class);
  StartActivity (intent);

The following code enables to launch dialer facility to the user from current running application only it uses implicit intents that requests an action be performed on a phone number.

  if (SomethingUnusual andanditlookwiered)
  {
  Intent intent=newIntent (Intent.ACTION_DIAL);
  uri.parse ("tel: 02024222242"));
  StartActivity (intent);
  }

Example of Intent
- We use intent for start another activity from one activity. Here, we create application intent and activity with name class file – IntentDemoActivity1.java and
  xmlfile_intent_demo_activity1.xml.
- Also, we create another activity with name IntentDemo_activity1.xml.
  and we create another activity with name IntentDemoActivity2.java and
  intent_demo_activity2.xml.
- Add another activity details in AndroidManiFest.xml file as follws :
  < activity android:name="com.example.intent.IntentDemoActivity2"
    android:label=(a)string/app_name">
  </activity>

- In our first activity, IntentDemoActivity1.java onClick of btnsubmit. We create object of intent using class file name as follows :
    Intent i=newIntent(this,IntentDemoActivity2class);
- Also we pass information username to the next activity using method of intent as :
    i.putExtra (string key, string value);
    Then, we can start next activity by using method – StartActivity(i);

xmlfile_intent_demo_activity1.xml

```xml
<?xmlversion="1.0"encoding="utf-8"?>
<manifestxmlns:android="http://schemas.android.com/apk/res/android"
package="com.example.intent"
android:versionCode="1"
android:versionName="1.0">

<uses-sdk
android:minSdkVersion="8"
android:targetSdkVersion="17"/>

<application
android:allowBackup="true"
android:icon="@drawable/ic_launcher"
android:label="@string/app_name"
android:theme="@style/AppTheme">
<activity
android:name="com.example.intent.IntentDemoActivity1"
android:label="@string/app_name">
<intent-filter>
<actionandroid:name="android.intent.action.MAIN"/>

<categoryandroid:name="android.intent.category.LAUNCHER"/>
</intent-filter>
</activity>
<activity
android:name="com.example.intent.IntentDemoActivity2"
android:label="@string/app_name">
</activity>
</application>

</manifest>
```

intent_demo_activity2.xml

```xml
<LinearLayoutxmlns:android="http://schemas.android.com/apk/res/android"
    xmlns:tools="http://schemas.android.com/tools"
    android:id="@+id/LinearLayout1"
    android:layout_width="match_parent"
    android:layout_height="match_parent"
    android:orientation="vertical"
    tools:context=".IntentDemoActivity1">

    <TextView
        android:id="@+id/tv1"
        android:layout_width="wrap_content"
        android:layout_height="wrap_content"
        android:text="This is FIRST activity"/>

    <TextView
        android:id="@+id/tv2"
        android:layout_width="wrap_content"
        android:layout_height="wrap_content"
        android:text="By clicking on button will start second activity"/>

    <TextView
        android:id="@+id/tv3"
        android:layout_width="wrap_content"
        android:layout_height="wrap_content"
        android:text="User name will pass to second activity"/>

    <TextView
        android:id="@+id/tv4"
        android:layout_width="wrap_content"
        android:layout_height="wrap_content"
        android:text="ENTER USER NAME     :"
        android:textAppearance="?android:attr/textAppearanceLarge"/>

    <EditText
        android:id="@+id/etusername"
        android:layout_width="match_parent"
        android:layout_height="wrap_content"
        android:ems="10"
        android:hint="Please type your name here">

        <requestFocus/>
    </EditText>
```

```xml
<Button
android:id="@+id/btnsubmit"
android:layout_width="wrap_content"
android:layout_height="wrap_content"
android:layout_gravity="center"
android:text="SUBMIT"/>

</LinearLayout>

<?xmlversion="1.0"encoding="utf-8"?>
<LinearLayoutxmlns:android="http://schemas.android.com/apk/res/android"
android:layout_width="match_parent"
android:layout_height="match_parent"
android:orientation="vertical">

<TextView
android:id="@+id/tv1"
android:layout_width="wrap_content"
android:layout_height="wrap_content"
android:text="This is SECOND activity"/>

<TextView
android:id="@+id/tv2"
android:layout_width="wrap_content"
android:layout_height="wrap_content"
android:text="User name retrieved passed from first activity"/>

<TextView
android:id="@+id/tv3"
android:layout_width="wrap_content"
android:layout_height="wrap_content"
android:textAppearance="?android:attr/textAppearanceLarge"
android:text="Entered User Name Is    :     "/>

<EditText
android:id="@+id/etname"
android:layout_width="match_parent"
android:layout_height="wrap_content"
android:ems="10"
android:enabled="false"
android:hint="Name Is Not Entered">

<requestFocus/>

</EditText>

</LinearLayout>
```

IntentDemoActivity1.java

```java
package com.example.intent;

import android.app.Activity;
import android.content.ContentValues;
import android.content.Intent;
import android.os.Bundle;
import android.view.View;
import android.view.View.OnClickListener;
import android.widget.Button;
import android.widget.EditText;

public class IntentDemoActivity1 extends Activity implements OnClickListener {

    EditText name;
    Button submit;

    @Override
    protected void onCreate(Bundle savedInstanceState) {
    super.onCreate(savedInstanceState);
    setContentView(R.layout.intent_demo_activity1);

    name=(EditText) findViewById(R.id.etusername);
    submit=(Button) findViewById(R.id.btnsubmit);
    submit.setOnClickListener(this);
    }

    @Override
    public void onClick(View arg0) {

    Intent i=new Intent(this,IntentDemoActivity2.class);
        i.putExtra("username",name.getText().toString());
        startActivity(i);
    }
}
```

IntentDemoActivity2.java

```java
package com.example.intent;

import android.app.Activity;
import android.content.Intent;
import android.os.Bundle;
import android.widget.EditText;
```

```
public class IntentDemoActivity2 extends Activity {

    EditText uname;
    @Override
    protected void onCreate(Bundle savedInstanceState) {
        // TODO Auto-generated method stub
        super.onCreate(savedInstanceState);
setContentView(R.layout.intent_demo_activity2);
        Intent i=getIntent();
        String username=i.getStringExtra("username");
uname=(EditText) findViewById(R.id.etname);
uname.setText(username);
    }
}
```

Working Mechanism:

In first activity, we will enter user name in the edittext enterusername, and it will pass to next activity when we click on submit button. Next activity will start with username entered in previous activity shown in edittext entername which we can not modify by setting properly of edittext-android:enabled="false"

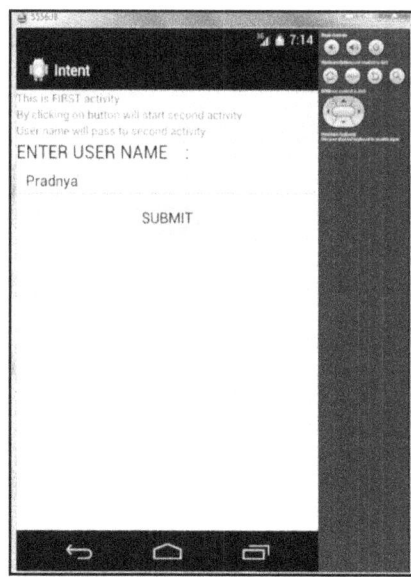

Fig. 9.10: Intent first activity   **Fig. 9.11: Intent second activity**

Introducing Adapters
- An adapter is an object that acts as a bridge between an AdapterView and the underlying data for the view.
- Adapter provides access to the data items .The adapter is also responsible for making View for each item in the data set.
- These are classes which binds data to user-interface views. It creates child views to represent each item.
- The user interface controls the support to adapters, it must extent AdapterView class.
- The developer can create AdapterView controls and new Adapter classes to bind them.
- Android has its own native adapters. Adapter has two tasks to be performed.
  (1) Supplying data
  (2) Selecting views that represent each item

Adapters :
(1) Array Adapter – It binds adapter views to an array of objects.
- Array Adapter binds them to string value of each object to a TextView control which is defined within layout.

ArrayAdapter: Extends BaseAdapter, implements Filterable

Class Overview
java.lang.Object
   android.widget.BaseAdapter
↳
      android.widget.ArrayAdapter<T>
↳

- A concrete Base Adapt er that is backed by an array of arbitrary object. By default this class expects that the provided resource id references a single TextView. That field id should be reference a TextView in the larger layout resource.
- The textview is referenced, it will be filled with the to string() of each object in the array the list of arrays of custom objects and these determined what text will be displayed for the item in the list.
- To use something other than Text Views for the array display, for instance, ImageViews, or to have some of data besides toString() results fill the views; override getView (int, View, ViewGroup) to return the type of view you want.

Public Constructors
ArrayAdapter(Context context, int resource)
Constructor
ArrayAdapter(Context context, int resource, int textViewResourceId)
Constructor

ArrayAdapter(Context context, int resource, <T> objects) Constructor	
ArrayAdapter(Context context, int resource, int textViewResourceId, <T> objects) Constructor	
ArrayAdapter(Context context, int resource, List<T> objects) Constructor	
ArrayAdapter(Context context, int resource, int textViewResourceId, List<T> objects) Constructor	
Public Constructor	
void	add(T object) Adds the specified object at the end of the array.
void	addAll(Collection<? extends T> collection) Adds the specified Collection at the end of the array.
void	addAll(T... items) Adds the specified items at the end of the array.
void	clear() Remove all elements from the list.
static ArrayAdapter<CharSequence>	createFromResource(Context context, int textArrayResId, int textViewResId) Creates a new ArrayAdapter from external resources.
Context	getContext() Returns the context associated with this array adapter.
int	getCount()
View	getDropDownView(int position, View convertView, ViewGroup parent) Get a View that displays in the drop down popup the data at the specified position in the data set.
Filter	getFilter() Returns a filter that can be used to constrain data with a filtering pattern.
T	getItem(int position)
long	getItemId(int position)
View	getPosition(T item) Returns the position of the specified item in the array.

void	insert(T object, int index) Inserts the specified object at the specified index in the array.
void	notifyDataSetChanged() Notifies the attached observers that the underlying data has been changed and any View reflecting the data set should refresh itself.
void	remove(T object) Removes the specified object from the array.
void	setDropDownViewResource(int resource) Sets the layout resource to create the drop down views.
void	setNotifyOnChange(boolean notifyOnChange) Control whether methods that change the list (add(T), insert(T,int), remove(T), clear()) automatically callnotifyDataSetChanged().
void	sort(Comparator<? super T> comparator) Sorts the content of this adapter using the specified comparator.

Example of Array Adapter

We create an application arrayadapter with activity class file AdapterDemo.java and .xml file activity_adapter_demo.xml. Here, we take a listview of name list of operating systems.

In AdapterDemo activity, we take a array of operating_system and will create a object of arrayadapter aa by passing parameter context, layout and array as follws :

ArrayAdapter<String>aa=new ArrayAdapter<String>

(this, android.R.layout.simple_list_item1, operating-system); and will set adapter to listview as follows :

lvref.setAdapter(aa);

```
activity_adapter_demo.xml
<?xmlversion="1.0" encoding="utf"-8"?>
<LinearLayoutxmlns:android="http://schemas.android.com/apk/res/android"
xmlns:tools="http://schemas.android.com/tools"
android:id="@+id/LinearLayout1"
android:layout_width="match_parent"
android:layout_height="match_parent"
```

```xml
android:orientation="vertical"
android:paddingBottom="@dimen/activity_vertical_margin"
android:paddingLeft="@dimen/activity_horizontal_margin"
android:paddingRight="@dimen/activity_horizontal_margin"
android:paddingTop="@dimen/activity_vertical_margin"
tools:context=".AdapterDemo">

<TextView
android:id="@+id/textView1"
android:layout_width="wrap_content"
android:layout_height="wrap_content"
android:text="Listing of Operating system  :"
android:textAppearance="?android:attr/textAppearanceLarge"/>

<ListView
android:id="@+id/listofos"
android:layout_width="match_parent"
android:layout_height="375dp">

</ListView>

</LinearLayout>
```

AdapterDemo.java

```java
package com.example.arrayadapter;

import android.app.Activity;
import android.os.Bundle;
import android.view.View;
import android.widget.AdapterView;
import android.widget.AdapterView.OnItemClickListener;
import android.widget.ArrayAdapter;
import android.widget.ListView;
import android.widget.Toast;

public class AdapterDemo extends Activity implements OnItemClickListener {
```

```java
    String[] operating_sytem={"Android",
            "ios",
            "Windows 8",
            "Windows 7",
            "Windows Xp",
            "Windows Vista",
            "Linux",
            "Unix",
            "Minix",
            "MS-DOS",
            "QNX",
            "L4",
            };

@Override
protected void onCreate(Bundle savedInstanceState) {
    super.onCreate(savedInstanceState);
    setContentView(R.layout.activity_adapter_demo);
    ArrayAdapter<String> aa=new ArrayAdapter<String>(this,android.R.layout.simple_list_item_1,operating_sytem);
    ListView lvref=(ListView) findViewById(R.id.listofos);
    lvref.setAdapter(aa);

    lvref.setOnItemClickListener(this);
    }


    @Override
    public void onItemClick(AdapterView<?> arg0, View v, int position, long id) {
        Toast.makeText(this,"Selected Operating System Is :"+operating_sytem[position],Toast.LENGTH_LONG).show();
    }
}
```

Working Mechanism :

When application starts, it will show you a list view having names of operating system. When we click on the item in list, it will show you a toast message.

Note : You can create your own array adapter class file by extending a ArrayAdapter class.

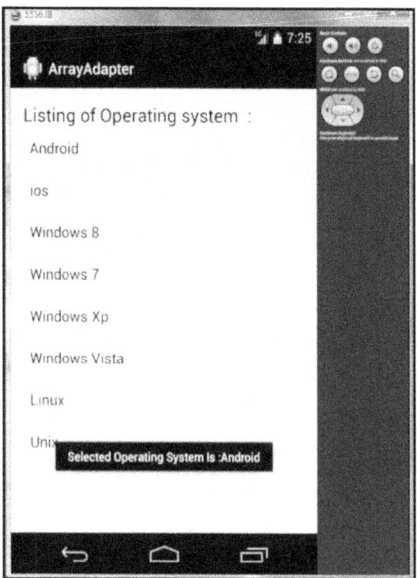

Fig. 9.12: Array adapter

(2) SimpleCursorAdapter : It binds to views to cursors returned from content provider queries. You specify a XML layout definition and then bind the value to each column.

SimpleCursorAdapter

extends ResourceCursorAdapter

Class Overview

java.lang.Object
    android.widget.BaseAdapter

↳
        android.widget.CursorAdapter

  ↳
            android.widget.ResourceCursorAdapter

    ↳
                android.widget.SimpleCursorAdapter

      ↳

- The XML file may contain TextViews or ImageViews, and to map columns from a cursor to these TextViews or ImageViews the specific views can be mapped to the specific columnsand XML files that specify the appearance of these views .the binding occurs in two phases.

- First, if a SimpleCursorAdapter.ViewBinder is available, setViewValue(android.view.View, android.database.Cursor, int) is invoked. If the returned value is true, binding has occurred. If the returned value is false and the view to bind is a TextView, setViewText(TextView, String) is invoked. If the returned value is false and the view is to bind to an ImageView, setViewImage(Image View, String) is invoked. If no appropriate binding can be found, an IllegalStateException is thrown. This adapter is used with filtering, for instance in AutoCompleteTextView.

Nested Classes

interface	SimpleCursorAdapter.CursorToStringConverter	This class can be used by external clients of SimpleCursorAdapter to define how the Cursor should be converted to a String.
interface	SimpleCursorAdapter.ViewBinder	This class can be used by external clients of SimpleCursorAdapter to bind values from the Cursor to views.

Inherited Constants

▶ From class android.widget.CursorAdapter

▶ From interface android.widget.Adapter

Public Constructors

SimpleCursorAdapter(Context context, int layout, Cursor c, String[] from, int[] to)
This constructor was deprecated in API level 11. This option is discouraged, as it results in Cursor queries being performed on the application's UI thread and thus can cause poor responsiveness or even Application Not Responding to errors. As an alternative, use LoaderManager with a CursorLoader.

SimpleCursorAdapter(Context context, int layout, Cursor c, String[] from, int[] to, int flags)
Standard constructor.

Public Methods

void	bindView(View view, Context context, Cursor cursor) Binds all of the field names passed into the "to" parameter of the constructor with their corresponding cursor columns as specified in the "from" parameter.
void	changeCursorAndColumns(Cursor c, String[] from, int[] to) Change the cursor and change the column-to-view mappings at the same time.

CharSequence	convertToString(Cursor cursor) Returns a CharSequence representation of the specified Cursor as defined by the current CursorToStringConverter.
SimpleCursorAdapter.CursorToStringConverter	getCursorToStringConverter() Returns the converter used to convert the filtering Cursor into a String.
int	getStringConversionColumn() Return the index of the column used to get a String representation of the Cursor.
SimpleCursorAdapter.ViewBinder	getViewBinder() Returns the SimpleCursorAdapter.ViewBinder used to bind data to views.
void	setCursorToStringConverter(SimpleCursorAdapter.CursorToStringConverter cursorToStringConverter) Sets the converter used to convert the filtering Cursor into a String.
void	setStringConversionColumn(int stringConversionColumn) Defines the index of the column in the Cursor used to get a String representation of that Cursor.
void	setViewBinder(SimpleCursorAdapter.ViewBinder viewBinder) Sets the binder used to bind data to views.
void	setViewImage(ImageView v, String value) Called by bindView() to set the image for an ImageView but only if there is no existing ViewBinder or if the existing ViewBinder cannot handle binding to an ImageView.
void	setViewText(TextView v, String text) Called by bindView() to set the text for a TextView but only if there is no existing ViewBinder or if the existing ViewBinder cannot handle binding to a TextView.
Cursor	swapCursor(Cursor c) Swap in a new Cursor, returning the old Cursor.

9.2.1 Using SimpleCursorAdaptor
- This adapter helps you bind columns from a cursor to a list view using a custom layout definition.
- Current context, a layout resource, cursor and two arrays are passed to this adapter.
  (1) One array stores names of columns
  (2) Another one contains resource IDs for the views which displays each column's data value.

  string uristring="content://contacts/people/";
  Cursor MyCursor=managedQuery(uri.parse(uristring), null, null, null, null);
  String [ ] from columns=new string[ ] {people.NUMBER,people.Name};
  int { } tolayoutIDS=new int [ ] {R.id.nameTextView,R.id.numberTextView};
  SimpleCursorAdapter MyAdapter;
  myAdapter=new simpleCursorAdapter (this, R.layout.SimpleCursorLayout,
       myCursor,
       fromcolumns,
       tolayoutIDs)
  myListView.SetAdapter(myAdapter);

9.3 Using Internet Resources
- The internet resources are used to create internet based applications. There are certain reasons to create the native applications for thick and thin client rather to depend on web based solutions.
  - **(1) Bandwidth:** By creating the application, developer can restrict the bandwidth requirements to only data updates. E.g. applications like images, layouts and sound are expensive for data consumers on devices.
  - **(2) Caching:** Mobile internet access is not supported to the mark. The internet service may give interrupted applications. A native application can cache data to provide as much functionality as possible.
  - **(3) Native Features:** The devices that run on an android provide a platform to run a browser, but they also includes location based services, camera hardware features. By creating native applications the data available online can be combined with hardware features.
- Android provides three connection techniques for internet connectivity. Each is offered to application layer:
  - **(1) GPRS, EDGE and 3G:** These are the carriers through which mobile offers different data plans.
  - **(2) Wi-Fi:** Wi-Fi receivers and mobile hot-spots are becoming increasing more common.

9.3.1 Connecting to an Internet Resource

- Before accessing to internet resources, INTERNET uses-permission this node to be added to application manifest.

    <uses-permission android:name="android.permission.INTERNET"/>

- The following skeleton code shows the basic pattern for opening an internet data stream: string myFeed=getstring(R.string.my_feed);

```
try
{
    URL url=new URL(myFeed);
    URLConnection connection=url.openconnection();
    httpURLconnection httpconnection=(httpURLconnection) connection;
    int responsecode=httpconnection.getResponsecodec);
    if (responsecode=httpURLconnection.HTTP_OK)
    {
        In.putstream in=httpconnection.getInputStream();
        [… Process the input stream as required…]
    }
}
catch(malformeddURLEXCEPTION e)
{
}
catch(IOException e)
{
}
```

9.4 Introducing Dialogs

- Dialog boxes are a common UI metaphor in desktop and web applications. These are used to help users to answer questions, make selections, confirm actions, and read warning or error messages. It is floating window that partially obscures the activity and launched it.
- Dialog boxes are not full screen and these are partially transparent. Using blur or dim filter the dialogs boxes are obscure the Activities.
- The following are the ways to implement dialog boxes:

    (1) Using a dialog class descendent: Android includes various specialist classes that extend dialog. Each one provides specific dialog-box functionality. These are created within their calling activity. No need to be registered in the manifest and life cycle of dialog box is controlled by its calling Activity.

(2) **Dialog:** Themed activities dialog theme is applied to a regular activity to give it the appearance of a Dialog box.

(3) **Toasts:** These are non-transient message_boxes, these are used by broadcast receivers and background services that notifies user events.

9.4.1 Introduction of Dialog Class

- Dialog class implements a simple floating window i.e. constructed entirely within an activity.
- Dialog d=new dialog (MyActivity.this);
  //the new window that blurs the window it obscures
  window window=d.getwindow();
  window.setflags(WindowManager.LayoutParams
  FLAG_BLUR_BEHIND,WindowManager.LayoutParams,
  FLAG_BLUR_BEHIND);
  d.SetContentView(R.layout.dialog_view);
  TextView text=(TextView)d.FindViewById
  (R.id.dialogTextView);
  text.SetText("This is the text");
  with d.show(); you can display the dialog box.

9.4.2 Alter Dialog Class

- This is the dialog implementations. This let the developer to create screens for some most common Dialog_box use cases, which includes:
  (1) Presenting a message to the user offering 1 - 3 options in the form of alternative buttons. E.g. Ok, Cancel, Yes or No.
  (2) List of options in the form of checkboxes or radio buttons.
  (3) Providing a text entry box for user input.
  AlterDialog.BUILDER ad=new AlterDialog.BuilderContext;
- The following code shows the two options that are created with the help of AlterDialogbox.

```
Context Context=MyActivity.this;
String title="It is Programming";
String Message="Android is about to start";
String button1 String="OK"'
String button2 String="Cancel";
AlterDialog.Builder ad=new AlterDialog.Builder(context);
ad.SetTitle(title);
ad.SetMessage(message);
ad.SetPositiveButton(button1string,
```

```
    new OnClickListner()
    {
public void OnClick (DialogInterface dialog, int arg1)
    {
    OK();
    }
    });
ad.SetNegativeButton(button2string, new OnClickListner()
    {
public void OnClick(DialogInterface dialog, int arg1)
    {
    //  do nothing
    }
    });
ad.SetCancelable(true);
ad.SetOnCancelListner(new OnCancelListner()
    {
public void OnCancel(DialogInterface dialog)
    {
    OK();
    }
    });
To display call
ad.show();
```

9.4.3 Specialist Input Dialogs

- Dialog box provides an interface for user input. Android includes several specialist dialog boxes that encapsulate controls which are used for common user input requests.

    (1) DatePickerDialog: DatePickerView is selected by user to select the date.

    (2) TimePickerDialog: Similar to above TimePickerView is used to select the time.

    (3) ProgressDialog: A dialog that displays a progress bar to a message textbox.

```
<TableLayoutxmlns:android="http://schemas.android.com/apk/res/android"
xmlns:tools="http://schemas.android.com/tools"
android:id="@+id/TableLayout1"
android:layout_width="match_parent"
android:layout_height="match_parent"
android:paddingBottom="@dimen/activity_vertical_margin"
```

```xml
android:paddingLeft="@dimen/activity_horizontal_margin"
android:paddingRight="@dimen/activity_horizontal_margin"
android:paddingTop="@dimen/activity_vertical_margin"
tools:context=".MainActivity">

<Button
android:id="@+id/btnalert"
android:layout_width="wrap_content"
android:layout_height="wrap_content"
android:onClick="customfun"
android:text="Click To Display Custom DialogBox"/>

<Button
android:id="@+id/btnalert"
android:layout_width="wrap_content"
android:layout_height="wrap_content"
android:onClick="alertfun"
android:text="Click To Display Alert DialogBox"/>

<Button
android:id="@+id/btnprogress"
android:layout_width="wrap_content"
android:layout_height="wrap_content"
android:onClick="progressfun"
android:text="Click To Display Progress DialogBox"/>

<Button
android:id="@+id/btnprogressbar"
android:layout_width="wrap_content"
android:layout_height="wrap_content"
android:onClick="progressbarfun"
android:text="Click To Display Progress Bar"/>

</TableLayout>

<?xmlversion="1.0"encoding="utf-8"?>
<LinearLayoutxmlns:android="http://schemas.android.com/apk/res/android"
```

```xml
    android:layout_width="match_parent"
    android:layout_height="match_parent"
    android:orientation="vertical">

    <TextView
    android:id="@+id/heading"
    android:layout_width="wrap_content"
    android:layout_height="wrap_content"
    android:layout_gravity="center"
    android:text="This is custom dialog box"
    android:textAppearance="?android:attr/textAppearanceLarge"/>

    <Button
    android:id="@+id/btnalert"
    android:layout_width="wrap_content"
    android:layout_height="wrap_content"
    android:layout_gravity="center"
    android:text="Click Me Please"/>

</LinearLayout>
```

```java
package com.example.assignalertdialog;

import android.app.Activity;
import android.app.AlertDialog;
import android.app.AlertDialog.Builder;
import android.app.Dialog;
import android.app.ProgressDialog;
import android.content.Context;
import android.content.DialogInterface;
import android.content.DialogInterface.OnClickListener;
import android.os.Bundle;
import android.view.View;
import android.widget.Button;
import android.widget.Toast;
```

```java
public class MainActivity extends Activity {

    public Context con;
    ProgressDialog pd;
    @Override
    protected void onCreate(Bundle savedInstanceState) {
        super.onCreate(savedInstanceState);
        setContentView(R.layout.activity_main);
        con=this;
    }

    public void alertfun(View v)
    {
        AlertDialog.Builder b=newBuilder(con);
        b.setTitle("My Alert Box")
        .setPositiveButton("YES", new OnClickListener() {
            @Override
            publicvoid onClick(DialogInterface arg0, int arg1) {
            Toast.makeText(con, "You Clicked On YES", Toast.LENGTH_LONG).show();
            }
        })
        .setNegativeButton("NO", new OnClickListener() {

            @Override
            publicvoid onClick(DialogInterface arg0, int arg1) {
            Toast.makeText(con, "You Clicked On NO", Toast.LENGTH_LONG).show();
            }
        })
        .setNeutralButton("CANCEL", new OnClickListener() {

            @Override
            publicvoid onClick(DialogInterface arg0, int arg1) {
            Toast.makeText(con, "You Clicked On CANCEL", Toast.LENGTH_LONG).show();
            }
        });
        AlertDialog a=b.create();
        a.show();
    }
```

```java
public void progressfun(View v)
{
    pd=new ProgressDialog(con);

    pd.setTitle("PROGRESSING");
    pd.show();

    new Thread(){
        public void run() {
            try {
                sleep(3000);
            } catch (InterruptedException e) {
                e.printStackTrace();
            }
            pd.dismiss();
        }
    }.start();
}

public void progressbarfun(View v)
{
    pd=new ProgressDialog(con);

    pd.setTitle("PROGRESSING BAR");
    pd.setProgressStyle(ProgressDialog.STYLE_HORIZONTAL);
    pd.show();

    new Thread(){
        public void run() {
            try {
                for(int i=1;i<=10;i++)
                {
                    sleep(1000);
                    pd.setProgress(i*10);
                }
            } catch (InterruptedException e) {
                e.printStackTrace();
            }
            pd.dismiss();
        }
    }.start();
}
```

```
public void customfun(View v)
{
final Dialog d=new Dialog(con);
d.setTitle("My Custom Dialog Box");
d.setContentView(R.layout.mydialog);
d.show();
Button b=(Button) d.findViewById(R.id.btnalert);
b.setOnClickListener(new View.OnClickListener() {
    @Override
    public void onClick(View arg0) {
        Toast.makeText(con, "You Clicked On Button!!Thank You", Toast.LENGTH_LONG).show();
        d.dismiss();
    }
});
}
}
```

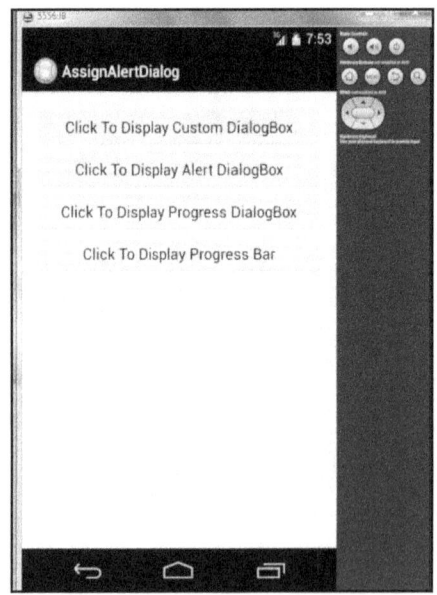
Fig. 9.13: Assign alert dialog

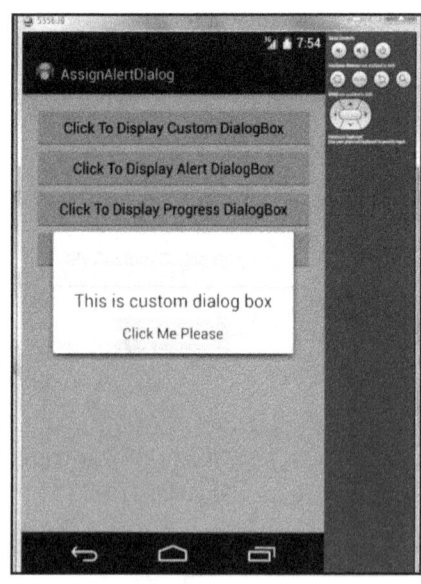
Fig. 9.14: Custom dialog box

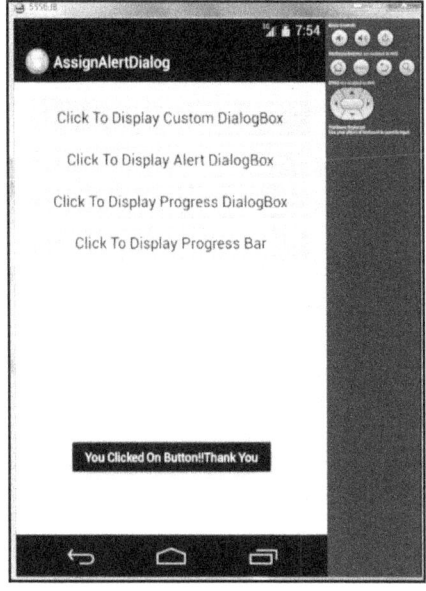

Fig. 9.15: Click event of dialog box

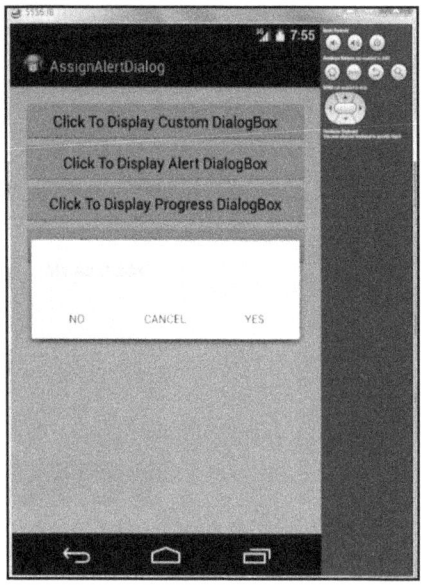

Fig. 9.16: Alert dialog box

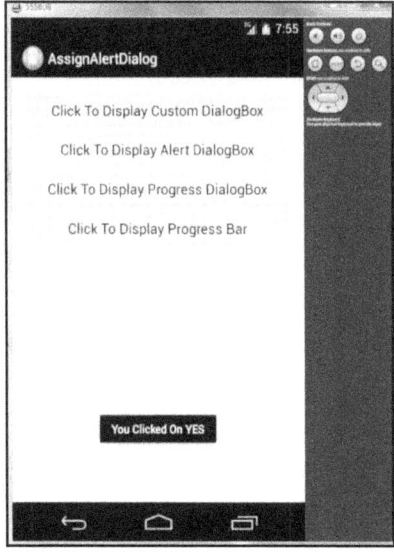

Fig. 9.17: Click to display progress bar

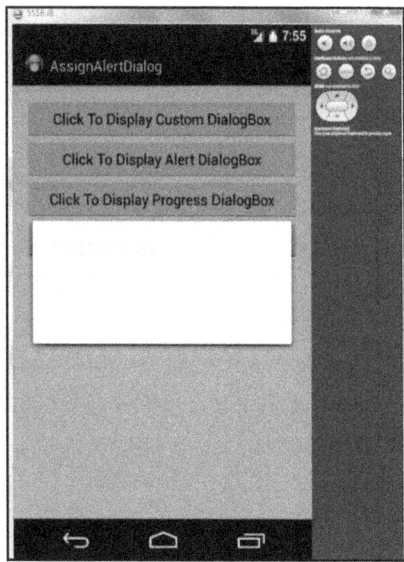

Fig. 9.18: Display progressing

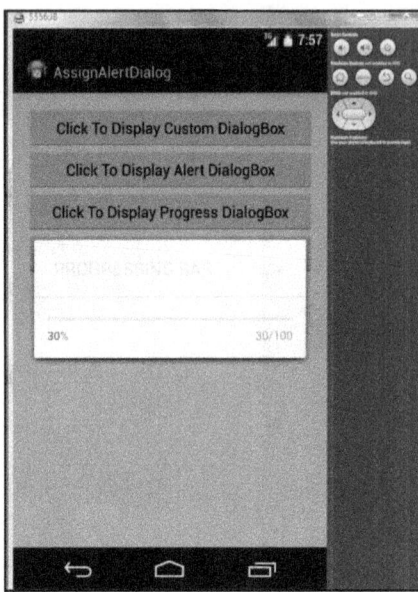

Fig. 9.19: Display progress bar

9.5 Example of Date Picker Control

We can create a date picker control dynamically. Here we created application DatePickerDemo with activity class file – DatePickerDemo.java and UI file – activity_date_picker_demo.xml

```
activity_date_picker_demo.xml
<LinearLayoutxmlns:android="http://schemas.android.com/apk/res/android"
xmlns:tools="http://schemas.android.com/tools"
android:id="@+id/LinearLayout1"
android:layout_width="match_parent"
android:layout_height="match_parent"
android:orientation="vertical"
android:paddingBottom="@dimen/activity_vertical_margin"
android:paddingLeft="@dimen/activity_horizontal_margin"
android:paddingRight="@dimen/activity_horizontal_margin"
android:paddingTop="@dimen/activity_vertical_margin"
tools:context=".DatePickerDemo">

<Button
android:id="@+id/button1"
android:layout_width="wrap_content"
android:layout_height="wrap_content"
```

```xml
android:layout_gravity="center"
android:text="Click Here To Select Date"
android:onClick="datefun"/>

</LinearLayout>
```

DatePickerDemo.java
```java
packagecom.example.datepickerdemo;

importjava.util.Calendar;
importandroid.app.Activity;
importandroid.app.DatePickerDialog;
importandroid.app.DatePickerDialog.OnDateSetListener;
importandroid.content.Context;
importandroid.os.Bundle;
importandroid.view.View;
importandroid.widget.DatePicker;
importandroid.widget.Toast;

public class DatePickerDemo extends Activity {

    public Context con;

    @Override
    protected void onCreate(Bundle savedInstanceState) {
        super.onCreate(savedInstanceState);
        setContentView(R.layout.activity_date_picker_demo);
        con=this;
    }

public void datefun(View v)
{
        Calendar c=Calendar.getInstance();
        finalint y=c.get(Calendar.YEAR);
        finalint m=c.get(Calendar.MONTH);
        finalint d=c.get(Calendar.DATE);
    DatePickerDialogdp=new DatePickerDialog(con, new OnDateSetListener() {

        @Override
        public void onDateSet(DatePicker arg0, intyy, int mm, intdd) {
        Toast.makeText(con, "Selected Date Is : "+dd+" / "+(mm+1)+" / "+yy+"",
Toast.LENGTH_LONG).show();
        }
    }, y, m, d);
    dp.show();
}
}
```

Working Mechanism :

In activity class file, we have written a function datefun() for button click, where we show DatePickerDialog as – dp.show();

In this function, we get instance of calender and obtained current date which is passed as parameter to DatePickerDialog constructor as follows :

Calender c=Calender.getInstance();

Final int y=c.get(Calender.YEAR); Then, we create DatePickerDialog object dp as follows – DatePickerDialog dp=new DatePickerDialog();

where parameters passed are – context, onClickListener, int year, int month, int date. Here, we created anonomous class onDateSetListener where we override onDateSet() method in which we show selected date using toast message.

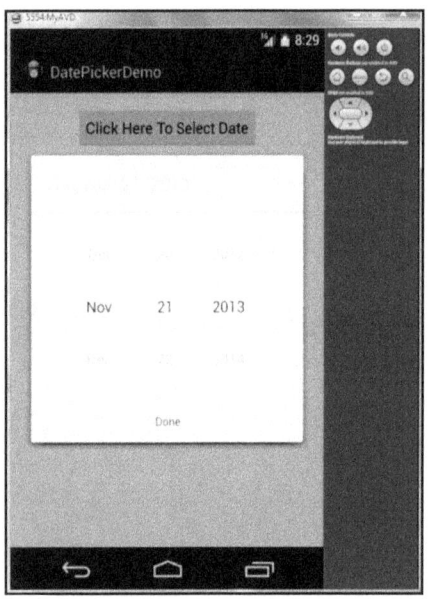
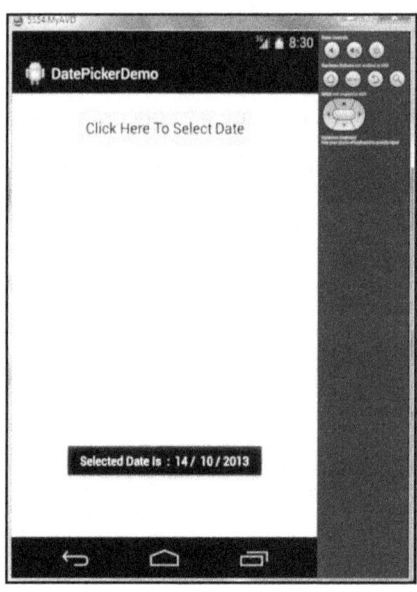

Fig. 9.20: Date picker   Fig. 9.21: Selecting date in date picker

9.6 Example of Time Picker Control

Similar to DatePickerControl, we created a project TimePickerDemo.

```
<LinearLayoutxmlns:android="http://schemas.android.com/apk/res/android"
xmlns:tools="http://schemas.android.com/tools"
android:id="@+id/LinearLayout1"
android:layout_width="match_parent"
android:layout_height="match_parent"
android:orientation="vertical"
android:paddingBottom="@dimen/activity_vertical_margin"
```

```xml
android:paddingLeft="@dimen/activity_horizontal_margin"
android:paddingRight="@dimen/activity_horizontal_margin"
android:paddingTop="@dimen/activity_vertical_margin"
tools:context=".TimePickerDemo">

<Button
android:id="@+id/button1"
android:layout_width="wrap_content"
android:layout_height="wrap_content"
android:layout_gravity="center"
android:text="Click Here To Select Time"
android:onClick="timefun"/>

</LinearLayout>
```

```java
packagecom.example.timepickerdemo;

importjava.util.Calendar;

importandroid.app.Activity;
importandroid.app.TimePickerDialog;
importandroid.app.TimePickerDialog.OnTimeSetListener;
importandroid.content.Context;
importandroid.os.Bundle;
importandroid.view.View;
importandroid.widget.TimePicker;
importandroid.widget.Toast;
public class TimePickerDemo extends Activity {
    public Context con;

    @Override
    protected void onCreate(Bundle savedInstanceState) {
        super.onCreate(savedInstanceState);
        setContentView(R.layout.activity_time_picker_demo);
        con=this;
    }

public void timefun(View v)
{
        Calendar c=Calendar.getInstance();
        finalint h=c.get(Calendar.HOUR);
        finalint m=c.get(Calendar.MINUTE);
        finalboolean vi=true;
```

```
TimePickerDialogdp=new TimePickerDialog(con, new OnTimeSetListener() {

    @Override
    public void onTimeSet(TimePicker arg0, int arg1, int arg2) {

        Toast.makeText(con, arg1+" :  "+arg2, Toast.LENGTH_LONG).show();
    }
}, h, m, vi);
    dp.show();
}
}
```

Working Mechanism:

On button click, timefun() is called in which we created a object of TimePickerDialog dp by passing parameter context, onTimeSetListener, int hour, int minute, boolean is 24 Hour View as follows : TimePickerDialog dp=new TimePickerDialog(); and we show it as follows – dp.show();

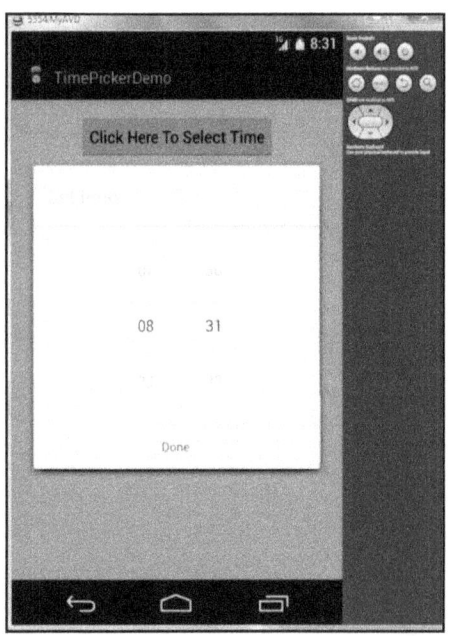
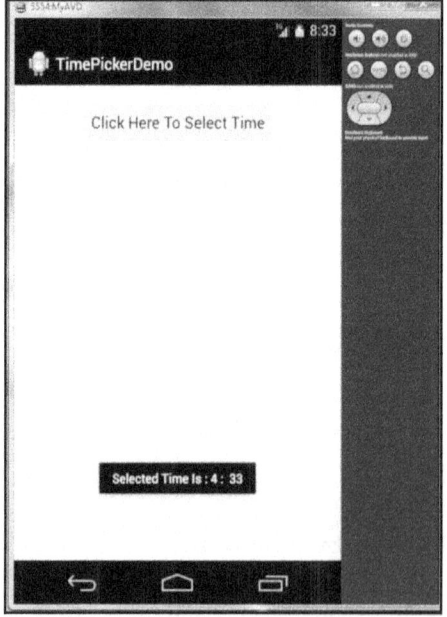

Fig. 9.22: Time picker **Fig. 9.23: Selecting time of Time Picker**

Practice Questions

1. What do you mean by Intent ? Explain with example.
2. Explain the concept of adapter.
3. What is dialog box ? How to implement dialog box.
4. Explain the concept of application components in Android.
5. Write short notes on :
   (a) Activity
   (b) Service
   (c) Content provider
   (d) Broadcast receiver
   (e) Using Internet resources.

Chapter 10...

ACCESSING LOCATION BASED SERVICES APPLICATION

10.1 Introduction
    10.1.1 Following is the Introduction How you can Obtain User Location in Android
10.2 Selecting Location Provider
    10.2.1 Finding the Available Location Providers
    10.2.2 Finding Location Providers by specifying criteria
10.3 Finding Your Current Location
    10.3.1 Location Privacy
    10.3.2 Finding the Last Known Location
    10.3.3 Flow for Obtaining the User Location
10.4 Creating Map-Based Activities
    10.4.1 Introduction
    10.4.2 Introduction to Map View and Map Activity
    10.4.3 How to Get MAP API Keys
    10.4.4 Creating Map Based Activity
    10.4.5 Configuration and Use of MapViews
    10.4.6 MapFragment
    10.4.7 Markers
    10.4.8 Changing the GoogleView
    10.4.9 Example
- Practice Questions

10.1 Introduction

Location based services are mainly used to find the physical location of the device. The accuracy of the returned location is dependent on the hardware available and the permissions requested by an application.

- Location awareness is one of the basic tasks performed by android. Location based services (LBS) are the services that let you find the user's current location. Few methods are GPS (Global Positioning System), Google's cell based location technology and Wi-Fi based location sensing techniques.

- LBS uses latitude and longitude to find the geographical location and android provides decoder that supports forward and backward geocoding that means to be mapped with real world address the conversion of latitude and longitude can be reversed.
- Map based activities can be created with Google maps as a UI element. It provides options such as alter zooming, moving to centered location etc.
- Location based services, maps and geocoding are used as a toolkit which accesses the location of mobile device.
- LBS include various technologies to find the device's current location. It has two elements such as:

  (1) Location Manager: It provides hooks to the location-based services.

  (2) Location Provider: Different location tracing technologies are used to determine the device's current location.

The following tasks are performed by using Location Manager:
1. Obtain your current location
2. Follow movement
3. Set proximity alerts for detecting movement into and out of a specified area
4. Find available Location Providers
5. Monitor the status of the GPS receiver

(1) Location Strategies

- The applications in which the location awareness is required user can utilize GPS and Android's network Location provider to acqiure user location.
- GPS service is most efficient and accurate, but it only works in outdoor and consumes battery power and doesn't return the location as quickly as users want.
- Android's Network Location Provider determines user location using cell tower and Wi-Fi signals, providing location information in a way that works indoors and outdoors, responds faster, and uses less battery power. To obtain the user location in your application, you can use both GPS and the Network Location Provider, or just one.

(2) Challenges in Determining User Location

- Tracing the users location by using mobile can be complicated. There are several reasons why a location reading can contain errors and be inaccurate. Some sources of error in the user location include the following:

1. **Multitude of location sources:** GPS, Cell-ID, and Wi-Fi can each provide a clue to user's location. Determining which to use and trust is a matter of trade-offs in accuracy, speed, and battery-efficiency.

2. **User movement:** Because of frequent change in device location, user must re-estimate device location every often.
3. **Varying accuracy:** Location estimates coming from each location source are not consistent in their accuracy. A location obtained 10 seconds ago from one source might be more accurate than the newest location from another or same source.
   - These problems can make difficult to obtain a reliable user location reading. This document provides information to help you meet these challenges to obtain a reliable location reading.

10.1.1 Following is the Introduction How you can Obtain User Location in Android

Requesting User Permissions

- In order to receive location updates from NETWORK_PROVIDER or GPS_PROVIDER, you must request user permission by declaring either the ACCESS_COARSE_LOCATION or ACCESS_FINE_LOCATION permission, respectively, in your Android manifest file. For example:

```
<manifest ... >
<uses-permission android:name="android.permission.ACCESS_FINE_LOCATION" />
<uses-permission android:name="android.permission.ACCESS_COARSE_LOCATION" />

...
</manifest>
```

- Without these permissions, your application will fail at runtime when requesting for location updates.
- When NETWORK_PROVIDER and GPS_PROVIDER both are used in the code then you need to request only the ACCESS_FINE_LOCATION permission, because it includes permission for both providers. ACCESS_FINE_LOCATION permission provides higher accuracy than ACCESS_COARSE_LOCATION permission.

Accessing the Location Manager

- Location Manager is used to access the location based services. To access the Location Manager, request an instance of the LOCATION_SERVICE using getSystemService() method as follows:

```
String servicestr=Context.LOCATION_SERVICE;
LocationManager lm= (LocationManager) getSystemService (servicestr);
```

Requesting Location Updates

- Getting user location in Android works by means of callback. You indicate that you'd like to receive location updates from the LocationManager.

- By Creating the object of LocationManager lm, we call requestLocationUpdates() which requests the LocationManager to update the object of LocationListener, which is passed as a parameter to this method.

```
LocationManager lm= (LocationManager) getSystemService (LOCATION_SERVICE);
MyLocationlistener ll=new MyLocationListener (this);
// Register the listener with the Location Manager to receive location updates
lm.requestLocationUpdates (LocationManager.GPS_PROVIDER, 1000, 0, ll);
```

- RequestLocationUpdates() is the method of location provider to use, it will display the Network Location provider for cell tower and Wi-Fi based location. By using second and third parameter which are the frequency at which your listener receives updates. The second is the minimum time interval between notifications and the third is the minimum change in distance between notifications—setting both to zero, requests location notifications as frequently as possible. The last parameter is your LocationListener, which receives callbacks for location updates.
- To request location updates from the GPS provider, substitute GPS_PROVIDER for NETWORK_PROVIDER. You can also request location updates from both the GPS and the Network Location Provider by calling requestLocationUpdates() twice—once for NETWORK_PROVIDER and once for GPS_PROVIDER.
- The MyLocationListener is a class which implements LocationListener interface. This class must be implement several callback methods that the Location Manager calls when the user's location changes or when the status of the service changes.

Those methods are as follows:

```
public void onLocationChanged (Location location) {    }
public void onStatusChanged (String provider, int status, Bundle extras) {}
public void onProviderEnabled (String provider) {}
public void onProviderDisabled (String provider) {}
```

- **Using the emulator with Location Based Services:**
    - To find the current location of the device, location based services are dependent on device hardware (emulator).
    - By using this hardware, device is likely to stay in pretty much the same location.
    - To componset android includes the hooks that enable you to emulate Location Providers for testing the location based applications.
  - Use the location controls available from the DDMS perspective in Eclipse, to push location changes directly into the emulator's GPS Location Provider.

- Here, we can provide longitude and latitude values manually as shown below.

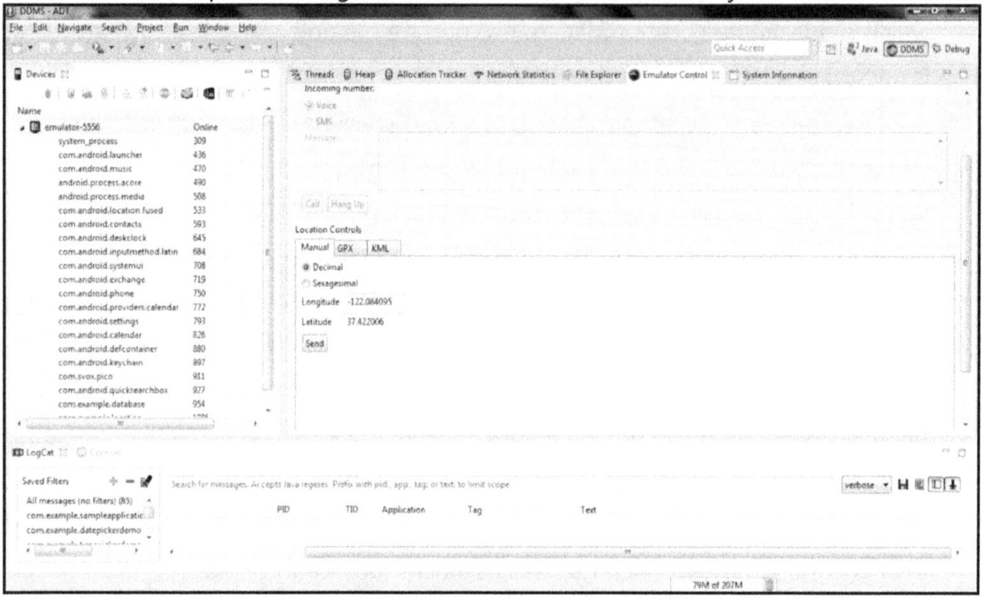

Fig. 10.1: Manually Location Control

10.2 Selecting Location Provider

- There are different technologies/location providers that are used to get the current location of device. Each one is different from others in following aspects - Power consumption, cost, accuracy, ability to calculate altitude, speed or headers.

10.2.1 Finding the Available Location Providers

The following are the static string constants that return the providers name for the common location providers.

(1) LocationManager.GPS_PROVIDER
(2) LocationManager.NETWORK_PROVIDER

GetProvider() method retrieves the current location provider snippet is shown below.

```
String providername=LocationManager.GPS_PROVIDER;
LocationProvider gpsprovider;
GpsProvider=LocationManager.getProviders (ProviderName);
```

- By calling getProviders() method, using a Boolean to indicate the information regarding all enabled location providers.

```
Boolean enableonly=true;
List<String> providers=LocationManager.getProviders (enableonly);
```

- All location based services automatically stores the user's current location. The location's accuracy is based on the location permissions you've requested and location sensors that are currently active for the device.

10.2.2 Finding Location Providers by specifying criteria

- In most of the application user want to explicitly choose a location provider to be used. The best practice is to specify the requirements and let android determine the best technology to use.
- The criteria class is used to detect the requirements of a provider in terms of accuracy, power use (low, medium, high), financial cost and the ability to return value for latitude, speed and heading.
- The following snippet shows a criterion which requires coarse accuracy, low power consumption, no need for altitude, bearing or speed. The provider is permitted to have an associated cost.

  ```
  Criteria Cr=new Criteria();
  Cr.setAccuracy (Criteria.ACCURACY_COARSE);
  Cr.setPowerRequirement (Criteria.POWER_LOW);
  Cr.setAltitudeRequired (false);
  Cr.setBearingRequired (false);
  Cr.setSpeedRequired (false);
  Cr.setCostAllowed (true);
  ```

- The coarse/fine values passed in to the setAccuracy() method which represents a subjective level of accuracy, where fine represents GPS or better and coarse represents any technology significantly less accurate than that.
- Android 3.0 introduced several additional properties to the Criteria class. It is designed for more control over the level of accuracy you require. The following is the extension of above snippet which specifies that a high horizontal (latitude/longitude) and medium vertical (elevation) accuracy are required. Requirements for the accuracy of returned bearing and speed are set to low.

  ```
  Cr.setHorizontalAccuracy (Criteria.ACCURACY_HIGH);
  Cr.setVerticalAccuracy (Criteria.ACCURACY_MEDIUM);

  Cr.setBearingAccuracy (Criteria.ACCURACY_LOW);
  Cr.setSpeedAccuracy (Criteria.ACCURACY_LOW);
  ```

- In terms of horizontal and vertical accuracy, high accuracy represents a requirement for results correct within 100 m. Low accuracy providers are correct to more than 500 m, whereas medium accuracy providers represent accuracy between 100 and 500 meters.
- When specifying accuracy requirements for bearing and speed, only ACCURACY_LOW and ACCURACY_HIGH are valid parameters.
- Having defined the required Criteria, you can use getBestProvider() to return the best matching Location Provider or getProviders() to return all the possible matches.

- The following snippet demonstrates the use of getBestProvider() to return the best Provider for your criteria where the Boolean value enables you restrict the result to a currently enabled Provider:

  ```
  String bestproviderobj=LocationManager.getBestProvider (Cr, true);
  ```
- If more than one Location Provider matches your criteria, the one with the greatest accuracy is returned. If no Location Providers meet your requirements, the criteria are loosened, in the following order, until a provider is found:
  - Power use
  - Accuracy of returned location
  - Accuracy of bearing, speed and altitude
  - Availability of bearing, speed and altitude
- The criterion for allowing a device with monetary cost is never implicitly relaxed. If no provider is found, null is returned.
- To get a list of names for all the providers matching your criteria, use getProviders().
- It accepts a criteria object and returns a String list of all Location Providers that matchs it, As with the getBestProvider() call, if no matching providers are found, this method return null or an empty list.

  ```
  List<String> matchingprovidersobj=LocationManager.getProviders (Cr, false);
  ```

10.3 Finding Your Current Location

10.3.1 Location Privacy

Privacy is an important aspect when an application uses the device's location. Particularly, when it is regularly updating the position. Ensure that an application uses the device location data in a way that respects the user's privacy by :

1. Only using and updating location when necessary for an application.
2. Notifying users of when application tracks their locations, and if and how that location information is used, transmitted and stored.
3. Allowing users to disable the location updates, and respecting the system setting for location based services preferences.

10.3.2 Finding the Last Known Location

- The last location of the device can be determined by location provider using getLastKnownLocation() method, by passing name of location provider. The following snippet shows how to retrieve the last location fix taken by the GPS provider.

  ```
  String provider=LocationManager.GPS_PROVIDER;
  Location location=LocationManager.getLastknownLocation (provider);
  ```

- The location object returned includes all the position information available from the provider. It also includes accuracy of the location, latitude, longitude, bearing, altitude and speed.

10.3.3 Flow for Obtaining the User Location

The challenge in obtaining the user location with preserving battery power makes it more complicated. The mentioned following code is a typical flow to obtain the user's location.

(1) Start application.
(2) Start listening for updates from desired location providers.
(3) Maintain a "current best estimate" of location by filtering out new, but less accurate fixes.
(4) Stop listening for location updates.
(5) Take benefit of last estimate of location update.

- Android states three ways to obtain the location of the user.

  (1) Cell_ID: Location area code contains the cell_ID which is assigned to exact tower location. Your phone stores the cell_ID and (Location Area Code) LAC of every tower the user's device gets connected.

  (2) Wi-Fi: Mobile device periodically sends anonymous data to GOOGLE with among other things such as your last location and any WiFi network you were connected at the time. The accumulated data builds on a database begun by travelling Google street view cars that recorded Wi-Fi networks available along their routers.

  (3) GPS: Your android device requests its distance from satellites in the GPS network and plots the intersection points along the boundary of the described spheres.

  The Following snippet shows how to obtain the location:

Create a new android application named as location with single activity LocationDemo.java and UI file – activity_location_demo.xml. Also create a new java class named as MyLocationListener which implements LocationListener. And add the permissions in AndroidManifest.xml file.

AndroidManifest.xml file :

```
<?xml version="1.0" encoding="utf-8"?>
<manifest
xmlns:android="http://schemas.android.com/apk/res/android"
    package="com.example.location"
    android:versionCode="1"
    android:versionName="1.0" >

    <uses-sdk
```

```xml
            android:minSdkVersion="8"
            android:targetSdkVersion="17" />
<uses-permission
android:name="android.permission.ACCESS_FINE_LOCATION"/>
<uses-permission
android:name="android.permission.ACCESS_COARSE_LOCATION"/>

    <application
        android:allowBackup="true"
        android:icon="@drawable/ic_launcher"
        android:label="@string/app_name"
        android:theme="@style/AppTheme" >
        <activity
            android:name="com.example.location.LocationDemo"
            android:label="@string/app_name" >
            <intent-filter>
                <action
android:name="android.intent.action.MAIN" />

                <category
android:name="android.intent.category.LAUNCHER" />
            </intent-filter>
        </activity>
    </application>

</manifest>
```

Activity location demo.xml file :

```xml
    <RelativeLayout
xmlns:android="http://schemas.android.com/apk/res/android"
    xmlns:tools="http://schemas.android.com/tools"
    android:layout_width="match_parent"
    android:layout_height="match_parent"
  tools:context=".LocationDemo" >

    <Button
        android:id="@+id/btngetlocn"
        android:layout_width="wrap_content"
        android:layout_height="wrap_content"
        android:layout_centerHorizontal="true"
        android:layout_centerVertical="true"
        android:onClick="btngetlocnfun"
        android:text="Get Location" />
```

```xml
        <Button
            android:id="@+id/btnstop"
            android:layout_width="wrap_content"
            android:layout_height="wrap_content"
            android:layout_below="@+id/btngetlocn"
            android:layout_centerHorizontal="true"
            android:text="Stop Updates"
            android:onClick="stopfun" />

    </RelativeLayout>
```

MyLocationListener.java file:

```java
package com.example.location;

import android.content.Context;
import android.location.Location;
import android.location.LocationListener;
import android.os.Bundle;
import android.widget.Toast;

public class MyLocationListener implements LocationListener {

    Context c;

     public MyLocationListener(Context con) {

c=con;
    }

    @Override
    public void onLocationChanged(Location arg0) {

        Toast.makeText(c, "location changed ", Toast.LENGTH_LONG).show();


        if (arg0!=null)
        Toast.makeText (c, "Current Location Is : Latitude = "+arg0.getLatitude()+" Longitude = "+arg0.getLongitude(), Toast.LENGTH_LONG).show();
        else
            Toast.makeText(c, "no Location Found ", Toast.LENGTH_LONG).show();

    }

    @Override
```

```java
        public void onProviderDisabled(String arg0) {
            Toast.makeText(c, "Provider disabled ", Toast.LENGTH_LONG).show();
        }
        @Override
        public void onProviderEnabled(String arg0) {
            Toast.makeText(c, "provider enabled ", Toast.LENGTH_LONG).show();
        }
        @Override
        public void onStatusChanged(String arg0, int arg1, Bundle arg2) {
            Toast.makeText(c, "status changed ", Toast.LENGTH_LONG).show();
        }
}
```

LocationDemo.java file:

```java
package com.example.location;

import android.app.Activity;
import android.location.LocationListener;
import android.location.LocationManager;
import android.os.Bundle;
import android.util.Log;
import android.view.View;
import android.widget.Toast;

public class LocationDemo extends Activity {

    LocationManager lm;
    LocationListener ll;

    @Override
    protected void onCreate(Bundle savedInstanceState) {
        super.onCreate(savedInstanceState);
        setContentView(R.layout.activity_location_demo);
    }

    public void btngetlocnfun(View v)
    {

        Toast.makeText(this,    "Location    will    be    recieved    now..."    Toast.LENGTH_LONG).show();
        lm=(LocationManager) getSystemService(LOCATION_SERVICE);

        boolean flaggps=lm.isProviderEnabled(LocationManager.GPS_PROVIDER);
```

```
        boolean flagnw=lm.isProviderEnabled(LocationManager.NETWORK_PROVIDER);

        ll=new MyLocationListener(this);
        try {
        lm.requestLocationUpdates(LocationManager.GPS_PROVIDER, 1000, 0, ll);
        }
        catch (Exception e) {
            e.printStackTrace();
        }

    }


    public void stopfun(View v)
    {
        if(ll!=null)
            lm.removeUpdates(ll);

    }
}
```

How it Works :

1. **Click on get Location :**

Fig. 10.2: Obtaining Location

2. **Enter the values for latitude and longitude :**

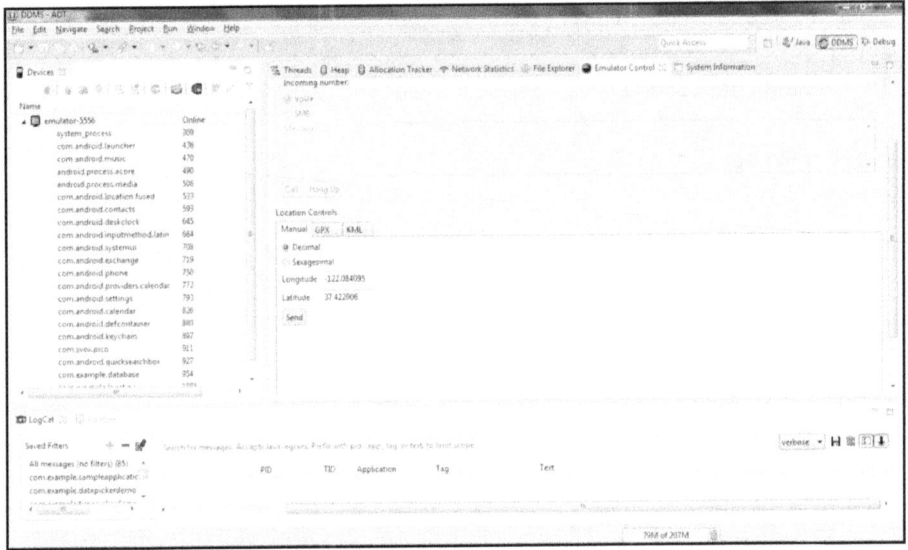

Fig. 10.3: Adding values of latitude and longitude

3. **It Wil Show you toast message that location is changed :**

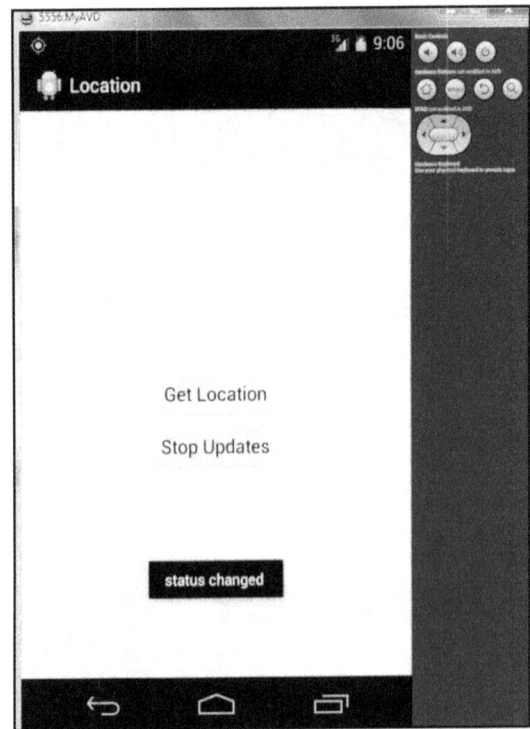

Fig. 10.4: Show toast message

10.4 Creating Map-Based Activities

10.4.1 Introduction

To provide map in an application is the most intuitive way to provide context for a physical location or address.

- MapView class is used to locate a physical location or address which creates activities that includes an interactive map.

The following are the tasks done with the help of MapView.

(1) It supports annotation using overlays and by pinning views to geographical locations.

(2) It offers full programmatic control of the map display, it offers to zoom the screen.

10.4.2 Introduction to Map View and Map Activity

The following is package hierarchy for MapActivity class:

java.lang.object

    |_ android.content.context

        |_ android.content.context Wrapper

          |_ android.view.context Theme Wrapper

            |_ android.app.Activity

              |_com.google.android.maps. MapActivity

- The permission snippet should be added to manifest .xml file as

  <uses-library android: name="com.google.android.maps"/>

Following are the classes that are used to support android maps:

(1) MapView : It is user interface element that displays the map.

(2) MapActivity : It is the base class extended to create an activity that include a MapView. MapActivity handles the life cycle of an application and background service management required for displaying maps.

(3) Overlay : Using overlays, canvas is provided to draw onto any number of layers displayed on the top of a MapView.

(4) MapController : It is used to control the map, enable you to set the center location and zoom levels.

(5) MyLocationOverlay : It is used to display the current position and orientation of the device.

(6) ItemizedOverlays and OverlayItems : These are used together to create a layer of map markers, displayed using drawables and associated text.

10.4.3 How to Get MAP API Keys

1. Google Maps Android API
- Google Maps Android API, by using this APIs you can add maps to your application that are based on Google Maps data. The API automatically handles access to Google Maps which serves, data downloading, map display and touch gestures on the map. You can also use API calls to add markers, polygons and overlays, and to change the user's view of a particular map area.
- The key class in the Google Maps Android API is MapView. A MapView displays a map with data obtained from the Google Maps service. When the MapView has focus, it will capture key presses and touch gestures to pan and zoom the map automatically including handling network requests for additional maps tiles. It also provides all of the UI elements necessary for users to control the map. Your application can also use MapView class methods to control the map programmatically and draw a number of overlays on top of the map.
- The Google Maps Android APIs are not included in the Android platform, but are available on any device with the Google Play Store running Android 2.2 or higher, through Google Play services.
- The library provides the com.google.android.gms.maps.MapFragment class and the MapView class for displaying the map components.

Install google play services:

Open the Android SDK Manager and install Extras → Google Play services

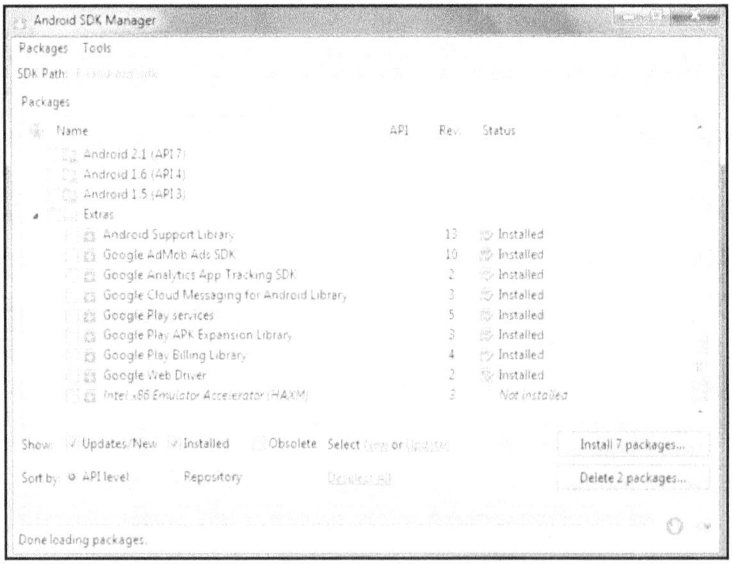

Fig. 10.5: Installing Google Play services

2. To obtain MD5 fingerprint:

- Eclipse with ADT plug-in is used to debug the android application. These are signed with the default debug certificate stored in the debug key store.
- Select

    Windows→Preferences→Android→Build

    In this Default Debug Keystore, the API key is stored.

    Following are the platforms where debug keystore is stored.

    (1) Windows Vista - \users\<username>\.android\debug.keystore

    (2) Windows XP - \Documents and Settings\<username>\.android\debug.keystore

    (3) Linux or Mac - <\.android\debug.keystore

- Every computer (Laptop) has different debug certificate and MD5 value.
- Keytool command from your Java installation is used to find MD5 fingerprint of your debug certificate.

    Generate your machine certificate fingerprint by using following command:

    ```
    keytool.exe -list -alias androiddebugkey -keystore
    "C:\Users\user\.android\debug.keystore" -storepass
    android -keypass android
    ```

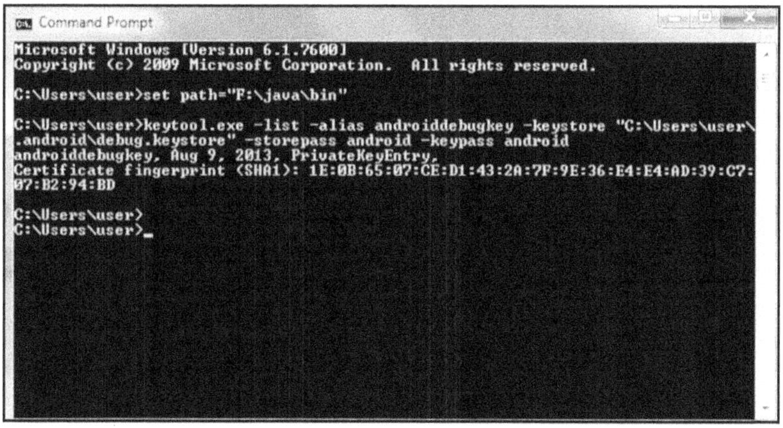

Fig. 10.6: Generate machine certificate fingerprint

Output key will be:
```
Certificate   fingerprint   (SHA1):   1E:0B:65:07:   CE:
D1:43:2A:7F:9E:36:E4:E4: AD: 39:C7:07:B2:94: BD
```

3. Obtain a Google Maps API key

If your application is registered with the Google Maps Android API v2 service, then you can request an API key. It's possible to register more than one key per project.

1. Register your project in Google APIs Console.

   For e.g. com.example.mapdemo

2. Navigate to your project in the Google APIs Console.

3. In the left navigation bar, click API Access.

4. In the resulting page, click Create New Android Key.

5. In the resulting dialog, enter the SHA-1 fingerprint, then a semicolon, then your application's package name. For example:

   1E:0B:65:07: CE: D1:43:2A:7F:9E:36:E4:E4: AD: 39:C7:07:B2:94: BD; com.example.mapdemo

- The Google APIs Console responds by displaying Key for Android apps (with certificates) followed by a forty-character API key.

For example:

AIzaSyCxRPQ8oPnX8U6uCK3oS0iqv5p-raYA0bU

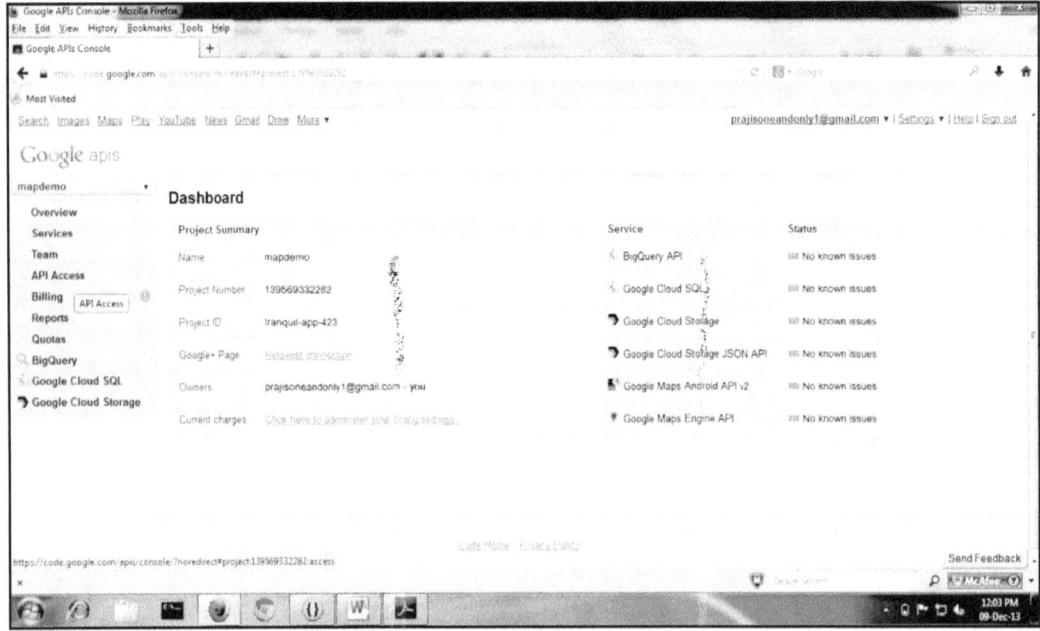

Fig. 10.7: Obtain Google Maps API key

Click on create new android key:

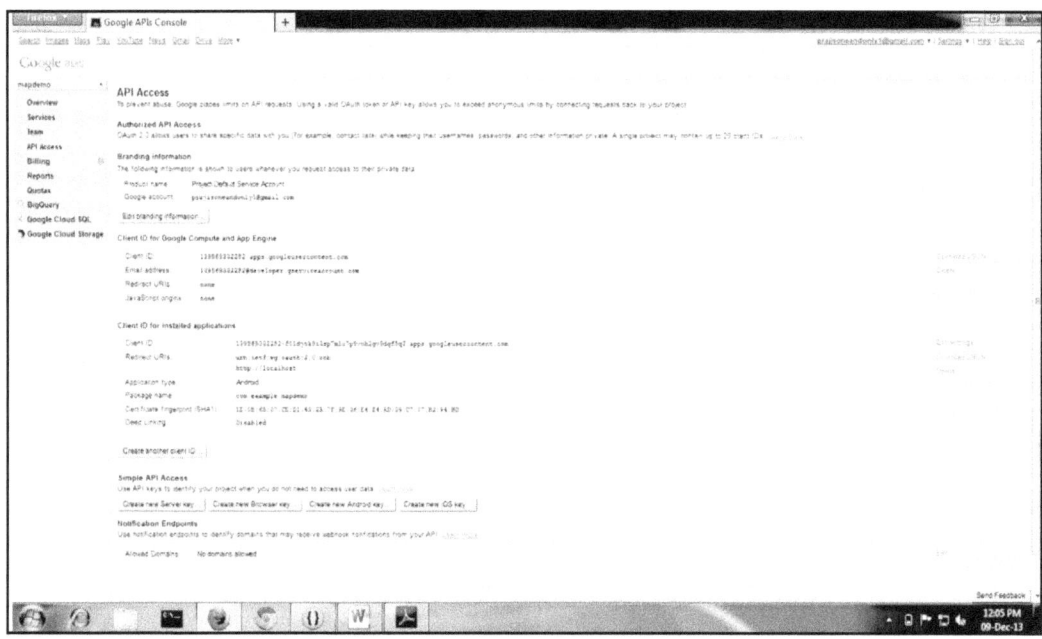

Fig. 10.8: Google API's Console

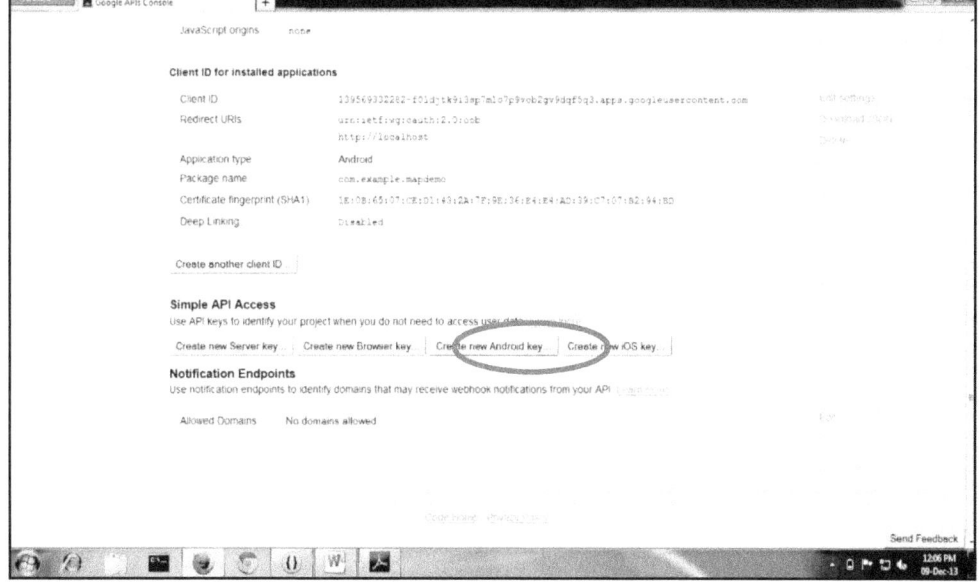

Fig. 10.9: Creating New Android key

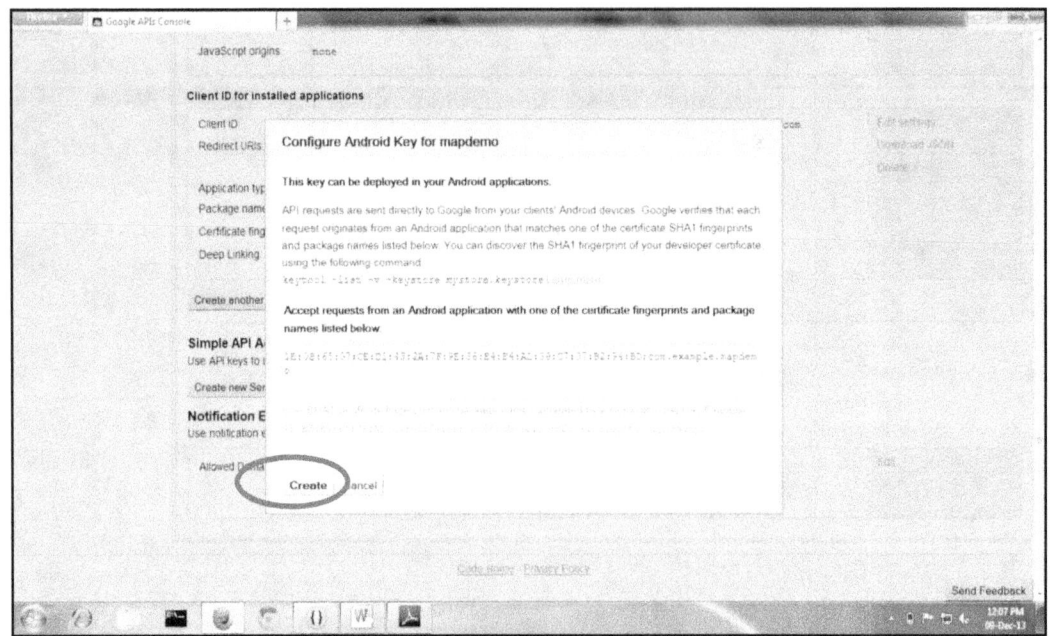

Fig. 10.10: Configure Android key for Map Demo

Output API key is:

AIzaSyCxRPQ8oPnX8U6uCK3oS0iqv5p-raYA0bU

10.4.4 Creating Map Based Activity

- Android supports only one MapActivity and MapView per application.
- The map package is not part of standard android open source (ASOP) project. It is provided with the android SDK by Google and it is available on all android devices.

How to create MapActivity.

1. Create an android application with activity MyMapActivity that extends MapActivity class.
2. Import google_play_services_lib library as follows: Import the library which was downloaded into Eclipse via File → Import → Android → Existing Android Code into Workspace. To use this library define a library dependency in your Android project.
3. MapView needs to include a uses-permission for internet access. For this, uses-permission needs to be added to application manifest file for internet.
   <uses-permission android:name="android.permission.INTERNET/">
4. Update the AndroidManifest.xml file with google API key which we have previously obtained for our application

```
<?xml version="1.0" encoding="utf-8"?>
<manifest
xmlns:android="http://schemas.android.com/apk/res/android"
```

```xml
package="com.example.mapdemo"
android: versionCode="1"
android:versionName="1.0" >
<uses-sdk
android:minSdkVersion="8"
android:targetSdkVersion="17" />
<permission
android:name="com.vogella.android.locationapi.maps.permission.MAPS_RECEIVE"
android:protectionLevel="signature" />
<uses-feature
android:glEsVersion="0x00020000"
android:required="true" />
<uses-permission
android:name="com.vogella.android.locationapi.maps.permission.MAPS
_RECEIVE" />
<uses-permission android:name="android.permission.INTERNET" />
<uses-permission
android:name="android.permission.WRITE_EXTERNAL_STORAGE" />
<uses-permission
android:name="com.google.android.providers.gsf.permission.READ_GSE
RVICES" />
<uses-permission
android:name="android.permission.ACCESS_COARSE_LOCATION" />
<uses-permission
android:name="android.permission.ACCESS_FINE_LOCATION" />
<application
android:allowBackup="true"
android:icon="@drawable/ic_launcher"
android:label="@string/app_name"
android:theme="@style/AppTheme" >
<activity
android:name="com.example.mapdemo.MyMapActivity"
android:label="@string/app_name" >
<intent-filter>
<action android:name="android.intent.action.MAIN" />
<category android:name="android.intent.category.LAUNCHER" />
</intent-filter>
</activity>
<meta-data
android:name="com.google.android.maps.v2.API_KEY"
android:value="your_apikey" />
```

```
            </application>
        </manifest>
```

Following is the snippet for creating new map-based activity:
```
        import.com.google.android.maps.MapActivity;
        import.com.google.android.maps.MapController;
        import.com.google.android.maps.MapView;
        import.android.OS.Bundle;
        public class MyMapActivity extends MapActivity
        {
        private MapView MapView;
        private MapController MapController;
        //override
        public void OnCreate(Bundle SavedInStanceState)
        {
        super.OnCreate (SavedInstanceState);
        SetContentView(R.layout.map_layout);
        MapView= (MapView) FindViewById(R.id.map_view);
        }
        //override
        protected boolean IsRouteDisplayed()
        {
        }
        }
```

10.4.5 Configuration and Use of MapViews

- By default, MapView shows the standard street map, in addition to display the satellite view and expected traffic overlay, as shown in following snippet.

    ```
    MapView.SetSatellite(true);
    MapView.SetTraffic(true);
    ```
- You can also query the MapView to find the current and maximum available zoom levels.

    ```
    int maxzoom=MapView.getMaxZoomLevel();
    int CurrentZoom=MapView.getZoomLevel();
    ```
- Current longitude and latitude span can be obtained by Geocoder.

    ```
    Geopoint Center=MapView.getMapCenter();
    int latspan=MapView.getLatitudeSpan();
    int longspan=MapView.getLongitudeSpan();
    ```
- SetBuiltInzoomControls() method is used to display the standard map zoom controls.

    ```
    MapView.SetBuiltZoomControls (true);
    ```
- MapController is used to pan and zoom a MapView.

    ```
    MapController mapcontroller=MapView.getController();
    ```

10.4.6 MapFragment

The MapFragment class extends the Fragment class and provides the life-cycle management and the services for displaying a GoogleMap widget. GoogleMap is the class which shows the map. The MapFragment has the getMap() method to access this class. The LatLng class can be used to interact with the GoogleView class.

10.4.7 Markers

You can create markers on the map via the Marker class. This class can be highly customized.

The following code shows an example.

```
public class MainActivity extends Activity {
static final LatLng location name = new LatLng(Latitude,Longitude);
static final LatLng KIEL = new LatLng(53.551, 9.993);
private GoogleMap map;
@Override
protected void onCreate(Bundle savedInstanceState) {
super.onCreate(savedInstanceState);
setContentView(R.layout.activity_main);
map = ((MapFragment) getFragmentManager().findFragmentById(R.id.map))
.getMap();
if (map!=null){
Marker Location name = map.addMarker(new MarkerOptions().position(Location name)
.title("Location Name"));
.icon(BitmapDescriptorFactory
.fromResource(R.drawable.ic_launcher)));
}
}
```

- On the GoogleMap you can register a listener for the markers in your map via the set OnMarkerClickListener(OnMarkerClickListener) method. The OnMarkerClickListener class defines the onMarkerClicked (Marker) method which is called if a marker is clicked.

10.4.8 Changing the GoogleView

The GoogleMap can be highly customized.

```
static final LatLng Location name = new LatLng(53.558, 9.927);
private GoogleMap map;
map.moveCamera(CameraUpdateFactory.newLatLngZoom(HAMBURG, 15));
map.animateCamera(CameraUpdateFactory.zoomTo(10), 2000, null);
```

10.4.9 Example

1. Create a new Android project called com.example.mapdemo with an activity called MainActivity.
2. Change the AndroidManifest.xml file to the following code. Add the following permissions to your application.

```xml
<?xml version="1.0" encoding="utf-8"?>
<manifest xmlns:android="http://schemas.android.com/apk/res/android"
package="com.example.mapdemo"
android:versionCode="1"
android:versionName="1.0" >
<uses-sdk
android:minSdkVersion="17"
android:targetSdkVersion="17" />
<permission
android:name="com.vogella.android.locationapi.maps.permission.MAPS_RECEIVE"
android:protectionLevel="signature" />
<uses-feature
android:glEsVersion="0x00020000"
android:required="true" />
<uses-permission
android:name="com.vogella.android.locationapi.maps.permission.MAPS
_RECEIVE" />
<uses-permission android:name="android.permission.INTERNET" />
<uses-permission android:name="android.permission.WRITE_EXTERNAL_STORAGE" />
<uses-permission
android:name="com.google.android.providers.gsf.permission.READ_GSE
RVICES" />
<uses-permission android:name="android.permission.ACCESS_COARSE_LOCATION" />
<uses-permission android:name="android.permission.ACCESS_FINE_LOCATION" />
<application
android:allowBackup="true"
android:icon="@drawable/ic_launcher"
android:label="@string/app_name"
android:theme="@style/AppTheme" >
<activity
android:name="com.example.mapdemo.MainActivity"
android:label="@string/app_name" >
<intent-filter>
<action android:name="android.intent.action.MAIN" />
<category android:name="android.intent.category.LAUNCHER" />
</intent-filter>
</activity>
<meta-data
android:name="com.google.android.maps.v2.API_KEY"
android:value="your_apikey" />
</application>
</manifest>
```

1. Adjust layout file

In this example we use the MapFragment. Change your layout file to the following code.

```
<RelativeLayout
xmlns:android="http://schemas.android.com/apk/res/android"
xmlns:tools="http://schemas.android.com/tools"
android:layout_width="match_parent"
android:layout_height="match_parent"
tools:context=".MainActivity" >
<fragment
android:id="@+id/map"
android:layout_width="match_parent"
android:layout_height="match_parent"
class="com.google.android.gms.maps.MapFragment" />
</RelativeLayout>
```

Fig. 10.11: Adjust layout

2. Activity class file

Change your activity to the following.

```
package com.example.mapdemo;
import android.app.Activity;
import android.os.Bundle;
import android.view.Menu;
```

```java
import com.google.android.gms.maps.CameraUpdateFactory;
import com.google.android.gms.maps.GoogleMap;
import com.google.android.gms.maps.MapFragment;
import com.google.android.gms.maps.model.BitmapDescriptorFactory;
import com.google.android.gms.maps.model.LatLng;
import com.google.android.gms.maps.model.Marker;
import com.google.android.gms.maps.model.MarkerOptions;
public class MainActivity extends Activity {
static final LatLng HAMBURG = new LatLng(53.558, 9.927);
static final LatLng KIEL = new LatLng(53.551, 9.993);
private GoogleMap map;
@Override
protected void onCreate(Bundle savedInstanceState) {
super.onCreate(savedInstanceState);
setContentView(R.layout.activity_main);
map                        =                        ((MapFragment)
getFragmentManager().findFragmentById(R.id.map))
.getMap();
Marker hamburg = map.addMarker(new MarkerOptions().position(HAMBURG)
.title("Hamburg"));
Marker kiel = map.addMarker(new MarkerOptions()
.position(KIEL)
.title("Kiel")
.snippet("Kiel is cool")
.icon(BitmapDescriptorFactory
.fromResource(R.drawable.ic_launcher)));
// Move the camera instantly to hamburg with a zoom of 15.
map.moveCamera(CameraUpdateFactory.newLatLngZoom(HAMBURG, 15));
// Zoom in, animating the camera.
map.animateCamera(CameraUpdateFactory.zoomTo(10), 2000, null);
}
@Override
public boolean onCreateOptionsMenu(Menu menu) {
getMenuInflater().inflate(R.menu.activity_main, menu);
return true;
}
}
```

3. Map is displayed on real device :

Note : For using the Google Maps you have to test the application on a real device as the emulator is not supported.

Practice Questions

1. What are the steps for finding User Location in Android ?
2. List all the classes that support map based activities.
3. How to create map based activity ?
4. How to get Map API key ?
5. Explain the concept of configuration and use of map views.
6. Write short notes on :
   (a) Location privacy.
   (b) Flow or obtaining the user location.
   (c) Map fragment.
   (d) Map view and map activity.

Chapter 11...

DATA STORAGE, RETRIEVAL AND SHARING

11.1 Introduction
11.2 File System in Android
    11.2.1 Introduction
    11.2.2 Techniques
    11.2.3 Shared Preferences
11.3 Internal and External Storage
    11.3.1 Introduction
    11.3.2 Internal Storage
    11.3.3 External Storage
    11.3.4 Choosing Best Storage Options
    11.3.5 Including Static Files as Resources
11.4 Saving and loading files
    11.4.1 Introduction
    11.4.2 Using Internal Storage
    11.4.3 Using External Storage
    11.4.4 Checking Media Availability
    11.4.5 How to Create Private Application File.
    11.4.6 Using the Application File Cache
    11.4.7 How to Store Publicly Readable Files.
    11.4.8 Example of internal Storage
    11.4.9 Example of External Storage
11.5 File Management Tools
- Practice Questions

11.1 Introduction

- Most of the applications in android need saving and loading data, which requires minimum user interface.
- Saving and loading data is essential for most of the applications. An activity should be stored in user interface state before it becomes inactive to ensure the same UI is presented it restarts, for this reason you need to save user preferences and UI selections.

- Android's application and activity state lifetime make the UI state and application data between sessions important as application process may be killed and it is activated again before returning.

11.2 File System in Android
11.2.1 Introduction
- A File is defined as object used for reading or writing large amounts of data which is needed for the application. For example, it's good for image files or anything exchanged over a network.
- File object helps in reading or writing a large amount of data, which is also shared among network.
- These file systems are also used in android which is similar to disk based file systems on other platforms. There are FILE API's that enable to work with android file to read and write.
- To work with android files, there is a need of aware of basics of Linux file system and the standard file input/output APIs in java.io.
- Like most Linux systems, there are several file systems in Android, many of which are used to boot and run the system. While we will touch on several of the file systems, the primary focus is on partitions where user data are stored, in particular EXT, FAT32, and YAFFS2 file systems.
- The physical memory, file systems, and data structures present on an Android device are the fundamental building blocks for data storage. Having a deep understanding of the structures will not only enable you to understand an Android device button but also perform your own research and development when presented with new file systems and data structures.
- To determine what file system Linux kernel (and thus Android) supports, you can examine the contents of the file /proc/filesystem. For a reference HTC , it contains the following file systems:
  ahoog@ubuntu:~$ adb shell cat /proc/filesystems
  nodev   sysfs
  nodev   rootfs
  nodev   bdev
  nodev   proc
  nodev   cgroup
  nodev   tmpfs
  nodev   debugfs

nodev   sockfs
nodev   pipefs
nodev   anon_inodefs
nodev   inotifyfs
nodev   devpts
        ext3
        ext2
nodev   ramfs
        vfat
        yaffs
        yaffs2

1. **Extended File System(EXT)**
   - The extended file system (EXT) is the de facto file system for Linux developed specifically for the operating system. As you already know, Linux supports a large number of file systems. However, the default is EXT. Since the original version of EXT was developed in 1992; there have been three additional releases: EXT2, EXT3, and EXT4.
   - Although EXT has been integral to most laptop, desktop, and server Linux distributions, I t was not found in early Android devices.
   - In 2010, EXT began to show up in devices, and on December 9, 2010, Google announced in their Android Developer blog that an increasing number of Android devices were going to move from YAFFS to the EXT (Android developer's blog).The move from YAFFS to EXT seems to be driven by several factors that were discussed online, including
     - more Android devices are moving from raw NAND flash to regular block device (eMMC).
     - EXT4 is a standard Linux file system that supports full Unix permissions.
     - EXT4 is stable and offers high performance.
     - YAFFS is single threaded, which would experience bottlenecks on forthcoming dual-core systems.
   - The first Android device to use EXT4 is the Google Nexus S, and it is expected that many tablet devices running Android's Honey comb release will also use this new file system. As only one Android device currently uses EXT4, many changes are expected overtime. Currently, the Nexus uses EXT4 in the following mount points:
     1. System image (read-only, /system)
     2. Local user data (read write, /data/data)
     3. Cache partitions (read write, /cache and possible others)

2. **FAT32/VFAT**
   - Android devices often have one or more Microsoft FAT32 partitions, generally on the SD card and eMMC. There as on for leveraging this venerable file system is not due to superior design but is due to sheer compatibility with other operating systems.
   - Microsoft's FAT32 file system was widely supported in most operating systems including Mac OSX, all Windows versions (obviously), Linux, and more. This means that Android data stored on the FAT32 partitions can be easily read, modified, or even deleted on other file systems.
   - In Linux, the file system driver for a FAT32 partition is called VFAT, not to be confused with Microsoft's earlier Virtual FAT file system that bridged the FAT16 and FAT32 implementation by adding, among other features, long file name support.
   - The HTC Incredible, there are three mount points that use FAT32:
     1. /mnt/sdcard
     2. /mnt/secure/asec
     3. /mnt/emmc

3. **YAFFS2**
   - It was developed by Aleph One Ltd. a Company based in New Zealand driven by customer requests, Aleph One began YAFFS design in December 2001 and released the first publicly available source code in May2002.
   - The primary developer (or certainly the most visible) is Charles Manning who is described as "The Embedded Janitor" and has been developing and "mopping up" embedded systems for 20 years (YAFFS: the NAND specific flash, n. d.). Charles is quite active on the YAFFS mailing list and is the de facto expert on YAFFS and YAFFS2.
   - YAFFS2 was built specifically for the growing NAND flash devices and has a number of important features that address the stringent needs of this medium. YAFFS2 is a log-structured file system (which protects data even through unexpected power outages) provides built in wear-leveling and error correction.

11.2.2 Techniques
- Android offers three techniques to serve the task of storing data which are preferences, local files, and SQLite database.
  1. Preferences are nothing but key value pair mechanism which saves the application's data.
  2. The local files are accessed by specialized methods and Java.IO classes. i.e. internal and external storage will see in next point 11.3.
  3. Android provides SQLite database library, which offers powerful native SQL database, which we will see in next chapter.

11.2.3 Shared Preferences

- Shared preferences are simple, Name/Value Pair (NVP) mechanism which is used for storing the application data, most commonly user's application preferences. Android offers for recording application state within activity's lifecycle handlers, as well as providing access to local file system by using specialized methods and java.io class.
- Shared preference is not strictly used for saving the user preferences such as ringtone which has been selected by user. PreferenceActivity is used for creating user preferences for application, which provides an activity framework for, which will be automatically persisted.
- To get a SharedPreferences object for your application, use one of two methods:
    1. **getSharedPreferences()** - Use this if you need multiple preferences files identified by name, which you specify with the first parameter.
    2. **getPreferences()** - Use this if you need only one preferences file for your activity. Because this will be the only preferences file for your activity, you don't supply a name.
- To write values:
    1. Call edit() to get a SharedPreferences.Editor.
    2. Add values with methods such as putBoolean() and putString().
    3. Commit the new values with commit()
- To read values,
    1. Use SharedPreferences methods such as getBoolean() and getString().
- Creating and saving shared preferences:

Shared Preferences class is used and Name/Value Pairs are used to store the sessions and application components running within the same application sandbox.

To create or modify shared preferences, call getSharedpreferences() on the current context, passing in the name of shared preferences to change.

```
Sharedprefernces . mysharedPreferences=
    getSharedpreferences(MY_PREFS,Activity.MODE_PRIVATE);
```

Shared preferences are stored within the application's sandbox, so they can be shared between an application's components but aren't available to other applications.

To modify shared preferences, use the SharedPreferences. Editor class, the Editor object is created by calling edit on the Shared Preferences object.

```
Sharedprefernces.Editor editor= mysharedPreferences.edit();
```

Use the put<type> Methods to insert or update the values associated with the specified name.

```
Editor.putBoolean("istrue",true);
Editor.putInt("wholenumber",2);
Editor.putString("Entryvalue","Not Empty");
```

To save edits apply() or commit() methods on the Editor object to save the changes asynchronously or synchronously respectively.

```
//commit the changes
Editor.apply();
```

Apply method was introduced in Android API level 9, calling it causes asynchronous write of the shared preferences Editor object to be performed. And commit() is called when confirmation is needed from earlier releases of commit().

Retrieving Shared Preferences:
- To access shared preferences getsharedPreferences() method is used.
- By using the type specification as get<type> method to extract saved values.

```
//retrieve saved values
Boolean is True = MySharedPreferences.getBoolean("isTrue",false);
Float lastFloat = MySharedPreferences.getFloat("lastFloadt",0f);
```

11.3 Internal and External Storage

11.3.1 Introduction
- All android devices have two storage areas. The terms internal and external are referred to the device's memory which is used for storage.
   1. Internal – Built-in non volatile storage.
   2. External – Micro SD Card.
- Even some devices offer internal and external partitions within built-in storage only. The API behavior remains same for external storage which may be removable.

11.3.2 Internal Storage
- By default, the applications which are stored on your devices can access this storage which is built-in and always available.
- Whenever the application which is using the internal storage is deleted, the space also removes all the files that are needed for that application.
- Internal storage sums what gives the private access to the data.
- The files can be stored directly on device's internal storage. By default, the private files of an application are stored internal storage and other applications are restricted to access these files. When the user uninstalls the application these files are removed.

11.3.3 External Storage
- It is mounted as USB storage so it is removable storage which is not always available.
- The mode for these file is world readable that is device or application don't have any control on the access of these files.

- If user saves the files in getExternalFileDir() then if application removed, then the files which are stored in this directory are removed.
- A shared external storage is used to save the files, this can be removable storage media (such as SD card) or an internal (non-removable storage). Files saved to external storage can be modified by the user when USB mass storage is enabled which transfers files on a computer.
- It's possible that a device using a partition of the internal storage for the external storage may also offer an SD card slot. In this case the SD card is not part of the external storage and the application and cannot access it. The extra storage is intended only for user provided media that the system scans.
- External storage can become unavailable if the user mounts the external storage on a computer or removes the media, and there is no security enforced upon files saved to the external storage. All applications can read and write files place.

11.3.4 Choosing Best Storage Options

Shared Preference, Internal Storage and External Storage are the ways to store the files and data related to an Android Application.

The following are some suggestions to choose one of the way to store the data and files.

- If the data which is to be stored is in key/value pair then use Shared Preferences object. For example, if you want to store user preference data such as user name, background color, data of birth, last login then Shared Preference can store all this information ideally, it will not emphasize on how data is stored.
- If you need to store ad-hoc data then internal storage should be used for example, application may need to download images from the Web for display. In this scenario images are to be stored to an internal storage.
- The scenario where applications needs to share the application data with other users. For example, you may create an Android application that logs the coordinates of the locations of a user, and need to be share all the data with that user. In this scenario, you can store application files to SD card of the device so that users can easily transfer the data to other devices for later use.

11.3.5 Including Static Files as Resources

- Creating and using files dynamically during run time, it is possible to add the package during design time so that these can be used it during run time.
- For example, some files may bundle in help files with the package so that proper help messages when users need it. In this case, you can add the files to the res/raw folder of your package.
- To make use of the file in the code, use the getResources() method to return a Resources object and then use its openRawResouces() method to open the file contained in the res/raw folder.

- If the application needs any resource that means any external file, these files must be included in distribution package by placing them in the res/raw folder of your project hierarchy.
  OpenRawResourcemethod accesses the read only file resources.
  `Resources myResources=getResources();`
  `InputStream myFile=myResources.openRawResource(R.raw.myFilename);`
- Android's resource mechanism lets you specify resource files for different languages, locations or hardware configurations. Example, dictionary resource file may be accessed in another application.
- The static files of an application should be stored in the project res/raw/directory.
- These files can be opened with openRawResource(), passing the R.raw.<filename> resource ID. This method returns an InputStream that you can use to read the file (but you cannot write to the original file).

11.4 Saving and loading files

11.4.1 Introduction

Many application developer chooses files to store the data. As they don't want to rely on Android's managed mechanism.

Example: multimedia files.

- The applications create or download the files that are specific to these applications. These can be stored internally or externally.
- Android offers two methods through the application context, both methods returns the file object that contains the path to the internal and external application file storage directory.
  (1) getDir()
  (2) getExternalFilesDir()
- When application gets uninstalled, all the files related to its applications are deleted from directories and subfolders. The files that are created for the application can be stored in its own directory in the following path.
  getExternalFilesDir() : i.e. /Android/data/(Your package name)/files.

11.4.2 Using Internal Storage

To create and write a private file to the internal storage:
1. Call openFileOutput() with the name of the file and the operating mode. This returns a FileOutputStream.
2. Write to the file with write().
3. Close the stream with close().

To read a file from internal storage:
1. Call openFileInput() and pass it the name of the file to read. This returns a FileInputStream.
2. Read bytes from the file with read().
3. Then close the stream with close().

```
String FILE_NAME="temp1.text";
//create new input file
FileInputStream fis=OpenFileInput(FILE_NAME);
//create output file which is private to this application.
FileOutputStream fos=OpenFileOutput (FILE_NAME, context.MODE_PRIVATE);
```

- FileOutputStream opens existing file, but if it does not exist, it will create the file with that name.
- To append the file open it with context.MODE_APPEND.
- Context.MODE_PRIVATE specifies the files opened to this application are private and access of these files is denied to other applications.
- With the help of content providers, file is shared between the applications. The Context.MODE_WORLD_READABLE or Context.MODE_WORLD_WRITEABLE makes the files to be accessed by other applications.
- File() constructor is used to create a new file in these directories. The filename is passed to this constructor.

  ```
  File file=new File (context.getFilesDir(), filename);
  ```

- Instead of calling File constructor the OpenFileOutput() method to retrieve FileOutputStream.

  ```
  String filename="myfile';
  String string="Hello Android';
  FileOutputStream outputstream;
  try
  {
  outputstream=OpenFileOutput (filename, Context.MODE_PRIVATE);
  (String.getBytes());
  OutputStream.close();
  }
  catch (Exception e)
  {
  e.PrintStackTrace();
  }
  ```

- To cache the files CreateTempFile() should be used. It extracts the file name from a URL and creates a file with that name into the applications internal storage.

```
public File getTempFile (Context context, String Url)
{
File file;
try
{
String fileName=Uri.parse (url).getLastPathSegment();
file=File.CreateTempFile (fileName, null, context.getCacheDir());
Catch (IOException)
{
//Error while creating file
}
    return file;
}
```

11.4.3 Using External Storage

- The application which is about to store the files into an external storage must verify about the storage that it is mounted or not. The state external storage can be retrieved by calling getExternalStorageState() method. If this returns MEDIA_MOUNTED value then user can read or write files to it.
- External storage have two categories of files :

  (1) Public Files : These files are freely available to other apps and user too. These files remains in storage even if the application is uninstalled by user. e.g. photos captured by the app.

  (2) Private Files : Files are deleted when the application using these files is uninstalled. e.g. additional resources by the app or temporary media files.
- To store the public files to the external storage, use getExternalStoragePublicDirectory() method to get file representing appropriate directory on an external storage.
- To store the private files to external storage getExternalStorageDirectory() method is used and the name of directory is passed to it. Each directory created by this method is added to parent and encapsulates all your application's external storage files.

```
public File getAlbumStorageDir (String albumName)
{
File file=new File (Environment.DIRECTORY_PICTURES), albumName);
if (! file.mkdirs())
    {
Log.e (LOGTAG, "Directory not created");
    }
return file;
    }
```

Following code demonstrate how to create a directory for an individual photo album.

```
public file=new file
    (Context.getExternalFileDir(Environment.DIRECTORY_PICTURES), albumName;
If (! file.mkdirs())
    {
Log.e (LOG_TAG. "Directory not created");
    }
        return file;
    }
```

- getFreeSpace() and getTotalSpace() – these two methods can be used to get the total free available space for storage.

11.4.4 Checking Media Availability

The availability of media should be checked before user save any work to external storage by calling getExternalStorageState(). The media might be mounted to a computer, missing, read-only or in some other state.

```
boolean mExternalStorageAvailable = false;
boolean mExternalStorageWriteable = false;
String state = Environment.getExternalStorageState();

if (Environment.MEDIA_MOUNTED.equals(state))

{
    mExternalStorageAvailable = mExternalStorageWriteable = true;
}
    else if (Environment.MEDIA_MOUNTED_READ_ONLY.equals(state))

{
    mExternalStorageAvailable = true;
    mExternalStorageWriteable = false;
} else

{
    mExternalStorageAvailable = mExternalStorageWriteable = false;
}
```

The given snippet checks whether the external storage is available to read and write. The getExternalStorageState() method returns other states that user might want to check, such as whether the media is being shared (connected to a computer), is missing entirely, has been removed badly, etc. developer can use these to notify the user with more information when your application needs to access the media.

Accessing files on external storage
- If developer is using API level 8 or greater, use getExternalFilesDir() to open a file that represents the external storage directory where user should save the files.
- This method takes a type parameter that specifies the type of subdirectory you want, such as DIRECTORY_MUSIC and DIRECTORY_RINGTONES (pass null to receive the root of your application's file directory).
- By properly specifying the type of directory Android's media scanner will categorized the files in the system. For example, ringtones are identified as ringtones and not music. If the user uninstalls your application, this directory and all its contents will be deleted.
- If you're using API Level 7 or lower, use getExternalStorageDirectory(), to open a File representing the root of the external storage. You should then write your data in the following directory:
  /Android/data/<package_name>/files/

The <package_name> is your Java-style package name, such as "com.example.android.app".
- If the user's device is running API Level 8 or greater and they uninstall your application, this directory and all its contents will be deleted.

Hiding your Files from the Media Scanner

Include an empty file named .nomedia in your external files directory (note the dot prefix in the filename). This will prevent Android's media scanner from reading your media files and including them in apps like Gallery or Music.

11.4.5 How To Create Private Application File.
- OpenFileInput and OpenFileOutput methods are used to reading and writing streams from and to files stored in the application's sandbox.
  ```
  String FILE_NAME="temp1.tmp";
  //create new file that is private to the application
  FileOutputStream fos=OpenFileOutput (file_name, context.MODE_PRIVATE);
  //create a new file input stream
  FileInputStream fis=OpenFileInput (file_name);
  ```
- These methods support only those file in current application's directory.
- FileOutputStream opens existing file, if the file does not exist android creates that file. Default mode is to overwrite the file. For appending the existing file, the mode in which it is open is to be modified.
  Context.MODE_APPEND
- Files which are created by using OpenFileOutput() method are private for that application. Private files can be accessed by only one application. Public files that are created can be shared by multiple applications. Content provider can be used to share the public files.

- Context.MODE_WORLD_READABLE or context.MODE_WORLD_WRITEABLE – These two mode are used to share the files publicaly.
  ```
  String OUTPUT_FILE="publicfile.txt";
  FileOutputStream fos=OpenFileOutput (OUTPUT_FILE, Context.MODE_WORLD_WRITEABLE);
  ```
- The location of file can be detected by using getDir() method. This will return absolute path to the files created using OpenFileOutput.
  ```
  File file=getFilesDir();
  Log.d ("OUTPUT_PATH", file.getAbsolutePath());
  ```

11.4.6 Using the Application File Cache

- The temporary files can be stored by using internal managed cache or external unmanaged cache by Android. These files can be accessed by using getCacheDir() and getExternalCacheDir() method from the current context.
- The files stored in cache are deleted when application is uninstalled. Files stored in the internal cache can be erased by the system when it running slow on storage. Files that are stored on an external cache will not be erased by system, as system does not kept a track of available storage on external media.

Sometimes the application needs the files which are temporary such files can be cached. for this getCacheDir() is used which opens a file that represents the internal directory where the application n should save cache files.

If you're using API Level 8 or greater, use getExternalCacheDir() to open a File that represents the external storage directory where you should save cache files.

If you're using API Level 7 or lower, use getExternalStorageDirectory() to open a File that represents the root of the external storage, then write your cache data in the following directory:

/Android/data/<*package_name*>/cache/

The <*package_name*> is your Java-style package name, such as "com.example.android.app".

Other Useful Methods

1. **getFilesDir()**

Gets the absolute path to the file system directory where your internal files are saved.

2. **getDir()**

Creates (or opens an existing) directory within your internal storage space.

11.4.7 How To Store Publicly Readable Files.

- Usually when application is deleted the files relative to those applications are deleted. If user want to save that files which are specific to an application but it is not gets deleted when the application is uninstall.
- In API Level 8 or greater, use getExternalStoragePublicDirectory(), passing it the type of public directory you want, such as DIRECTORY_MUSIC, DIRECTORY_PICTURES, DIRECTORY_RINGTONES, or others. This method will create the appropriate directory if necessary.

- The above mentioned method accepts a string parameter that determines which subdirectory is to be accessed by using a series of environment static constants as follows.

    (1) DIRECTORY_ALARAM: Audio files that should be available as user-selectable alarm sound.

    (2) DIRECTORY_DCIM: Pictures and videos taken by devices.

    (3) DIRECTORY_DOWNLOADS: Files downloaded by user.

    (4) DIRECTORY_MOVIES: Movies

    (5) DIRECTORY_MUSIC: Audio files that represent music.

    (6) DIRECTORY_NOTIFICATION: Audio files that should be available as user-selectable notification sounds.

    (7) DIRECTORY_PICTURES: Pictures.

```
String FILE_NAME="mymusic.mp3";
file path=Environment.getExternalStoragePublicDirectory (Environment.DIRECTORY_MUSIC);
File file=new file (path, FILE_NAME);
try
    {
path.mkdirs();
[…write files…]
    } catch (IO Exception e)
    {
Log.d (TAG, "Error writing" + FILE_NAME e);
    }
```

- If returned directory does not exist, then it must be created first.
- If you're using API Level 7 or lower, usegetExternalStorageDirectory() to open a File that represents the root of the external storage, then save your shared files in one of the following directories:

    Music/ - Media scanner classifies all media found here as user music.

    Podcasts/ - Media scanner classifies all media found here as a podcast.

    Ringtones/ - Media scanner classifies all media found here as a ringtone.

    Alarms/ - Media scanner classifies all media found here as an alarm sound.

    Notifications/ - Media scanner classifies all media found here as a notification sound.

    Pictures/ - All photos (excluding those taken with the camera).

    Movies/ - All movies (excluding those taken with the camcorder).

    Download/ - Miscellaneous downloads

11.4.8 Example of internal Storage

```xml
<LinearLayout xmlns:android="http://schemas.android.com/apk/res/android"
    xmlns:tools="http://schemas.android.com/tools"
    android:id="@+id/LinearLayout1"
    android:layout_width="match_parent"
    android:layout_height="match_parent"
    android:orientation="vertical"
    android:paddingBottom="@dimen/activity_vertical_margin"
    android:paddingLeft="@dimen/activity_horizontal_margin"
    android:paddingRight="@dimen/activity_horizontal_margin"
    android:paddingTop="@dimen/activity_vertical_margin"
    tools:context=".InternalStorage" >

    <TextView
        android:id="@+id/textView1"
        android:layout_width="wrap_content"
        android:layout_height="wrap_content"
        android:text="Enter The Data Here :"
        android:textAppearance="?android:attr/textAppearanceLarge" />

    <ScrollView
        android:id="@+id/s"
        android:layout_width="match_parent"
        android:layout_height="100dp" >

    <EditText
        android:id="@+id/etdata"
        android:layout_width="match_parent"
        android:layout_height="wrap_content"
        android:ems="10"
        android:inputType="textMultiLine" >

        <requestFocus />

    </EditText>
    </ScrollView>
```

```xml
<Button
    android:id="@+id/savebtn"
    android:layout_width="wrap_content"
    android:layout_height="wrap_content"
    android:onClick="savefun"
    android:text="Click Here To Save Your Data In File" />

<Button
    android:id="@+id/displaybtn"
    android:layout_width="wrap_content"
    android:layout_height="wrap_content"
    android:onClick="displayfun"
    android:text="Click Here To Display Your Data In File" />

<TextView
    android:id="@+id/textView2"
    android:layout_width="wrap_content"
    android:layout_height="wrap_content"
    android:text="Saved Data In file Is    :"
    android:textAppearance="?android:attr/textAppearanceLarge" />

<ScrollView
    android:id="@+id/sv"
    android:layout_width="match_parent"
    android:layout_height="100dp" >

    <TextView
        android:id="@+id/etrdata"
        android:layout_width="match_parent"
        android:layout_height="wrap_content"
        android:text="No Data To Display"
        android:textAppearance="?android:attr/textAppearanceMedium" />
</ScrollView>
```

```xml
<Button
    android:id="@+id/clearbtn"
    android:layout_width="wrap_content"
    android:layout_height="wrap_content"
    android:onClick="clearfun"
    android:text="Click Here To Clear Data In File" />

</LinearLayout>
```

```java
package com.example.internalstorage;

import java.io.FileInputStream;
import java.io.FileOutputStream;
import java.io.InputStreamReader;
import java.io.OutputStreamWriter;

import android.app.Activity;
import android.os.Bundle;
import android.view.View;
import android.widget.EditText;
import android.widget.TextView;
import android.widget.Toast;

public class InternalStorage extends Activity {

    EditText etdata;
    TextView etrdata;
    String data="",readdata="";
    FileOutputStream out;
    OutputStreamWriter w;
    FileInputStream in;
    InputStreamReader r;
    private String filename="myfile.txt";
```

```java
@Override
protected void onCreate(Bundle savedInstanceState) {
    super.onCreate(savedInstanceState);
    setContentView(R.layout.activity_internal_storage);
    etdata=(EditText)findViewById(R.id.etdata);
    etrdata=(TextView)findViewById(R.id.etrdata);
}

public void savefun(View v)
{
    char[] buffer=new char[100];

    data="";
    data=etdata.getText().toString();
    if(data.equals(""))
    {
    Toast.makeText(getApplicationContext(), "Enter Data To Save!!",
                                    Toast.LENGTH_LONG).show();
    }
    else
    {
    try
    {
        out = openFileOutput(filename, MODE_APPEND);
        w=new OutputStreamWriter(out);
        w.append("\n"+data);
        w.flush();
        w.close();
        out.close();

        Toast.makeText(getApplicationContext(), "Your Text Saved
                            Successfully!!", Toast.LENGTH_LONG).show();
        etdata.setText("");
```

```java
            etrdata.setText("click Display Button To See New data");
        }
        catch (Exception e)
        {
            e.printStackTrace();
        }
    }
}

public void displayfun(View v)
{
    char[] buffer=new char[100];
    etrdata.setText("");
    readdata="";
    try
    {
        in=openFileInput(filename);
        r=new InputStreamReader(in);
        int chlength;
        while((chlength=r.read(buffer))>0)
        {
            String str=String.copyValueOf(buffer, 0, chlength);
            readdata+=str;
        }
        if(readdata.equals(""))
        {
            etrdata.setText("No Data To Dispaly");
            Toast.makeText(getApplicationContext(), "No Data To Display!!",
                                             Toast.LENGTH_LONG).show();
        }
        else
            etrdata.setText(readdata);
        in.close();
        r.close();
    }
```

```
        catch (Exception e)
        {
            e.printStackTrace();
        }
    }

    public void clearfun(View v)
    {
        try
        {
            out = openFileOutput(filename, MODE_PRIVATE);
            w=new OutputStreamWriter(out);
            w.write("");
            w.flush();
            w.close();
            out.close();
            Toast.makeText(getApplicationContext(), "Your File Data Deleted
                                    Successfully!!", Toast.LENGTH_LONG).show();
            etrdata.setText("No Data To Dispaly");
        }
        catch (Exception e)
        {
            e.printStackTrace();
        }
    }
}
```

Fig. 11.1: Enter the data in internal storage

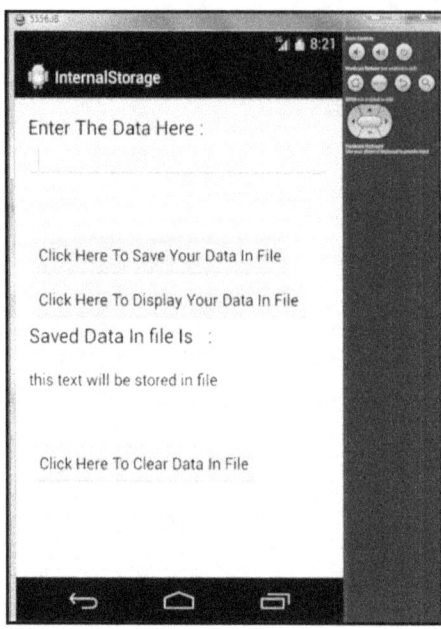

Fig. 11.2: Store data in internal storage

Fig. 11.3: Updating data in internal storage

Fig. 11.4: Deleting data from internal storage

11.4.9 Example of External Storage

```xml
<?xml version="1.0" encoding="utf-8"?>
<manifest xmlns:android="http://schemas.android.com/apk/res/android"
    package="com.example.externalstorage"
    android:versionCode="1"
    android:versionName="1.0" >

    <uses-sdk
        android:minSdkVersion="8"
        android:targetSdkVersion="17" />
    <uses-permission
android:name="android.permission.WRITE_EXTERNAL_STORAGE"/>

    <application
        android:allowBackup="true"
        android:icon="@drawable/ic_launcher"
        android:label="@string/app_name"
        android:theme="@style/AppTheme" >
        <activity
            android:name="com.example.externalstorage.ExternalStorage"
            android:label="@string/app_name" >
            <intent-filter>
                <action android:name="android.intent.action.MAIN" />
```

```xml
            <category android:name="android.intent.category.LAUNCHER" />
        </intent-filter>
    </activity>
</application>
</manifest>

<LinearLayout xmlns:android="http://schemas.android.com/apk/res/android"
    xmlns:tools="http://schemas.android.com/tools"
    android:id="@+id/LinearLayout1"
    android:layout_width="match_parent"
    android:layout_height="match_parent"
    android:orientation="vertical"
    android:paddingBottom="@dimen/activity_vertical_margin"
    android:paddingLeft="@dimen/activity_horizontal_margin"
    android:paddingRight="@dimen/activity_horizontal_margin"
    android:paddingTop="@dimen/activity_vertical_margin"
    tools:context=".ExternalStorage" >

    <TextView
        android:id="@+id/textView1"
        android:layout_width="wrap_content"
        android:layout_height="wrap_content"
        android:text="Enter The Data Here :"
        android:textAppearance="?android:attr/textAppearanceLarge" />

    <ScrollView
        android:id="@+id/s"
        android:layout_width="match_parent"
        android:layout_height="100dp" >

    <EditText
        android:id="@+id/etdata"
        android:layout_width="match_parent"
        android:layout_height="wrap_content"
        android:ems="10"
        android:inputType="textMultiLine" >
        <requestFocus />
    </EditText>
    </ScrollView>
```

```xml
<Button
    android:id="@+id/savebtn"
    android:layout_width="wrap_content"
    android:layout_height="wrap_content"
    android:onClick="savefun"
    android:text="Click Here To Save Your Data In File" />

<Button
    android:id="@+id/displaybtn"
    android:layout_width="wrap_content"
    android:layout_height="wrap_content"
    android:onClick="displayfun"
    android:text="Click Here To Display Your Data In File" />

<TextView
    android:id="@+id/textView2"
    android:layout_width="wrap_content"
    android:layout_height="wrap_content"
    android:text="Saved Data In file Is    :"
    android:textAppearance="?android:attr/textAppearanceLarge" />

<ScrollView
    android:id="@+id/sv"
    android:layout_width="match_parent"
    android:layout_height="100dp" >

    <TextView
        android:id="@+id/etrdata"
        android:layout_width="match_parent"
        android:layout_height="wrap_content"
        android:text="No Data To Display"
        android:textAppearance="?android:attr/textAppearanceMedium" />
</ScrollView>

<Button
    android:id="@+id/clearbtn"
    android:layout_width="wrap_content"
    android:layout_height="wrap_content"
    android:onClick="clearfun"
    android:text="Click Here To Clear Data In File" />
</LinearLayout>
```

```java
package com.example.externalstorage;

import java.io.File;
import java.io.FileInputStream;
import java.io.FileOutputStream;
import java.io.InputStreamReader;
import java.io.OutputStreamWriter;

import android.app.Activity;
import android.os.Bundle;
import android.os.Environment;

import android.view.View;
import android.widget.EditText;
import android.widget.TextView;
import android.widget.Toast;

public class ExternalStorage extends Activity {
    EditText etdata;
    TextView etrdata;
    String data="",readdata="";
    FileOutputStream out;
    OutputStreamWriter w;
    FileInputStream in;
    InputStreamReader r;
    private String filename="myfile.txt";
    File sdcard,dir,file;

    @Override
    protected void onCreate(Bundle savedInstanceState) {
        super.onCreate(savedInstanceState);
        setContentView(R.layout.activity_external_storage);
        etdata=(EditText)findViewById(R.id.etdata);
        etrdata=(TextView)findViewById(R.id.etrdata);

        sdcard=Environment.getExternalStorageDirectory();
        dir=new File(sdcard.getAbsolutePath()+"/myfolder");
        dir.mkdirs();
```

```java
        file=new File(dir, filename);;
        Toast.makeText(getApplicationContext(), "myfile.txt and myfolder is
                                    created!!",Toast.LENGTH_LONG).show();
    }
    public void savefun(View v)
    {
            data="";
        data=etdata.getText().toString();
        if(data.equals(""))
        {
            Toast.makeText(getApplicationContext(), "Enter Data To Save!!",
                                        Toast.LENGTH_LONG).show();
        }
        else
        {
        try
        {
            out = new FileOutputStream(file);
            w=new OutputStreamWriter(out);
            w.append("\n"+data);
            w.flush();
            w.close();
            out.close();
            Toast.makeText(getApplicationContext(), "Your Text Saved
                            Successfully!!", Toast.LENGTH_LONG).show();
            etdata.setText("");
            etrdata.setText("click Display Button To See New data");
        }
        catch (Exception e)
        {
            e.printStackTrace();
        }
        }
    }
```

```java
public void displayfun(View v)
{
    char[] buffer=new char[100];
    etrdata.setText("");
    readdata="";
    try
    {
        in=new FileInputStream(file);
        r=new InputStreamReader(in);
        int chlength;
        while((chlength=r.read(buffer))>0)
        {
        String str=String.copyValueOf(buffer, 0, chlength);
                                    readdata+=str;
        }
        if(readdata.equals(""))
        {
                etrdata.setText("No Data To Dispaly");
            Toast.makeText(getApplicationContext(), "No Data To Display!!",
                                    Toast.LENGTH_LONG).show();
        }
        else
                            etrdata.setText(readdata);
        in.close();
        r.close();
    }
    catch (Exception e)
    {
        e.printStackTrace();
    }
}
public void clearfun(View v)
```

```
{
    try
    {
        out = new FileOutputStream(file);
        w=new OutputStreamWriter(out);

        w.write("");
        w.flush();
        w.close();
        out.close();
        Toast.makeText(getApplicationContext(), "Your File Data Deleted
                            Successfully!!", Toast.LENGTH_LONG).show();
                                etrdata.setText("No Data To Dispaly");
    }
    catch (Exception e)
    {
        e.printStackTrace();
    }
  }
}
```

Fig. 11.5: Enter data in external storage

Fig. 11.6: Store data in external storage

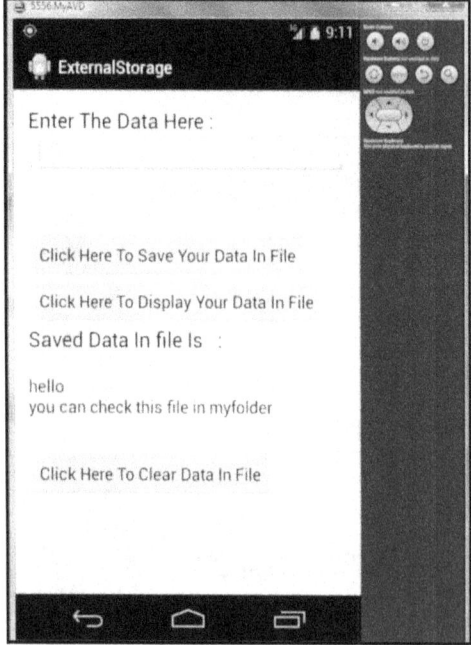

Fig. 11.7: Updating data in external storage

Fig. 11.8: Deleting data from external storage

11.5 File Management Tools

- Android offers some basic file management tools to help to deal with file system. These utilities mostly located within the java.io.File package.
- Mostly all Java file management utilities are used to manage the working of files. Android uses default utilities and also provides some specialized utilities for file management that are available from the application context.
  1. **fileList :** It returns a string array that includes all the files created by the current application.
  2. **deleteFile :** It enables to remove files created by the current application.
     For example-
     (a) MyFile.delete();
     (b) MyContext.deleteFile (filename); - When file stored on internal storage, with the help of context you can delete the files.
- All cached files may be manually deleted by using getCacheDir() on regular basis.
- These methods explicitly used for cleaning up temporary files that are left behind when the application crashes or killed.

Practice Questions

1. Explain the concept of file management tool.
2. How file system works in Android Operating Systems ?
3. How to create private application file ?
4. How to store publicly readable files ?
5. Write short notes on :
   (a) Shared preferences   (b) Internal storage
   (c) External storage   (d) Check media availability.

Chapter 12...

INTRODUCTION TO SQLite

12.1 SQLite
- 12.1.1 What is SQLite ?
- 12.1.2 Adoption
- 12.1.3 SQLite in Android
- 12.1.4 Introduction to Android Databases

12.2 Working with Android Database-SQLite
- 12.2.1 Introduction of SQLiteOpenHelper
- 12.2.2 Opening and Creating by Using Application Context
- 12.2.3 Creating and Updating Database with SQLiteOpenHelper

12.3 Content Values and Cursor
- 12.3.1 Cursor
- 12.3.2 Extracting Values from a Cursor
- 12.3.3 Database and Data Model
- 12.3.4 Security and ContentProvider
- 12.3.5 Using ContentProvider
- 12.3.6 SQLite Database and CursorLoader
- 12.3.7 Cursors and Loaders

12.4 Querying a Database
- 12.4.1 Adding, Updating and Removing Rows
- • Practice Questions

12.1 SQLite

There are many relational database management systems, these are the separate processes that can access the database from client application. In mobile devices SQLite relational database management system is used which contains in a small c programming library. And it is not separate process but it is an integral part of it.

SQLite implements most of the SQL standard and ACID compliant, using dynamically and weakly typed syntax that does not guarantee the domain integrity.

SQLite is popular amongst embedded database for local/client storage in application software such as web browser. SQLite has many bindings to programming languages, it is most widely deployed database engine and this is used by many browsers, operating system and embedded system.

The source code for SQLite is in the public domain.

Design

The SQLite engine has no standalone processes with which application program communicates. The SQLite library is linked in and becomes integral part of the application the library can also be called dynamically. By calling simple function calls the application program uses the SQLite's functionality, which reduces latency in database access. Function calls within a single process are more efficient than inter process communication.

The entire database (definitions, tables, indices, and the data itself) is stored as a single cross platform file on the host machine the simple locking system is applied on entire database file during writing. SQLite read operations can be multitasked, though writes can only be performed sequentially.

12.1.1 What is SQLite ?

- SQLite is an in-process which implements self contained, server less, zero-configuration transactional SQL Database engine. It is open source and can be implemented for commercial as well as private applications.
- It is server less that means it reads and writes from and to ordinary disk files. It is cross-platform, it can be copied between 32-bit and 64-bit systems.
- SQLite supports the data types TEXT (String in Java), integer (long in Java) and REAL (double in Java). All other types are converted into one of these.
- The database requires a less memory at runtime (250 Kbyte). So, it is best to be embedded in another application.

History

D. Richard Hipp designed SQLite in the year 2000 working for General Dynamics contract with the United States Navy. The design goals of SQLite were to allow the program to be operated without installing a database management system or requiring an administrator. In august 2000, version 1.0 of SQLite was released based on GNU database manager.

Hipp in 2011 announced his plans to add an UNQL interface to SQLite databases and to develop UnQLite an embeddable document oriented database.

Features

SQLite implements most of the SQL-92 standard for SQL but it lacks in some features for example it has partial support for triggers and it can't write to views, complex queries are supported by it still has limited ALTER_TABLE support, as it can't modify or delete columns.

SQLite uses an unusual type system for an SQL compatible DBMS. Instead of assigning a type to a column as in most SQL database systems, types are assigned to individual values. In language terms it is dynamically typed. This adds flexibility to columns, especially when bound to a dynamically typed scripting language. However, the technique is not portable to other SQL products. The SQLite web site describes a "strict affinity" mode, but this feature has not yet been added. However, it can be implemented with constraints like CHECK (typeof(x) ='integer').

The same database can be accessed by many computer processes or threads concurrently. Several read accesses can be satisfied in parallel. But the write access can be provided to only one of the processes or threads. Otherwise write access fails with error code. This concurrent access situation would change when dealing with temporary tables. This restriction is relaxed in version 3.7 which enables concurrent reads and writes.

A standalone program called SQLite 3 is provided that can be used to create a database, define tables within it, insert and change rows, run queries and manage an SQLite database file. This program is a single executable file on the host machine. It also serves as an example for writing applications that use the SQLite library. SQLite is a popular choice for local/client SQL storage within a web browser and within a rich internet application framework.

SQLite also has bindings for a large number of programming languages, including BASIC, C, C++, Clipper//Harbour, Common Lisp, C#, Curl, D,Delphi, Free Pascal, Haskell, Java, Livecode, Lua, newLisp, Objective-C (on OS X and iOS), OCaml, Perl, PHP, Pike, Python, REBOL, R,REALbasic, Ruby, Scheme, Smalltalk, Tcl, Visual Basic, and JavaScript. An ADO.NET adapter, initially developed by Robert Simpson, is maintained jointly with the SQLite developers since April 2010. An ODBC driver has been developed and is maintained separately by Christian Werner. Werner's ODBC driver is the recommend connection method for accessing SQLite from OpenOffice.org. There is also a COM (ActiveX) wrapper making SQLite accessible on Windows to scripted languages such as JScript and VBScript. This adds database capabilities to HTML Applications (HTA)

Before each release of SQLite, it undergoes regression testing. More than 2 million tests are run as part of a release's verification. Starting with the August 10, 2009 release of SQLite 3.6.17, SQLite releases have 100% branch test coverage, one of the components of code coverage.

SQLite development stores revisions of its source code in Fossil, a distributed version control system that is itself built upon a SQLite database.

12.1.2 Adoption

Web Browsers
- The configuration data like bookmarks, cookies, contacts etc. is stored through Mozilla Firefox and Mozilla Thunderbird and this is internally managed SQLite databases, and even offer an add on to manage SQLite database.
- The opera internet suite and browser uses SQLite 3.7.9 for managing WebSQL databases. This is noted in opera about, although without the mention of WebSQL (databases can be managed through opera webdatabases).
- SQLite is added to the HTML 5 web storage standard. After discussion inside the W3C Web Applications Working Group the WebSimpleDB API proposal was developed.

Web Application Frameworks
- Django, a Python web framework, supports SQLite3 by default.
- As of version 7, Drupal, a PHP-based content management system for making websites and blogs, has an option to install using SQLite.
- Ruby on Rails' default database management system is also SQLite.
- web2py, a Python web framework, default database management system is also SQLite.
- Skype is a widely deployed application that uses SQLite.
- Adobe Systems uses SQLite as its file format in Adobe Photoshop Lightroom, a standard database in Adobe AIR, and internally within Adobe Reader.
- Xmarks, the bookmark sharing tool has also reported to use SQLite to manage the bookmarks for each user.
- The Service Management Facility, used for service management within the Solaris and OpenSolaris operating systems, uses SQLite internally.
- Flame, a malware program used for cyberespionage, used SQLite to store the data it collects.
- Spiceworks, the popular free IT systems management, inventory, and help desk software application uses SQLite.
- WikidPad, a personal desktop wiki, implemented in Python, uses SQLite for metadata, and wiki-pages, if chosen.
- Anki, learning software, stores its decks in SQLite format, version 3.

Operating systems

Because of its small size, SQLite is well suited to embedded systems, and is also included in:
- Blackberry's BlackBerry 10 OS
- Microsoft's Windows Phone 8
- Apple's iOS

- Symbian OS
- Nokia's Maemo
- Google's Android
- Linux Foundation's MeeGo
- LG's webOS
- NetBSD
- OpenBSD

This is also suitable for desktop operating system .Apple adopted it as an option in OSX's core Data API from the original implementation in Mac OS X 10.4 onwards and also for administration of videos and songs on the iPhone.

12.1.3 SQLite in Android
- SQLite is embedded into every Android device. Using a SQLite database in Android does not require a setup procedure or administration of the database.
- User have to define the SQL statements for creating and updating the database. Afterwards the database is automatically managed for user by the Android platform.
- To access SQLite database files should be accessed, this process is slow. Therefore it is recommended to perform database operations asynchronously
- If application creates a database, this database is by default saved in the directory DATA/data/APP_NAME/databases/FILENAME.

The following rules are used to construct the directories

1. DATA is the path which the Environment.getDataDirectory() method returns. APP_NAME is your application name.FILENAME is the name you specify in your application code for the database.

- **Why SQLite in Android:**

Due to benefits of SQLite as it is open source and requires less memory at runtime. Developers of Android applications use this database. Additionally in android, it does not require any setup procedure or administration in database.

- Android platform automatically manages database once it is created and updated.
- When application creates a database it gets stored in DATA/data/APP_Name/_database/FILENAME.
- SQLite manager is responsible for the setup. In case this can also be done by using SQLite database browser.

12.1.4 Introduction to Android Databases
- Android provides structured data through a combination of SQLite databases and Content providers
- The application SQLite data can be managed and stored in a structured format. Android offers a full SQLite relational database Library. Each application can create its own databases over which it has a complete control.

- Content Providers are well defined interface for using and sharing data which provides abstraction from the underlying data store.

SQLiteDATABASE
- SQLite database is the base class for working SQLite database in android and it provides methods to open, query, update and close the database. It has insert(), update() and delete() methods. Additionally it provides execSQL() method, which allows execution of SQL command directly.
- The creation of attributes in the table is done with the help of an object content values which is in the key/value pair. Key represents column identifier and value represents the content for the table record in this column. It can be used for inserts and updates of database entries.
- It has implemented as a compact C library that is included as a part of the Android software stack.

12.2 Working with Android Database-SQLite

- Android encapsulates the database and exposes only public methods and constants that are required to interact with the database.
- Contract or helper is the two classes that are used to interact with database.
- This class exposes database constants, column names, which will be required by populating and querying a database. The following snippet shows a skeleton for database constants that are made public by using helper class.

    public static final string key_id="_id";

//The name and column index of each column in the database.

    public static final string KEY_GOLD_HOARD_NAME_COLUMN=
    GOLD_HOARD_NAME_COLUMN";

    Public static final string.

12.2.1 Introduction of SQLiteOpenHelper
- SQLiteOpenHelper class is used to implement the patterns for creating, opening and upgrading databases.
- The new database creation and upgradation of old database is done by extending SQLiteOpenHelper class and overriding constructor OnCreate and OnUpgrade.
- OnUpgrade method drops the existing instance and creates it with new definition of database.
- To create and upgrade the database, it must be opened in a writeable form.
- How Android database stores the data ?

The following Android specific considerations are to be followed :
(1) Files (such as bitmaps or audio files) are not stored within the database. Use a string to store a path to the file, preferably a fully qualified URI.
(2) All tables should include an auto-increment key field as a unique index field for each row.
- Android database creation and upgradation can be done by using SQLiteOpenHelper class or directly with application context's methods.

12.2.2 Opening and Creating by Using Application Context
- OpenOrCreateDatabase() method is used by application context.
  ```
  SQLiteDatabasedb=context.openOrCreateDatabase(Database_name,context.MODE_PRIVATE, null);
  ```
- After creating db instance, creation and upgradation logic is handled by OnCreate and OnUpgrade of SQLiteOpenHelper. exeCSQL() method is used to create and drop tables.
- Following snippet shows database creation by using SQLiteOpenHelper class.

```
    Private Static Class newDBOpenHelper extends SQLiteOpenHelper
{
    Private static final String DATABASE_NAME="mydata.db";
    Private static final String _TABLE="dbclient";
    Private static final int DATABASE_VERSION=1;
    Public void onCreate (SQLiteDatabase db)
{
}
    Public void onUpgrade(SQLite db,old value ,new value)
    {
    }
}
```

Package:

Android.database this package contains all necessary classes which helps working with database. android.database.sqlite this package has SQLite specific classes.

12.2.3 Creating and Updating Database with SQLiteOpenHelper
- In Android application, to create and update the database, developer needs to create a subclass of SQLiteOpenHelper class. In the constructor of subclass, call super() method of SQLiteOpenHelper, which specifies the database name and the current database version.
- The following methods are used for creation and updatation on data.
    (1) onCreate(): It is called by the framework, if the database is accessed but not yet created.

(2) onUpgrade(): It is called, when database version of the application increased. It updates a database schema or it drops the previous and create by using OnCreate() method.
- Both above stated methods receives SQLiteDatabase object as a parameter which is Java representation. This object is accessed by getReadableDatabase() and getWriteableDatabase() methods. These methods belong to SQLiteOpenHelper class.
- Separate class per table is created while creating tables. So that each class have its own defined static onCreate() and onUpgrade() methods.

Content Providers
- Content providers an interface for publishing and consuming data, based around a simple URI addressing model using the content: //schema.
- Content providers can be shared between applications, queried for results, have their existing records updated or deleted and have new records added.
- Several native Content Providers have been made accessible for access by third party application, including the contact manager, media store, calendar.

12.3 Content Values and Cursor

- A query returns a cursor object. It basically points to one row of query result. This helps android to buffer the query result, as it does not have to load data into memory.
  The cursor provides following methods:

  (1) getCount(): To count the number of elements in resulting query.

  (2) movetofirst(), movetonext (): These methods are used to move between rows of a table.

  (3) isAfterlast(): To check the last row of table appears.

  (4) getLong(columnindex): getString(columnindex) i.e. it provides get *() method to access the column data for the current position of the result.

  (5) getColumnIndex() or Throw (string) which allows getting the column index for a column name of the table.

  (6) close(): This method is called to close the cursor.
    - Content Values are used to insert new rows into tables. Each ContentValues object represents a single table row as a map of column names to values.
- Cursors are the returned object by database queries. Cursors are nothing but the pointer to the database. Cursors are used to control the position (row) in the result.

Set of Database Query:
- Content values are used to insert new rows into tables. Each ContentValues object represents a single table row as a map of column names to values.

- Following are the some of navigation functions that are used by cursor:

    (1) moveToFirst(): Moves the cursor to the first row in the query result.

    (2) moveToNext(): Moves cursor to the next row.

    (3) moveToPrevious(): Moves cursor to the previous row.

    (4) getCount(): Returns the number of rows in the result set.

    (5) getColumnIndexorThrow(): It returns zero-based index for the column with the specified name.

    (6) getColumnName(): Returns the name of specified column index.

    (7) moveToPosition(): Moves cursor to specified row.

    (8) getPosition(): Returns current position of cursor.

12.3.1 Cursor

- A query returns a cursor object. A cursor represents the result of a query and points to one row of the query result. This way Android can buffer the query results efficiently. And the data is not loaded into memory.
- getcount() method is used to count the number of elements of the resulting query.
- To move between individual data rows, you can use the moveToFirst() and moveToNext() methods. The is afterlast() method allows to check if the end of the query result has been reached.
- Cursor provides typed get*() methods, e.g. getLong(columnIndex), getString (columnIndex) to access the column data for the current position of the result. The "columnIndex" is the number of the column you are accessing.
- Cursor also provides the getColumnIndexOrThrow(String) method which allows getting the column index for a column name of the table.
- A Cursor needs to be closed with the close() method call.

ListViews, ListActivities and SimpleCursorAdapter

- ListViews are Views which allow displaying a list of elements.
- ListActivities are specialized *activities* which make the usage of ListViews easier.
- To work with databases and ListViews you can use the SimpleCursorAdapter. The SimpleCursorAdapter allows setting a layout for each row of the ListViews.
- You also define an array which contains the column names and another array which contains the IDs of Views which should be filled with the data.
- The SimpleCursorAdapter class will map the columns to the Views based on the Cursor passed to it.
- To obtain the Cursor you should use the Loader class.

12.3.2 Extracting Values from a Cursor

- To extract values from a cursor, fist use the moveTo<location> methods that are described earlier to position the cursor at the correct row, and then use the type-safe get<type> methods to return. The value stored at the current row for the specified column.
- To find the column index of a particular column within a result cursor, for that getColumnIndexorThrow(), getColumnIndex() methods.

  ```
  int ColumnIndex=cursor.getColumnIndex (KEY_COLUMN_1_NAME);
  if (ColumnIndex >-1)
  {
      string code-ColumnValue=cursor.getString(ColumnIndex);
  }
  else
  {
      if column doesn't exist.
  }
  code e.g. Extracting values from a cursor.
  ```

12.3.3 Database and Data Model

- Create the MySQLiteHelper class. This class is responsible for creating the database. The onUpgrade() method will simply delete all existing data and re-create the table. It also defines several constants for the table name and the table columns.

Content provider and sharing data

- A SQLite database is private to the application which creates it. If user wants to share data with other applications user can use a content provider.
- A *content provider* allows applications to access data. In most cases this data is stored in SQLite database.
- A content provider can be used within an application to access data. It is typically used to share data with other application. As application data is by default private, a *content provider* is a convenient to share user data with other application based on a structured interface.
- A *content provider* must be declared in the AndroidManifest.xml file.

Accessing a content provider

- The access to a *content provider* is done via an URI. The basis for the URI is defined in the declaration of the ContentProvider in the AndroidManifest.xml file via the android:authorities attribute.
- Many Android datasources, e.g. the contacts, are accessible via content providers.

Own ContentProvider
- To create your own ContentProvider you have to define a class which extends android.content.ContentProvider. You have to also declare your ContentProvider in the AndroidManifest.xml file. This entry must specify the android:authorities attribute which allows identifying the ContentProvider. This authority is the basis for the URI to access data and must be unique.

```
<provider android:authorities="de.vogella.android.todos.contentprovider"
    android:name=".contentprovider.MyTodoContentProvider" >
</provider>
```

- Your ContentProvider must implement several methods, e.g. query(), insert(), update(), delete(), getType() and onCreate(). In case you do not support certain methods its good practice to throw an UnsupportedOperationException().
- The query() method must return a Cursor object.
- Query in database is created by using query() or rawquery() or SQLiteQUERYBUILDER class.

    (1) rawQuery() : It accepts SQL stmt as an input.

    Cursor cursor=getReadableDatabase()

    rawQuery("select*from Demo where_id=?", new string[] {id});

    (2) query() : It provides structured interface for specifying SQL query.

    return database.query(Database_Table, new string[] {key_Rowid, key_category, key_summary, key_description},

    null, null, null, null, null);

- **RawQuery() Example**

    The following gives an example of a rawQuery() call.

    ```
    Cursor cursor = getReadableDatabase ().
    rawQuery("select * from todo where _id = ?", new String[] { id });
    ```

- **query() Example**

    The following gives an example of a query () call.

    ```
    return database.query(DATABASE_TABLE,
    new String[] { KEY_ROWID, KEY_CATEGORY, KEY_SUMMARY, KEY_DESCRIPTION },
     null, null, null, null, null);
    ```

    The method query() has the following parameters.

Table 12.1: Parameters of the query() method

Parameter	Comment
String dbName	The table name to compile the query against.
String[ ] columnNames	A list of which table columns to return. Passing "null" will return all columns.
String whereClause	Where-clause, i.e. filter for the selection of data, null will select all data.
String[ ] selectionArgs	You may include? S in the "whereClause"". These placeholders will get replaced by the values from the selectionArgs array.
String[ ] groupBy	A filter declaring how to group rows, null will cause the rows to not be grouped.
String[ ] having	Filter for the groups, null means no filter.
String[ ] orderBy	Table columns which will be used to order the data, null means no ordering.

- If a condition is not required you can pass null, e.g. for the group by clause.
- The "whereClause" is specified without the word "where", for example a "where" statement might look like: "_id=19 and summary=?"
- If you specify placeholder values in the where clause via, you pass them as the selectionArgs parameter to the query.

12.3.4 Security and ContentProvider

- By default content provider is available from version 4.2. As of Android 4.2 a *content provider* must be explicitly exported.
- To set the visibility of your *content provider* uses the android:exported=false|true parameter in the declaration of your *content provider* in the AndroidManifest.xml file.

Thread Safety

- If different operators from different process are accessing the same database and have many writes concurrently its raises the issue of data integrity.
- The ContentProvider can be accessed from several programs at the same time, therefore user must implement the access thread-safe.
- The easiest way is to use the keyword synchronized in front of all methods of the ContentProvider, so that only one thread can access these methods at the same time.
- If user do not require that Android synchronizes data access to the ContentProvider, set theandroid:multiprocess=true attribute in user's <provider> definition in the AndroidManifest.xml file. This permit an instance of the provider to be created in each client process, eliminating the need to perform interposes communication.

12.3.5 Using ContentProvider

Loader
- The Loader class allows user to load data asynchronously in an activity of fragment. They can monitor of the data and deliver new results when content changes. the data persist between configuration changes.
- If the result is retrieved by the Loader after the object has been disconnected from its parent (activity or fragment), it can cache the data.
- Loaders have been introduced in Android 3.0 and are part of the compatibility layer for Android versions as of 1.6.

Implementing a Loader
- abstract AsyncTaskLoader class can be used as the basis for the Loader implementations.
- The LoaderManager of an activity or fragment manages one or more Loader instances. The creation of a *Loader* is done via the following method call.

    # start a new loader or re-connect to existing one
    getLoaderManager().initLoader(0, null, this);

- The first parameter is a unique ID which can use by the callback class to identify that Loader later. The second parameter is a bundle which can be given to the callback class for more information.
- The third parameter of initLoader() is the class which is called once the initialization has been started (callback class). This class must implement the LoaderManager. LoaderCallbacksinterface. It is good practice that an activity or the fragment which uses a *Loader* implements the LoaderManager.LoaderCallbacks interface.
- The third parameter of initLoader() is the class which is called once the initialization has been started.
- The Loader is not directly created by the getLoaderManager().initLoader() method call, but must be created by the callback class in the onCreateLoader() method.
- Once the Loader has finished reading data asynchronously, the onLoadFinished() method of the callback class is called.

12.3.6 SQLite Database and CursorLoader
- Android provides a Loader default implementation to handle SQLite database connections, the CursorLoader class.
- For a *ContentProvider* based on a *SQLite* database you would typically use the CursorLoader class. This *Loader* performs the database query in a background thread so that the application is not blocked.
- The CursorLoader class is the replacement for Activity-managed cursors which are deprecated now.

- If the Cursor becomes invalid, the onLoaderReset() method is called on the callback class.

12.3.7 Cursors and Loaders

- To manage the life-cycle you could use the managedQuery () method in *activities* prior to Android 3.0.
- As of Android 3.0 this method is deprecated and you should use the Loader framework to access the ContentProvider.
- The SimpleCursorAdapter class, which can be used with ListViews, has the swapCursor() method. Your *Loader* can use this method to update the Cursor in its onLoadFinished() method.
- The CursorLoader class reconnects the Cursor after a configuration.

12.4 Querying a Database

- Each database query is returned as a Cursor. query() method is used to execute a query on database. The following values are passed to it:
    (a) An optional boolean that specifies if the result set should contain only unique values.
    (b) The name of the table to query.
    (c) A projection, as an array of strings, that lists the columns to include in the result set.
    (d) A where clause that defines the rows to be returned. Wildcards that will be replaced by the values passed in through selection parameter.
- A group by clause how the resulting rows will be grouped.
- A having clause that defines which row groups to include if you specify a group by clause.
- A string that describes the order of the returned rows.
- A string that defines the maximum number of rows in the result set.

12.4.1 Adding, Updating and Removing Rows

The SQLite Database classes exposes insert, delete and update methods that encapsulate the SQL.execSQL() method executes any valid SQL statements on your database tables.

- Anytime updates happen to a database cursor also should be updated by running a new query.
- **Inserting Rows :**

To add a new row to table, construct a ContentValues object and use its put method to add name/value pair, which represents each column name and its associated value.

```
ContentValues newValues=new= ContentValues();
    newValues.put (,);
```

```
newValues.put (,);
newValues.put (,);
SQLiteDatabase db=DBOpenHelper.getWritableDatabase();
db.insert (.DATABASE_TABLE, null, newValues);
```

- The second parameter used in insert method is null column hack.
- When new row gets inserted at least once column name is must to be declared with associated value, latter it can be kept null.
- By keeping the second parameter null column hack to null, it will throw an exception when an empty content values are stored into object SQLite.
- **Updating Rows :**

ContentValues are used to update the row in a table.

Steps :

(1) Create ContentValues object, using put methods to assign new values to each column gets to be updated. Call update() method on database, the name of table updated ContentValues object, and where clause which specifies the rows to be updated.

```
ContentValues updatedValues=new ContentValues();
updatedValues.put( , );
String where=KEY_ID+"="+Id;
String WhereArgs[]=null;
SQLiteDatabase db=,getWriteableDatabase
dp.update(.DATBASE_TABLE, updateValues, where, WhereArgs);
```

- **Deleting Rows :**

To delete a row, delete() method is called on database, specifying table name and a where clause that returns the rows you want to delete.

```
//specify a where clause that determines which row(s) to delete.
//specify where arguments as necessary.
String where=+"="+0;
String WhereArgs[]=null;
//Delete the rows that match the where clause.
SQLiteDatabase db=.getWritableDatabase();
db.delete (.DATABASE_TABLE, where, WhereArgs);
```

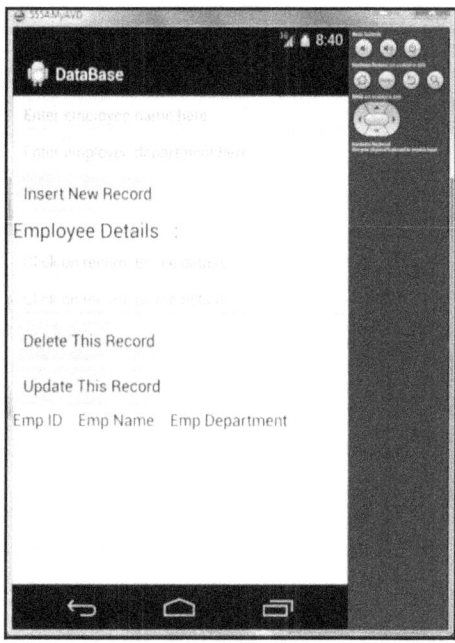

Fig. 12.1: Database

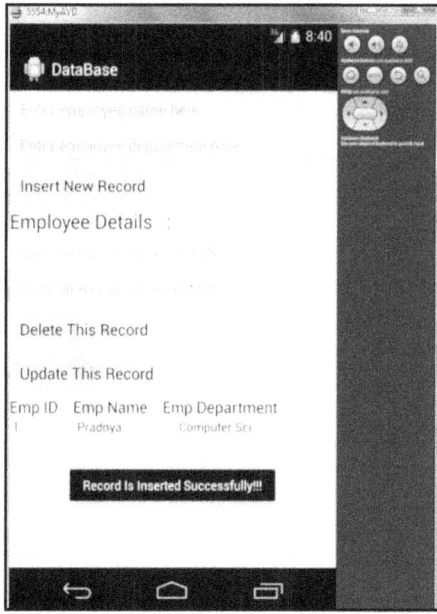

Fig. 12.2: Inserting record in Database

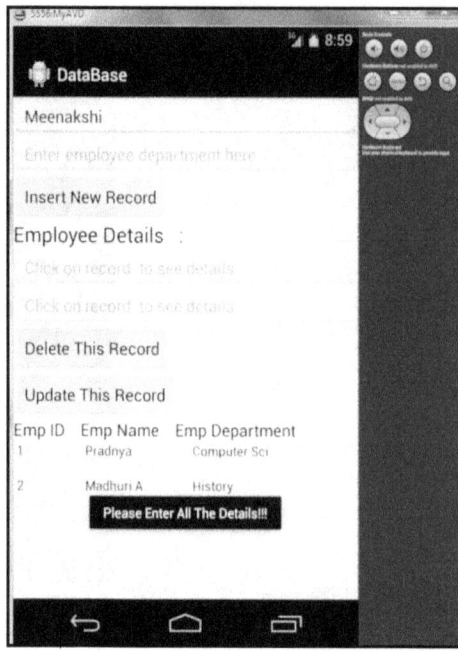

Fig. 12.3: Insert Name in Database

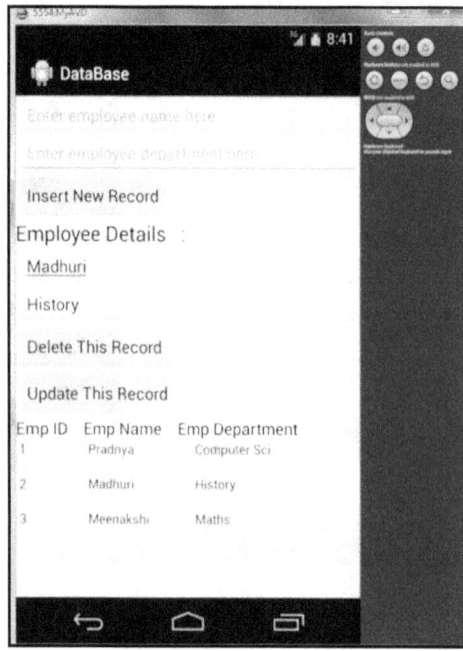

Fig. 12.4: Inserting Name and Department in Database

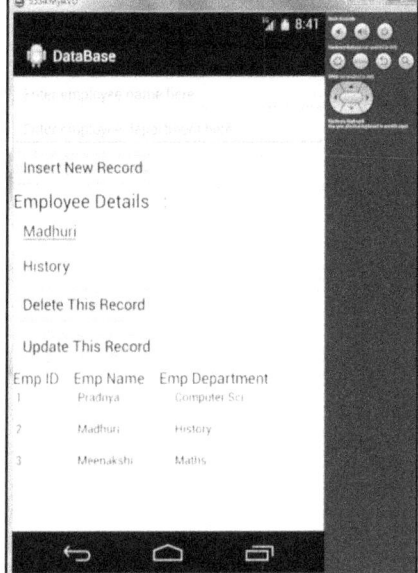 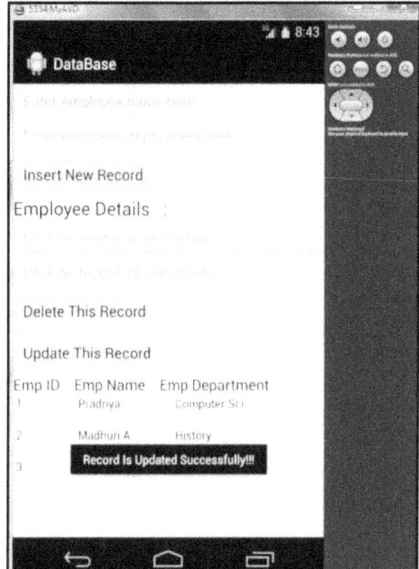

Fig. 12.5: Updating Database   Fig. 12.6: Delete Record from Database

Practice Questions

1. What is meant by SQLite? State its features.
2. Write a detailed note on SQLite Open Helper Class.
3. Discuss about addition, deletion and updation of records in database.
4. How to extract values from cursor.
5. Write short notes on :
   (a) SQLite in Android.
   (b) Cursors and Loaders.
   (c) Database and Model
   (d) Content Provider

Chapter 13...

PEER-TO-PEER COMMUNICATION

13.1 Introduction
13.2 Introduction of Android Instant Messaging
13.3 GTalk Services: Using, Binding and Making Connection
    13.3.1 Using the GTalk Service
    13.3.2 Binding to the GTalk Service
    13.3.3 Making a GTalk Connection and Starting an IM Session
13.4 Managing Chat Session
    13.4.1 How to Start or Join a Chat Session
13.5 Sending and Receiving Data Messages
    13.5.1 Sending Instant Text Messages
    13.5.2 Receiving Data Messages
    13.5.2 Chat Rooms and Group Chats
13.6 Introduction of SMS
13.7 Sending SMS, Listening SMS Messages
    13.7.1 Sending SMS
    13.7.2 Listening SMS
- Practice Question

13.1 Introduction

- Android application uses peer-to-peer communication for exchanging text and data. Specifically instant messaging (SMS) uses peer-to-peer communication protocols. For example: The applications are developed, which communicates between direct devices. The application such as multiplayer games and collaborative mobile social applications.
- The first evolution towards instant messaging (IM), based on GTalk services, it includes the functionality like to send and receive text messages, set user status through present and determine the presence of IM contacts.
- Android uses this technology to be used for sending text IM messages and broadcasting intents to remote devices that is device-to-device communication in real time. Due to security concerns IM API is removed from that version. I.e. Android 1.0

- Android uses SMS functionality, to send and receive the messages within your application with added functionality as, user can create own SMS client application to replace the native applications available as part of the software stack.

13.2 Introduction of Android Instant Messaging

- The released version of android after android SDK 1.0, exposed the suite of instant messaging through XMPP based IM service. This includes management of contact rosters, presence notification and other transmission and receipt of IM. (XMPP-Extensible Messaging and Presence Protocol).
- Google Talk is peer-to-peer communication protocol for instant messaging. It maintains socket connection to server once it establishes the connection, it provides fast access and low latency.
- GTalk facilitates the developers by using the ability to broadcast intents Over The Air (OTA) between android devices using data messaging. These messages received by a remote device and re-broadcast as Intents locally.
- GTalk provides a framework to build various applications such as multi-user, social or collaborative applications. It ranges from dynamic route guidance system, gaming system, distributed emergency warning system, family social network.
- Android includes all relevant interfaces to create Google talk instant messaging clients, which has control over presence management and subscription handing.

13.3 GTalk Services: Using, Binding and Making Connection

Google Talk
- **Google Talk** is an instant messaging service that provides both text and voice communication. The instant messaging service is known as "GTalk" or "Gchat" to its users, although Google does not endorse this name.
- Google offers Google Talk which is the client application to access the service. Google Talk applications were available for Microsoft Windows (XP server 2003, Vista, Windows 7, Android, Blackberry and Chrome OS operating system. Because the Google Talk servers communicate with clients using an open protocol, (Extensible Messaging and Presence Protocol) XMPP, the service can also be accessed using any other client that supports XMPP. Such clients are available for a number of operating systems that not supported by the Google Talk client.
- Google Talk used extensions to XMPP for voice/video signaling and peer-to-peer communication. As of August 2012, Google Talk's implementation differs slightly from the draft XMPP Jingle specifications. In 2012, Google had stated that an update was under way. Since May 2013, support for the XMPP instant messaging protocol is dropped.

History of Interoperability
- Interoperability was the major goal of the Google Talk service. Google Talk used XMPP to provide real-time extensible Messaging and Presence events (XMPP), including offline messaging and voice mailing. Google Talk supported messaging with any service provider that supports the XMPP protocol. This included Earthlink, Gizmo Project, Tiscali, Netease, Chikka, MediaRing, and, according to Google, "thousands of other ISPs, universities, corporations and individual users."

Product integration
- Google Talk service is integrated into Gmail. Users can send instant messages to other Gmail users. As it works within a browser, the Google Talk client does not need to be downloaded to send instant messages to Gmail users.
- Conversation logs are automatically saved to a Chat area in the user's Gmail account. This allows users to search their chat logs and have them centrally stored in their Gmail accounts. For a long time it wasn't possible to directly download chat logs that are not attached to an e-mail conversation. A new feature is introduced on September 15, 2011 that is Google Takeout program that allows users to download chat logs via IMAP.
- Google Talk is a web based module that may be embedded in iGoogle and other web pages, allowing text chat. Google+ is integrated into Google Talk. In the standalone client and the Google Talk widget embedded into Gmail and Google+, Google+ contacts appear in the contacts list, their respective circles are shown in Google+'s iteration of the widget.

Voice and Video
- By using Google Talk within Gmail it is possible to place and receive phone calls. For availing this facility the user must upgrade to a full Google voice account. Initially, users outside of the US cannot upgrade to a full Google Voice account and cannot receive phone calls in Gmail. (Outbound calling though gmail does not require Google Voice and is available in many countries outside the US.) Google Talk allows users to leave a voicemail for a contact whether or not they are signed into Google Talk. Messages can be up to 10 minutes long and are sent to the recipient's email. Messages can be sent with or without first ringing the recipient's phone number.
- Google also provides a Voice and Video Chat browser plug-in (not to be confused with the standalone Google Talk client) that supports voice and video chat between Gmail users. The plug-in is available for Windows (XP, Vista, and 7), Mac OS X (only on Intel-based Macs), and Linux(Debian, Ubuntu, Fedora, and OpenSUSE packages).

Encryption
- The connection between the Google Talk client and the Google Talk server is encrypted, except when using Gmail's chat over HTTP, a federated network that doesn't support encryption, or when using a proxy like IMLogic end-to-end messages are unencrypted. . It is possible to have end-to-end encryption over the Google Talk network using OTR (Off-The-Record) encryption using other chat clients like Adium (for Mac) or Pidgin (for Linux and Windows).
- Google's version of "Off the Record" is not OTR (off-the-record) encryption. Enabling "Off The Record" inside Gmail's Chat turns off logging of messages, but does not enable encryption.

Offline Messaging
- Google introduces offline messages to Google talk on October 31, 2006. This allows users to send messages on their contacts, even that user is offline. They will get the messages when they appear online.
- This only works between gmail-accounts though, that doesn't work between Google Talk servers and other XMPP servers.

Mobile Device Compatibility
- On June 30, 2006, Nokia released new software for their Nokia 770 Internet Tablet that included Google Talk as one of the compatible (Voice over IP) VoIP clients, because of the XMPP-based software. Another Google Talk-compatible device is Sony's mylo, released on September 15, 2006. A Google Talk client is also available for BlackBerry devices from the Blackberry site. Google Talk support is also integrated in Google Android devices, but does not support voice and video calls below Android version 2.3.4. This was released in April 2011 for the Google Nexus S.
- Google Talk provides XMPP protocol, most mobile phones for which a suitable XMPP client exists could also offer Google Talk service, at least theoretically (depending on the handset, the user may encounter security warnings because of unsigned Java ME midlets or limits put in place by the mobile service provider). Mobile clients specially designed for Google Talk exist as well.
- Most phones support the IMPS protocol, and there are hybrid XMPP/IMPS networks (through XMPP transports, or specially designed hybrid servers), which can also contact Google Talk users. The Google Talk service itself is unusable from IMPS (that means, you cannot log with your Gmail account, but you can talk with your Gmail friends with your IMPS account from your mobile phone).
- For most smart phones, including Symbian-based as well as Android, third-party applications such as Nimbuzz and Fring include support for Google Talk accounts, including VoIP calls.

Text formatting
- Google talk does not provide text formatting features such as making text bold and italic. To write message in bold, a user should type the required text between two asterisks (*), for example *this text would be bold in Google Talk*. Similarly for making text italic, one should put text between underscores (_) and for strike-through in text content one should put text in between dashes (-). This only function in some of the Google native tools, and does not always function as expected when received from other XMPP clients.

History
- On December 15, 2005, Google released libjingle, a C++ library to implement Jingle, "a set of extensions to the IETF's Extensible Messaging and Presence Protocol (XMPP) for use in voice over IP (VoIP), video, and other peer-to-peer multimedia sessions." Libjingle is a library of the code that Google uses for peer-to-peer communication, and was made available under a BSD license.
- On January 17, 2006, Google enabled server-to-server communications, federating itself with any XMPP server that supports the dialback protocol.
- On February 7, 2006, Gmail added the ability to chat with a built-in XMPP client.
- On February 7, 2006, Gmail received chat functionality, using Ajax for server–browser communication, and was integrated with Google Talk.
- In 2006 Google reported that they were working on adding new features such as supporting SIP in a future release, which would broaden the user base for the program.
- In August of that year Google's and eBay's announced that they would look into making Google Talk users able to communicate with Skype: "The companies will also explore interoperability between Skype and Google Talk via open standards to enable text chat and online presence." However with Microsoft's acquisition of Skype on May 10, 2011 such interoperability might have been suspended between Google and eBay.
- Google integrated Google Talk with Orkut on November 8, 2006.
- Google releases the Google talk gadget on March 14, 2007. an Adobe Flash-based Talk module that can be added to iGoogle (formally the Google Personalized Homepage) or embedded in any web page, thus, allowing one to chat from any operating system which is supported by Adobe as long as Adobe Flash Player is installed.
- On May 18, 2007 a screen shot is presented as Google App presentation showing some phone integration in Google talk. A Google engineer confirmed they have been using it internally for some time on March 2, 2008.

- On November 26, 2007, Google Talk released Group Chat capabilities. Before this, users could chat with only one person per window. Group chat allows many users to chat with each other in an environment similar to IRC.
- Google upgraded its Gmail integrated chat to include AOL Instant Messenger chat capability. Gmail users are allowed to login into AIM chat service and communication with any AIM user still signed to Google talk services.
- On November 11, 2008, Google Chat (voice and video chat) was launched enabling computer to computer voice and video chat.
- Google came out with a Voice and Video Chat browser plug-in, in 2008.

Fig. 13.1: Gtalk Window

- On April 20, 2012, Google announced that it was shutting down the mobile web app for Google Talk.
- On May 15, 2013, Nikhyl Singhal stated at Google I/O, the move to 'Google+ Hangouts' will mean that XMPP (the protocol that allowed Google Talk to interoperate with other vendors and applications) will no longer be supported. This also ends the Google "open offer to interoperate forever", that Larry Page stated on the same day when talking about the Google Instant Messaging service.

13.3.1 Using the GTalk Service

- Before implementing the GTalk services, developer needs to import the GTalk service library into your application with a uses-library tag inside the application node of the project manifest,

  <uses-library android:name="com.google.android.gtalkservice"/>
- Developer also needs to add the GTalk uses-permission tag as of XML.

`<uses-permission android:name="android.permission.GTalk"/>`

- The following interfaces are used while developing Android Instant Messaging functionality.

  (1) IGtalkService: It is used to connect access and manage GTalk connections.

  (2) IGtalkConnection: A GTalk connection represents a persistent socket connection between the device and the server connecting to. This service creates a default connection upon start-up that you can access it by getDefaultConnection() on GTalk service object.

  (3) IIMSession: This interface is used for the implementation of most important functionality. It is used to retrieve the IM roster, set the presence of user, obtains the presence of contacts, and manages the chat session. getDefaultSession() method is used to create a default session.

  (4) IChatSession: IChatSession interface takes care of chat messages by creating chat or joining existing ones, from an IM session object. New chat messages, invite new participants to a group chat and return a list of people involved in a chat.

  (5) IChatListner: The implementation of this interface is to listens for messages in an IM session or chat session. This handler listens to incoming messages, new chat participants, people leaving a chat etc.

  (6) IGroupChatInvitationListner: This interface listens for invitations to join group chats. On Invitation Received handler is passed to a GroupChatInvitation that includes the username of the inviter, the room address, a "reason" and password you need to join the group chat.

  (7) IRosterListner: It monitors your IM contacts roster, the presence of the people on it, by implementing the IRosterListner interface. The Roster listener includes event handlers that are fired when there are changes in a contact's presence as well as upon the addition and removal of contacts from the roster.

13.3.2 Binding to the GTalk Service

- **Bind service:** This Component bounds the application to the GTalk service. This method accepts two input parameters, an intent, which specified a component to bind to, and Service Connection implementation.
- Bound GTalk service represents a connection between your application and GTalk service API. There is need to initiate GTalkConnection, before using this service to Android's instant messaging functionality.

13.3.3 Making a GTalk Connection and Starting an IM Session

- A GTalk connection is a channel between device and GTalk server. All the instant messages which belongs to a session flows through this channel.
- A device needs a single GTalk connection supporting a single IMSession that uses the device's username.

- DefaultConnection and session using getDefaultConnection() and getDefaultSession() methods on the GTalk service.
  IGTalkConnection gTalkConnection=gtalkService.getDefaultConnection();
  IIMsession imsession =gTalkConnection.getDefaultIMSession();
- Imsessions are used to send text and data messages, set user present, IM contact roster and manage group chats.
- In Android application, IM session is a primary interface which handles instant messaging. Service connection is used to bind the GTalkService to the application. It ensures that an IM object is always valid.

13.4 Managing Chat Session

- What is mean by chat session? Chat session which is created within IM session and is used to manage and participate in person-to-person chats and chat rooms. Chat session has various kinds of instant messages. All text-based instant messages are handled by using IChatSession interface. This interface is responsible for sending text and adding new participants to chat. The incoming messages are notified by attaching chat listener to chat session.
- Implementation of chat session :
  (1) It integrates text messaging within user's own application.
  (2) A chat room can be formed, for multi-player game or integrate person-to-person within mobile social network application.

13.4.1 How to Start or Join a Chat Session

- A chat session represents all instant messaging communication with target user passes, only single chat session per contact per IM session.
- getChatSession() or CreateChatSession() methods are used to create a chat session through an IM session.
- How these method works :
  (1) If a chat session already exists for a given contact, retrieve it by passing in the username of person with whom one wants to communicate. If there is no active chat session with the specified user, this returns null.
  IChatSession cs=imSession.getChatSession (targetContactEmailAddress);

New Chat Session with particular user, it is created by using CreateChatSession() method, passing in the target contact's username. If the IMSession is unable to create a new chat session, it will return null.

IChatSession ChatSession=imsession.CreateChatSession (targetContactEmailAddress);
IChatSession ChatSession=imsession.getChatSession (targetContactEmail/Address);
if (ChatSession=null)
ChatSession=imsession.createChatSession (targetContactEmailAddress);

13.5 Sending and Receiving Data Messages

- The GTalk service has the functionality data messages between applications running on different devices. This transaction of the data is not visible to user.
- In GTalk Services, data messages enables user to broadcast intents over the Air (OTA) to remote user devices.
- On the receiving device, GTalk Service extracts the intent from the received message and rebroadcast it locally, where it is handled by intent resolution mechanism in the same way as locally broadcast intents.
- The result is an interface for broadcasting intents on remote devices using instant messenger contacts.
- By using data messages multiuser applications on distributed mobile devices as instant messaging architecture facilitates with low latency and rapid response time.

13.5.1 Sending Instant Text Messages

(1) When active chat session is opened SendChatMessage() method is used to send messages to the contact(s) in that session, ChatSession.sendChatMessage ("Hello world");

This message is transferred to all the contacts which are in current chat session.

13.5.2 Receiving Data Messages

- IChatListner interface is used to listen for incoming messages by overriding its new MessageReceived handler.
- This ChatListner is registered with the help of specific chat session or the generic session. IM Session, using the addRemoteChatListner() method.
- IChatListner interface includes a stub class that developer should extend when creating your own ChatListner implementation.

13.5.2 Chat Rooms and Group Chats

- The GTalk supports chat rooms and group chats. These are managed by using IChatSession interface.
- CreateGroupChatSession() method is used to create a chat room, nickname for the room is passed to invoke the group or room along with that a list of users to invite.
  String nickname="Android Implementation";
  String[ ] contacts={"ABC", "XYZ"};
  imsession.CreateGroupChatSession (nickname, contacts);
- Join the group IGroupChatInvitationListner. This interface listens group chat invitations. Each invitation includes the address and password needed to join an existing chat room.
- To join the existing chat room, use the joinGroupChatSession method from an active IMSession, passing in the address of the room one can want to join:
  imsession.joinGroupChatSession (address, nickname, password);

- **Managing Group Chat Sessions:**
  (1) getParticipants() method gives a list of participants in a chat session. inviteContact() method invites new members to chat session. Leave() method lets you exit a chat room and the end session.
  (2) With Normal Chats, you can listen to chat room messages by implementing and registering an IChatListner.

13.6 Introduction of SMS

- Over two decades and more SMS technology is familiar to all mobile phones. This substitutes phone calling by delivering short text messages with a capacity of 160 characters and data messages that are needed to run some of the applications.

How to Use SMS in the Application :
- SMSManager handles the SMS functionality within your android phone. Using SMSManager, new application can be created which is used to send text messages, react to incoming text, or use SMS as data transport layer.
- SMS in not used in real-time responsiveness where you get timely delivery of SMS.
- SMS are used to communicate between android and non-android users compared to instant messaging, SMS is a mechanism which is very slow, possibly expensive and it suffers from high latency inspite it is supported everywhere, where latency and update frequency is not an issue.
- SMS messaging in android is handled by the SMSManager. In android SMSManager is a class which extends object android.telephony.SMSManager package is included in java.lang.object
- The object is invoked by calling static method SMSManager.getDefault().
  SMSManager SMSManager=SMSManager.getDefault();
- Android requires permission needed by an application to be specified in AndroidManifest.xml file, using following code :
  <uses-permission android:name="android.permission.SEND_SMS"/>

13.7 Sending SMS, Listening SMS Messages

13.7.1 Sending SMS
- In android it is handled by SMSManager. To send text messages use SendTextMessage from SMS Manager, passing in the address (phone number) of your recipient and the text messages.

  (1) public void SendTextMessage (String destinationAddress, String SCAddress, String text, PendingIntent SentIntent, Pending Intent DeliveryIntent)

Parameters :
destination Address_the address to send message

SCAddress : is the service center address or null to use the current default SMSC.

text : The body of the message to send.

SetIntent : If not null, this PendingIntent is broadcast when message delivery is successful or failed. The result code will be.

ACTIVITY.RESULT_OK for success and error messages as follows.

RESULT_ERROR_GENERIC_FILURE

RESULT_ERROR_RADIO_OFF

RESULT_ERROR_NULL_PDU

DeliveryIntent : If not null, this PendingIntent is broadcast when the message is delivered to the recipient.

String sendTo="9481...";

String MyMessage="Android supports SMS"!;

SMSManager.SendTextMessage (SendTo, null, MyMessage, null, null);

13.7.1.1 Tracking and Conforming SMS Message Delivery

- The last two parameters of the method SendTextMessage are used to tract and confirm of SMS message delivery. For this implementation of broadcast receivers, it should be used to listen to the specific actions.
- The fourth parameter is SetIntent is fired to track about successful transmission of message. The result is of the following form which is received by broadcast receiver.
  (1) Activity.RESULT_OK SUCCESS
  (2) SMSManager.RESULT_ERROR_GENERIC_FAILURE : It indicates a nonspecific failure.
  (3) SMSManager.RESULT_ERROR_RADIO_OFF : Whenthe connection radio is turned off.
  (4) SMSManager.RESULT_ERROE_NULL_PDU: To indicate PDU failure.
- The fifth parameter PendingIntent, DeliveryIntent, is fired only after the DestinationAddress receives messages. The following code shows how the pending intents are defined and broadcast receiver registered.

13.7.1.2 Conforming Maximum Size of Message

- The size of SMS is restricted to the 160 characters, the longer messages are partitioned into smaller sizes. This is done by using DivideMessage() method, it has following parameters.
  (1) String as an input, which is divided into an ArrayList of messages and SendMultiplePartTextMessage() method is used to transmit. This array of messages.

Arraylist <String> MessageArray=SMSManager.divideMessage (MyMessage);

Arraylist <pendingIndent> SetIntents=new ArrayList <pendingIntent> ();

For (int i=0; i<messageArray.size(); i++)

sentIntents.add(sentPI);

SMSManager.SendMultipartTextMessage (sendTo, null, messageArray, SetIntents, null);

13.7.2 Listening SMS

- A new SMS is received by the destination device, a new broadcast intent is fired with the android.provider.Telephony.SMS_RECEIVED action.
- <uses_permission android:name="android.permission.RECEIVE_SMS"/>
- To extract the array of SMS Message objects which are packaged within the SMS broadcast Intent bundle, to convert each PDU byte.
- Incoming message are listened, by registering the Broadcast Receiver using an Intent Filter that listens for android.provider.Telephony.SMS_RECEIVED action string.
  Final string SMS_RECEIVED="android.provider.Telephony_SMS_RECEIVED";
  IntentFilter filter=new IntentFilter (SMS_RECEIVED);
  Broadcast Receiver receiver=new IncomingSMSRECEIVED();
  register Receiver (receiver, filter);

Example of Sending Data Messages

- The binary data is send by SMS using the SendDataMessage method on a SMSManager. The SendDataMessage method works much like SendTextMessage. It includes additional parameters for destination port and an array of bytes.

Intent SentIntent=new Intent (SENT_SMS_ACTION);
PendingIntent sentPI=pendingIntent.getBroadcast(getApplicationContext(), 0, SetIntent, 0);
short destport=80;
byte[ ] data={...user data]
SMSManager.SendDataMessage (sendTo, null, destinationPort, data, sentPI, null);

- Data messages are received in the same way as a normal SMS text message and it is extracted same as it is.
- getUserData() and getUserDataHeader() methods are used to extract it.
  byte[ ] Data=msg.getUserData();
  SMSHeader header=msg.getUserDataHeader();
- getUserData method returns a byte array of the data while getUserDataHeader() method returns an array of metadata elements used to describe the data contained in the message.
- Using android, we can send message programmatically. Consider an android application of name MessageDemo and activity with class file- MessageDemo.java, UI file- activity_message_demo.xml.
- Also create a class file ReceiveMessage.java extendingBroadcastReceiver class which will be useful for listening incoming message.

Add receiver using java class file ReceiveMessage.java for an action *"android.provider.TelephonySMS_RECEIVED"* and permission to AndroidManifest.xml file as follows -

```xml
<LinearLayoutxmlns:android="http://schemas.android.com/apk/res/android"
xmlns:tools="http://schemas.android.com/tools"
android:id="@+id/LinearLayout1"
android:layout_width="match_parent"
android:layout_height="match_parent"
android:orientation="vertical"
android:paddingBottom="@dimen/activity_vertical_margin"
android:paddingLeft="@dimen/activity_horizontal_margin"
android:paddingRight="@dimen/activity_horizontal_margin"
android:paddingTop="@dimen/activity_vertical_margin"
tools:context=".MessageDemo">

<TextView
android:id="@+id/txtto"
android:layout_width="wrap_content"
android:layout_height="wrap_content"
android:text="To : "/>

<EditText
android:id="@+id/etto"
android:layout_width="match_parent"
android:layout_height="wrap_content"
android:ems="10"
android:inputType="phone">

<requestFocus/>
</EditText>

<TextView
android:id="@+id/tvmsg"
android:layout_width="wrap_content"
android:layout_height="wrap_content"
android:text="Text Message    :"/>

<EditText
android:id="@+id/etmsg"
android:layout_width="match_parent"
android:layout_height="wrap_content"
android:ems="10"
android:inputType="textMultiLine"/>

<Button
```

```xml
android:id="@+id/btnsend"
android:layout_width="wrap_content"
android:layout_height="wrap_content"
android:onClick="sendmsgfun"
android:text="Send Message"/>

</LinearLayout>
```

```java
packagecom.example.sendmessage;

importandroid.app.Activity;
importandroid.app.PendingIntent;
importandroid.content.BroadcastReceiver;
importandroid.content.Context;
importandroid.content.Intent;
importandroid.content.IntentFilter;
importandroid.os.Bundle;
importandroid.telephony.SmsManager;
importandroid.view.View;
importandroid.widget.EditText;
importandroid.widget.Toast;

public class MessageDemo extends Activity {
    EditTextph,msg;
    PendingIntentpi,dpi;
    @Override
    protected void onCreate(Bundle savedInstanceState) {
        super.onCreate(savedInstanceState);
        setContentView(R.layout.activity_message_demo);
        ph=(EditText) findViewById(R.id.etto);
        msg=(EditText) findViewById(R.id.etmsg);

    pi=PendingIntent.getBroadcast(getApplicationContext(), 0, new Intent("SENT"), 0);

        registerReceiver(new BroadcastReceiver() {

            @Override
            public void onReceive(Context context, Intent intent) {
                                switch (getResultCode()) {

                                        caseActivity.RESULT_OK:

    Toast.makeText(context, "MESSAGE SENT", Toast.LENGTH_LONG).show();
                                                                            break;

                            caseSmsManager.RESULT_ERROR_GENERIC_FAILURE:

    Toast.makeText(context, "MESSAGE FAILURE", Toast.LENGTH_LONG).show();
                                                                            break;

                                caseSmsManager.RESULT_ERROR_NO_SERVICE:
```

```
                Toast.makeText(context, "NO SERVICE", Toast.LENGTH_LONG).show();
                                                                        break;

                              caseSmsManager.RESULT_ERROR_NULL_PDU:
                Toast.makeText(context, "NULL PDU", Toast.LENGTH_LONG).show();
                                                                        break;

                              caseSmsManager.RESULT_ERROR_RADIO_OFF:
                Toast.makeText(context, "RADIO OFF", Toast.LENGTH_LONG).show();
                                                                        break;

                                                        default:
                                                                        break;
                                                }

                        MessageDemo.this.unregisterReceiver(this);


                }

        }, new IntentFilter("SENT"));
dpi=PendingIntent.getBroadcast(getApplicationContext(), 0, new Intent("DELIVERED"), 0);

                registerReceiver(new BroadcastReceiver() {

                        @Override
                        public void onReceive(Context context, Intent intent) {
                                        switch (getResultCode()) {

                                                caseActivity.RESULT_OK:
                Toast.makeText(context, "MESSAGE DELIVERED", Toast.LENGTH_LONG).show();
                                                                        break;

                                              caseActivity.RESULT_CANCELED:
                Toast.makeText(context, "MESSAGE NOT DELIVERED", Toast.LENGTH_LONG).show();
                                                                        break;
                                                }
                        MessageDemo.this.unregisterReceiver(this);

                }

        }, new IntentFilter("DELIVERED"));
}
```

```java
    public void sendmsgfun(View v)
    {
        String phoneno=ph.getText().toString();
        String message=msg.getText().toString();
        android.telephony.SmsManager m=android.telephony.SmsManager.getDefault();
        m.sendTextMessage(phoneno, null, message, pi,dpi);
    }
}

packagecom.example.sendmessage;
importandroid.content.BroadcastReceiver;
importandroid.content.Context;
importandroid.content.Intent;
importandroid.os.Bundle;
importandroid.telephony.SmsMessage;
importandroid.widget.Toast;

public class ReceiveMessage extends BroadcastReceiver {

    @Override
    public void onReceive(Context con, Intent intent) {

         Bundle b=intent.getExtras();
        SmsMessage[] m=null;
        String msg="";
        if(b!=null)
        {
            Object [] pdus=(Object[]) b.get("pdus");
            m=new SmsMessage[pdus.length];
            for(int i=0;i<m.length;i++)
            {
                m[i]=SmsMessage.createFromPdu((byte[]) pdus[i]);
            msg+=" SMS FROM - "+m[i].getOriginatingAddress()+" \n";
                    msg+=m[i].getMessageBody().toString();

            }
            Toast.makeText(con, msg, Toast.LENGTH_LONG).show() ;

        }

    }

}
```

Working Mechanism:

Run MessageDemo application on the two emulators. Using one emulator, send message to another emulator. So that another emulator can listen message, and will show it in toast message.

In onCreate() method of MessageDemo class, we have created pending intents 'pi' for 'SENT' and 'dpi' for 'DELIVERED' and registered an intent receiver that listens for the intent using BroadcastReceiver.

When we click on button 'Send Message', sendmsgfun() method will be called in which we obtained object of SmsManager m and send message using method sendTextMessage(StringdestinationAddress i.e. phoneno,StringscAddress, String message, PendingIntentsentIntent i.e. pi, PendingIntentdeliveryIntent i.e. dpi);

Where the Parameters are

destinationAddress	the address to send the message to
scAddress	is the service center address or null to use the current default SMSC
text	the body of the message to send
sentIntent	if not NULL this PendingIntent is broadcast when the message is successfully sent, or failed. The result code will be Activity.RESULT_OK for success, or one of these errors: RESULT_ERROR_GENERIC_FAILURE RESULT_ERROR_RADIO_OFF RESULT_ERROR_NULL_PDU For RESULT_ERROR_GENERIC_FAILURE the sentIntent may include the extra "errorCode" containing a radio technology specific value, generally only useful for troubleshooting. The per-application based SMS control checks sentIntent. If sentIntent is NULL the caller will be checked against all unknown applications, which cause smaller number of SMS to be sent in checking period.
deliveryIntent	if not NULL this PendingIntent is broadcast when the message is delivered to the recipient. The raw pdu of the status report is in the extended data ("pdu").

On another emulator, using class ReceiveMessage.java and BroadcastReceiver, it will call onReceive() method when new message arrives. In this method, we retrieves a map of extended data from the Intent object 'intent' which is passed as a parameter using method

Also we retrieve message using method getMessageBody()which returns the message body as a String, if it exists and is text based. And getOriginatingAddress() returns the originating address (sender) of this SMS message in String form or null if unavailable. And display it using a Toast object.

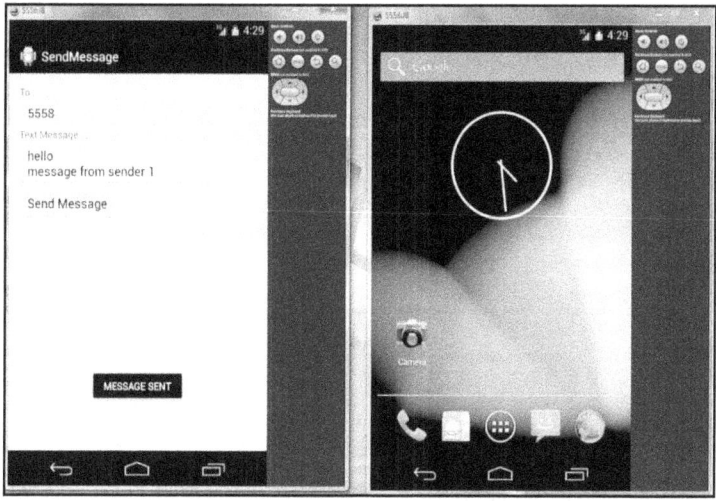

Fig. 13.2: Sending message

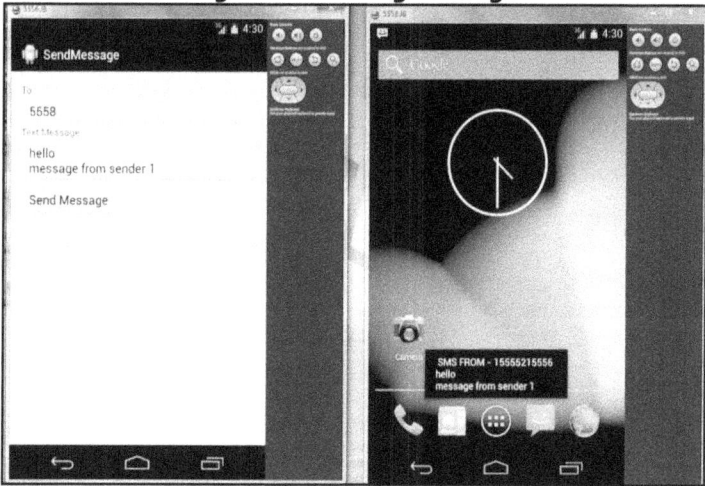

Fig. 13.3: Receiving message

Practice Questions

1. Explain the interfaces that are used while instant messaging in Android.
2. Explain in brief. How to make a GTalk connection ?
3. Explain in brief. How to Start Im session.
4. How the data messages are transmitted (send and receive) in GTalk services.
5. Write short notes on :
   (a) SMS
   (b) Receiving Data Messages
   (c) Listening SMS

Chapter 14...

ACCESSING ANDROID HARDWARE

14.1 Introduction
14.2 Media APIs
    14.2.1 Playing Media Resources
    14.2.2 State Machine for Media Player Object
    14.2.3 Recording Multimedia
    14.2.4 Using the Camera
14.3 Introduction to Sensor Manager
    14.3.1 Sensor Framework
14.4 Android Telephony
14.5 Bluetooth
    14.5.1 Managing the Local Bluetooth Device Adapter
    14.5.2 Device Discoverability
    14.5.3 Discovering Remote Devices
    14.5.4 Bluetooth Communication
    14.5.5 Communication by Opening
    14.5.6 Selection of Remote Devices for Communication
    14.5.7 Opening a Client Bluetooth Socket Connection
    14.5.8 Transmission of Data Using Bluetooth Sockets
14.6 Manage Network and Wi-Fi Connections
    14.6.1 Introduction of Connectivity Manager
    14.6.2 Supporting User Preferences for Background Data Transfers
    14.6.3 Finding and Monitoring Network Connectivity
    14.6.4 Managing Wi-Fi
    14.6.5 Monitoring Active Wi-Fi Connection Details
    14.6.6 Scanning for HotSpots
    14.6.7 Managing Wi-Fi Configuration
    14.6.8 Creating Wi-Fi Network Configuration
    14.6.9 Transfering Data using Wi-Fi Direct
- Practice Questions

14.1 Introduction

The Android OS is implemented on increasingly diverse hardware that is available on mobile devices. Every application i.e. APIs provides low level access to these hardware. The development for any application should consider the ability to monitor and control the hardware features on devices.

Hardware APIs Includes :
1. To play and record multimedia contents including audio, video and camera which is used to capture images and live videos.
2. To monitor hardware by using sensors which are present in Sensor Manager?
3. To examine telephony package for monitoring phone calls as well as phone status.
4. Communication libraries for managing Bluetooth, network and Wi-Fi connections.

With increasing popularity nowadays mobile phones are becoming de facto portable digital media player. Specifically this is leading to cloud-based music players, combined with modern phones with ever increasing storage capacities.

There are many Android APIs for controlling audio and video playback, controlling the audio focus of a device.

Android 4.0 use remote control client mechanism which provides a mechanism for showing users details on the media playing and which allows user to control the playback from device's lock screen.

These mobiles are embedded with high-resolution cameras, and it is substituting non-SLR digital cameras. Android camera APIs helps to take pictures, live videos as well as new media effect. APIs provides a way to modify video images in real time from within an application.

Android's open platform provides agnostic philosophy and ensures that it offers a multimedia API capable of playing and recording a wide range of image, audio and video formats both locally and streamed.

14.2 Media APIs

- The modern technology like portable digital media player defeats over a traditional mobile system.
- Android's open source platform exposes the multimedia library (which is capable of playing and recording a wide range of media formats) to the user's application.
- Android supports following multimedia formats :
    (i)   JPEG
    (ii) PNG
    (iii) OGG
    (iv) mpeg-4
    (v)   3GPP
    (vi) MP3

Playing Audio and Video :

Android 4.0.3 (API level 15) supports the following multimedia formats for playback as part of the base framework.

Note : Some devices may support playback of additional file formats.

Audio :
- AAC LC/LTP.
- HE AAC V1 (AAC+)
- HE AAC V2 (Enhanced AAC+)

Images :
- Video.
- N/W protocols.

14.2.1 Playing Media Resources

- Multimedia library in Android is handled by media player class. The media which is stored as application resources, local files can be accessed by using the class.

Introduction of Media Player :

Media Player class is used to playback of audio and video within Android application. Using media player user can stored in application resources, local files, content providers, or streamed from a network URL. The media player's management of audio and video files and streams is handled as a state machine transitions from state machine can be described as follows :

1. Initialize the media player with media to play.
2. Prepare the media player for playback.
3. Start the playback.
4. Pause or stop the playback prior to its completing.
5. The playback is complete.

- New media player instance is needed to be created for playing media resource. Initialize it with a media source, and prepare it for playback. To stream internet media using the media player, application must include the INTERNET permission.
  `<uses-permission android:name="android.permission.INTERNET"/>`

- Android supports a limited number of simultaneous media player objects, not releasing them can cause runtime exceptions when the system runs out. When user finishes playback, call release on media player object to free the associated resources :
  mediaplayer.release();

- To play a media resource, a new instance of media player class is created and it is assigned to source which can be played by using SetDataSource() method.
  ```
  String MEDIA_FILE = Settings.System.DEFAULT_RINGTONE_URI.tostring();
  ```

```
        MediaPlayer mpfile = new MediaPlayer();
try
{
   mpFile.SetDataSource (MEDIA_FILE_PATH);
   mpFile.prepare();
   mpFile.start();
}
   Catch (IllegalArgumentException e) {  }
   Catch (Illegal StateException e) {  }
   Catch (IOException e) {  }
```
- Once Media Player is prepared, call start to begin the playback of the associated media resource.

    mpFile.start();
- Media Player also includes stop, pause and seek methods to control playback, as well as methods to find the duration, position and image size of the media.

14.2.2 State Machine for Media Player Object

Playback control of audio and video files and streams is managed as a state machine. The diagram shows the life cycle of media player object.

Preparation Audio for Playback :

The following are the ways which are used for playing audio content by using media player :
1. Include media player as an application resource.
2. Play it from local files or content providers or stream it from a remote URL.

To include audio content as an application resource, add it to the res/raw folder of resources hierarchy. Raw resources are not compressed or manipulated in any way when packaged into user's application.

Initializing Audio Content for playback :

To play back audio content using a media player object and set the data source of an audio. This can be done by using static create() method passing in the Activity Context and any of the following audio sources :
- A resource identifier (typically for an audio file stored in the res/raw resource folder).
- A URI to a local file (using the file ://schema)
- A URI to a row within a content provider that returns an audio file.

    // Load as audio resource from a package resource.
    ```
    MediaPlayer Resource Player = MediaPlayer.Create (this, R.raw.my_audio);
    ```
- The another alternative is to use the SetDataSource method on an existing media player instance shown this follow listing method accepts a file path, content provider URI, streaming media URL path or File Descriptor. When using the SetDataSource method, it is important to call prepare on the media player before playback.

- Preparing video for playback.
- Playback of video content is slightly more involved than audio. To play a video, you need a surface to watch it.
- There are two alternatives for the playback of video content. The first technique, using the VideoViewClass encapsulates the creation of surface and allocation and preparation of video content using a media player.

  The second technique allows user to create own surface and manipulate the underlying media player instance directly.

Playing Video Using the Video View :

A video view is used to playback video. The video view includes a surface on which the video is displayed and encapsulates and manages a media player instance that handles the playback. This video view is then coded into user interface and video can be assigned which is to play by calling SetVideoPath() or SetVideoURI() methods to specify the path to a local file or the URI of either a content provider or remote video stream.

```
final VideoView VideoView=(VideoView) findViewById(R.id.VideoView);
//Assign a local file to play.
Videoview.SetVideopath("/sdcard/video1.3gp");
//Assign a URL of a Remote Video Stream VideoView.SetVideouri
(myAwsomeStreamingSource);
```

- When the video is initialized, it is controlled by using the start, StopPlayback, pause and seekTo methods.
- The video view also includes the SetkeepScreenOn() method to apply a screen wake LOCK that will prevent the screen from being dimmed while playback is in progress without requiring a special permission.
- The following code used to assign a video to a video view. It uses a media controller to control playback.

```
//Get a reference to the video view final VidewView VideoView = (Videoview)
      findViewByID (R. id. VideoView);
//Configure the video view and assign a source video.
      VideoView.SetkeepScreenOn (true);
      VideoView.SetVideoPath ('/sdcard/video.3gp")
//Attach a media controller.
      MediaController mediacontroller = new mediaController(this);
      VideoView.SetmediaController (mediaController);
```

Creating a Surface for Video Playback :

Media player directly used to view video content is to prepare a surface onto which the video will be displayed.

- It is done by using SurfaceView object. The surface View class is wrapper around the surface holder object, which in turn, is a wrapper around the surface that is used to support visual updates from background threads.
- The media player uses a SurfaceHolder object to display video content, assigned using SetDisplay method. To include SurfaceHolder in your UI layout, use the SurfaceView class which is shown in layout .XML file.

Surface Holders are created asynchronously. Before surface Holder object is assigned to media player SurfaceCreatedHandler should be fired by implementing surfaceHolder. Call back interface. After creating and assigning the SurfaceHolder to media player, SetDataSource() method is called to specify the path, URL, or Content Provider URI of the video resource to play.

- After media source is selected prepare() is called to initialize the media player in preparation for playback.

Controlling Media Player Playback :
- When a media player is prepared, call start to begin playback of the associated media.
    MediaPlayer.start();

Use stop and pause methods to stop or pause playback, respectively. The media player also provides the getDuration() method to find the lengths of the media being played and the GetCurrentPosition() method to find the playback position.

SeekTo() method is used to jump to a specific position in the media. Common media control buttons which is controlled by MediaController which is standard control included by Android. This controller is associated with the video playback view, the media controller will be visible only when it is set as visible.

If VideoView is used to display its video ontent, SetMediaController() method is used to assign mediacontroller.

    //Attach a media controller
    MediaController mediaController = new MediaController (this);
    VideoView.SetMediaController (mediacontroller);

To control a media player, or other audio or video source directly to implement a new MediaController.MediaPlayerControl.

- The SetAnchorView() method to determine which view should anchor the media controller when it's visible, and call show or hide to show or hide the controller.
    MediaController.SetAnchorView (myView);
    MediaController.show();

- **Managing media playback output :**
  The media player also provides control for controlling the tasks such as volume of the output, lock the screen brightness, during playback, and set the looping status.

- The volume of each channel can be controlled during playback using the SetVolume() method. It takes a scalar float value between 0 and 1 for both the left and right channels (where 0 is silent and 1 is maximum volume).
    ```
    MediaPlayer.SetVolume (0.5f, 0.5f);
    ```
- To force the screen to stay on during video playback, the SetScreen on while playing method is used as follows :
    ```
    MediaPlayer.SetScreenOnWhilePlaying (true);
    ```

Responding to the Volume Control :

It is important the current application responds to correctly to handle users pressing the volume and any attached media playback control keys. By default using the volume key on either device or an attached headset, changes the volume of whichever audio stream is currently playing. If there is no volume key, it will after the ringtone. Activity's SetVolumeControlStream() method typically within its OnCreate() method allows specifying which audio stream should be controlled by the volume keys while the current activity is active.

When media player is used user should specify the STREAM_MUSIC stream to make it focus of the volume key.

14.2.3 Recording Multimedia

- MediaRecorder class handles the multimedia. To record the audio or video a new object of MediaRecorder class :
  MediaRecorder MediaRecorder = new media recorder ();
- Before recording media, application needs a permission the following tag is added in manifest.xml file.
    ```
    <uses-permission android:name="android.permission.RECORD_AUDIO"/>
    <uses-permission android:name="android.permission.RECORD_VIDEO"/>
    ```
- The Media Player configures the video and audio sources (generally the camera and microphone), output format, video size and frame rate and the video, audio encoders.
    ```
    //Set the audio source.
        MediaRecorder.SetAudioSource (MediaRecorder.AudioSource.MIC);
    //Set the output form
        MediaRecorder.SetOutputFormat (MediaRecorder.outputformat.DEFAULT);
    //Set the audio encoder to use.
        MediaRecorder.SetAudioEncoder (MediaRecorder.AudioEncoder.DEFAULT);
    ```
- SetoutputFile method is used to store the recorded media.
    ```
    MediaRecorder.SetOutPutFile ("myoutputfile.mp4");
    ```
    This method must be called before prepare and after SetOutPutFormat or it will throw exception.

Recording can be start by calling prepare and followed by start method.

    `MediaRecorder.Prepare();`

    `MediaRecorder.Start();`

- The playback is stopped by using stop() and MediaRecorder resources are freed by calling release() method.

    `MediaRecorder.Stop();`

    `MediaRecorder.Release();`

How to share the media with other applications?

To share the media created by one application with another application, media store content provider is assigned with metadata and specific file location is selected.

- The new object of ContentValues is created to add new record to a media store. The metadata includes title, time stamp and geocoding information for new media file.

    `ContentValues content=new ContentValues (3);`

    `Content.Put (Audio.Audiocolumn, TITLE, "TheSunisBrightest");`

    `Content.put (Audio.AudioColumns.DATE_ADDED, system.CurrentTimeMillis()/1000);`

    `Content.put (Audio.Media.MIME_TYPE, "audio/amr");`

    -Absolute path of the media file is added by using :

    `Content.Put(MediaStore.Audio.Media.DATA, "OutputFile.mp4");`

- To insert this file into media store of other application. ContentResolver of that application is accessed.

`ContentResolver resolver=getContentResolver();`

    `Uri uri=resolver.insert(Audio.Media.EXTERNAL_CONTENT_URI, Content);`

- The availability of the newly added media file into the application is published by using Broadcast Intents.

    `SendBroadCast(new Intent(Intent.ACTION_MEDIA_SCANNER_SCAN_FILE, uril));`

14.2.4 Using the Camera

- To access camera hardware on Android mobile phones, the permissions to use the CAMERA must be added to manifest .XML file of your application. The following snippet grants access to camera services.

    `<uses-permission android:name="android.permission.CAMERA"/>`

    `<uses-feature android:name="android.hardware.camera">`

- The 'Camera' class enables user to adjust camera settings, taking pictures and manipulating camera previews.
- The static open() method is used to access camera services and all the resources hold by this services are released by release() method.

    `Camera Camera=Camera.open();`

    `Camera.release();`

- Camera settings are done with camera parameters object and GetParameters() method on the camera accesses parameters of camera. Set* methods are used to modify the settings of camera and changes are applied by using SetParameters() method.
- Camera parameters are used to state the image, preview size, image format, frame rate

    ```
    camera.Parameters parameters=camera.getParameters();
    parameters.SetPictureFormat(PixelFormat.JPEG);
    camera.SetParameters (Parameters);
    ```

Taking a Picture :

Before taking picture <u>preview</u> must be started stated as above.

- The picture is taken by calling TakePicture on a camera object, which has following parameters.

    ```
    camera.shuttercallback, camera.picturecallback,
    camera. picturecallback, camera.picturecallback.
    public void takepicture()
    ```

```
{
camera.takepicture (shutter callback, raw callback, jpegcallback);
}
ShutterCallBack ShutterCallBack=new shutter call back()
    {
public void onshutter()
    {//code
    }
};
PictureCallBack rawcallback=new picturecallback()
    {
public void onPictureTaken(byte[]_data, camera_camera)
    {
    //code
    }
};
Picturecallback jpegcallback=new PictureCallBack()
    {
public void onpicturetaken (byte[]_data, camera_camera)
    {
    //code
    }
}
```

Using the Camera Preview :
- Android applications uses this functionality to incorporate live videos. Camera preview can be displayed in real time onto a surface, as shown below :

    `Camera.SetPreviewDisplay(Surface);`

    `Camera.SetPreview();`

    `Camera.StopPreview();`

    StartPreview() method is called which starts updating the surface and after setting preview picture has taken. Every time when picture is to be taken it is done by calling StartPreview() method and finished with StopPreview().

- release() is called to release the camera for use by other application. OnPause() method also it stop immediately and camera is available to other applications OnResume() it resumes to previous application only.

14.3 Introduction to Sensor Manager

- Android devices have built-in sensors that senses the motion, orientation and different environmental conditions. These sensors provides a raw data with high precision and accuracy. Android supports broad categories of sensors :

    1. **Motion Sensor :** This measures acceleration forces and rotational forces along with three axes. It has accelometers, gravity sensors etc.
    2. **Environmental Sensor :** This measures environmental parameters like air temperature and pressure, humidity and illumination. This includes barometers, thermometers.
    3. **Position Sensors :** These measures the physical location of a device, it includes orientation sensors, magnetometer.

- Some of the sensors are hardware based and some are software based. These are called virtual sensor also.

    Virtual sensor collects the information from hardware based sensors and evaluates the result from it.

14.3.1 Sensor Framework

- The sensor framework is a part of android hardware package and it includes following classes and interfaces.
    1. **SensorManager :** This class is used to create an instance of the sensor service. This provides various methods to access and listen sensors, registering and unregistering sensor event listeners.
    2. **Sensor :** This class is used to create an instance of specific sensor.

3. **SensorEvent :** This class is used to create a sensor event object, which provides information about a sensor event, raw sensor data, type of sensor that generates the event, accuracy of data and timestamp of an event, this information is retrieved using this class.
4. **SensorEventListener :** This interface is used to create two call back methods that receives notifications when sensor values change or when sensor accuracy changes.

- SensorManager is used to manage the sensor hardware. get_system_service() method is used to get a reference to the sensor service.

    ```
    String Service_name=context.SENSOR_SERVICE;
    SensorManager SensorManager= (SensorManager)
    getSystemService (service_name);
    ```

- SensorListner interface is used to listen for sensor value and accuracy changes. OnSensorChanged() method is implemented to react to value changes. The sensor parameter i.e. passed to this method identifies the sensor triggered the event, and the new values detected by this sensor is added to values float array.
- For accuracy notification OnAccuracyChanged() method is used to sense the accuracy. This parameter identifies the sensor triggered on the event, accuracy parameter indicates the new accuracy.

    Following are the constant values that are used to notify the accuracy of the sensor :

    1. **SensorManager.SENSOR_STATUS_ACCURACY_HIGH :** It indicates that sensor is reporting with highest possible accuracy.
    2. **SensorManager.SENSOR_STATUS_ACCURACY_LOW :** It indicates that sensor is reporting with low accuracy.
    3. **SensorManager.SENSOR_STATUS_ACCURACY_MEDIUM :** It indicates that sensor is with medium accuracy and need to be improve the readings.
    4. **SensorManager.SENSOR_STATUS_ACCURACY_UNRELIABLE :** It indicates the sensor data is unreliable, meaning that either improvement is required or readings are not done properly.

- To identify which sensor is triggered in an event, sensor manager needs some of the constants. These sensors are dependent upon the hardware for your application which is available on the host device.

    1. **SensorManager.SENSOR_ACCELEROMETER :** This is an accelerometer sensor which returns the current acceleration along the three axes in m/s^2.
    2. **SensorManager.SENSOR_ORIENTATION :** This returns the current orientation on three axes in degrees.
    3. **SensorManager.SENSOR_LIGHT :** That returns a single value describing the ambient.

4. **SensorManager.SENSOR_MAGNETIC_FIELD :** It is a sensor used to determine the current magnetic field measured in microteslas (μT) along three axes.
5. **SensorManager.SENSOR_PROXIMITY :** It is proximity sensor that returns a single value describing the distance between the device and the target in meters (m).
6. **SensorManager.SENSOR_TEMPERATURE :** This is a thermometer sensor that returns the ambient temperature is Celsius (C).

    SensorManager.registerListner
    (mySensorListner,
    SensorManager.SENSOR_TRICORDER,
    SensorManager.SENSOR_DELAY_FASTEST);

registerListner() will listen to the sensor, it specifies the sensor which trigger and which rate the sensor should get updated.

14.4 Android Telephony

- Android's Telephony API monitors mobile voice and data connections as well as incoming and outgoing calls and to send and receive short messages.
- There is need to check telephony hardware which monitors phone state and phone calls, as well as initiating calls and monitoring incoming call details.

Making Telephony as a required hardware feature:

- Some of the devices do not support for telephony hardware. An application that provides reverse number lookup for incoming calls or a replacement SMS client simply won't work on WiFi devices.
- To specify that an application requires telephony support to function, user can add a uses-feature node to specify an application manifest.

    <uses –feature android: name="android.hardwrae.telephony"
        Android: required="true"/>

Checking for android hardware:

- If user is using telephony APIs but that are not strictly required for an application, then the existence of telephony hardware can be checked before attempting to make use of related APIs. It is checked in application's lifecycle only so that UI and behavior can be adjusted accordingly.
- Use the Package Manager's hasSystemFeature() method, specifying the FEATURE_TELEPHONY feature. The Package manager includes constants to query the existence of CDMA and GSM specific hardware.

Using Telephony

- The Android telephony hardware enables user to create own dialer or integrate call handling and phone state which monitors an application.

1. **Initiating phone calls**
   - For initiating the phone calls use Intent. ACTION_DIAL Intent, specifying the number to dial by setting the intents data using a tel: schema
     ```
     Intent towhomyoucall=new intent(Intent.ACTION_DIAL,uri.parse(tel:552-2367));
     startActivity(towhomyoucal);
     ```
   - The above action starts a dialer activity and it prepopulated with the number which is specified. The default dialer Activity allows user to change the number before explicitly initiating the call.
   - Intent is used to announce intention to dial a number, and an application stays decoupled from the dialer implementation used to initiate the call.

2. **Replacing a native dialer**
   - It involves two steps:
     1. Intercept intents serviced by the native dialer.
     2. Initiate and manage outgoing calls.
   - The native dialer application responds to Intent actions which corresponds to a user pressing the hardware call button, asking to view data using tel: schema, or making ACTION_DIAL request using the tel: schema.
   - The intent-filter in manifest file is included to intercept these requests. Replacement dialer Activity that listens for the following actions:
     1. **Intent.ACTION_CALL_BUTTON:** This action broadcasts when the device's hardware call button is pressed the intent filter is created for listening this default action.
     2. **Intent.ACTION_DIAL:** This intent action described, is used by applications that want to initiate a phone call. The Intent Filter used to capture the actions that are default as well as browsable and must specify tel: schema to replace existing dialer functionality.
     3. **Intent.ACTION_VIEW:** The view action is used by applications wanting to view a piece of data. Ensure that the Intent Filter specifies the tel: schema to allow new activity used to view telephone numbers.
   - After the activity started it should provide a UI that allows users to enter or modify the number to dial and to initiate the outgoing call. To place the call there are two options that is to use existing telephony stack or own alternatives. to use existing telephony stack use Intent. ACTION_CALL.

To initiate the call by using the system in call Activity and system manages dialling, connection and voice handling, the following action is performed.

```
Intent towhomyoucall=new intent( Intent.ACTION_CALL,uri.parse(tel:552-2367));
startActivity(towhomyoucal);
```

To use this action, an application must request the CALL_PHONE uses permission.

<uses-permission android:name="android.permission.CALL_PHONE"/>

3. **Accessing Telephony Properties and Phone State:**
   - Access to the telephony APIs is managed by the Telephony Manager, Accessible using the getSysytemService method.

   ```
   String srvcname=Context.TELEPHONY_SERVICE;
   TelephonyManager telephonyManager=(TelephonyManager) getSysytemService(srvcname);
   ```
   - The telephony manager provides direct access to many of the phone properties, including devices, network, Subscriber Identity Module (SIM) and data state details.
   - Some connectivity status information can be obtained by using Connectivity Manager.

4. **Reading Phone Device Details:**
   - Using the Telephony Manager, user can obtain the phone type(GSM,CDMA or SIP), unique ID(IMEI or MEID), software version and phone numbers
   - This action needs the uses permission which is added to manifest file which reads each of the properties.

   <uses-permission android name:"android.permission.READ_PHONE_STATE"/>

5. **Reading Network Details:**
   - Ice is connected to a network, Telephony Manager is used to read the mobile country code and Network code, the country ISO code ,and the network operator code and the type of a network using getNetworkOperators, getNetworkCountryIso, getNetworkOperatorName and getNetworkOperatorName() methods as follows.
   - These commands work only when user is connected to a mobile network and can be unreliable if it is a CDMA network.use the getPhoneType method to determine which phone type is being used.

6. **Reading SIM Details:**
   - When application is running from GSM device then it will have SIM card. Telephony Manager can query the details of SIM card such as ISO country code, operator name, operator MCC and MNC.
   - If user has included the READ_PHONE_STATE uses permission in an application manifest, it enables to obtain the serial number for the current SIM using getsimSerial Number method when the SIM is ready state.

7. **Reading Data Connection and Transfer State Details:**
   - Using the getdataState and getDataActivity methods, user can find the current data connection state and transfer Activity.
8. **Monitoring Incoming Phone Calls:**
   - If an application respond to incoming phone calls only while it is running, override onCallStateChanged method in Phone State Listener implementation. And register it to receive notification when the call state changes:

14.5 Bluetooth

Bluetooth is a communication protocol which is designed for short-range, low bandwidth devices within range. By initiating the Bluetooth APIs, user can search for, and connect to, other Bluetooth devices. It also can initiate a communication link using Bluetooth sockets and then transmit and receive streams of data between devices from within an application

Android provides APIs to manage and monitor Bluetooth settings :

(a) To control discoverability.

(b) To discover nearby Bluetooth devices.

(c) To use Bluetooth as proximity based.

(d) Peer-to-peer transport layer for an application.

14.5.1 Managing the Local Bluetooth Device Adapter

- BluetoothAdapter class controls the local Bluetooth devices, which represents the host Android device on which application is running.
- By calling getDefaultAdapter() method the default Bluetooth adapter is accessed.
    ```
    BluetoothAdapter Bluetooth = BluetoothAdapter. get DeaultAdapter ();
    ```
- To read any of the local Bluetooth adapter properties, initiate discovery, or find bonded devices, it include the Bluetooth permission in application manifest.
- To modify any of the local device properties, the BLUETOOTH_ADMIN permission is also required.
    ```
    <uses-permission android:name="android.permission.BLUETOOTH"/>
    <uses-permission android:name="android.permission.BLUETOOTH_ADMIN"/>
    ```
- The Bluetooth adapter offers methods for reading and setting properties of the local Bluetooth hardware.
    isEnabled() method is used to confirm the device is enabled, after which user can access the Bluetooth adapter's name and hardware name address, using the getName() and getAddress() method.
    ```
    if (bluetooth.isEnabled() )
    ```

```
{
    String address=bluetooth.getAddress();
    String name=bluetooth.getName();
}
```
- If user have the BLUETOOTH_ADMIN permission user can change the friendly name of the Bluetooth adapter using SetName() method.
  ```
  Bluetooth.SetName("Blackfang");
  ```
- To find more detailed description of the current Bluetooth adapter state, use the getState() method, which returns one of the following Bluetooth adapter constants.
    1. STATE_TURNING_ON
    2. STATE_ON
    3. STATE_TURNING_OFF
    4. STATE_OFF
- To conserve battery life and optimize security, most users will keep Bluetooth disabled.
- To enable the Bluetooth adapter, user can start a system preference activity using the BluetoothAdapter. ACTION_REQUEST_ENABLE static constant as a StartActivity ForResult action string.
  Start Activity for Result
  (new Intent (BluetoothAdapter.ACTION_REQUEST_ENABLE, 0);
- It prompts a user to turn on Bluetooth and asks for confirmation, if user agrees the SubActivity will close and return to the calling Activity when the Bluetooth Adapter has turned on.

14.5.2 Device Discoverability

The process two devices of finding each other to connect is called discovery. Before a link establishment Bluetooth socket for communication, the local Bluetooth Adapter must communicate with remote device.

Before connecting devices must discover each other.

Managing Device Discoverability :

For an Android device to find local Bluetooth Adapter during a discovery scan. The Bluetooth Adapter's discoverability is indicated by its scan mode, this is found using getScanMode() method on the BluetoothAdapter object. It will return one of the following BluetoothAdapter constants :

1. **SCAN_MODE_CONNECTABLE_DISCOVERABLE :** This is true then the device is discoverable from any Bluetooth device performing a discovery scan both page and inquiry scan are valid.

2. **SCAN_MODE_DISCOVERABLE :** Page scan is enabled but inquiry scan is not. This means that devices that have previously connected and bonded to the local device can find it during discoverability.
3. **SCAN_MODE_NONE :** Discoverability is turned off. No remote devices can find the local Bluetooth Adapter during discoverability.

StartActivityForResult
(new Intent (BluetoothAdapter.ACTION_REQUEST_DISCOVERABLE), DISCOVERY_REQUEST
- By default discoverability will be enabled for 2 minutes. User can modify this setting by adding an EXTRA_DISCOVERABLE_DURATION extra to the launch intent, specifying the number of seconds up to which discoverability lasts.

14.5.3 Discovering Remote Devices

Discovery process can take some time to complete (up to 12 seconds). User can check if the local Bluetooth Adapter is already performing a discovery scan by using the is Discovering() method. To initiate the Discovery process, call StartDiscovery() on the Bluetooth discovery :

```
If (bluetooth.isEnabled() )
    bluetooth.StartDiscovery();
```

To cancel a discovery in progress, call CancelDiscovery().

The discovery process is asynchronous. Android uses BroadCast Intents to notify user of the start and end of discovery as well as remote devices disconnect during the scan.

Discovered Bluetooth Devices are returned via Broadcast Intents by means of the **ACTION_FOUND broadcast action.**
- Each broadcast Intent includes the name of the remote device in an extra indexed as BluetoothDevice. EXTRA_NAME, and an immutable representation of the remote Bluetooth device as a Bluetooth Device parceble object stored under the BluetoothDevice. EXTRA_DEVICE

14.5.4 Bluetooth Communication

The Android Bluetooth communications APIs are wrappers around RFComm, the Bluetooth radio frequency communications protocol. RFComm supports RS 232 serial communication over the logical link control and adaption protocol (L_2CAP) layer.

The following classes are used to establish an RFComm communication channel for bidirectional communication.

1. **Bluetooth Server Socket :** It is used to establish a listening socket for initiating a link between devices. To establish a handshake, one device acts as a server to listen for, and accept, incoming connection requests.
2. **Bluetooth Socket :** It is used to create a new client to a listening Bluetooth Server Socket. Also returned by the Bluetooth Server Socket after a connection established.

Once a connection is established, Bluetooth sockets are used by both the server and client to transfer data streams.
- When application is created which uses Bluetooth as a peer-to-peer transport layer, there is a need to implement both a Bluetooth Server Socket to listen for connections and a Bluetooth Socket to initiate a new channel and handle communications.
- When connected, the Bluetooth Server Socket returns a Bluetooth socket that's then used by the server device to send and receive data. This server side Bluetooth Socket is used in exactly the same way as the client socket.

The designation of server and client are relevant only to how the connection is established. It doesn't affect how data flows after that connection is made.

14.5.5 Communication by Opening

Bluetooth Server Socket Listner :

A Bluetooth server socket is used to listen for incoming Bluetooth socket connection requests from remote Bluetooth devices. In order for two Bluetooth devices to be connected, one node should be as a server and the other as a client. After the two are connected, the communication between the server and host devices are handled through a Bluetooth socket at both ends.
- Bluetooth adapter acts as a server and incoming requests are responded by calling its listen Using RFComm with service record method to listen for incoming connection requests. The name is passed to identify the server and universally unique identifier (UUID). This method will return a BluetoothServerSocket object.
- Call accepts on the server socket, optionally passing in timeout duration to have it start listening for connections. The server socket will now block until a remote Bluetooth Socket Client with a matching UUID attempts to connect.
- If connection request is made from a remote device that is not paired with the local Bluetooth Adapter, the user will be prompted to accept pairing request before the accept call returns. This can be intimated as a Notification, or a Dialog :
- If an incoming communication request is successful, accept will return a Bluetooth Socket connected to client device. This socket is used to transfer data.

14.5.6 Selection of Remote Devices for Communication

- To listen Bluetooth Server Socket from within an application, BluetoothSocket class can be used on the client device to initiate a communication channel. It is also returned by the Bluetooth server socket listener after a connection to a client device has been established.
- Create a client side Bluetooth Socket by calling CreateRFCommSocket(). To service record on a Bluetooth device object that represents the target remote server device.

- Bluetooth device connection requirement. To establish a connection between Bluetooth Socket to a remote Bluetooth device, the following conditions must be true.
  1. The remote device must be discoverable.
  2. The remote device must be accepting connections through a Bluetooth Server Socket.
  3. The local and remote devices must be paired. If the devices are not paired, the users of each device will be prompted to pair them when the connection request is initiated.

14.5.7 Opening a Client Bluetooth Socket Connection
- To initiate a communications channel to a remote device, create a Bluetooth socket using the BluetoothDevice object that represents it.
- To create a new connection, call CreateRFComm() socket to service record on the Bluetooth device object representing the target device. Pass in UUID of its open Bluetooth Server Socket Listner.
- If users attempt to connect to a Bluetooth Device that has not yet been paired with the host device, it will prompt to accept the pairing before the connect call completes. The users must accept the paring request on both the host and remote devices for the connection to be established.

14.5.8 Transmission of Data Using Bluetooth Sockets
- After a connection has been established, Bluetooth socket should be there on both the client and server devices. There is no specific differentiation between client or server side Bluetooth socket.
- Data transfer across Bluetooth sockets is handled via standard Java InputStream and OutputStream object. By using getInputStream() and getOutputStream() methods are used to obtain from a Bluetooth Socket.
  The first is used to send a string to a remote device using an output stream, and second is used to listen for incoming strings using an Input Stream. The same technique is used to transfer any streamable data.

14.6 Manage Network and Wi-Fi Connections
- To ensure the applications are running efficiently and responsively, application should know and manage the connections such as network technologies (Wi-Fi, GPRS, 3G, LTE and so on). On these technologies the speed, reliability and cost of internet connectivity.
- Android broadcasts intents that allows monitoring changes in network connectivity and offers APIs that provide control over network settings and connections.
- Android networking is handled via the Connectivity Manager, which is a service that monitors the connectivity state, sets preferred network connection and manage connectivity.

14.6.1 Introduction of Connectivity Manager

- It represents the network connectivity service. It is used to monitor the state of network connections, configure fail over settings and control the network radio.
- To use the connectivity manager, application needs read and write network state access permissions.

    <uses-permission android:name="android.permission.ACCESS_NETWORK_STATE"/>
    <uses-permission android:name="android.permission.CHANGE_NETWORK_STATE"/>

- To access connectivity manager, use getSystemService(), passing in context.CONNECTIVITY_SERVICE() as the service name as shown below :

    String service=context.CONNECTIVITY_SERVICE;

    connectivityManager connectivity=(Connectivity Manager) getSystemService(Service);

14.6.2 Supporting User Preferences for Background Data Transfers

- Until Android 4.0 (API level 14), user preferences for background data transfers were enforced at the application level meaning that pre-android 4.0 platforms.
- To obtain the background data setting, call the getBackgroundDataSetting() method on the Connectivity Manager object.

    booleanBackgroundEnabled=connectivity.getBackgroundDataSetting();

- If background data setting is disabled, application should transfer data only when it is active and in the foreground.
- If user changes background data preference, the system will send a broadcast intent with the connectivity manager's ACTION_BACKGROUND_DATA_SETTING_CHANGED action.
- To monitor these changes, create register a new Broadcast Receiver that listens for this broadcast intent.
- In Android 4.0, getBackgroundData() setting will always returns true. Users have control over the network data usage of applications including setting individual data limits and restricting background data.
- These preferences are taken at system level that is if data transfer is unavailable for an application, attempts to transfer data or check the network connectivity status will fail with device appearing offline.
- To prevent users from limiting or disabling an application data transfer is to :
    1. Minimize the data transfer.
    2. Modify the data usage based on the connection type.
    3. Provide user preferences for modifying data usage.
- By adding MANAGE_NETWORK_USAGE Intent filter to the preference activity's manifest node, users can make the changes within system settings when user inspects application's data usage.

14.6.3 Finding and Monitoring Network Connectivity

- Connectivity manager provides a high-level view of the available network connections. The getActiveNetworkInfo() method returns a NetworkInfo object that includes details on the currently active network.

  `NetworkInfo ActiveNetwork=Connectivity.getActiveNetworkInfo();`
- getNetworkInfo() method is used to find details on an inactive network of the type specified.
- The return NetworkInfo() is used to find the connection status, network type and detailed state information of the returned network.

  Before transferring data, configure a repeating alarm or schedule a background service that performs data transfer, use the connectivity manager to check that user is actually connected to the internet and it also used to verify which type of connection is in place.
- By finding the connectivity status and network type, downloads and uploads can be temporarily disabled, which alters refresh frequency or defer large downloads based on the bandwidth available.
- To monitor network connectivity, create a Broadcast Receiver that listens for Connectivity Manager.CONNECTIVITY_ACTION() broadcast intents.
- These intents include extras that provides additional details on the change to the connectivity state. Static constants which are available in ConnectivityManager class evaluate these 'extras'.
- EXTRA_NO_CONNECTIVITY extra contains a Boolean that returns true if the device is not connected to any network otherwise, it is FALSE.

14.6.4 Managing Wi-Fi

The Wi-Fi manger, which represents the android Wi-Fi connectivity service, that can be used to configure Wi-Fi network connections, manage the current Wi-Fi connection, scan for access points and monitor changes in Wi-Fi connectivity.

- To use the Wi-Fi manager, application must have <uses-permissions> for accessing and changing the Wi-Fi state included in its manifest.

  `<uses-permission android:name="android.permission.ACCESS_WIFI_STATE"/>`

  `<uses-permission android:name="android.permission.CHANGE_WIFI_STATE"/>`

getSystemService() method, is passed in context.WIFI_SERVICE constant, to access the Wi-Fi manager.

setWiFiEnabled() method is used to enable or disable Wi-Fi hardware or to request for current Wi-Fi state using getWiFistate or isWiFiEnabled method.

Monitoring Wi-Fi Connectivity.

Connectivity manager monitors changes in Wi-Fi connectivity. However, the Wi-Fi manager does broadcast intents whenever the connectivity status of the Wi-Fi network changes, using an action from one of the following constants defined in WiFiManager class.

- Connectivity Manager is used to monitor changes in WiFi connectivity. WiFi Manager does broadcast intents whenever the connectivity status of the Wi-Fi network changes, using one of the following constants which are defined below:
  1. **WIFI_STATE_CHANGED_ACTION:** This indicates that WiFi hardware has changed, moving between enabling, enabled, disabling, disabled and unknown. it also includes two extra values keyed on EXTRA_WIFI_STATE and EXTRA_PREVIOUS_STATE that provides the new and previous Wi-Fi state.
  2. **SUPPLICANT_CONNECTION_CHANGE_ACTION:** This is a broadcast intent and it is displayed whenever the connection state with the active supplicant (access point) changes. It is fired when a new connection is established or on existing connection is lost, using EXTRA_NEW_STATE Boolean extra, which returns true.
  3. **NETWORK_STATE_CHANGED_ACTION:** It is fired whenever the Wi-Fi connectivity state changes. This intent includes two extras the first, EXTRA_NETWORK_INFO, includes the network info object that details the current network state, whereas second EXTRA_BSSID includes BSSID of the access point where user connected to.
  4. **RSSI_CHANGED_ACTION:** User can monitor current signal strength of the connected Wi-Fi network by listening for the RSSI_CHANGED_ACTION intent. This broadcast intent includes an integer extra, EXTRA_NEW_RSSI, that holds the current signal strength.

Scanning for Hotspots :

Wi-Fi Manager conducts access point scans using the start scan method. Intent with the SCAN_RESULTS_AVAILABLE_ACTION action will be broadcast to asynchronously announce that the scan is complete and results are available.

14.6.5 Monitoring Active Wi-Fi Connection Details

- When an active Wi-Fi connection has been established, user can use getConnectionInfo method on the Wi-Fi Manager to find information on the connection's status. The returned Wifi Info object includes the SSID, BSSID, MAC address and IP address of the current access point as well as the current link speed and signal strength.
- The following snippet shows how the active connection is detected
  ```
  WifiInfo info=wifi.getconnectioninfo();
  If( info.getBSSID()!=null)
  int strength=Wifimanager.calculatesignallevel(info.getRssi(),5);
  int speed= info.getLinkspeed();
  String units=WifiInfo.LINK_SPEED_UNITS;
  String ssid=info.getSSID();
  String cSummary=String.format("connected to %S
  at%S%S.Strength%s/5",ssid,speed,units,strength);
  ```

14.6.6 Scanning for HotSpots

- WiFiManager is used to conduct access point scans using the startscan method. Intent with the SCAN_RESULTS_AVAILABLE_ACTION() action will be broadcast to asynchronously announce that the scan is complete and results are available.

- The getScanResults() method is called to display scan Result objects as a list. Each scanResult() includes the details retrieved for each access point detected, including link speed, signal strength, SSID, the authentication techniques.
- The following snippet shows how to initiate a scan for access points that displays a Toast indicating the total number of access points found and the name of the access point with the strongest signal.

14.6.7 Managing Wi-Fi Configuration
- Wi-Fi Manager is used to manage the configured network settings and control which networks to connect to. The additional details can be taken as it gets connected to active network connection.
- To get the list of current network configurations use getConfiguredNetworks(). The Wi-fiConfiguration objects returns the network ID, SSID and the other details of each configuration.
- To use the particular network configuration, use the enableNetwork() method, passing in the network ID to use and specify true for the disableALLOthers() parameters.

14.6.8 Creating Wi-Fi Network Configuration
- To get connected to Wi-Fi, user need to create and register a configuration. This can be done by using native Wi-Fi configuration settings, but this cannot be performed from own application. For doing this there is a need of replacing the native Wi-Fi configuration Activity.
- Network Configurations are stored as Wi-FiConfiguration objects. The following is a non-exhaustive list of public fields that are available for each Wi-Fi configuration
    1. **BSSID:** The BSSID for an access point.
    2. **SSID:** The SSID for a particular network.
    3. **NetworkID:** A unique identifier used to identify this network configuration on the current device.
    4. **Priority:** The network configuration's priority to use when ordering the list of potential access points to connect to.
    5. **Status:** The current status of this network connection, which will one of the Wi-FiConfiguration.Status.ENABLED(), Wi-FiConfiguration.Status. DISABLED, Wi-FiConfiguration.Status.CURRENT().
- The Wifi configuration also contains the supported authentication and the keys used previously to authenticate with this access points.
- To add the new network with configuration, the addnetwork method is used simillarly updateNetwork() lets user update a network configuration by passing in a Wi-Ficonfiguration that is populated with networked(). User also can remove the network by using removeNetwork() by passing NetworkID() to it.

14.6.9 Transfering Data using Wi-Fi Direct
- Wi-Fi Direct is communication protocol which is designed for medium range, high bandwidth peer to peer communications. Android 4.0 (API level 14) supported Wi-Fi direct communication as compared to Bluetooth it is more faster and reliable, and works over greater distances.

- Using Wi-Fi Direct APIs user can search for and connect to other Wi-Fi configuration and direct devices within the range.
- Using sockets a communication link is instantiated which can enable to transmit and receive the data between supported devices (including printers, cameras, scanners and televisions) and between instances of an application running on the different devices.
- Wi-Fi direct is mostly suitable for media streaming and media sharing.
  Initializing the WiFi Direct Framework:
  - To use Wi-Fi direct an application requires the ACCESS_WIFI_STATE,CHANGE_WIFI_STATE() and internet permissions:
    <uses-permission android:name="android.permission.ACCESS_WIFI_STATE"/>
    <uses-permission android:name="android.permission.CHANGE_WIFI_STATE"/>
    <uses-permission android:name="android.permission.INTERNET"/>
  - Wi-Fi direct connections are initiated and managed using the Wifip2pManager system service, which can be accessed using the getSystemService() method, passing in the context.WIFI_P2P_SERVICE().

  `wifiP2pManager=(wifiP2pManager) getSystemService (context.WIFI_P2P_SERVICE);`
  - Before using Wi-Fi P2P Manager's initialize method, create a channel to the Wi-Fi Direct Framework using the wifip2pManager's initialize method. ChannelListener listens the loss of channel connection.
  - By initializing Wi-Fi P2P Manager is done within the onCreate() handler of an activity.

  Most actions such as peer discovery and connection attempts are done by using Wi-Fi P2P Manager and which intimates on success or failure by using an ActionListner.

  When it is successful it returns associated actions that are obtained by receiving Broadcast Intents.

Practice Questions

1. Explain the concept of Media API's
2. What is sensor manager ?
3. What is the use of Bluetooth ?
4. How to manage Wi-Fi connection ?
5. What is an Importance of Sensor Framework ?
6. What is Bluetooth Communication ?
7. Write short notes on :
   (a) Playing media resources.
   (b) Transmission of data using Bluetooth Socket.
   (c) Managing Wi-Fi.

Chapter 15...

PUBLISHING ANDROID APPLICATION TO MARKET

15.1 Preparing for Publishing
15.2 Preparing an Application for Release
15.3 Deploying APK Files
15.4 abd install "C:\Users\Mydemo\Desktop\Firstdemo.apk"
15.5 Releasing Your Applications on Google Play
    15.5.1 Releasing Your Application on Google Play is a Simple Process that Involves Three Basic Steps
15.6 Submitting an Application

15.1 Preparing for Publishing

- Google has made the application deployment easy so that it will be available for the end users application developers can release the application through application marketplace, such as Google Play. The another way to release the application by sending them directly to users or by letting users download them from your own website.
- Publishing is the general process that makes an Android applications available to users. When developers publish an Android application there is need to perform two main tasks:
- **Prepare the application for release:**
  During the preparation step, build a release version of an application, which users can download and install on their Android-powered devices.
- **Release the application to users:**
  During the release step, publicize, sell, and distribute the release version of your application to users.
- The following figure shows the overall android application development process, the publishing process is performed after the testing phase of the application has been completed testing is done in debug environment debugging done to meet the release criteria of the application which performs respective to functionality, performance and stability before the publishing process.

15.2 Preparing an Application for Release

Preparing an application for release is a multi-step process that involves the following tasks:

1. Export an application as an APK (Android Package) file.
2. Generate own self signed certificate and digitally sign an application with it.
3. Deploy the signed application.
4. Use the Android Market for hosting and selling an application.

Generation of APK file involves multiple steps that are mentioned below:

- Configuring your application for release.

    Starting with version 1.0 of the Android SDK, the androidManifest.xml file of every Android application includes the two attributes such as android:versionCode and android:versionName .

    To publish an application to an android market (www.android/market/), the androidManifest.xml file must have the following attributes:

    1. android:versionCode (within the <manifest> element)
    2. android:versionName. (within the <manifest> element)
    3. android:icon (within the <application> element)
    4. android:label (within the <application> element)

For android application developed it is mandatory to get the version code of an application ,to configure an application to the current Android Market versioning.

```
<?XML version="1.0" encoding ="utf-8"?>
<?xml version="1.0" encoding="utf-8"?>
<manifest xmlns:android="CDMA, example FirstDemo
    package="net.learn2develop.FirstDemo
    android:versionCode="1"
    android:versionName="1.0">
<application android:icon="@drawable/icon" android:label="@string/app_name">
<uses-library android:name="com.google.android.maps"/>
```

The android:versionCode attribute represents the version number of an application ,for every updation of an application this number should be increased by 1,so that programmatically it will differentiate the newest version from the previous one. This value is never used by Android market but this is useful to android application to configure an application with newest environment of android market.

The android:versionName attribute contains versioning information that is visible to the users, it should contain values in the format:<major>.<minor>.<point>.if the application undergoes a major upgrade, you should increase the major by 1. For small incremental upgrades you can increase the <minor> or <point> by 1. For example, a new application may have a version name of"1.0.0", for small incremental upgrades it might be changed to "1.1.0"or"1.0.1"and for the next major upgrade it might change to"2.0.0"

The android:icon displayed the launcher icon for an application and android:label attribute specifies the name of an application, this name will be displayed in the setting->Applications->Manage Application, section of an Android device. The following snippet shows where the android label is specified as application element.

```xml
<?xml version="1.0" encoding="utf-8"?>
<manifest xmlns:android="http://schemas.android.com/apk/res/android"
    package="net.
    android:versionCode="1"
    android:versionName="1.0">
<application android:icon="@drawable/icon" android:label="FirstDemo">
<uses-library android:name="com.google.android.maps"/>
```

The minimum version of SDK that an application needs to run on any lower versions of an android, this can be specified in Androidmanifest.xml file using the <uses-sdk> element.

```xml
<?xml version="1.0" encoding "utf-8"?>
<?xml version="1.0" encoding="utf-8"?>
<manifest xmlns:android="http://schemas.android.com/apk/res/android"
    package="net.learn2develop.FirstDemo"
    android:versionCode="1"
    android:versionName="1.0">
<application android:icon="@drawable/icon" android:label="FirstDemo">
<uses-library android:name="com.google.android.maps"/>
    <activity android:name=".MainActivity"
        android:label=@string/app_name">
        <intent-filter>
        <action android:name="android.intent.action.MAIN"/>
        <category android:name="android.intent.category.LAUNCHER">
        </intent-filter>
    </activity>
</application>
    <uses-sdk android:minSdkVersion="7"/>
    <uses-permission android:name="android.permission.INTERNET"/>
    <uses-permission android:name="android.permission.ACCESS_FINE_LOCATION"/>
    <uses-permission
android:name="android.permission.ACCESS_COARSE_LOCATION"/>
</manifest>
```

The above snippet shows the minimum SDK version is 7 that is Android 2.1. Generally it is a good practise to set the minimum version of SDK so that wider users will be able to run an application.

Building and signing a release version of an application:
- All android applications must be digitally signed before they are allowed to be deployed onto a device (or Emulator) for some mobile platforms there is need of purchasing the digital certificates from a Certificate Authority (CA) to sign an application self signed certificates can be used to sign Android applications.
- When Eclipse is used to develop an Android application then press F11 to deploy it to an emulator, Eclipse automatically signs it. This can be verified by Windows->Preferences in Eclipse ,expanding the android item, and selecting Build.
- Eclipse uses default debug keystore ("debug.Keystore") to see an application. This Keystore is known as digital certificate.
- For publishing an android application, it must be signed with developer's own certificate the applications signed with debug certificate cannot be published. Own signed certificates can be generated by using Keytool.exe utility provided by the Java SDK, eclipse has made it easy by including a wizard that shows the steps to generate a certificate.
- **Testing the release version of your application.**
  Before you distribute your application, you should thoroughly test the release version on at least one target handset device and one target tablet device.
- **Updating application resources for release.**
  You need to be sure that all application resources such as multimedia files and graphics are updated and included with your application or staged on the proper production servers.
- **Preparing remote servers and services that your application depends on.**
  If your application depends on external servers or services, you need to be sure they are secure and production ready.

15.3 Deploying APK Files

- When you are finished preparing your application for release developer has to sign .apk file that application can be distributed to users.
  There are three methods to deploy APK files:
  1. Deploying manually using the adb.exe tool.
  2. Hosting the application on a web server.
  3. Publishing through the Android market.

- Besides this the applications can be installed on end user devices by sending e-mails, SD cards. As an APK file is transferred to user's device, it can install the application.
- The easiest and quickest way to release your application is to send it to a user through email. To do this, you prepare your application for release and then attach it to an email and send it to a user. When the user opens your email message on their Android-powered device the Android system will recognize the APK and display an **Install Now** button in the email message (see figure 1). Users can install your application by touching the button.

Fig. 15.1

1. Using the adb.exe tool

Once the android application is signed it can be deployed to an emulators and devices using adb.exe (Android Debug Bridge) tool (located in the platform-tools folder of the Android SDK).

Using the command prompt on windows, navigate to the"<Android_SDK>/platform-tools"folder.

- To install an application to an emulator/device the following command is issued (assuming the emulator is currently up and running or only one device is currently connected)

The currently connected devices to the computer can be shown by using the devices option with adb, D:\Android 2.3\android-sdk-windows\platform-tools>adb devices (List of devices attached) the following result is showing the connected devices to the computer.

List of devices attached:

1. emulator-5554
2. emulator-5556

- For using a particular device the command should indicated adb-s option with the specification of the device as follows

    adb-s emulator-5556 install Firstdemo.apk

- If the apk file already exists on the particular device it will show an error message,

    Failure [INSTALL_FAILED_ALREADY_EXISTS]

    - Inspection of a launcher on Android device/emulator, the icon FirstDemo is launched on screen. The application is stored on following location as

        Setting->Applications->Manage Applications on Android device.

15.4 abd install "C:Users\Mydemo\Desktop\Firstdemo.apk"

- An application can be uninstall by using adb.exe ,this can be done by using shell option.

    abd shell rm/data/app/net.Firstdemo.apk

Using a Web Server:

- Web server can be used for hosting own application by the developer team this is ideal if own website hosting services can be used as an applications can be provided free of cost to end users (or certain group of people can be restricted. But once apk file is downloaded the application will get installed on particular devices.)
- To demonstrate the use web server Internet Information Server(IIS) on windows 7, copy the signed Firstdemo.apk file to C:\inetpub\wwwroot\.

    In addition, create a new HTML file named Install.html with the following content:

    <html>
    <title>FirstDemo</title>
    <body>
    Download the FirstDemo <a href ="FirstDemo.apk">here</a>
    </body>
    </html>

- On web server register a new MIME type for the APK file. the MIME type for the .apk extension is application/vnd.android.package-archieve.
- To install apk file over the web, SD card should be implied onto device or emulator as .apk files are stored in download folder which is created by SD card.
- By default all applications are installed from the Android market on almost all devices with the help of emulators or device.

  Hence for allowing the installation of applications from a web server, android emulator or device should be configured to accept applications from non market sources.
- From the application settings menu check for "Unknown Sources" item, which prompt with a warning message then Click on OK. By checking this item emulator or device, allow to install an applications from other non-Market sources, (such as web server).

Publishing on the Android Market

Releasing through an App Marketplace:

- So far we learned how to package an android application and distribute it in various ways-via web server, the adb.exe file, email, SD card and so on these ways does not provide a suitable access to explore an application world.
- If you want to distribute your apps to the broadest possible audience, releasing through an app market place such as Google Play is ideal.
- Google Play is the premier marketplace for Android apps and is particularly useful if you want to distribute your applications to a large global audience. However, you can distribute your apps through any app marketplace you want or you can use multiple marketplaces.

15.5 Releasing Your Applications on Google Play

- Google Play is a robust publishing platform that helps developers publicize, sell, and distribute an Android applications to end users around the world. When developer release an applications through Google Play, users have access to a suite of developer tools that let developers analyze sales, identify market trends, and control to whom the applications are being distributed.
- Developers also provided with access to several revenue-enhancing features such as in-app billing and application licensing. The rich array of tools and features,

coupled with numerous end-user community features, makes Google Play the premier marketplace for selling and buying Android applications.

- Creating a developer profile
    - The first step towards publishing application on the Android market is to create a developer profile at http://market.android.com/publish/Home. For this you need a Google account (Gmail account). Once logged in to the Android market, firstly create developer profile.
    - The one time registration fees should be paid for publishing an application on android market. Click Google Checkout button to redirect to a page where registration fees can be paid. Click Continue link.
    - Developer needs to agree to the Android Market developer Distribution Agreement. Check the "I agree" checkbox and click "I agree Countinue " link.

15.5.1 Releasing Your Application on Google Play is a Simple Process that Involves Three Basic Steps

15.5.1.1 Preparing Promotional Materials

To fully leverage the marketing and publicity capabilities of Google Play, developers need to create promotional materials for an application, such as screenshots, videos, graphics, and promotional text.

15.5.1.2 Configuring Options and Uploading Assets

Google Play lets you target applications to a worldwide pool of users and devices. By configuring various Google Play settings, you can choose the countries you want to reach, the listing languages you want to use, and the price you want to charge in each country. You can also configure listing details such as the application type, category, and content rating. When you are done configuring options you can upload your promotional materials and your application as a draft (unpublished) application.

15.5.1.1 Publishing the Release Version of Your Application

If you are satisfied that your publishing settings are correctly configured and your uploaded application is ready to be released to the public, you can simply click **Publish** in the developer console and within minutes your application will be live and available for download around the world.

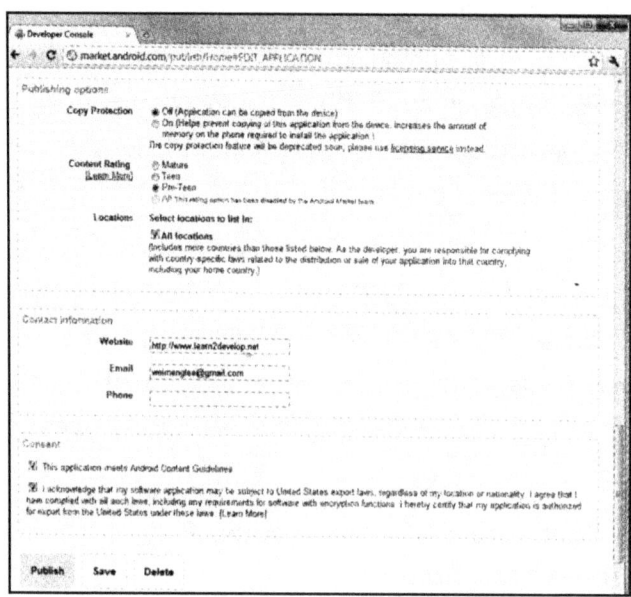

Fig. 15.2

15.6 Submitting an Application

- Once all setup formalities are done, an application is ready to submit an Android market. If developer wants to charge for an application, Setup Merchant Account Link should be clicked. additional information such as bank account and Tax Id should be entered and for free applications click Upload Application Link.

- Some more details should be supplied while uploading an application.

Among all details the following mentioned details are manadatory:

1. The application in APK format

2. At least two screenshots. You can use DDMS perspective in Eclipse to capture screenshots of an application. It may run on emulator or a real device.

3. A high resolution application icon, the size of this image must be 512 × 512 pixels.

Fig. 15.3

Above figure shows FirstDemo.apk is uploaded to an Android market. Based on APK file uploaded user may be asked for such permissions which are required to an application to be installed on a device. For example GPS access, or Network configuration.

Title of an application, its description as well as recent changes.

- When guidelines and agreements are properly followed, click on Publish to Publish an application on the Android Market.
- That's it!! now application can be available on the Android Market .and developer can monitor any comments submitted on an application, as well as bug reports and total number of downloads.

www.ingramcontent.com/pod-product-compliance
Lightning Source LLC
Chambersburg PA
CBHW081423230426
43668CB00016B/2337